West of Harlem

CultureAmerica

Erika Doss and Philip J. Deloria
SERIES EDITORS

Karal Ann Marling
EDITOR EMERITA

West of Harlem
African American Writers and the Borderlands

Emily Lutenski

UNIVERSITY PRESS OF KANSAS

Published by the University Press of Kansas (Lawrence, Kansas 66045), which was
organized by the Kansas Board of Regents and is operated and funded by Emporia
State University, Fort Hays State University, Kansas State University, Pittsburg State
University, the University of Kansas, and Wichita State University

Library of Congress Cataloging-in-Publication Data
Lutenski, Emily.
West of Harlem : African American writers and the borderlands / Emily Lutenski.
    pages cm. — (CultureAmerica)
Includes bibliographical references and index.
ISBN 978-0-7006-2086-9 (cloth : alk. paper)
 1. American literature—African American authors—History and criticism.   2. American
literature—20th century—History and criticism.   3. African Americans in literature.   4. Race
relations in literature.   5. West (U.S.)—In literature.   6. Southwestern States—In literature.
I. Title.
PS153.N5L88 2015
810.9'896073—dc23
2015004304

British Library Cataloguing-in-Publication Data is available.

Printed in the United States of America

10 9 8 7 6 5 4 3 2 1

For Anne

Contents

Acknowledgments

I am sincerely grateful for the support I received while completing this project from colleagues, friends, and family.

For helping me lay the intellectual groundwork for this book, thanks are due to those with whom I worked at the University of Michigan, especially my mentors Anne Herrmann, Phil Deloria, María Cotera, and Josh Miller. They are all tremendously kind and intellectually brave and have provided me with excellent models of how to do academic work. Sidonie Smith gave me advice about publishing on which I continue to rely. And I truly appreciate my friends Kelly Williams, Elspeth Healey, Aaron McCollough, Tamara Bhalla, Gavin Hollis, Ji-Hyae Park, John Cords, and others who made up a lively, funny, and nurturing intellectual community during the time I first began to think about the intersection of race and place in American literature. Dan Mrozowski deserves extra special thanks not only for his participation in that community but also for reading the manuscript and being an overall great friend.

When I first conceptualized this book, I was working at Bowling Green State University. From my time there, I am especially thankful for Matthew Mace Barbee, who read the manuscript and is one of my best critics and favorite people. I am also truly glad to know Bill Albertini, Candace Archer, Jolie Sheffer, Sarah Rainey, Ramona Bell, and Clayton Rosati, who became supporters and friends during those years. Members of the Department of Ethnic Studies and my writing group coordinated through the Institute for the Study of Culture and Society also helped me grow as a thinker and writer. Thank you all.

I could not have written this book without the year I spent as a fellow at Princeton University's Center for African American Studies. There, I was fortunate to receive the encouragement of many generous people and tremendous scholars, including Eddie Glaude, Noliwe Rooks, Tera

Hunter, and Imani Perry. I am especially grateful for the mentorship of Daphne Brooks, who continues to inspire me with her creative, interdisciplinary thinking about race and gender. Special gratitude is also reserved for Thadious Davis of the University of Pennsylvania and Mary Pat Brady of Cornell University, who traveled to Princeton to workshop the manuscript for this book, which is now immeasurably stronger as a result of their sage advice. And I shared my year at Princeton with Danielle Clealand, who helped me extend my thinking about race in comparative and transnational ways and was the best co-fellow I could ever ask for.

Since then, I have been tremendously lucky to land at Saint Louis University, where I received a Mellon Faculty Development Grant from the College of Arts and Sciences to help bring this work to completion. I have an amazing group of colleagues in the Department of American Studies who support me in countless ways: Matthew Mancini, Cindy Ott, Heidi Ardizzone, Kate Moran, and Ben Looker. I am lucky to work with such great scholars, teachers, and friends. I am especially thankful for Ben Looker and his attentive reading of the manuscript; it is so much better for having had his eyes on it. I am grateful, too, for all the help I received from staff member Terri Foster and from graduate students Mie Wang, Anna Schmidt, Robert Hansee, Aretha Butler, and Elizabeth Eikmann, who served as my research assistants. Outside of American studies, Mary Gould, Nadia Brown, Amanda Izzo, Bukky Gbadagesin, Jonathan Smith, Lorri Glover, Torrie Hester, Toby Benis, Georgia Johnston, and other affiliates of African American studies, women's and gender studies, and English deserve my sincere gratitude, and I am glad they are part of my intellectual community. Last, I extend profound thanks to Flannery Burke. Before I had ever spoken to her, Flannery read an early version of the manuscript, and her rigorous questions and smart feedback shaped it in fundamental ways. I am so happy to have an office down the hall from her now.

Other scholars in African American studies, American studies, history, and literature have been instrumental to my work. I am indebted to Davarian Baldwin, Minkah Makalani, Martha Cutter, Melody Graulich, Rudolph P. Byrd, Henry Louis Gates Jr., and Daniel Heath Justice, who, as editors of journals and collections, encouraged and bettered my scholarship on race and place. I am also thankful for Cary Wintz, Douglas Flamming, and Michael Johnson, who were incisive critics and inspirations as I pursued the project of linking African American studies with western literature and history. Jesse Gant has been a willing ear for all my ideas about this book since its inception, and he has always been honest about which ones were good and which ones were not, while being unwavering in his support.

I am grateful to the librarians and archivists who helped with this work, particularly at the Special Collections Research Center at Syracuse University and the Beinecke Rare Book and Manuscript Library at Yale University. Thanks, too, go to all the kind people—at presses, archives, agencies, journals, and private collections—who helped me locate materials and gave me permission to use them. Jill Quasha and Susan Sandberg were particularly generous in this regard, along with Anita Green and the rest of the Anita Scott Coleman family. Thanks are also due to Cynthia Davis and Verner Mitchell, who kindly put me in touch with the Coleman descendants to further this project. I gratefully acknowledge Craig Tenney of Harold Ober Associates, who aided me in securing permission to use material by Langston Hughes and Arna Bontemps. "Strong Men, Riding Horses," by Gwendolyn Brooks, is reprinted by consent of Brooks Permissions.

I also owe the entire team at the University Press of Kansas my sincerest thanks. Phil Deloria first encouraged me to propose this book for the CultureAmerica series, and he and Erika Doss, the series editors, have been encouraging and insightful ever since. The staff members at the press, new and old, have been unendingly patient and accessible and have given great advice at all stages of this project. In this regard, I especially appreciate all the work of Editor in Chief Michael Briggs.

Finally, I thank my parents, who taught me to love reading, who did everything they could to make my education possible, and who have supported me in so many other ways.

Lester after the Western

Strong Men, riding horses. In the West
On a range five hundred miles. A Thousand. Reaching
From dawn to sunset. Rested blue to orange.
From hope to crying. Except that Strong Men are
Desert-eyed, except that Strong Men are
Pasted to stars already. Have their cars
Beneath them. Rentless, too. Too broad of chest
To shrink when the Rough Man hails. Too flailing
To re-direct the Challenger, when the challenge
Nicks; slams; buttonholes. Too saddled.

I am not like that. I pay rent, am addled
By illegible landlords, run, if robbers call.

What mannerisms I present, employ,
Are camouflage, and what my mouths remark
To word-wall off that broadness of the dark
Is pitiful.
I am not brave at all.
—Gwendolyn Brooks, "Strong Men, Riding Horses" (1959)

Introduction

Going to the Territory

Why have most of the serious writers of this generation
turned up their noses at America's greatest source of
material: the West? I am sure that Dumas or Hugo or
Tolstoy or Shakespeare would not have neglected it
had they lived in our time and place. And why has the
western been the last thing to attract the Negro writer?
We've missed a bet.
—*Arna Bontemps to Langston Hughes (April 30, 1956)*

During the 1893 World's Fair in Chicago, a young historian named
Frederick Jackson Turner delivered a lecture titled "The Significance
of the Frontier in American History." This presentation, given at the
annual meeting of the American Historical Association on July 12,
catapulted him to professional stardom and provided a touchstone for
countless scholarly discussions of American identity and the American
West—including this one—for generations to come. The World's Columbian Exposition, which hailed US imperialism and exceptionalism,
was a fitting milieu for Turner's speech, in which he proclaimed that
uniquely American character traits such as "dominant individualism,"
a "practical, inventive turn of mind," and the "buoyancy and exuber-
ance which comes with freedom" were due to the westward march of
imperium.[1] The delivery of Turner's speech is a well-worn story among
western historians, who have both reified Turner's thesis and contested
it—but never forgotten it—during the intervening 120-odd years.

Playing Indian: an African American child in a headdress rides his trusty tricycle steed in the Wild West of Los Angeles, 1923. (Los Angeles Public Library Photo Collection)

While Turner's place as progenitor in the field of western history is secure, western historians are probably less likely to remember another speech given at the Columbian Exposition just a month after Turner's, on August 25, by another Frederick—Frederick Douglass—who was the headliner for the sole "Colored American Day" during the events in Chicago. African Americans had struggled for years to gain representation in planning for the fair, as well as in exhibiting and obtaining employment at the event. Ida B. Wells even distributed a lengthy coauthored pamphlet, *The Reason Why the Colored American Is Not in the World's Columbian Exposition*, which critiqued the fair's exclusionary practices as symptomatic of US racism. After years of struggle, Colored American Day was merely a panacea for black activists; by limiting the African American presence to a single day, it even hailed the segregationist practices of Jim Crow. Wells, outraged, boycotted the events. Those who participated barely managed to stave off the inclusion of minstrelsy, the mocking presence of vendors hired to sell watermelon for the occasion, and aggressive white-supremacist hecklers. Despite such setbacks, the aging Douglass delivered an impassioned and well-reasoned speech to explain to "our transatlantic friends why we have a share so slender in this World's Columbian Exposition." Whereas Turner had recently spoken about the frontier, Douglass set his sights on another major problem in American history: not a "Negro problem," he insisted, but a "National problem." "The problem," he told his 2,500-person audience, "is whether the American people have the honesty enough, loyalty enough, patriotism enough to live up to their own Constitution."[2]

Through Turner's and Douglass's speeches, the 1893 World's Fair unwittingly brought together two of the most vexing problems in American history: the problem of the frontier as a process, a place, or a symbol, and the problem of black marginalization and oppression. Yet for too long, these narratives have remained separate—so much so that in 1972, in his foundational collection *Long Black Song: Essays in Black American Literature and Culture*, critic Houston A. Baker Jr. contended:

The tales of pioneers enduring the hardships of the West for the promise of immense wealth are not the tales of black America.

When the black American reads Frederick Jackson Turner's *The Frontier in American History*, he feels no regret over the end of the Western frontier. To black America, *frontier* is an alien word; for, in essence, all frontiers established by the white psyche have been closed to the black man.[3]

If western historians are unlikely to consider Turner's speech with Douglass's, scholars of African American studies are probably just as unlikely to see the West as a crucial site for the examination of black identity and culture. Historian Richard White once juxtaposed Turner's speech at the fair with the unofficial presence of Buffalo Bill Cody, who set up his popular Wild West Show just outside its gates. Of this pairing, White eloquently remarked, "Turner and Cody followed separate but connected strands of a single mythic cloth. And as in Chicago one hundred years ago, their seemingly contradictory stories make historical sense only when told together." Unlike the stories of Turner and Cody, the stories of Turner and Douglass appear to be unrelated even by contradiction. This book, however, suggests that the stories represented by these figures—stories of the West and stories of African America—are intrinsically connected.[4]

When he spoke of the West, Douglass observed that it had little to offer African Americans. He was clearly aware of the impact place had on African American experiences, even titling his first abolitionist paper the *North Star*, thereby tying geographic mobility to African American freedom. This, however, had its limits. Douglass rightfully decried the racist efforts of the American Colonization Society to resettle blacks, and he frowned on African American immigration to Canada as a response to the 1850 Fugitive Slave Act. He was attentive, however, to both northern and southern borderlands and their impact on African American lives; he spoke out against expansionist efforts in the West and in Mexico. Douglass opposed the United States–Mexico War, deeming it "a murderous" act toward the Mexicans and characterizing it "as a war against the free states—as a war against freedom, against the Negro, and against the interests of workingmen in this country—and as a means of extending that great evil and damning curse, negro slavery." He could not, however, condone the dreams of African Americans who imagined the West and both its northern and southern borderlands as spaces for black freedom. In 1879, speaking about the African American Exoduster movement to Kansas, he stated that while he understood why blacks would leave the South, he considered it "a surrender, a premature, disheartening surrender, since it would make freedom dependent on migration rather than protection; by flight, rather than by right."[5]

For his part, it seems unlikely that Turner ever envisioned his intrepid American pioneers as black. Indeed, "The Significance of the Frontier in American History" obscured the historical linkages between the frontier and black experience—most obviously the history of bondage and emancipation, with which Douglass's activism was so enmeshed. In this history, westward expansion and Indian removal provided more land for a plantation economy built on the backs of enslaved people, and the admittance of each state to the westward-moving union raised the sectional question of whether it would be slave or free. But Turner merely glossed this point when he stated, "Even the slavery struggle . . . occupies its important place in American history because of its relation to westward expansion"—enfolding, obscuring, and forgetting the fact of blackness as a central component of the frontier experience. Such obfuscation contributed to a popular western mythos that remained dominant throughout much of the twentieth century and was centered on rugged, white, male individuals interacting with a symbolic "virgin land."[6]

Despite these exclusions, silences, and seeming lack of intersections, a few short years after Baker's essay collection helped midwife black literary criticism and African American studies more generally, a giant in African American letters, Ralph Ellison, delivered an address that undermined the alleged mutual exclusivity of black experience and frontier experience. In this lecture, titled "Going to the Territory," the Oklahoman writer remarks that, for African Americans, "geography was fate." He insists, "Not only had [African Americans] observed the transformation of individual fortune made possible by the westward movement along the frontier, but the Mason-Dixon Line had taught them the relationship between geography and freedom." With this contention, Ellison is participating in an exceptionalist frontier ethos much like the one so famously articulated by Turner back in 1893.

Playing cowgirl: an African American child poses on a pony in Los Angeles, 1944. (Los Angeles Public Library Photo Collection)

While his emphasis on black experience in "the [Indian] territory" serves as a corrective to dominant depictions of the frontier, it also tends to make African Americans the subject of plots that echo those narrated by Turner. Like Turner, who describes pioneers and colonists confronting the wilderness and being rewrought in a new and uniquely American image, Ellison favors a narrative of individual success—a hearty, masculine frontierism where blacks know not only the frontier experience but also the geography of North and South, which he paints as a geography of freedom and oppression. In Ellison's speech, these geographic trajectories are separate rather than overlapping or intersectional. His linguistic mapping detaches the axes of North-South and East-West, and in doing so, he furthers the notion that westward movement is unique and that the West is a place that stands alone—this time, in terms of the possibilities it offers African Americans, just as it did for white fortune seekers.[7]

Elsewhere in "Going to the Territory," Ellison insists, "we possess two basic versions of American history: one which is written and as neatly stylized as ancient myth, and the other unwritten and as chaotic and full of contradictions, changes of pace, and surprises as life itself. Perhaps this is to overstate it a bit, but there's no denying that Americans can be notoriously selective in the exercise of historical memory." When this statement is applied to the West as a symbol and myth of America—as it has so often been treated from Turner's time onward—the African American presence is forgotten in the American historical memory. Ellison wants to bring black history back into the fold, unveiling the surprising black presence woven into the American fabric as the very threads that keep it together. He argues:

> By ignoring such matters as the sharing of bloodlines and
> cultural traditions by groups of widely differing ethnic origins,
> and by overlooking the blending and metamorphosis of cultural
> forms which is so characteristic of our society, we misconceive
> our cultural identity. It is as though we dread to acknowledge
> the complex, pluralistic nature of our society, and as a result we
> find ourselves stumbling upon our true national identity under
> circumstances in which we least expect to do so.

When America forgets its racial histories, Ellison suggests, it misapprehends what it means to be American. Thus, if the frontier has been treated, time and time again, as one of the driving symbols of the nation, one must examine not only how blacks share a western history but also how they are fundamental to it. When Ellison argues for the excavation and retention of a fuller American historical memory, he does not question the West's centrality to this memory or to American identity more generally. Rather than introducing an entirely new story or an entirely different geography, he uses the same familiar tropes but uncovers the unexpected presence of black subjects who "learned . . . that freedom was to be attained through geographical movement, and that freedom required one to risk his life against the unknown"—in other words, the frontier, the virgin land, of American history.[8]

To examine Ellison's engagement with the West disrupts the "two basic versions of American history"—the neat, mythologized history and the contradictory, surprising history—he describes in "Going to the Territory." Depictions of the African American West have, indeed, often been dominated by two major narratives that continue to be alluded to and in some cases undermined by contemporary scholarship. In the first, blackness is subject to erasure. The legacy of the "slavery struggle," as Turner put it, is encompassed by a greater master narrative of the frontier and thereby minimized to the point of invisibility. As a result, once the existence of vibrant black communities in the West becomes impossible to ignore—for example, through social movements and unrest in places like Watts and Oakland in the 1960s—the westernness of the sites housing these communities tends to be forgotten, and the urban environment tends to be emphasized. But well before the 1960s—in 1922—the neighborhood of South Central Los Angeles became legible to Chandler Owen, the Harlem-based editor of the *Messenger*, not as the West but as a "veritable little Harlem."[9]

If minimization, erasure, obfuscation, and forgetting characterize the first dominant discourse of the African American West, in the second narrative the region is seen as a land of opportunity, a place where one can find freedom from prejudice and oppression. Here, blacks become participants in a landscape populated by fortune-seeking gold miners and homesteaders; the West is a refuge for escaped and former slaves.

Yet the very presence of a black West comes as a surprise, and it is thought to consist of only scattered individuals such as, in the words of historian Quintard Taylor, "rowdy, rugged *black* cowboys, gallant *black* soldiers, and sturdy but silent *black* women, . . . stereotype[s] of the black westerner as a solitary figure loosened from the moorings of family, home, and community." At the center of these stories is the individual black westerner—who, like the white westerner, is characterized as a lone adventurer taming the wilderness and forging a new, free life in a new place.[10]

Ellison demonstrates this breed of thinking about the black West when he describes the Oklahoma where he grew up as "wild mainly in the sense of it being a relatively unformed frontier state." Like Turner, he elaborates on how encounters with this wildness inform the American character, essentially propounding a rugged individualism: "I have stressed in this country that geography has performed the role of fate, but it is important to remember that it is not geography alone which determines the quality of life and culture. These depend on the courage and personal culture of the individuals who make their home in any given locality." He continues, "Today most of the geographical frontier is gone, but the process of cultural integration continues along the lines that mark the hierarchical divisions of the United States." The way this line resonates with Turner's earlier speech is obvious. Nearly ninety years apart, both speakers see the frontier as closed; yet the frontier as both a process and a geography remains linked to the formation of courageous individual character, which endures as a definitive trait of American identity. Because of this link, if American culture is to be maintained, new frontiers must be created. In Turner's time, the idea of the frontier was extrapolated beyond the contiguous United States to encompass the nation's imperial interventions during the Spanish-American War. Ellison's frontier differs greatly, remaining within the national boundaries and focused on the "hierarchical divisions" of race that continue to persist long after emancipation. Unlike Turner, whose frontier subsumes black enslavement and vanishes Indians, Ellison's frontier is, crucially, a racial frontier. The imperative of integration in the post–civil rights era is this new frontier for Ellison, one that maintains the central paradigm of American experience.[11]

As a result, it may come as no surprise that Ellison sees the West as having deep roots in the African American imagination: "Freedom," he claims, "was also to be found in the west of the old Indian Territory. . . . It is no accident that much of the symbolism of our folklore is rooted in the imagery of geography." When Ellison makes this connection to folklore, he locates the black West in a time long before his speech, the title of which is taken from a Bessie Smith song, "Work House Blues," recorded in 1924. An imagined West where blacks can escape discrimination, terror, and violence after the subversion of Reconstruction was common when Smith recorded her song, which is steeped in folkloric traditions. It was released when the African American literary upstarts of the New Negro movement were also turning to black folklore as a source for their art. As Tiya Miles and Sharon P. Holland contend, "By the late nineteenth century and early twentieth century, many African Americans had come to see the Western lands called Indian Territory as a refuge in America, and more, as a potential *black space* that would function metaphorically and emotionally as a substitute for the longed-for African homeland." This was true despite the occurrence of events such as the devastating Tulsa race riots of 1921, right near the heart of Indian Territory, during which the city's Greenwood business district, known as "black Wall Street," was entirely destroyed. But regardless of this situation and others like it, a hopeful vision of the West as a place for blacks to access American freedom was expanded in the 1920s, moving beyond Indian Territory to other regions. As a result, a mere four years after the Tulsa riots, writer, activist, and promoter of the black literati James Weldon Johnson could claim in the *Denver Post*, "Your West is giving the Negro a better deal than any other section of the country. . . . There is more opportunity for my race, and less prejudice against it in this section of the country than anywhere else in the United States."[12]

As Johnson's comment about Denver or Owen's about Los Angeles indicates, African Americans in the 1920s and 1930s, including the New Negro generation associated with the production of literature, art, and music during this period, were thinking about the American West. But clearly, Ellison's need to remind audiences of the black West as late as 1979 indicates that this connection had been—and often continues to be—forgotten. When the "New Negro" comes to mind, scholars and

critics are likely to locate this well-known paradigm of black intellectu-
alism, modernity, politics, and artistic production squarely in Harlem.
This generation of black artists and intellectuals is typically seen as
one that broke away from the constraints of the post-Reconstruction
South and the legacy of slavery to forge new lives in booming modern
metropolises in the North—industrial cities like Chicago and Detroit
and, most famously in terms of the arts, the "culture capital," as Johnson
termed it: New York's Harlem.[13] This Great Migration narrative characterizes the modern black experience and African American literature
squarely as an outgrowth of the urban environment. And during the
early twentieth century, the West was rarely imagined as urban, even
though western cities experienced booming growth.

Black literary endeavors during these years were largely situated
within a New York–based publishing milieu, which was fixated on black
creative writing because, as Langston Hughes remarks in *The Big Sea*
(1940), "the negro was in vogue." The dialectic of North-South constructed in narratives of the Great Migration is, indeed, common in
African American literature emerging from the New Negro movement
in the 1920s and 1930s. For example, Jean Toomer's *Cane* (1923), often
considered the harbinger of the New Negro renaissance, is organized
in three parts moving from South to North and then South again—
emblematic of a New Negro impulse to recover and promote a seemingly "authentic" and often southern black identity in the face of both
mainstream racist parody and a modernist primitivism that upheld a
fantasy of black life as natural, atavistic, uncultivated, and a way to heal
the wounds of an overcivilized age. This impulse acted, too, in defiance
of an older generation of black intellectuals who championed respectability and assimilation to (white) middle-class norms. Participating in
the aesthetic zeitgeist of the interwar period, the "talented tenth" of the
United States' most paradigmatically modern metropolis made its mark
in American literary and intellectual history. Given its prominence, it is
perhaps unsurprising that criticism still tends to locate African American
literary production in the 1920s and 1930s almost exclusively in Harlem
or, when it extends beyond Harlem, to the interplay between Harlem
and the South (by the 1940s, Gwendolyn Brooks and Richard Wright,
among others, would put Chicago more squarely on the literary map).[14]

This is not to say that scholarship has failed to extend the scope of African American history and literature beyond a North-South binary. Key works in African American and Africana studies have vigorously taken on and opened up the concept of diaspora and its relationship to black modernity and African American modernism. One of the most notable examples is, of course, Paul Gilroy's influential *The Black Atlantic: Modernity and Double-Consciousness*, wherein he describes the modern emergence of a circum-Atlantic and transnational black culture and politics: "In opposition to . . . nationalist or ethnically absolute approaches," he suggests, "cultural historians could take the Atlantic as one single, complex unit of analysis in their discussions of the modern world and use it to produce an explicitly transnational and intercultural perspective." Brent Hayes Edwards has built on this concept, with particular reference to the New Negro movement, in *The Practice of Diaspora: Literature, Translation, and the Rise of Black Internationalism.* Edwards emphasizes, "To note that the 'New Negro' movement is at the same time a 'new' black internationalism is to move against the grain of much of the scholarship on African American culture in the 1920s, which has tended to emphasize United States–bound themes of cultural nationalism, civil rights protest, and uplift in the literary culture of the 'Harlem Renaissance.'" African American and Africana literary cultures in the 1920s extended both far beyond and in tandem with Harlem, and Edwards locates these cultures in both the Anglophone and Francophone circum-Atlantic world through the lenses of translation and *décalage*. In works like Gilroy's and Edwards's, Harlem—and indeed, the nation—loses its exceptionalism and centrality, becoming just one of many nodes in a network of literary, cultural, and political formations constituting and being constituted by transnational black experience.[15]

Yet even in scholarship like this, which rethinks black geographies so significantly, there is little consideration of region and of how region can play a part in—and perhaps complicate—such constructs of the transnational. In fact, there is little mention of nonurban locations (or those imagined as nonurban) in these depictions of black modernism and modernity, which tend to connect New York with other metropolitan centers—such as the cosmopolitan cities of Paris and London—more than with African or Caribbean colonial peripheries. If the urban environment and the black Atlantic remain the central frames of reference for black diasporic experience, the African American West continues to be left out of this picture. Even Gilroy's image of a ship, which he uses as a metaphor to describe circum-Atlantic black culture and politics, seems to have little application in the arid, desert landscape of the borderlands West.[16]

Although concepts such as the black Atlantic and black internationalism have considerably disrupted the binary of North-South, the rural South remains the most prominent nonurban location in African American studies. (It is worth noting that in much of the literature of the 1920s and 1930s—most famously in the work of the white writers known as the southern agrarians, but also in the work of African American writers—the South, like the West, tends to be imagined as primarily rural.) There is no denying that the South occupies a crucial place in African American history and the African American imagination—perhaps even the most important place. As Thadious Davis argues, black literature from at least the 1970s onward has included "the recovery of a later black identity that is rooted in the South as grounded manifestation of the ever-desired formative 'homeplace.'" This southern imagination may also be present in the work of earlier black writers such as Zora Neale Hurston or Arna Bontemps.[17]

Nevertheless, the South is not the only region of importance in the African American cultural imagination, as Ellison's "Going to the Territory" points out. There are counternarratives of black mobility that break from the circum-Atlantic frame and the North-South binary by turning toward the West. One example is recorded in Arna Bontemps and Jack Conroy's collection of African American migration narratives, *Anyplace but Here* (originally, and tellingly, published as *They Seek a City* in 1945):

"Where you bound?" a Negro tenant farmer in Mississippi asked a neighbor who was waiting with two bulging imitation-leather suitcases beside a back-country road. "Goin' North to Chicago-Deetroit [*sic*]?"

"Naw! Too many already gone there and ain't making it so good. I want to strike out to some place where colored folks ain't already crowded up like sardine fish. I'm taking that Liberty Special for Frisco; California, here I come!"[18]

This dialogue raises a series of questions about the current map of African American studies. How does paying attention to the geography it produces change our historical memory of both internal and transnational black migration and its literary outgrowths? How are central paradigms of African American studies, such as the black Atlantic or black internationalism, changed or expanded when the black American West is taken into account? How are scholarly conceptions of black modernity challenged when it becomes located in a place—the West—so long depicted as antimodern (and, in groundbreaking works such as Krista Comer's *Landscapes of the New West: Gender and Geography in Contemporary Women's Writing*, as postmodern)? Finally, how does bringing New Negro writers into the West change our understanding of the West and, by extension, when the West remains a central problem and trope in American studies, our understanding of American identities?

Attempts to answer such questions emerged in the new western history and literary studies that appeared in the 1980s and 1990s, when scholars such as Patricia Nelson Limerick, Richard White, Susan Lee Johnson, Annette Kolodny, and Krista Comer more thoroughly integrated race, gender, class, and sexuality as categories of analysis in scholarship on the West. Since then, work on the black West continues to grow. African American western history is comprehensively represented in Quintard Taylor's *In Search of the Racial Frontier: African Americans in the American West, 1528–1990*, and it has been approached in important and nuanced ways in Douglas Flamming's *Bound for Freedom: Black Los Angeles in Jim Crow America*, Daniel Widener's *Black Arts West: Culture and Struggle in Postwar Los Angeles*, Josh Sides's *L.A. City Limits: African American Los Angeles from the Great Depression to the Present*, and Herbert G. Ruffin II's *Uninvited Neighbors: African Americans in Silicon Valley, 1769–1990*, among others. In literary and cultural studies, scholarly monographs dedicated to African American writers in the West include Blake Allmendinger's *Imagining the African American West*, Eric Gardner's *Unexpected Places: Relocating Nineteenth-Century African American Literature*, and Michael K. Johnson's *Black Masculinity and the Frontier*

Myth in American Literature and *Hoo-Doo Cowboys and Bronze Buckaroos: Conceptions of the African American West.* Through its focus on the black West in the 1920s and 1930s, this book adds to the dialogue initiated by these scholars.[19]

Indeed, there was a deep and pervasive interest in the West during the interwar period. Amply apparent in mass culture, such as pulp fiction and film, and in the rise of the western tourism industry (especially with the formation and expansion of the National Park Service), this interest was also evident among the self-styled avant-gardists of the art world. Modernist attention to the West occurred primarily in the form of primitivism that sought to regenerate white society, which was thought to have become flaccid, deracinated, and overcivilized. This regeneration took place through contact with Mexican American and Native American people in the West (and, in the East, through contact with African Americans) and through the use of folk forms as inspiration for modern art. Exploring the cultures, art, and folkways of these ethnic communities, modernists adapted them to serve their own often highly stylized or highly stereotyped ends. Native American folk art, for example, was exhibited in galleries alongside the work of Dadaists. The imagist *Poetry: A Magazine of Verse* released a special "Indian Issue" in February 1917, after assistant editor Alice Corbin Henderson moved to Santa Fe. A well-known photograph of Willa Cather—taken in 1936 by Carl Van Vechten, a white promoter of the New Negro movement—shows her posed underneath a New Mexican santo. Art patron, *salonnière*, and writer Mabel Dodge Luhan introduced Cather, Georgia O'Keeffe, Ansel Adams, Marsden Hartley, Andrew Dasburg, and D. H. Lawrence (among others) to the West when she hosted them at her pueblo revival-style compound in Taos, New Mexico. The literary and visual art they produced there often presented pristine, untouched, and uncanny landscapes and primitive, simultaneously simple and savage Indian and Mexican people.[20]

White modernists' attraction to the West was largely an attraction to Native Americans and Mexican Americans as racial others. When they formed their own community, white writers who traveled to Luhan's compound hoped to imitate the tribal world of the nearby Taos pueblo. Helen Carr notes that this circle of writers and artists "saw the Pueblos

Willa Cather photographed under a New Mexican santo by Carl Van
Vechten, 1936. (Library of Congress, Prints and Photographs Division, Carl
Van Vechten Collection; courtesy of the Carl Van Vechten Trust)

as a world of beauty and harmony, a welcome retreat from 'Mechanical' America."[21] The West, and the borderlands of the Southwest in particular, became known for the natural beauty of both its landscapes and its racialized native inhabitants.

Such an alliance of race and region is evident in one of the most popular texts published about the Southwest during this period: *Our Southwest* (1940), by New Mexican tour guide and travel writer Erna Fergusson. Born and raised in Albuquerque and known today as "New Mexico's First Lady of Letters," Fergusson was a recognized authority on the region. Yet her book opens with a chapter titled "What Is the Southwest?" When she takes on this definitional project, she focuses on race and culture. She claims that although the region is hard to define geographically, it remains distinct because it is a "mestizo" place: "The Southwest is a crossing of South and West," she writes, "but in the sense of breeding to produce offspring. It is neither South nor West, but a mestizo partaking of the characteristics of both parents, and like a child, baffling to both." Importantly, Fergusson's allusion to *mestizaje*, or racial mixing, is not merely metaphorical or biological; it is also cultural. During the interwar period, when white tourists and modernists arrived in the Southwest, it was largely the Indians of the pueblos and, to a lesser degree, the Mexican Americans of the towns who drew them to immerse themselves in places like Taos and Santa Fe.[22]

Of course, what is missing from this multiracial figuration is a black presence. Another of Fergusson's books starkly demonstrates the limits of her mestizo West, right in the title: *New Mexico: A Pageant of Three Peoples* (1950). The three peoples under study are, unsurprisingly, Native Americans, Mexican Americans, and Anglo-Americans. There are no African Americans (or, for that matter, Asian Americans) to be seen. How quickly *mestizaje* changed from the way it was envisioned by Mexican intellectual José Vasconcelos's 1925 *La raza cósmica* (The Cosmic Race)! There, *mestizaje* incorporates blackness, as Vasconcelos describes "a new race, a synthetic race that aspires to engulf and express everything human in forms of constant improvement." This vision contrasts greatly with the rigid "color-line" of the United States—cited by DuBois as the "problem of the Twentieth Century." Vasconcelos, indeed, critiques the United States' "inflexible line that separates the

Blacks from the Whites, and the laws, each time more rigorous, for the exclusion of the Japanese and Chinese from California." This is far different from the way he characterizes the "Latin continent," which he claims thrives on "increasing and spontaneous mixing which operates among all peoples." In short, although white moderns were attracted to the West precisely because it was a multiethnic landscape, it remained a multiethnic landscape where a black presence seemed unthinkable.[23]

As a result, it becomes easier to understand how a figure like Mabel Dodge Luhan could, on the one hand, marry a Pueblo Indian and become a champion of Indian self-determination (although, admittedly, her activism was often clouded by the lens of privilege) and, on the other hand, exhibit a loathing toward the African Americans she encountered at her New York salon. Luhan's famous "hospitality did not extend to black New Yorkers," writes Christine Stansell in *American Moderns: Bohemian New York and the Creation of a New Century.* When Carl Van Vechten brought black performers—a singer and a dancer—to her apartment in Greenwich Village, "Dodge quailed at the straight-on dose of African American popular culture. The combination of black people and 'low' culture seemed to impinge upon her very sense of herself, calling up racial stereotypes of predatory sexuality." Stansell uses Luhan's memoirs to illustrate this antipathy toward blacks: "An appalling Negress danced," Luhan writes. "The man strummed a banjo and sang an embarrassing song while she cavorted and they both leered and rolled their suggestive eyes and made me feel first hot and then cold, for I had never been so near this kind of thing before." When the West is conceptualized by white modernists as an Indian or a Mexican—but not as a black—place, it explains the contradictions in the stories told by figures like Luhan, whose autobiography documents her hostility toward blacks and her attraction toward Indians. Since both groups are, in her imagination, allied with places (New York and New Mexico, respectively), in such cultural mappings, African Americans are written out of the ethnic landscape of the West. As a result, when white modernists move there, fantasizing about contact with untouched landscapes and quaint, communal people, their fantasies are also predicated on evacuating western blacks. In doing so, they further their "escape"—to use Luhan's term to describe her move to the West—from the problems of the twentieth century by forgetting the black-white color line, by forgetting black art, by forgetting black politics, and by forgetting black literature. In short, the West enables them to attempt to forget blacks entirely. Perhaps it is this kind of willful forgetting that also enables modernists to neglect the multiple dimensions of political struggle for other people of color in the West—by supporting Native self-determination, for example, only when it emphasizes cultural preservation rather than when it emphasizes change, modernization, or a greater allocation of resources (even for things as vital as water or plumbing on reservations).[24]

To reinsert blacks into the scope of the mestizo West is to bring African American studies into dialogue with Chicana and Chicano studies. Whereas the dominant spatial tropes of black studies continue to be diaspora, the black Atlantic, and black internationalism, Chicana and Chicano studies have conceptualized transnationalism by looking to the borderlands. In *Border Matters: Remapping American Cultural Studies*, José David Saldívar draws a parallel between his work on borders and Gilroy's on the black Atlantic. He writes, "the culture of the United States–Mexico borderlands, like the black Atlantic diaspora culture, cannot be reduced to any nationally based 'tradition.'" To look at the black West brings these transnational cultural forms together.

Additionally, Chicana and Chicano studies' borderlands have been critical to rethinking formulations of the American West as, fundamentally, a transnational West. As Saldívar suggests, attention to the *frontera* exposes the limitations of the frontier as the central "field-Imaginary" in American studies by bringing the study of race and ethnicity into the frame; this attention has led to the rethinking of what "American" means when it initiates a transhemispheric perspective. The language of Chicana and Chicano studies, indeed, has reshaped dialogues on the American West and has worked in tandem with—and as a presage to—the new western history and literary studies. Mary Pat Brady's essay "Scaling the West Differently" describes the impact of Chicana and Chicano studies on studies of literature and region in the American West. She remarks, "when we realize that western literature might also be *norteño* literature, the presuppositions buried beneath 'western' are unveiled. Turning 'the West' into 'the North,' or *el norte*, reveals western literature's dependence upon a hidden locus of observation or controlling center, such as New York or New England, and begins the process of revealing the impact such loci may have on the material studied." Concepts of diaspora and transnationalism emerging in black studies have informed borderlands discourses in Chicana and Chicano studies; these borderlands discourses, in turn, have informed studies of the American West and the idea of "America" more generally. As a result, this book participates in recent scholarship of the African American West that considers it in its proper multiethnic context, such as Scott Kurashige's *The Shifting Grounds of Race: Black and Japanese Americans in the Making of Modern Los Angeles,* David Chang's *The Color of the Land: Race, Nation, and the Politics of Landownership in Oklahoma, 1832–1929,* and Stacy Smith's *Freedom's Frontier: California and the Struggle over Unfree Labor, Emancipation, and Reconstruction,* among others. Given this conceptual feedback loop, an exploration of how black cultural production interacts with and perhaps interrupts this cycle makes sense, particularly for an important moment in African American literary history, when authors were informed by new national and transnational vocabularies of race and their complicated imbrications with regional identity. To do so exposes that "the West" is in conversation with more than "the East," and it is also more than Mexico's "North." As José E. Limón points out in *American Encounters: Greater Mexico, the United States, and the Erotics of Culture,* "the West" (including Greater Mexico) also exists in conversation with "the South" and a range of places even more unexpected, all touched by African American migratory and diasporic experience.[25]

This book, then, emerges from the linkages among black studies, Chicana and Chicano studies, western literature and history, and American studies. It asks where the black Atlantic and black internationalism converge with the borderlands and the "*transfrontera* contact zone"— "the social space of subaltern cultures, the Janus-faced border line in which people geopolitically forced to separate themselves now negotiate with one another and manufacture new relations, hybrid cultures, and multiple-voiced aesthetics." In envisioning this convergence, the "borderlands West" examined in this book largely comprises areas that were once parts of Mexico or Indian Territory—sites that complicate notions of both race and nation. This complication is compounded by the presence of African American residents, intellectuals, and writers who lived in, thought about, and traveled through these areas. Some of these places are still within the Mexican nation-state, but most were ceded in 1848 and are now within the geopolitical borders of the United States, such as New Mexico, California, and Utah; other places were once part of Indian Territory—after the Kansas-Nebraska Act, the land that became Oklahoma in 1907. My focus on this borderlands West is not meant to imply that black people did not live in other parts of the western United States or that they did not document their experience via literature and other publications. As Eric Gardner has demonstrated, nineteenth-century blacks were already producing journalism in the Pacific Northwest. And in the early twentieth century, noted filmmaker and writer Oscar Micheaux homesteaded in South Dakota, which inspired his books *Conquest: The Story of a Negro Pioneer* (1913) and *The Homesteader: A Novel* (1917). *The Homesteader* was also adapted as a film in 1919, demonstrating that blacks have always participated in popular constructions of the American West. Furthermore, during the New Negro movement, singer and entertainer Taylor Gordon, a contemporary of the writers examined at length in this book, told "Wild West" stories about his hometown of White Sulphur Springs, Montana, in his published memoir *Born to Be* (1929). My borderlands West is not meant to occlude but to be in dialogue with these voices, while at the same time locating African Americans in geographic, national, and racial borderlands—contested terrain. Additionally, my focus on the borderlands that were once Mexico and Indian Territory is not meant to insinuate that these are the only borderlands in the West—or even the only international borderlands. Historian Kornel Chang has written profitably of the United States–Canada borderlands, and as literary critic Claudia Sadowski-Smith has aptly demonstrated, Latina and Latino, Asian, and Native American border fictions have been produced as well.[26]

By coupling "borderlands" with "West," this book participates in what Krista Comer has called "an emergent critical regionalism or postnational West." She continues, "Revisionist readings of what variously is called the 'glocal' or 'transregional' will . . . be on the horizon of American cultural studies for some time, which means that 'the West'—in all its multiple invocations—necessarily must be at the center of multiple field debates." The complex geographies of regional writing are not provincial; rather, they are reflections of a global milieu—and this is certainly seen in black western writing. In making connections among local, regional, and transnational geographies, Comer insists that "the most difficult and productive challenge" is "to critique the keyword [West] while refusing to vacate a dialogue with it, because to concede the term would be to permit its most regressive political and social effects." Although this book focuses on the borderlands that were once Mexico and Indian Territory, by using the term "West," it also acknowledges the reality that regions do not exist in isolation; they are always relational. I thereby use the term "borderlands West" as a kind of intentional slippage, meant to invoke the networks that bind both adjacent and transnational sites. These networks take many shapes: the dialogue between neighborhoods (such as Los Angeles's Central Avenue district and its Furlong Tract in chapter 2), the dialogue between rural areas and cities (such as the classic binary between the province and the metropolis), the dialogue between regions (such as the West and the South), and the dialogue between nations—not just at the borders where they touch, like the United States–Canada and United States–Mexico borders (see chapter 4), or even the borders between Native American nations and the surrounding United States, but also the dialogues between more surprising and geographically disconnected sites (such as the West's conversation with India in chapter 5).[27]

This book thus aims to revise dominant narratives about both the American West and American literary cultures in the time between Turner's proclamation of "The Significance of the Frontier in American History" and Ellison's "Going to the Territory." It was this period when the West became familiar through frontier myth and was, perhaps, at its most powerful, percolating throughout popular culture and, as Richard Slotkin has argued, national ideology and policy. Taken collectively, the writers I examine at length in this book bore witness to almost this entire span of time. Anita Scott Coleman was the oldest, born in 1890; Arna Bontemps lived the longest, passing away in 1973. Although these writers gained their initial notoriety as "New Negroes" during their youth, all of them—except for Wallace Thurman, who suffered from ill health and died in 1934 at age thirty-two—continued to write well after the New Negro movement declined in the 1930s, whether they published prolifically, sporadically, or rarely. Langston Hughes remained at the forefront of African American literature throughout his life and traveled worldwide as a speaker while maintaining a home base in Harlem. Bontemps also published frequently and lectured publicly, although he was a somewhat quieter figure, devoted to his family and his career as head librarian at Fisk University. A busy mother, foster mother, and community member, Coleman's literary output was scarcer, but she continued to write articles, stories, and poetry; her final work, a children's book titled *Singing Bells*, was published posthumously in 1961. The paucity of Jean Toomer's post-*Cane* (1923) publishing record is well known by scholars, but he too continued to write, and much of his writing has since been archived. In addition to living through these years of powerful frontier mythology and ideology of the West, these writers experienced cataclysmic shifts in black identity politics that informed the publishing industry and the reception of African American literature from the rise of the New Negro movement to its recovery during the civil rights era. And in their work, they brought these stories together.[28]

The chapters that follow explore these writers' varied relationships to the borderlands West through both their literature and their biographies, through their published work and archived manuscripts. Although I consider these writers, for the most part, in separate chapters, it is not my intention to isolate them and reproduce the solitude prized in the tradition of frontier individualism. Rather, my structure and method are derived from feminist theorizing, often by women of color, that has long considered the nexus of race, gender, and region. In *Extinct Lands, Temporal Geographies: Chicana Literature and the Urgency of Space*, Mary Pat Brady contends, "Chicana . . . literature has been particularly attuned to the complex ways race, gender, sexuality, and class emerge simultaneously, if unevenly, through both the discursive and the spatial." An intersectional approach to race, gender, sexuality, class, and the spatial is perhaps most familiar in Gloria Anzaldúa's *Borderlands/La Frontera: The New Mestiza*, which figures the ambiguities of the borderlands not only geographically but also as a complex, multiple "new *mestiza*" consciousness. As Brady points out elsewhere, the epistemological possibilities of this metaphorical borderlands promise fuller, more complete knowledge, yet the metaphorical usage of borderlands has also enabled academics to "locate an argument by apparently materializing it, while often dislocating it from any historically specific referents," thereby minimizing engagement with the realities of, for example, the violence and exploitation that often occur in "real" border spaces.[29]

In this book I strive for the epistemological fullness enabled by metaphorical borderlands, but I allow this metaphor to guide my scholarly method while endeavoring to produce historicized literary research. In doing so, I draw not only from Anzaldúa but also from a range of feminist thinkers who have considered the imbrications of race and gender in spatialized terms and who have insisted on the connections among theory, experience, and practice. Black feminist theorist bell hooks, for example, has written of the "margin" as the site where one can gain a more nuanced, clear, and complete knowledge. She notes, "I did not feel sympathetic to white peers who maintained that I could not expect them to have knowledge of or understand the life experiences of black women. Despite my background (living in racially segregated communities) I knew about the lives of white women, and certainly no white women lived in our neighborhood, attended our schools, or worked in our homes." As a result, she argues that those on the margin have a sort of epistemic advantage and makes a case for bringing the voices and perspectives of women of color to the center of feminist knowledge:

This lived experience may shape our consciousness in such a way that our world view differs from those who have a degree of privilege (however relative within the existing system). It is essential for continued feminist struggle that black women recognize the special vantage point our marginality gives us and make use of this perspective to criticize the dominant racist, classist, sexist hegemony as well as to envision and create a counter-hegemony.[30]

When I look to the borderlands West as a geographic margin of African American literature and history, as well as to writers of color (both black and nonblack) within that marginal geography, I draw from this feminist scholarship. Organizing chapters around a single writer and the borderlands West is one way to apply the insights of feminist theory to my scholarly method. Feminist standpoint epistemology, for example, has long envisioned identities and knowledge emerging from social locations, utilizing a spatial metaphor easily extended to the consideration of region alongside race, gender, and other categories of analysis. As a result of these locations, one's vision, experience, and knowledge can only be partial; however, when myriad "partial perspectives" are brought together, particularly by bringing the knowledge of marginalized groups to the center, they can collaboratively create a stronger objectivity, a clearer way of seeing the world. I envision each of my chapters as a way to focus on one writer's inevitably partial perspective, yet I see the chapters functioning together and speaking collectively in the book as a whole, forming a clearer picture of both New Negro experiences and the American borderlands West. Thus, when I ask these writers to speak together, I am interested in "making a hard turn from anomaly to frequency and unexpectedness," as articulated by Philip J. Deloria in *Indians in Unexpected Places.* By refusing to consider these writers' engagement with the West to be anomalous, I reject the idea that the West is anomalous in black history and experience.[31]

Part I of *West of Harlem* is therefore centered on "One Who Stayed" and foregrounds the presence of black women in the West. Chapter 1, "Home on the Range: Domesticity and a Black Woman's West," focuses on the writing of Anita Scott Coleman. Recently rediscovered in scholarship, Coleman largely *has* been treated as anomalous in terms of African American engagement with the West during the Harlem renaissance years. However, she is certainly not the only African American to write about the West. Nor is she the only black woman writer from the West, although she is the one who most explicitly discusses the West as a region. Born in Mexico, Coleman moved to New Mexico as a toddler, where she remained until adulthood. She then moved not to Harlem but to Los Angeles. Although she stayed in the borderlands West, she published prolifically in Harlem-based venues such as the *Crisis* and *Opportunity* in the 1920s. Her lifelong western residency is fairly uncommon among well-known New Negro writers, but in contrast to the assumptions of recent critics, her interaction with the West is by no means unique. Descriptions of Coleman as virtually the only New Negro writer in the West perpetuate mythologies of western individualism, furthering the idea that African Americans in the West were solitary, dislocated, and anomalous. Perhaps Coleman herself, who describes the paucity of black westerners in her essay "Arizona and New Mexico—The Land of Esperanza," exacerbates this sense. She claims that "here and there are Negroes, like straggly but tenacious plants growing . . . an isolated lot." Yet a closer look at Coleman's writing reveals a counternarrative of black domesticity, community, and nationalism, as well as the connections between multiethnic borderland communities and black communities that are not situated "home to Harlem," as Claude McKay wrote, but home in the borderlands West.[32]

Despite depictions (like Coleman's) of the West as an African American home during the years of the Great Migration, other New Negro writers reversed the westward trajectory, leaving the West for Harlem. Part II, comprising chapters on Arna Bontemps, Wallace Thurman, and Langston Hughes, focuses on "Those Who Went Away." Chapter 2, "The Two LAs: Los Angeles, Louisiana, and Geographies of Race," explores the western experiences and writings of Bontemps. Although born in Louisiana, Bontemps spent his formative years in Los Angeles, where he moved in 1906 when he was three years old. According to historian Douglas Flamming (the only scholar to date who has written about Bontemps and the West), Bontemps left for Harlem in 1924 because he felt a need to "re-establish ties with the African American culture he . . . had lost in the West." Bontemps's unpublished, archived works, however, expand this interpretation. These works—an autobiographical bildungsroman titled "The Chariot in the Cloud" (1929) and an unfinished novel with the working title "The Prizefighter and the Woman" (1947)—are set in the Los Angeles region. Rather than simply leaving the West behind, these texts create complicated triangulations between the West, the North (particularly Harlem), and the South, as well as intricate local geographies of Los Angeles. Taken together, they call the location and stability of African American culture into question.[33]

Wallace Thurman, the subject of chapter 3, "Revolt from the Provinces: Black Politics of Respectability and Black Sexual Politics," also moved from Los Angeles to Harlem in the mid-1920s. There, he would become known as a consummate Manhattanite, but he was born and raised largely in Salt Lake City, Utah, with stints in Boise, Idaho, and Los Angeles. Thurman's portrait of the black West at first seems largely negative. In one essay from 1926 he writes, "I am sorry . . . I have to write of the Utah Negro," because rather than inspire racial pride, "there has been and is certainly nothing about him to inspire anyone to do anything save perhaps drink gin with gusto and develop new technique for the contravention of virginity." He concludes his essay by lamenting, "Thus is Utah burdened with dull and unprogressive Mormons, with more dull and speciously progressive Gentiles, and with still more dull and not even speciously progressive Negroes. Everyone in the state seems more or less a vegetable." Yet despite his claims to New York chauvinism, a closer look at Thurman's western writing reveals critiques of New York as cutting as those of Utah—and Utah and the West provide historical fodder that makes the region more compatible with his queer black aesthetic than Harlem is.[34]

The work of Langston Hughes is explored in chapter 4, "Technicolor Places: Race and Revolution in Transnational America." Hughes preceded his colleagues Bontemps and Thurman in traveling from the borderlands West to Harlem. Hughes's borderlands, however, extend transnationally, originating in Toluca, Mexico, where he lived with his father during the summer of 1919 and from the summer of 1920 through the summer of 1921. In the winter of 1934–1935 Hughes returned to Mexico, this time to Mexico City, to settle his father's estate. Although his time there was limited, Mexico played a formative role in Hughes's transnational and antiracist vision, a politics and aesthetic long considered Pan-African but here also understood as multiethnic.

Part III turns to "One Who Arrived," Jean Toomer. While Hughes's biography and writing interrogate the transnational West across the conjoined borders of Mexico and the United States, Toomer's work extends this reach to transnational sites farther afield, as discussed in chapter 5, "Mapping the New American Race: From New York to New Mexico—and Beyond." For Toomer, who articulated a multiple, mixed-race identity, Harlem proved to be a site of oppression rather than liberation, and he looked elsewhere for a more fitting home. In New Mexico, where Toomer traveled and lived periodically from the 1920s through the 1940s, he found this home—a place not of whiteness or blackness but of *mestizaje*. He describes this in a 1940 essay titled "New

Mexico after India," where he contemplates the relationships among the racial landscapes of New Mexico, New York, and India, places he had traveled to while seeking spiritual, racial, and personal coherence.

These five chapters bring African American literature into the center of studies of the transnational American West, in part providing a counterdiscourse to writing by Anglo-American modernists, who tend to efface black westerners while affixing romantic, primitivist gazes on Native Americans and Mexican Americans. In contrast, the writing of Native Americans, Mexican Americans, and Asian Americans in the West does not occlude black westerners. These writings are the subject of the book's coda, "The Borderlands of Blackness: The Formation of a Multiethnic American Imagination." Osage Indian writer and historian John Joseph Mathews's autobiographical novel *Sundown* (1934), "proto-Chicano" writer and folklorist Américo Paredes's collection of poetry *Between Two Worlds* (published in 1991 but penned largely in the 1930s and 1940s), Mexican American writer Josefina Niggli's *Mexican Village* (1945), and Filipino writer and labor activist Carlos Bulosan's *America Is in the Heart* (1943) offer glimpses of the black West in conjunction with Native American, Mexican American, and Asian American histories and literatures during the period of this study. In these works, black westerners provide new ways for nonblack borderlands subjects to consider their own ethnic identities and place in the American racial order. In bringing this comparative perspective to ethnic literatures, I suggest the potential for mutual progress and critical dialogue across the field of ethnic studies and the broader project of interdisciplinary American cultural studies.

When I identify the West as the place where African American studies, Chicana and Chicano studies, and other ethnic studies converge, I point to a site that continues to be a force in the American imagination, a nexus that occupies a central place in American studies and, indeed, in debates about what it meant to be American during the first half of the twentieth century. Along the way, the modernist West of Anglo-American writers and artists, so tied to primitivist fantasies of Native and Mexican American people, arts, and folkways, is disrupted by an African American presence. African American subjects and African American writings call the dominant historical narratives of the black

West as either a space of absence or a space of individual opportunity into question. The persistent representation of the New Negro as an urban identity produced as an outgrowth of the Great Migration is dislocated by this new geographic context—one that rethinks the "practice of diaspora" beyond the black Atlantic and urban internationalism. Finally, the ethnic landscape of the borderlands West is complicated not only by considering the treatment of Mexican American, Asian American, and Native American westerners in African American writing but also by considering the representation of black Westerners in literature by nonblack people of color, where the black presence is surprising, given the manner in which African Americans have largely been absented from the West created by Anglo-American writing. Overall, this book seeks to discover two things: What happens to African American identity when it is placed in sites that have long been considered, as Erna Fergusson's writing reminds us, tricultural and exclusive of blacks? And how do conversations about race in the United States change when they happen predominantly among minority groups, rather than in conversations with Anglo America?

The answers to these inquiries are twofold. On the one hand, I argue that the West reveals things about African American literature and race that a focus on Harlem, or even on Harlem and the South, does not. Black nationalism and racial uplift become complicated, enriched, and even undermined when African American writers confront the minority groups and racial orders that proliferate in the borderlands. On the other hand, I contend that African American literature reveals things about the borderlands West that other literatures do not. For so long, the borderlands West has been imagined in two ways. In the first way, the Anglo frontier myth either vanishes or romanticizes Indians and Mexicans, ignores Asian immigration, forgets African Americans, and envisions a feminized, virgin land ripe for the American Adam. The second way, which counters this deracinated West, comes from Chicana and Chicano studies and fantasizes about a radically hybrid borderlands, a place of epistemic advantage and liberation from oppressive hierarchies. African American literature during the long New Negro movement tells us that, ultimately, the borderlands West is neither of these things—the black westerner undermines the deracinated Anglo frontier myth, while the long reach of Jim Crow is a sad reminder of the limits of borderlands metaphors. When Anita Scott Coleman calls Arizona and New Mexico "the land of esperanza," she describes exactly these paradoxes. Her choice to use the Spanish word for "hope" when writing for a largely African American, English-speaking audience indicates that the borderlands West was imagined as a multiethnic space for liberation, including African American liberation. Yet embedded in this word for hope is *esperar*, the verb for "to wait," which suggests that this space for multiethnic liberation is still in the making—still, as Langston Hughes would write of Harlem in 1951, "a dream deferred."[35]

PART I

One Who Stayed

What happens to a dream deferred?

Does it dry up
like a raisin in the sun?
Or fester like a sore—
And then run?
Does it stink like rotten meat?
Or crust and sugar over—
Like a syrupy sweet?

Maybe it just sags
Like a heavy load.

Or does it explode?
—Langston Hughes, "Harlem (2)" (1951)

CHAPTER I

Home on the Range

Domesticity and a Black Woman's West

> Indeed, to a Harlem Negro oppressed by moldering
> tenements, Watts might look like the promised land with
> its wide boulevards, grassy backyards and single- and
> two-story houses. Yet the psychic truth runs deeper: in
> the super-America of southern California, Watts weighs
> its lot not against the garbage-strewn streets of Harlem
> or the dusty "Niggertowns" of Dixie, but against the
> lush life of Hollywood Boulevard, the beaches of Santa
> Monica and the affluent traffic of the Harbor Freeway,
> which swoops over the ghetto.
> —"*After the Bloodbath,*" Newsweek *(August 30, 1965)*

From 1922 to 1925, the *Nation* published a series of essays collectively titled *These United States.* In it, writers like Willa Cather waxed poetically about places like Nebraska to demonstrate the diversity and variety among the states of the union and to capture their "spirit of place," to use D. H. Lawrence's term from 1923. With the exception of an essay on Georgia written by W. E. B. DuBois, none of the essays were by African Americans. The series inevitably and unavoidably discussed race, but without the voices of people of color. These essays written by well-meaning white progressives often fell woefully short in their discussions of race and racism. The essay on Mississippi, by Beulah Amidon Ratliff, traffics almost exclusively in racist stereotypes when she describes it as "undeniably a backward State." Clement Wood's essay on Alabama insists that "Alabama is both [white and black] races. If she forgets this, the cost to herself will be desolating," while largely discussing interracial sexuality and sexual exploitation. Ludwig Lewisohn's apologist essay on South Carolina positions a gentlemanly, aristocratic, paternalistic "Old South" against a new one that, among its other despicable qualities, "oppress[es] and bedevil[s] the Negro without the old gentry's vivid and human even if strictly feudal sympathy with his character and needs." Similarly, Douglas Freeman's essay on Virginia insists that, contrary to what his readers might assume, African Americans there are treated with great consideration by whites. Yet in the essays on other southern states—Arkansas, Louisiana, North Carolina, Tennessee, and West Virginia—there is little mention of black Americans. In essays on northern and midwestern states, they are almost entirely absent. In the borderlands West, Elizabeth Shepley Sergeant, who authored the essay on New Mexico, has to contend with Indians and "Spanish Americans," "two cultures as ancient as anything on our continent." Still, she sees them as "little modified by centuries and circumstance" and vacillates between vanishing them and praising their simplicity and spiritual freedom under a primitivist eye. From Mary Austin, who takes up Arizona, one also gets the sense that Indians are valued most when they are vanished or assimilated into whiteness: "The Indian tribes incorporated in the State," she writes, "are most of them of superior type. . . . In Arizona more individualistic cultures have made possible a more citizenly type of coordination, in which the Indians give promise of becoming, as an intelligent Navaho once put it to me, 'a pulse in the side of the white race.'"[1]

In response to the racial politics of *These United States*, the Harlem-based African American political, literary, and cultural magazine the *Messenger* published a series of essays titled *These "Colored" United States* from 1923 to 1926. In this series, the *Messenger* proclaimed, "a brilliant representative from each State that has a goodly proportion of Negroes will speak out . . . and say to the world in plain language just what conditions they face." Contributors to the series included Alice Dunbar-Nelson writing on Delaware, George Schuyler writing on New York, Wallace Thurman writing on Utah, and Anita Scott Coleman, a black woman from New Mexico who wrote an essay titled "Arizona and New Mexico—The Land of Esperanza." In this essay and throughout her

Anita Scott Coleman reads on her family's New Mexico ranch, 1915.
(Courtesy of the Anita Scott Coleman Family Collection)

written corpus, Coleman advanced her vision of the West and provided an alternative to the more prevalent spatial imaginings constructed by the contributors to *These United States*, particularly white female regionalists like Mary Austin. She did so not only by including African Americans in the scope of the borderlands West but also by rethinking western women's homemaking through the perspective of African American history and experience.[2]

Although largely forgotten in scholarly recollections of the New Negro movement, Coleman was not an unknown within the Harlem literary scene, having published in leading forums such as the *Crisis* and *Opportunity*, in addition to the *Messenger*. Her poems, short stories, and essays had also been published in black newspapers nationwide, including the *Baltimore Afro-American*, as well as in middlebrow African American women's magazines such as *Half-Century Magazine*. She won Spingarn literary prizes, presented by the *Crisis*, in 1925 and 1926, as well as *Opportunity*'s literary prize in 1925. Other winners would become New Negro luminaries, including Countee Cullen, Arna Bontemps, Zora Neale Hurston, and Langston Hughes. In 1928, at what was arguably the peak of the New Negro movement, the *Messenger* called Coleman "one of the best of the Negro writers," and as late as 1938, a review of the collection *Negro Voices: An Anthology of Contemporary Verse* counted Coleman among "those who have already established some reputations in the field of literature." Coleman continued to receive widespread recognition into the 1940s and remained well known to African American writers who would themselves become synonymous with the New Negro movement. For example, in 1943 Langston Hughes opened his column in the *Chicago Defender* by quoting a character from one of Coleman's short stories, treating her as a household name.[3]

Despite Coleman's notoriety in Harlem and in wider African American publishing networks, she remained geographically distant from New York for her entire life, always remaining in the West. This geographic trajectory sets Coleman apart from many of her New Negro contemporaries. Although other well-known writers, such as Thurman and Bontemps, grew up in the West, most abandoned it for the allure of Jazz Age Harlem. It is worth noting, however, that Coleman is not anomalous: a perusal of Spingarn prizewinners, for example, reveals many others from western locations, including other women. In 1925 a young poet named Bernice Love Wiggins self-published a book titled *Tuneful Tales* in El Paso. And in Los Angeles, where Coleman moved after leaving New Mexico in 1926, there was a lively writers' community. With the encouragement of *Opportunity* editor Charles S. Johnson, a black literary club, called the Ink Slingers, was created there, and Coleman participated in it.[4]

Despite her substantive publishing record, scholarly work on Coleman has only recently begun to surface. In 2008 two collections of her writing were published: *Unfinished Masterpiece: The Harlem Renaissance Fiction of Anita Scott Coleman*, edited by Laurie Champion and Bruce A. Glasrud, and *Western Echoes of the Harlem Renaissance: The Life and Writings of Anita Scott Coleman*, edited by Cynthia Davis and Verner D. Mitchell. Champion and Glasrud's introduction to their collection of Coleman's short stories situates her work among that of other New Negro writers, including other westerners such as Thurman and Bontemps, and in black publications of the 1920s and 1930s. Theirs is primarily a recovery project, much like those undertaken for so many other women writers of the New Negro movement and most famously described in Alice Walker's "In Search of Zora Neale Hurston." Davis and Mitchell's introduction to their collection takes a different approach. In addition to preserving and republishing Coleman's written corpus, they correct the scant prior scholarly record of Coleman's life and literary contributions. Relying largely on interviews with surviving family members, Davis and Mitchell remediate the inaccuracies reproduced in earlier scholarship and provide a more developed portrait of Coleman and her family. As a result, their work contains the most comprehensive biographical study of Coleman to date.[5]

As Davis and Mitchell document, Coleman was born Anita (Annie) Scott in 1890 in Guaymas, Sonora, Mexico, to Mary Ann Stokes and William Henry Scott. When she was a toddler, the family moved to Silver City, New Mexico, where she would live from 1893 until 1926. By then, she had married a man named James Harold Coleman. He relocated to Los Angeles in 1924 in search of work, and she and her children joined him in 1926. She would remain in Los Angeles for the rest of her life, passing away in 1960. During these years, the black West grew exponentially, and Coleman bore witness to these changes, which were most dramatic in cities like Los Angeles, where migrants and their progeny tended to be housed. As an example of this growth, it is worth noting that the black population of Los Angeles in 1880 was a mere 102; by 1900, it had grown to 2,131; and ten years later, in 1910, the black population of Los Angeles had reached 7,599. By 1920, six years before Coleman arrived, the black population totaled 15,579. This astounding growth would continue for decades. By the time of Coleman's death in 1960, blacks in Los Angeles numbered 334,916. An expanding African American population was also characteristic of Coleman's home state of New Mexico, although it was not nearly as dramatic. There, it wasn't until the "closure" of the frontier in the late nineteenth century that the territory opened significantly to African Americans. Whereas New Mexico was home to a mere 172 "Negroes" in 1870, this had increased nearly sixfold, to 1,015, in 1880. By the time of Coleman's birth in 1890, the black population of New Mexico had grown to 1,956. Of these, more than 30 percent (592) lived in Grant County, where Silver City is the county seat. Grant County thus had the greatest number of African Americans in New Mexico; there, the black-white ratio was approximately 1:15. By comparison, in San Miguel County, which had the greatest number of whites in New Mexico (22,986), there were nearly 178 whites for every African American. In sum, when Coleman arrived as a child in 1893, Silver City looked quite different from the majority of New Mexico; it had a far more prominent black presence than elsewhere in the territory. This would inform Coleman's depictions of New Mexico—particularly in terms of its strong black western community—in her written work.[6]

The surprising black presence in Grant County was largely due to a silver boom in the 1870s. According to Rodman Wilson Paul, "towns like Silver City became famous, and mines, mills, and smelters went to work in the hills of southern New Mexico even at a time when the railroad was still fifty miles away, the isolation severe, and the Apache danger very real." In 1881, reporting on an exhibition of "the finest silver ores ever seen in this city"—which originated from Grant County—the *Washington Post* declared, "all the reports of rich discoveries are not visionary, but real ones, and . . . New Mexico and Arizona will eventually furnish the bullion wealth of the world." With such press, Grant County's reputation as a boomtown was secured, and it was nicknamed "the treasure vault of New Mexico." As word spread about its mineral stores, Grant County began to look like mining areas elsewhere in the West. The difficult, dangerous work with erratic payoffs would have lured men of wide-ranging backgrounds, including African Americans. Miner and pioneer H. W. Ailman suggests as much in his memoirs, noting that old California gold miners resettled near Silver City, which implies that the heterogeneous culture of California gold mining may have carried over to New Mexico. He describes a multiethnic community of miners that was often in conflict with Indians who attempted to fend off encroachment on their homelands. Mexicans in the region, Ailman notes, were largely responsible for creating the smelting technology necessary to produce silver bullion. He also worked with a "raw Dutchman, just over," who "could talk five languages—German, Irish, Spanish, English, and American," an asset due to the multiethnic character of Silver City's mining labor. Newspapers as far away as Chicago gloated that in Silver City, "Mexican labor can be got in abundance at $1 to $1.25 per day," while a writer in the *Atlanta Constitution* complained, "Everybody" in Silver City "eats at Chinese restaurants." Although mentioned less often than the Mexicans, European immigrants, and even Asian immigrants of Silver City, African Americans were not absent from these descriptions of its boomtown years. As in mining communities elsewhere (such as Bisbee, Arizona), they were relegated to domestic duties, which were deemed unsavory in a largely masculine environment; for example, Ailman mentions his "Negro cook."[7]

These workers were not the only blacks to make their way to Silver City. To protect the claims of miners and settlers who were increasingly impinging on Apache homelands, Fort Bayard was built on the outskirts of Silver City in 1866. It housed active troops until 1899, including "colored troops" such as the Ninth and Tenth Calvary—the so-called buffalo soldiers enlisted in the service of manifest destiny. The presence of these troops contributed to Grant County's black population. Coleman's father had served with the Ninth Calvary in Texas from 1879 to 1889, and it is possible that the presence of this familiar community—as well as the economic opportunities offered by the mines and associated

industries—is what drew the Scott family there in 1893. There may have
been personal reasons as well. As Verner D. Mitchell records, Silver City
was home to "three tubercular sanitariums, including the largest one in
the country, which would have made it attractive to William Henry, as
Anita suffered from pulmonary ailments."[8]

Over Coleman's lifetime, however, the black community in New
Mexico transitioned in terms of both size and geographic distribution.
By the 1900 census, the number of black New Mexicans had dropped
precipitously, likely because of declining payouts from the mines in the
1890s, which made prospects bleaker for everyone in the area and likely
more so for blacks. By 1902, newspapers nationwide were claiming that
the town, once "a red hot, rip-roaring mining camp" that was "full of
life," now "tells by its dirt and dilapidation the pathetic story of Silver
City's decline." Along with a loss of population due to the collapse of
the mining industry, the eventual containment of Geronimo and the
Apaches led to the decommissioning of Fort Bayard, which became an
army sanitarium in 1899. Upon their discharge, soldiers were entitled
to free transportation back to where they had enlisted, and many blacks
took advantage of this offer and left the region. According to William A.
Doback and Thomas D. Phillips, however, "A survey of 418 black regulars'
pension files showed . . . 129 settled in the west outside of Texas in towns
from San Diego to St. Paul (Fort Snelling), Missoula to Silver City, New
Mexico (Fort Bayard). Clearly the army had taken these men places that
they would not have gone otherwise." Indeed, Davis and Mitchell report
that "obituary and census reports confirm . . . that a number of buffalo
soldiers . . . retired in Silver City," a fact that Coleman corroborates when
she describes black "Indian war fighter[s], who thought wearily upon
receiving [their] discharge[s] that 'here' was as good as 'way back there'
to settle down and rest." As a result, despite the general depopulation of
the region, a core group of black community members, referred to by
Silver City newspapers as "colored pioneers," remained. These included
the Scott family. Even after Coleman's departure from Silver City in the
1920s, its black community remained entrenched, and African American
newspapers in the East would occasionally report social events there.[9]

After 1900, the number of blacks in the area steadily increased
again, likely due to a growing service sector in the region, linked to the

railroad. When the railroad finally reached the area near Silver City, it provided employment (albeit difficult and sometimes demeaning) for African Americans, particularly men. It also provided geographic and some social mobility. As one of the largest employers of black men nationwide, railroads produced a collective voice for black workers, leading to greater political agency; this culminated in the 1920s with the formation of the Brotherhood of Sleeping Car Porters. Coleman's father was among those who found work on the railroad in Silver City. As a result, she may have grown up hearing conversations about black labor, civil rights, and place, which are echoed in her written work. It is not surprising, then, that Coleman submitted work to and received accolades from the *Messenger*, which was cofounded by A. Philip Randolph and Chandler Owen in 1917. The *Messenger* became both a major forum for the publication of New Negro literature and the official publication of the Brotherhood of Sleeping Car Porters after Randolph spearheaded the organization in 1925. Wallace Thurman (the subject of chapter 3) served as managing editor for the *Messenger* in 1925–1926, so he likely oversaw the publication of some of Coleman's work.[10]

Until the 1920s, Coleman and other blacks in New Mexico did not experience a legal doctrine of Jim Crow segregation. Although extralegal systems of white supremacy existed in New Mexico, blacks were relatively unlikely to be the targets of mob violence there. According to the Tuskegee data on lynching, between 1883 and 1962, there were thirty-six cases of lynching in New Mexico; only three of the victims were African American. This is not to say that white supremacy and racialized violence did not impact black life in New Mexico. As William D. Carrigan and Clive Webb have noted, the Tuskegee data do not demarcate beyond the simple binary of "black" and "white"; "white" therefore includes people of Mexican, Asian, and Native American descent or origin, even when they are denied the privileges of whiteness in terms of political power and social practice. Additionally, some instances of anti-Mexican mob violence were not included in the Tuskegee data at all. Carrigan and Webb suggest that New Mexico—along with Texas, California, and Arizona—had high rates of anti-Mexican violence. As a result, systems of racial terror were certainly present in New Mexico. Thus the specter of racialized violence likely haunted the lives of all

An African American Pullman porter in Albuquerque, New Mexico, ca.
1890s. (Center for Southwest Research, University Libraries, University of
New Mexico)

people of color, but it was a less obvious threat to African Americans
than to Mexican Americans.[11]

Although it was not free of racialized brutality, the West seemed to
promise African Americans a better environment than either the Jim Crow
South or the North, where blacks were susceptible to discrimination and
mob violence. Beginning most famously in the 1870s with the Kansas
group known as the "Exodusters," African Americans who traveled to the
West began to establish predominantly black towns. As Ellison's "Going
to the Territory" suggests, Oklahoma also became a major site of black
migration from the South during the late nineteenth and early twentieth
centuries, and it saw the establishment of many black towns. Advertisements persuaded African Americans to "give yourselves and children new
chances in a new land, where you will not be molested and where you will

be able to think and vote as you please," a place where "the negro can rest from mob law, here he can be secure from every ill of southern politics." Beyond Kansas and Oklahoma, blacks joined communities throughout the West as they left the post-Reconstruction South behind with the goal of fostering black freedom and autonomy in places that seemed less touched by Jim Crow. California, Colorado, and New Mexico became home to black municipalities. In New Mexico, the towns of Blackdom and Vado were formed in the early twentieth century. According to historian Gerald Horne, "Negroes flocked to . . . 'a dream in the desert,'" and some even "walked a year from Georgia to reach this site." Based on the lore surrounding the town's founding, "Blackdom represented attempts by blacks to escape the caste system imposed upon them by southern whites." Its founders, Francis (Frank) Boyer and Daniel Keyes, had "witnessed a black barber shot and killed by a white customer" in Georgia. "Tired of these slave conditions," they "started walking to New Mexico and freedom in 1896." Boyer had evidently grown up hearing tales about New Mexico from his father, who had served there as a solider during the Mexican-American War; the elder Boyer had described it as a place of relative freedom for blacks. After the settlement was established in 1901 under the provisions of the Homestead Act, more blacks were lured there by articles and advertisements placed in African American newspapers throughout the nation. In December 1912, for example, the *Chicago Defender* printed a letter to the editor from a Blackdom resident named Lucy Henderson. She sang the praises of homesteading there, passionately declaiming:

> I feel that I owe it to my people to tell them of this free land out here which is the equal of the best land to be found anywhere, and where the climate is ideal, where there is no "Jim Crowism" and where the constitution of the state cannot be changed for the coming twenty-five years. Here the black man has an equal chance with the white man. Here you are reckoned at the value which you place upon yourself. Your future is in your hands to be what you would have it be.

She concluded, "I have only this to say—that any one coming to Blackdom and deciding to throw in their lot with us will never have cause to regret it."[12]

Henderson's letter makes an interesting point about New Mexico during an important year of its history—the year it achieved statehood. Drama surrounding statehood had been occurring since the mid-nineteenth century, when New Mexico first became a territory. It initially petitioned for statehood in 1850, with a constitution that outlawed slavery. At that time, its territorial boundaries also included what is now Arizona, as well as parts of what is now Texas, Oklahoma, Utah, and Kansas. The Compromise of 1850 ground New Mexico's application for statehood to a halt and initiated a debate about whether it could ban slavery. Although there had never been many enslaved people in New Mexico, its antislavery stance was in fidelity with Mexican tradition. Black politics and Latina and Latino politics were entwined. Needless to say, slave states—particularly neighboring Texas—agitated against statehood for New Mexico, and during the Civil War, the territory faced more difficulties when Arizona seceded from New Mexico and set up a pro-Confederacy, pro-slavery provisional territorial government. Although there were few blacks in the region during these years, black politics was at the center of New Mexican and Arizonan politics—with New Mexico decidedly more antislavery than Arizona. The shadow of anti- and pro-slavery politics would haunt these two territories into the twentieth century. In 1906 Congress passed a joint statehood bill for New Mexico and Arizona, but it was rejected by Arizona on the basis of race. Arizonans protested to the Senate and cited "the decided racial differences between the people of Arizona and the large majority of the people of New Mexico, who are not only different in race and largely in language, but have entirely different customs, laws, and ideals and would have but little prospect of successful amalgamation." New Mexico, in short, had much larger Mexican American and Native American populations than Arizona did, and it hoped to implement policy that ensured these residents (particularly the *hispano*, or Spanish-descended, population) some measure of rights and protection under the law. Arizona balked at these more progressive politics. When New Mexico finally achieved statehood in 1912, its constitution included explicit protections for Spanish speakers (including bilingual education), as well as provisions for racial equality in voting and political office holding that would be very difficult to amend. In fact, these provisions (Article VII, Section

3, and Article XII, Section 10) came to be called the "unamendable" sections of the New Mexico Constitution. Although these provisions were not designed with African Americans in mind (and it is worth noting that they were a formidable obstacle to women's suffrage), it is possible that, as a result of such politics and policies, African Americans like Lucy Henderson saw New Mexico as a place where racial equality was possible.[13]

Despite Henderson's insistence that there was "no 'Jim Crowism'" in Blackdom, the existence of this community did not go uncontested by its white neighbors. Early responses to the settlement included virulent white-supremacist sentiments such as those expressed in a 1903 article titled "White Man's Country," in which Roswell resident W. R. Cummins wrote:

> This is a white man's government and ever since Roswell has been on the map white people have paid the taxes and managed the town. It is true that there have been one or two good old fashioned negroes here and they have had the respect and confidence of all the people. But now Roswell is threatened with an overflow of negroes run out of the panhandle of Texas and Oklahoma and the people are wondering what to do to protect their families and homes from these worthless blacks. Today they are threatening to invade our public schools, they are saucy and impudent.

This article is steeped in the language of racism, including the paternalistic suggestion that there are "good old fashioned negroes" who are loyal and subservient and welcome in the community as long as their labor can be exploited. Also evident is a paranoia about the new generation of blacks who presumably did not grow up under the yoke of slavery and thus are imagined by whites to be "threatening," "saucy," and "impudent" when they defy white-supremacist fantasies of black deference in order to seek economic, social, and political independence. Blacks from Texas, where poll taxes and white primaries had nearly completely disenfranchised African Americans in the former slave state, were particularly likely to migrate westward in the hope of shaking off Jim

Crow. (Oklahoma was still a territory—both Oklahoma Territory and Indian Territory—in 1903, and Jim Crow had not yet been legislated. It was, however, on its way.)[14]

When Roosevelt Boyer Sr., the son of Blackdom cofounder Frank Boyer, recalled growing up in the town, he commented on the racism among white New Mexicans and how it was inflected not just by black but also by white migration to the territory: "At first whites didn't mind [the Blackdom settlement]," he suggested. "They were all from the North and they all soon moved out and left the place to Southerners." The southerners "didn't like nobody. They was hard on us as they could be." When New Mexico became increasingly populated by migrants from many ethnic groups in the early twentieth century, white migrants brought their regionally inflected versions of antiblack racism with them. Northerners responded to the black settlement with a kind of early "white flight," and southerners responded with more obvious white supremacy, all rooted in fears of miscegenation (such as when Cummins wonders what whites can do "to protect their families") and racial segregation (such as Cummins's reference to the "overflow of negroes . . . threatening to invade our public schools"). Later, when Vado was settled, the Ku Klux Klan reportedly threatened the town, but the "settlers held their ground."[15]

Even when whites ostensibly supported Blackdom, they did so only when the black community was painted as accommodationist—as thrifty and industrious and, perhaps most important, as segregated. In 1915 the *Roswell Record* encouraged whites to attend the dedication of Blackdom's Baptist church, suggesting, "Blackdom is an enterprising community . . . and all should be interested in its progress. Negroes living a contented, prosperous, and communal life, are rare indeed and should be encouraged by white people." Like Cummins's article, this description of Blackdom as "contented," "communal," "enterprising," and "prosperous" perpetuates a white fantasy of "old fashioned negroes" who are subservient, whose value lies in their capacity as laborers, and who are seemingly content with segregation. The article goes on to note that "refreshments for white people will be served separately."[16]

In his memoirs, W. E. "Old Man" Utterback writes of being "truly among the pioneering families of southeastern New Mexico." He recalls,

"About ten miles west of Greenfield was a place called Blackdom. A number of Negroes homesteaded this land. They were a bunch of hard-working people and gave no trouble in any way." His statement participates in the paternalistic fantasies about black labor and obedience, while at the same time expressing surprise at black respectability and civility. Although Utterback compacts Blackdom's residents into these fantasies, he also intuits something deeply subversive about Blackdom. This comes, surprisingly and humorously, during his recollections of a baseball game:

> On Emancipation Day [Blackdom residents] invited the white folks out for a big feed; the women were excellent cooks. After the feed, the Negro men challenged the white men to a baseball game. . . . I caught the game and as we played on an open prairie with no backstop, I had to do a good job of catching. The field faced north and their big first baseman, whom they called Y. Z., hit one which I think landed in Orchard Park. I made the sad mistake of trying to block this Y. Z. from home plate. He came in head first and skinned my shin bone about a foot. Oh, by the way, we lost the ball game.

In Utterback's memories, Blackdom residents walked a fine line between meeting and challenging the expectations of their white neighbors. On the one hand, they were "hard-working people who gave no trouble" and fulfilled white ideals about black female domestication ("the women were [predictably] excellent cooks") and black male physicality (the formidable Y. Z.). Based on this description, Blackdom appeared to be a safe and satisfactory settlement to this white man's gaze. On the other hand, Blackdom was clearly a community that celebrated black independence. Its residents also challenged (perhaps playfully) white authority by besting their neighbors in a baseball game. (Lest we be tempted to downplay the seriousness of a baseball game as a challenge to white authority, recall that this was the era of boxer Jack Johnson's famous "Fight of the Century" and defeat of the "Great White Hope" James Jeffries—an event that led to nationwide unrest and violence. Sport often mirrors national tensions about race.) The residents of

Blackdom played subversively with white expectations—a trickster-like subversion that seems particularly at home in the West, where Native American and African American folk and narrative traditions, centered on archetypal trickster characters who represent patterns of resistance, meet and inform each other.[17]

New Mexico's predominantly black towns, Blackdom and Vado, do not go unconsidered in Coleman's writing. In her essay "Arizona and New Mexico—The Land of Esperanza," she refers to them as "the greatest outstanding feature of the Negro population . . . in New Mexico." This is high praise from someone who never lived in either town, and it suggests that while whites may have seen Blackdom as either a threat to racial purity or safely segregated, black New Mexicans saw the settlement quite differently. And although none of the Scott family ever lived in Blackdom or Vado, Anita would have had intimate knowledge of the dreams and goals of the Blackdom community because the man she married, James Harold Coleman, was an early settler and promoter of the town. Davis and Mitchell surmise that "James Coleman was born in Virginia and grew up in Washington, D.C. . . . [He] was a skilled printer and photographer who may have gone west to work as a chauffeur for a wealthy family. . . . Perhaps . . . James was disillusioned with New Mexico and wanted to return east." This biography, however, seems incomplete, given an advertisement placed in the *Crisis* in 1913, where Coleman implored blacks to settle in Blackdom: "WANTED 500 Negro families (farmers preferred) to settle in FREE government lands in Chaves County, New Mexico. Blackdom is a Negro colony. Fertile soil, ideal climate. No 'Jim Crow' Laws. For information write JAS. HAROLD COLEMAN Blackdom . . . New Mexico." Particularly noteworthy is the insistence that "Blackdom is a Negro colony." This sentence suggests that it was more than a place where blacks could slip beyond the reach of Jim Crow; James Coleman may have shared a more determined vision of black autonomy in the West that began with the Kansas Exodusters and Oklahoma's black towns and continued in New Mexico when Boyer and Keyes founded Blackdom and Anita Scott's father built his ranch outside of Silver City. These individuals took advantage of the 1862 Homestead Act, which went into effect on the same day that Abraham Lincoln issued the Emancipation Proclamation and was accessible to African Americans once they became citizens in

THE CRISIS

WANTED

500 Negro families (farmers preferred) to settle on FREE Government Lands in Chaves County, New Mexico. Blackdom is a Negro colony. Fertile soil, ideal climate. No "Jim Crow" Laws. For information write

JAS. HAROLD COLEMAN
Blackdom - - - - - New Mexico

James Harold Coleman's advertisement for Blackdom, New Mexico, published in the *Crisis* in August 1913.

1868—including women. In light of this convergence of black emancipation and homesteading, Blackdom's Emancipation Day baseball game takes on a more nuanced meaning as both a general celebration of African American freedom and a particular celebration of how that freedom was enacted through black landownership in New Mexico.[18]

Black homesteaders like Anita Scott Coleman's father and Frank Boyer provide historical precedents for the characters that populate much of Coleman's western writing. In her short story "Rich Man, Poor Man," for example, she describes "old big black double-jointed Daniel Evans. . . . So big was he that he towered above every other man in the community; so black, that his genial wrinkled old countenance shone strikingly where-ever he went; and so shrewd and industrious was he that the Evans ranch and the Bar-Crescent-E brand was as widely known as other longer standing ones." In her portrayal, Daniel takes on almost mythic proportions. Coleman plays on archetypically western characteristics, such as masculinity, industriousness, courage, individualism, independence, and economic advancement, and figures them as unabashedly black—"so black" is listed alongside all of Daniel's other admirable qualities. These characteristics come to bear during the lively conversations about the "race question" that are common on the Evans ranch. When Coleman conjoins the mythologies of the American frontiersman (in the tradition of Turner's thesis) with the "race question," she is able to insert black subjects into the larger American imagination. As a result, she defies both the expectation that western (and American) identity is a white identity and Houston A. Baker's assertion that "tales of pioneers enduring the hardships of the West for the promise of immense wealth are not the tales of black America."[19]

In "Arizona and New Mexico—The Land of Esperanza" Coleman again describes black westerners by appealing to characteristics such as self-reliance, independence, and solitude: "Here and there are Negroes," she writes, "like straggly but tenacious plants growing"; they are "an isolated lot." Yet she sees potential, opportunity, and hope for blacks in the West: "Criss-crossing in and out through the medley of adventure stalk the few in number black folks. Often, it is only the happy-go-lucky black gambler; again it is but the lone and weary black prospector—but ever and ever the intrepid, stalwart Negro home-seeker forms a small but valiant army in the land of esperanza." This "Negro home-seeker" harks back once again to the Homestead Act and the way it enabled landownership by black women and men who became agents in the national project of manifest destiny. Coleman hints at this when she writes, "mingled with the tales of Indians on warpaths are the stories of heroism performed by avenging whites and all interwoven with these deeds are mingled the deeds of solitary Negroes."[20]

The position of blacks in the imperial project is clearly a complicated one for Coleman. When she couples Indians with violence and tempers white heroism with vengeance, she both acknowledges black participation in acts of conquest and denies these roles by depicting blacks as "solitary" and detached, caught up in a network beyond their control. She briefly mentions the "fast dwindling tribes of Indians, living echoes of a by-gone day," and suggests that "most of the old settlers among Negroes in 'these parts' are descended or related to a hoary-haired and fast-passing, honorably discharged, Indian war fighter." Thus, she both recognizes Indian oppression and distances herself and other blacks from

4—1003-R.

The United States of America,

To all to whom these presents shall come, Greeting:

WHEREAS, a Certificate of the Register of the Land Office at **LAS CRUCES, NEW MEXICO,**

has been deposited in the General Land Office, whereby it appears that, pursuant to the Act of Congress of May 20, 1862,

"To Secure Homesteads to Actual Settlers on the Public Domain," and the acts supplemental thereto, the claim of

WILLIAM H. SCOTT

has been established and duly consummated, in conformity to law, for the **SOUTHWEST QUARTER OF SECTION FOUR-**

TEEN IN TOWNSHIP EIGHTEEN SOUTH OF RANGE FOURTEEN WEST OF THE NEW MEXICO ME-

RIDIAN, NEW MEXICO, CONTAINING ONE HUNDRED SIXTY ACRES,

according to the Official Plat of the Survey of the said Land, returned to the GENERAL LAND OFFICE by the Surveyor-General:

NOW KNOW YE, That there is, therefore, granted by the UNITED STATES unto the said claimant   the tract of Land above described; TO HAVE AND TO HOLD the said tract of Land, with the appurtenances thereof, unto the said claimant   and to the heirs and assigns of the said claimant   forever; subject to any vested and accrued water rights for mining, agricultural, manufacturing, or other purposes, and rights to ditches and reservoirs used in connection with such water rights, as may be recognized and acknowledged by the local customs, laws, and decisions of courts; and there is reserved from the lands hereby granted, a right of way thereon for ditches or canals constructed by the authority of the United States.

IN TESTIMONY WHEREOF, I,   **WILLIAM H. TAFT**

President of the United States of America, have caused these letters to be made

Patent, and the seal of the General Land Office to be hereunto affixed.

GIVEN under my hand, at the City of Washington, the   **TWENTY-THIRD**

(SEAL)   day of   **NOVEMBER**   in the year of our Lord one thousand

nine hundred and   **TWELVE**   and of the Independence of the

United States the one hundred and   **THIRTY-SEVENTH.**

By the President: *Wm. H. Taft*

By   *M. O. LeRoy* Secretary,

Recorder of the General Land Office.

RECORD OF PATENTS: Patent Number **301747**

6—3177

Land patent for the homestead claim of William H. Scott (Anita Scott Coleman's father), 1912.

it through the vehicle of nostalgia, focusing on honorable black military service to insert blacks into the national imagination. In doing so, she glosses over the fact that black autonomy via western landownership came at the expense of indigenous populations that had been removed from the land. At this moment, she uses an old tactic—vanishing Indians—to make way for another marginalized subject.[21]

Black autonomy via homesteading is emphasized both in Coleman's writing and in Blackdom's founding documents, which shed light on some of the hopes and dreams of African American settlers in New Mexico. Blackdom was established in 1903, and its thirteen-member board of directors described the object of the Blackdom Townsite Company as follows:

> In general it is proposed to obtain control of a large body of land in the County of Chaves and the Territory of New Mexico under the laws of the United States of America and there to establish and maintain a colony of negroes by means of the cultivation of crops, the growing of town and settlements and the general improvement of the inhabitants of such colony; to build, erect and equip school houses, colleges, churches and various educational and religious institutions for the improvement and upbuilding of the moral and mental conditions of said colony.

This passage contains language that suggests the influence of major African American thinkers of the late nineteenth and early twentieth centuries. Most clearly, the emphasis on "improvement" and "upbuilding" mimics the language of racial uplift articulated by Booker T. Washington in his famous "Atlanta Exposition Address" and in his autobiography, *Up from Slavery* (1901). The focus on education in Blackdom's Articles of Incorporation also reveals Washington's influence on the town's founders. It is not surprising that Frank Boyer and his wife Ella (who later founded Vado) were both trained as teachers—Frank studied at Morehouse and Fisk, and Ella attended Atlanta University. Indeed, oral history interviews conducted with former Blackdom residents describe the Boyers as education-minded: "Mr. and Mrs. Boyer, they were more or less like educators. . . . They had in mind having a school. Building a school out there that was something like Tuskegee, or some of those schools in agriculture. . . . I mean that was in their mind, that type of school out there—industrial school or something agricultural." Washington's influence was not uncommon among black homesteaders in the West. One of the most famous, Oscar Micheaux, wrote novels based on his experiences, including *The Conquest: The Story of a Negro Pioneer* (1913) and *The Homesteader* (1917). The latter was eventually adapted as a film, launching Micheaux's illustrious career as a director and producer. *The Conquest*, dedicated to Booker T. Washington, painted a picture of racial uplift through the provisions of the Homestead Act.[22]

James Coleman's advertisement in the *Crisis*, particularly its attempt to recruit farmers to Blackdom, shares this vision of uplift through industrial and agricultural education and economic advancement. But his advertisement also emphasizes Blackdom as a "negro colony" situated on a "large body of land." In other words, while Blackdom takes on the subtle, accommodationist tones of Washington, it also promotes autonomy, thereby presaging the union of black enterprise, cultural nationalism, and even territorial separatism that would most famously be given voice by Marcus Garvey and the Universal Negro Improvement Association a few years later. The blurry line between Washingtonian accommodation, middle-class industriousness, and respectability and Garveyite nationalism and enterprise contributes to the trickster-like subversions evident, for example, in Utterback's recollections of Blackdom's Emancipation Day baseball game.

In short, James Coleman's decision to join the Blackdom colony complicates descriptions of him as a chauffeur and a printer and as someone who was disaffected with the West. Instead, he was a dedicated race man who, according to oral history interviews, "was goin' to start a paper in Blackdom and he was a professor but never taught school there. He had a little office and he had a typewriter and such thing and he would get out a small paper there. White sheet more or less. I don't remember if it had a name but it didn't last too long." James was more than a skilled printer; he was a writer and editor as well. As such, he and Anita would have shared a vision for black publication in addition to their shared vision for black autonomy and self-determination. Both these visions are articulated in Anita's literature, as well as in James's legacy as "one of the first Negro newspapermen on the west coast." After the family's move to Los Angeles, James became an editor at the city's *New Age Dispatch* (formerly the *New Age*), where he continued to iterate his belief in the West as a site for back enterprise and self-determination. For example, in 1931 he encouraged Tuskegee's president, Robert Russa Moton, to travel to California and be entertained by Coleman and Frederick Madison Roberts—the founder of the *New Age*, a great-grandson of Sally Hemings, the first African American elected to the California State Assembly, and Marcus Garvey's host when he visited Los Angeles in 1922. Coleman pledged that he and Roberts "would do our level best to make a sitting for them which would be pleasing to Dr. and Mrs. Moton and beneficial to Tuskegee." Continuing to align western lands with black entrepreneurship, he noted, "We have a lot of very rich people in California, rich and abundantly generous. Come out to the Coast; we will see to it that the best is prepared for you and your friends. There is less meanness and more goodness in California than in any other part of the United States."[23]

As his touting of the "goodness" of California indicates, James Coleman's time in Blackdom and in New Mexico did not last forever. Due to a lack of water, the soil in Blackdom eventually grew too alkaline to farm successfully, and by the 1920s, the site was largely vacant. Many of the residents of Blackdom, however, remained in New Mexico or elsewhere in the West. Some moved to Roswell or Las Cruces, and the Boyers went on to establish New Mexico's other predominantly black town, Vado, where some of their descendants still live. James Coleman made his way to Silver City, where he met and married Anita Scott in 1916. They lived there for several years, which suggests that although they were aware of and concerned about the increasing reach of Jim Crow into New Mexico, they were relatively unhindered by the white community surrounding them.[24]

There was a long history of antiblack legislation in New Mexico, including an 1859 slave code that restricted enslaved African Americans from traveling, testifying in court, and bearing arms; however, during Anita Scott Coleman's time in New Mexico—the late territorial and early statehood years—there was not yet wholesale legal segregation of public accommodations or segregated schooling for black and *hispano* children. But as the years wore on and more blacks—and southern whites—arrived in New Mexico, the state ratcheted down black freedom. In 1925 a statute was introduced that allowed school segregation in cases "where, in the opinion of the County School Board or Municipal School board and on the approval of said opinion by the State Board of Education, it is for the best advantage and interest of the school that separate rooms be provided for the teaching of pupils of African descent, and said rooms are so provided, such pupils may not be admitted to school rooms occupied by pupils of Caucasian or other descent." Although not all New Mexican schools chose to segregate their students by race, some did—including those in Roswell and Las Cruces, where many Blackdom pioneers had relocated. Perhaps this is unsurprising, given that in his 1903 article, Cummins had already expressed anxiety about black New Mexicans and the possibility of their invading Roswell's public schools. These schools remained segregated well into the 1950s, until after the *Brown v. Board of Education* decision.[25]

By the time Anita Scott Coleman departed New Mexico in 1926, then, black civil liberties were becoming increasingly imperiled. As she notes in "Arizona and New Mexico—The Land of Esperanza," which was published the year she moved away:

> So far, in New Mexico, the Negro has not yet a bone to gnaw
> in politics. He is not legislated either pro or con, he is an
> unconsidered quantity, due to his inconsequential numbers. But
> what New Mexico may or may not do is evidenced in the fact
> that the influx of Negro children to Dona Ana County the center
> of the cotton activity were not allowed to attend the schools.
> Separate schools were immediately installed, also Roswell in
> Chav[e]s County maintains a separate school system.

Her tone in this passage is suggestive. She begins her first sentence with "So far," implying that it is only a matter of time before the Negro is "legislated." She intuits that the impact of this legislation is likely to be detrimental to blacks, given how quickly segregated schools appeared in certain communities well before statewide Jim Crow was put to paper. Indeed, as Davis and Mitchell point out, when Coleman was in high school, three of her contemporaries from Albuquerque were removed from the public high school in 1907 due to pressure from white students who did not want to graduate with them. Long before New Mexico legalized school segregation, it was already being put into practice. And in response, black New Mexicans began contesting these constraints, as Albuquerque residents did by forming a local branch of the NAACP in 1913.[26]

Although she left New Mexico in the mid-1920s, Coleman likely kept abreast of changes in the educational system in her home state. She had attended an integrated high school herself and had then trained to be a teacher at New Mexico Normal School (now Western New Mexico University). She even maintained, as a keepsake, correspondence between one of her teachers and Booker T. Washington, who had responded to a query about the possibility of Anita getting a teaching job in Washington, D.C. Coleman has been quoted as saying, "I did teach—long enough to consider it the most interesting work I've ever done." Given her long-standing commitment to African American education, the implementation of segregation in New Mexico almost certainly would have been a concern for Coleman, even after she moved to Los Angeles. It is also possible that the curbing of black freedom in New Mexico actually precipitated this move, which would explain some of the nostalgic tones in Anita's writing about the place where she grew up, and particularly about the establishment of independent black communities and domiciles there.[27]

Whereas New Mexico seems to be colored by nostalgic longing in Coleman's writing, Los Angeles has often been characterized as a "city of the future" (a vision that, as William Deverell contends, can be constructed only by effacing its Mexican past). For many black migrants, that future meant freedom from the legacy of slavery that was still alive in the South. W. E. B. DuBois—who would become a mentor to Coleman through the Spingarn literary competitions—commented on this in the August 1913 issue of the *Crisis*. He contributed an essay titled "Colored California" and dedicated the issue to exploring black life in the state. According to DuBois, although the growing city of Los Angeles was beset by racial discrimination and a clearly drawn color line, it held promise—a future—for its rapidly growing black community. This black future, as Paul Robinson and other scholars have noted, drew on a lengthy black past stemming from the time of Spanish colonization. Indeed, black Angelenos had long been intermingled with the Mexican, Native, Asian, and Anglo-Americans of their city. Consequently, in the early twentieth century, blacks in Los Angeles were part of a "sprawling, multiracial place where the rules of the game and the hierarchies of power seemed always in flux," as historian Douglas Flamming points out. By the time the Colemans arrived, the black community was experiencing a period of dramatic expansion and was becoming both more visible and more cohesive. The multifaceted and intermingled racial landscape of Los Angeles was still very much alive, however. The new African American migrants who moved there in the 1920s still tended to settle in racially mixed neighborhoods. It was not until the 1940s that distinct black enclaves became well established through the enactment of restrictive covenants that crowded additional migrants, largely from the South, into neighborhoods that were already becoming black, such as Coleman's in South Central Los Angeles.[28]

By the time Langston Hughes visited South Central Los Angeles in 1932, he described it as "more a miracle than a city . . . where . . . ordinary black folks lived in houses with 'miles of yards.'" Back in 1913, this is also what DuBois witnessed: "The colored population of Los Angeles," he remarked, "are without a doubt the most beautifully housed group of colored people in the United States." He commented on the "business establishments of colored people" and marveled at "above all, homes—beautiful homes." The photographs accompanying DuBois's article depicted African American families posed on their well-manicured lawns or in front of their freshly painted bungalows shaded by graceful palm fronds, and they demanded more space than the text. During these years, indeed, it was often home ownership that captured the African American imagination when it turned toward the West. Flamming points out that in 1910 Los Angeles, "a striking 36 percent of Los Angeles's black families owned their homes. Few cities in the North or Midwest had black homeownership rates of even 10 percent, and none exceeded 15 percent. Most southern states had rates similar to the North, perhaps slightly higher. Even in the West, where rates of black homeownership were higher, not all cities rated well." Quintard

Taylor agrees, contending that "Los Angeles led the way" in black home ownership, and with the exception of San Francisco, "western cities . . . usually had high levels of black homeownership." Despite her change in location, property ownership remained a consistent defining factor in Coleman's western experience—from the Scott family's 160-acre home-steaded ranch outside of Silver City to the Coleman family's bungalow in the burgeoning black community of South Central Los Angeles.[29]

These contexts of black homesteading in New Mexico and black home ownership in Los Angeles help make better sense of Davis and Mitchell's remark that, for Coleman, "home is not a restrictive place or a domestic prison, or even an escape from racist reality, but a site of agency for the African American family." In short stories such as "The Little Grey House," which is set in New Mexico, Coleman establishes a vision of black domesticity and family that runs counter to many white women's writings about the West during this period, such as Mary Austin's *Cactus Thorn* (written in 1927 but first published in 1994), which imagines white women being happily set free from marriage and domestic life in the West rather than happily entering into it. "The Little Grey House," first published in Chicago's *Half-Century Magazine* in 1922, appeals to its readership's bourgeois aspirations by placing black domestic life and the marriage plot in a western town called Hillsvale. There, an older black bachelor named Timothy Martin admires the construction of a compact house, which is described as "built of cement" but may in fact be adobe, given its "little squat chimney" and its location in the Southwest during the heyday of pueblo revival-style architecture. Each day, as he passes the house on his way to work, Timothy also passes a "plump little brown woman," Opal Kent. Both the house and the woman become triggers of fantasy for Timothy, who simultaneously imagines the finished house and laments past failures with women that have left him single. Meanwhile, the reader discovers that Opal, a spinster, has devoted the income from her deceased father's life insurance, as well as her savings from her job as a domestic for a white family, to the house's construction. She intends to rent it out while continuing to work for the white family, with whom she traveled West for the "wife's health." She anticipates saving the rent money until she can afford to move into the house on her own. But Opal's plans are spoiled when her employers

CALIFORNIA NUMBER

The CRISIS

AUGUST, 1913 TEN CENTS A COPY

Cover of the *Crisis*'s "California Number," showcasing the homes of black Angelenos, August 1913.

suddenly move away and the house remains vacant. She is forced to make the difficult decision to sell it. Timothy purchases the house, and upon his arrival there, he finds Opal crying in the kitchen. At the end of the story, Timothy assures Opal that the house is no good to him without a wife, and they kiss, foretelling their marriage.[30]

This domestic landscape is signaled by omnipresent descriptions of Opal's homemaking talents, always counterpoised with indications of Timothy's slovenly lifestyle. Opal is characterized almost entirely by thrift, industry, and her cooking, cleaning, and sewing skills: "All in the world she could do is cook and clean house," Coleman writes. As a result, when faced with the prospect of losing her dream home, Opal becomes "timid and self conscious and oppressed . . . , and like most homeless women, . . . afraid." Given her status as an unmarried, homeless woman, Opal even worries, "I must be funny, and, oh . . . oh, queer." (She is, of course, saved from the fate of bucking heteronormativity by the marriage foreshadowed by the story's tidy O. Henry ending.) Timothy, in contrast, is predictably incompetent in the domestic space. Although he is characterized as a successful workingman, he rents, not owns, his "untidy bachelor apartment." His "sink [is] overfilled with plates and cups," and he subsists on the culinary handouts of kindly older women or his own cooking, which falls pathetically short of his "vivid memory" of his mother's. To make his new house a home, Timothy needs Opal, and "The Little Grey House" creates a seemingly staid fiction of domestic bliss that would likely be critiqued as regressive by white feminist writers of Coleman's day, particularly when Timothy envisions himself as "Lord and Master of both the little woman and the little grey house."[31]

The text, it is true, presents a neat, familiar marriage plot. But it also unites this plot with gestures toward wider black politics. Early in the story, Timothy becomes distracted from his domestic fantasies by the "evening's paper," where the "front page . . . in great black type announced the sweeping victory of a political candidate who was especially distasteful to him." Given Coleman's deep interest in fostering and contributing to black publications, it is easy to imagine this paper as the *New Age Dispatch* or the *Chicago Defender* and to envision that Timothy is reacting to the election of an antiblack politician. Furthermore, Coleman alludes to Opal's mistreatment at the hands of the white families for whom she works. First, her dream of home ownership is crushed when her initial employers—the ones who brought her West—leave the region. Even more significantly, the next family she works for is described as "unendurable." At their hands, Opal is subjected to constant "contempt and rude treatment." Coleman suggests that although Opal is ideal (and idealized) in the domestic space, it is her housekeeping for these white families that forces her to sell her own little house and limits her agency as a worker, as an African American, and as a woman.[32]

Opal's homemaking thus plays two distinct roles in the narrative, and it is this tension that shapes the story's political valences. On the one hand, Opal will be an ideal homemaker as Timothy's wife. On the other hand, she is a domestic laborer who has been abandoned and mistreated by her white employers. When Coleman grapples with the politics of domesticity, she does so in the West, where black home ownership and domestic autonomy were far more common than in other parts of the country, yet where they were increasingly being circumscribed by restrictive covenants. Likewise, fewer black women in the West had to work for wages than they did elsewhere, yet they continued to be exploited as domestic laborers. In Los Angeles in 1930, for example, 87 percent of black women were domestic laborers. These tensions are revealed in Coleman's representation of the West, where black homes and families are more than just staid domestic fantasies. Instead, they are a reckoning with these statistics, which reveal the position of so many black women in the West—caught between exploitation and autonomy.[33]

Indeed, Coleman gained a reputation for her "bitterly amusing yarns about Negro domestics." "No one," claimed one newspaper, "understands the relations between colored and white, domestics and employers, better than Mrs. Coleman, as her numerous excellent stories attest." Although many of Coleman's short stories end like "The Little Grey House" does, in a happy marriage, a 1948 poem titled "Hands" describes black women's domestic servitude ending only in death:

> Hands, brown as snuff,
> Wash-tub hands,
> Curled like claws from clutching and squeezing

Heavy wet garments.
Water-soaked, sudsy, rheumy, old hands—
    Only when they are folded thus
    In the quiescent pose of death
    Are they stilled.

In another poem titled "Idle Wonder," first published in *Opportunity* in 1938, the speaker describes "poor Agnes," who "lives with the white folks / And they think she is contented / And actually delighted with being / Their house-maid."[34]

As a result of Coleman's grasp of the complexity of black women's relationships to domesticity, stories like "The Little Grey House"—in which she appears to subscribe to sedate notions of heteronormative marriage and domesticity, predictably gendered divisions of labor, and the kind of "true womanhood" historically attributed to white middle-class women (with black women existing as their foils)—are far more subversive. They participate in a wider black women's politics of respectability that, though fraught with class-bound visions of uplift, historically provided a foundation for successful political campaigns spearheaded by black women. Coleman's experience with autonomous black domesticity, via homesteading in New Mexico and home ownership in Los Angeles, provides a new historical context for this politics and a distinctively regional mode for subverting black women's exploitation.

One approach to Coleman, then, might be to locate the literary antecedents to her work in the tradition of black women's domestic fiction of the post-Reconstruction period, which, as Claudia Tate asserts, "aspired to intervene in the racial and sexual schemes of the public world . . . by plotting new stories about the personal lives of black women and men." Perhaps Coleman's mobilization of respectability politics is not surprising, given her mentorship by DuBois, who responded to her submissions to the *Crisis* and famously declared in his essay "Criteria of Negro Art" (1926) that "all art is propaganda" for uplifting the race. In embracing such a politics of respectability, Coleman diverges from the work of many of her New Negro contemporaries, both female and male. Some, like Wallace Thurman, railed against DuBois's dictum in the name of pure art. Others, like Zora Neale Hurston, constructed far more frank—and thus "disrespectable"—illustrations of black female sexuality in works such as *Their Eyes Were Watching God* (1937). But Thurman left the West, and Hurston was very much a southern writer. Coleman, who stayed in the West, found home in a context that enables this difference.[35]

The theme of "home seeking" derived from Coleman's western experience, which is so central to her corpus of work set in the West, is extended to other sites as well. She is by no means an exclusively western writer, for much of her work takes place in far more familiar nodes of the Great Migration, such as Chicago. But the concerns and possibilities that emerge through Coleman's preoccupation with black western homes permeate all her work, even when it is set in other places. In these locations, "home seeking" becomes even more complicated and perhaps more futile for African Americans. A telling example is her short story "Jack Arrives," in which a black family is torn asunder by economic need when patriarch Jack "quit his job, [left] the town, and [went] elsewhere [to] find decent employment that would afford him a living wage." A family that, at the outset of the story, appears to be the epitome of heteronormative domestic bliss—with an educated, ambitious male breadwinner; his supportive, sensitive female spouse; and their adorable male child—is broken apart because of racism. Jack, who has dreams of becoming a successful architect with clients who "come from far and near to have him plan their homes," finds that his "nut-brown face, his friendly black eyes and his big smiling mouth were more potent than leprosy, chasing away jobs which might have been his." Like the female domestics elsewhere in Coleman's writing, Jack's relationships to home and labor are entwined, and the always too-simple dichotomy of private and public is broken. In his quest to design others' homes, Jack's own home crumbles. His family is forced to put their "household goods in storage" and live separately for more than a year, not in houses but in mere "dingy little room[s]." At the end of the story, Jack realizes his dream when he wins an architectural contest to design a bungalow for an heiress (who is white). Prize in hand, Jack is finally "ready for home." Yet the domestic bliss that should accompany his financial success is uncertain. First, Jack has sold the blueprints he had drawn for his own "dream house," which he and his wife had fantasized about for years as "the kind of bungalow they would build when 'dreams come true.'" As a result, Jack cannot build their perfect house and ensure their happiness. Second, at the end of the story it is uncertain whether the family Jack left behind is intact at all. Along with the letter he receives notifying him of his prize, he receives another from his wife. An earlier letter from her had informed him that "Junior was ill," and "several days had passed without any other further word." In his haste to open the other envelope and his subsequent fervor to "toss his things together" to "get ready for home," Jack leaves his wife's letter unopened. Although he now dreams of a home built not by "wonderful architectural feats" but by "a trusting, winsome woman and a bonny little boy," the letter's contents—perhaps reporting on his son's illness or even his death—remain unknown, calling this future into question.[36]

Even in stories with more comforting, less ambiguous endings, the black nuclear family and domesticity remain central topics, and they appear to be more at risk in Coleman's tales set in the East. In "Rich Man, Poor Man," Drusilla, the daughter of a rich man (black western homesteader Daniel Evans), moves east with her new husband, a poor man, John Condon. Although Drusilla had been known to "quote a remembered fragment from some of the old arguments," such as "it's a sorry man who can't take care of his own family," she ends up selling all her fancy dresses to purchase a bakery shop and "work for" her husband, who had been injured in a car accident. This sacrifice fulfills his long-standing entrepreneurial dreams, but Drusilla's decision to enter the workforce goes against her vow that she would never "work for any man alive." Her sacrifice is met by John's loving "arms around [her]," a cozy picture of marital bliss that concludes the story. Still, this outcome is less than ideal in the heteronormative imaginary—it is threatening to John's manhood, and he initially protests Drusilla's purchase of the bakery, declaring, "No woman will ever remember working for me. I'm a man who wants only a man's chance—a man's chance, do you hear, and I'll do a man's part." Likewise, Drusilla's ability to prepare "spicy, tasty little dishes" and "keep their tiny rooms shining like mirrors and her own pretty self trim and neat as a rosebud" becomes uncertain when she agrees to "do the night work" and "sell [their wares] over the counter." Away from the homes and homesteads of the West—such as the successful ranch built by Drusilla's father—black homes are threatened. At first, these homes appear to be threatened by women's work; however, Coleman makes it clear that the ultimate threat is racism. Early in "Rich Man, Poor Man," back on the Evans ranch, the Evans family and their ranch hands are reading newspapers that describe atrocities "done to Negro[es]" in "unknown, far-off," and decidedly nonwestern places. Such atrocities cause them to ask, "How's a black man to support a wife and children on the mere pittance he gets a day" in places where "a black man can't get a good (?) job cleaning the streets; if some white man happens to want it." While black men in the East face unemployment due to racial discrimination, black women face exploitative employment, for they can always work as domestics, getting a "good (?) job in somebody's kitchen." Even Drusilla's mother had done domestic work in an effort to establish the western homestead: "To buy our first cow," she tells Drusilla, "I . . . washed and scoured from house to house."[37]

Likewise, "Phoebe and Peter up North" ends with a picture of domestic happiness: Peter promises Phoebe that she can quit her job because "we've got enough money now to start on that little home you wanted, out in the suburbs." Phoebe quickly changes from bragging that "I'm the only lady of Color on my job; . . . helper to the best candy artist in this old town," to declaring that, as a housewife, she'll be "the only lady on my job. I'll have homerule in my hands. Why, I'll be the helper to the best old scout on earth, Mr. Peter Nettleby." This domestic ideal, however, seemed unattainable when the Nettlebys first moved "up North" from the South, largely because Phoebe was "chuck full of country," a "staid, a-way-down-South-colored matron." Her husband hoped she would become more cosmopolitan and modern to fit with their new milieu in Chicago, the crucible of the Great Migration. As a result of Peter's discontent, Phoebe leaves him to work as an assistant to a candy maker, using the only "meager store of knowledge" she has, other than "the art of picking cotton." She remakes herself as an independent northern woman, albeit one who performs kitchen labor, under the tutelage of her rakish neighbor, Mayme Wilson, described as "city through and through." In the sequel to this story, "Phoebe Goes to a Lecture," the "snippy-snappy city life" of the North threatens the Nettlebys' domestic ideal again when Phoebe accompanies Mayme to a lecture at the "Wise Acres Women's Club." The speaker is the "foremost and most accurate authority on birth-control known," a Margaret Sanger–like figure who makes "Phoebe [feel] like it was indeed a heinous crime to be a mother." This contradicts "her old home training wherein, maternity had been upheld as a woman's crowning glory, and little ones as the Lord's anointed." Phoebe ultimately rejects the lecturer's suggestions, to the surprising approval of Mayme, who tells her, "I urged you to come, not that I thought you'd enjoy that especially, but get out, see with your eyes and hear with your ears, and give your brains an airing. That's what city life is for, to put the 'pep' in living." At the end of the story, Phoebe retreats "to home and Peter."[38]

"Phoebe Goes to a Lecture" illustrates what can be considered an antifeminist impulse in Coleman's oeuvre. Certainly, Coleman's depiction of black domesticity as a refuge is in stark contrast to the work of many writers influenced by the ethos of the "New Woman" and its offshoots, many of whom turned toward region—the West in particular—to find a more freely gendered space. For white women regionalists, gender roles seem to be increasingly disrupted as they move further from the eastern establishment. Some of these women, such as Mary Austin, grew up in the West. Others, such as Mabel Dodge Luhan and Alice Corbin Henderson, relocated there. Still others were travelers; Willa Cather, for instance, made the borderlands West the setting for her novels *The Song of the Lark* (1915), *The Professor's House* (1925), and *Death Comes for the Archbishop* (1927). For these women, western experiences enabled the invention of new and liberating gendered landscapes, largely through contact with indigenous people. Luhan, for example, built a domestic space in the West when she constructed her pueblo revival-style compound there in 1919; it was utterly unlike anything she had experienced before, largely because of her relationship with Pueblo Indian Antonio (Tony) Lujan, who seemingly liberated her from the constraints associated with female domesticity. This was not an uncommon fantasy. Austin's California-based *Cactus Thorn* critiques the institution of marriage, and even her essay on Arizona makes femininity more flexible and a central component of the state's culture: "Arizona women," she writes, "are a trifle less familiar with the 'patter' of culture east of the Mississippi; they are also a little more accessible to new points of view.

But that is a distinction that can be made in other Western States in direct ratio to the distance from New York." As the editors of the anthology *The Desert Is No Lady* insist, "women have located [freedom] in the Southwestern landscape." According to historian Flannery Burke, Austin and other Anglo women artists saw the Southwest as "the one place where they could freely and completely pursue their ambitions." If this freedom was also a freedom from marriage and domesticity, Coleman's scenes of domestic coupling present a decidedly different picture of the borderlands West.[39]

Groundbreaking gender historians such as Nancy F. Cott have suggested that the "bonds of womanhood" both constrain women to traditional domestic places and tie them together to agitate for rights. White middle-class women, like those who were the subjects of Cott's book, had long been twisted in the image of the "cult of domesticity" or the "cult of true womanhood." But black women's family lives had been imperiled by the brutal practices of the slave system, which refused them the institution of marriage and tore their families asunder, as well as by labor exploitation and discrimination that continued after emancipation and shaped their domestic experiences. As a result, as historian Elsa Barkley Brown suggests, "The family and the concept of community as family offered the unifying thread that bound African Americans together in a postslavery world." For African American women, freedom was always communal—it was not defined, as it was for white women, by individual equality in the liberal tradition.[40]

Within this context, then, it is possible to see Phoebe's retreat to the home and family not as simply regressive or antifeminist. When she is juxtaposed with the "foremost and most accurate authority on birth-control known"—and when many such authorities in the 1920s were also advocates of eugenics—it becomes possible to see Phoebe's endorsement of motherhood and domesticity as a far more radical act. This act, then, is accomplished when she "see[s] with [her] eyes and hear[s] with [her] ears" as a black woman confronting the politics of feminism, the politics of race, and the politics of domesticity in the interest of furthering the greater black community. During this time, black women's experiences of reproductive and racial science had been shaped by atrocities such as forced sterilization and gynecological experimentation, and as

Daylanne K. English has suggested, eugenics discourses informed US modernism and New Negro literature.[41]

Envisioning black domesticity and family as acts of resistance makes sense of one of the stirring artifacts uncovered by Davis and Mitchell's research into Coleman's life and family: a photograph of her son, Spencer, which he gave to his mother in 1952 and signed, "From your black son." Below it, in another family member's hand, is written, "This proves we knew about black power long before Stokely Carmichael did." The photograph and its jocular inscriptions emphasize family ties and racial pride and suggest a concept that emerges in Coleman's writing: that the black family and the black home, rendered through western fantasy and experience, can be conceptualized as the foundational unit of black politics. If the nineteenth-century cult of domesticity provided a fiction that maintained the apparition of white racial purity, in Coleman's twentieth-century work, black domesticity and family underpin black solidarity, autonomy, and power.

It is worth noting that later black power movements in the 1960s and 1970s also promoted the black family—replete with heteronormative gender roles—as a political foundation. Some scholars have attributed this touting of gender hierarchies and divisions of labor to the black male chauvinism that emerged in reaction to the 1965 Moynihan report and its infamous matriarchy thesis. E. Francis White has remarked, "In making appeals to conservative notions of appropriate gender behavior, African American nationalists reveal their ideological ties to other nationalist movements, including European and Euro-American bourgeois nationalists" who "turned to the ideology of respectability" to impose "proper order on" the nation-state's "upper and lower classes"—in the process, pathologizing the black family as a threat to such respectability. In short, to borrow Audre Lorde's metaphors, black nationalists attempted to use the "master's tools" (patriarchy) to dismantle the "master's house" (racism). Others have seen domestic narratives as apolitical at best; they are not even the feminized complement to the masculine project of nation building. At worst, as Houston A. Baker suggests about the work of Frances Harper, they are "an essentially conservative appeal to white public opinion." But some scholars, including Claudia Tate and Lora Romero, challenge all these positions and read the nexus of black

The family as the site of black power: Spencer Coleman's note to his mother from her "black son," 1952. (Courtesy of the Anita Scott Coleman Family Collection)

domesticity and black nationalism far differently. Romero contends that in black women's writing, "domesticity," rather than being "the quintessential marker of mindless capitulation," is "a symbolic system compatible with a range of political possibilities." It is in this context that Coleman's work, with its complicated interplay between black homes and black nationalism in the West, makes the most sense.[42]

None of these positions, however, fully captures Coleman's decidedly regionalist domesticity. This vision is not a separatist politics, for in Coleman's construction of the West, racial boundaries are permeated. She describes the region as "the home of the half-breed, the inevitable outcome, where two or more races meet and mingle in an un-accustomed freedom." Accordingly, western families are made up of multiracial kin, as revealed by another photograph of Coleman on the family ranch with her *Nuevo Mexicana* sister-in-law, Ida Gonzalez, and her mother, Mary Ann Stokes. In the West, home, homesteading, and home ownership are tied to more than black autonomy. They also cultivate interracial families. Sometimes an outgrowth of demographics, and sometimes a result of circumstance, these families were also a way to contend with the nativist policies instituted in the West in the late nineteenth and early twentieth centuries.[43]

Although the Homestead Act, for example, was accessible to immigrants, they had to declare their intent to become naturalized citizens. In accordance with the 1790 Naturalization Act (which was largely in effect until 1952), however, nonwhites could not become citizens. In the twentieth century, California's Alien Land Law (1913) prohibited landownership by aliens who were ineligible for naturalized citizenship. Asians were specifically targeted in *Takao Ozawa v. United States* (1922) and *United States v. Bhagat Singh Thind* (1923). After these cases, in places such as California's Imperial Valley, marriage provided one way for Asian (in this case, Punjabi) immigrants to secure land. New Mexico also had an Alien Land Law, implemented in 1921 and not repealed until 2006. There, as in California, marriage provided a way to circumvent the law, and such marriages occasionally involved African Americans. Even Blackdom, founded as a "Negro colony," was home to at least one such mixed marriage. According to Blackdom resident Mrs. F. L. Mehlop, one of its homesteaders was "a Negro woman by the name of

Mrs. Johnson. . . . Johnson was her maiden name." She "had a claim out west" because "her husband was Chinese, therefore an alien, and couldn't file."[44]

Coleman addresses this aspect of the western cultural landscape in her fiction and directs her readers to its regionally defining characteristics. In Coleman's short story "Three Dogs and a Rabbit," for example, the interracial family—albeit a very different one from Mrs. Johnson's in Blackdom—is definitely an outgrowth of the West. In the story, an elderly woman who is on trial for harboring a black fugitive is revealed to be a former slave herself. Previously, the narrator asserts:

> That she was anything other than a white American was
> improbable. . . . She, the widow of old Colonel Ritton . . . as
> dauntless and intrepid a figure as ever lived to make history for
> his country. His career as an Indian fighter, pioneer and brave
> open opposer of the lawlessness which held sway over the far West
> . . . is a thing that is pointed to with pride and made much of, by
> Americans.

Mrs. Ritton's racial ambiguity is a result not of phenotype but of marriage. Her hair is described as "crinkled almost to the point of that natural curliness which Negro blood imparts. The kind of curl that no artificial aid so far invented can duplicate." The emphasis on the "natural" curl that cannot be cultivated through "artificial aid" purports a biologically determinist view of race, a view that suggests it is natural, transmissible, and recognizable. If this were the case, however, Mrs. Ritton's hair—along with her "heavy-lidded" eyes, said to be a "purely Negro attribute," and her "mouth" exhibiting "a fullness, a ripeness, exceedingly—*African*"—would make her immediately and incontrovertibly identifiable as a black woman. But despite these characteristics, she becomes unrecognizable as black, a racial ambiguity resulting from her participation in an American mythology of the West through marriage, family, and domesticity. Through her marriage to a western archetype, Mrs. Ritton has learned to "forget the scars of serfdom" that decorated her beaten body and represented the experience of blackness under the regime of chattel slavery. She was brought together with her husband,

The multiracial family in the borderlands West: Anita Scott Coleman with her sister-in-law, Ida Gonzalez, and her mother, Mary Ann Stokes, in 1915. (Courtesy of the Anita Scott Coleman Family Collection)

she remarks, the same day she received those scars, and he subsequently "taught [her] . . . the joys of freedom." As a result of this marriage and the western mythology undergirding it, the interracial Rittons join a "family-tree" that "flourished like the proverbial mustard-seed, un-blighted before the world." In "Three Dogs and a Rabbit," the West initiates interracial domesticity and family, calling the categories of whiteness and blackness into question. Attending to such ambiguity and multiplicity in the West, however, does not destroy or erase the black family. Rather, Coleman's story incorporates African Americans into western families and African American families into the West, where they thrive in this new context. Mrs. Ritton, after all, is on trial for harboring a black man. In doing so, she maintains and protects her racial ties both by forming a fictive kinship with this fugitive as part of a larger struggle for communal freedom and by preserving her own memories of "the days of my bondage."[45]

"Three Dogs and a Rabbit," then, describes the coexistence of ra-cial multiplicity and black cohesion, imbrications that define much of Coleman's western writing. Her short story "The Brat," also set in the West, foregrounds these ties even more powerfully. "The Brat" is about the ties that bind a black mother and her son, who are torn asunder by racial violence even as their relationship is preserved by their cross-racial networks. Like "Three Dogs and a Rabbit," which is narrated by the fugitive Mrs. Ritton protects, "The Brat" is also a frame story. Its white narrator, Miss Aggie, retells what she heard from her "old wash-woman" Jennie, a withered black domestic. It centers on Jennie's survival during a race riot, likely patterned on Tulsa, given its western location. Back then, Jennie recalls, she was both a "wild young thing and a mother" to her year-old infant, whom she flippantly calls "the brat." They lived with Jennie's friend Biddy and her lover, Black Luke. Luke's nickname describes his countenance, but Biddy is described as a "fair, fair girl . . . with big blue eyes and straw colored hair," yet "nobody noticed her looks. 'Cause it is common, a common sight enough to see colored folks as white as white folks." "The brat," Jennie mentions, was also "of that kind." The three "young . . . and wild and foolish" adults were inebri-ated when the violence of the riot descended on them. Black Luke was murdered almost instantly, and Biddy and Jennie were both wounded.

Biddy was able to "save 'the brat'" and deliver him to her parents' house before dying from her wounds. Jennie was hospitalized for months.[46]

Before the riot, Jennie admits, she had a cold relationship with "the brat." When Biddy fled with him, Jennie admits to being "glad, glad, glad to be shed of 'the brat' forever." Once she recovered from her injuries, however, she had a change of heart and became determined to retrieve him. "I hadn't ever cared for him or wanted him before," she tells Miss Aggie, but "now my heart ached for him." She set off to Biddy's parents' house to be reunited with her child, but when she arrived she was stunned to discover that they were "white—white folks. White, Miss Aggie, like you." They were also comfortably middle or upper class, and thinking that "the brat" was Biddy's child, they were equipped to provide him with luxuries that Jennie could not. As a result, she claimed to be only "his old nurse" and left him behind, in the hope they could provide him with a more comfortable life. She checked in annually, but at age twelve "the brat" rejected these visits by his "ol' black mammy" due to teasing by his white friends. Clearly, the family ties between Jennie and the brat are severed by white hegemony: initially by mob violence, then by the wealth gap that forces Jennie to relinquish her son to Biddy's parents, and finally by the racist jeers of her son's white friends and his complicity with that racism when he rejects his mother's visits. At the same time, it was a white woman, Biddy, who "gave up her life to save him from death or a life far worse," and it is this sacrifice that motivates Jennie to reconnect with the brat when she begins "goin' straight and keepin' straight cause of [Biddy's] wantin' so much to have 'the brat' grow clean and wholesome." In other words, the black family in "The Brat" is both broken and mended by cross-racial interactions, leaving its status ambiguous.[47]

Such ambiguity is written onto "the brat's" body itself, as it was written onto Biddy's. At the end of the story, Jennie reveals to Miss Aggie that "the brat" is now known as "David Kane, one of America's greatest singers." His voice, Jennie insists, reveals his parentage: "I told you 'bout my singin'. Well, my boy sings, too. . . . His voice tells you what he is, is the thing that keeps him bound. He sings like only one of my race can sing, but he sings so fine, so fine, Biddy's race won't let him go. . . . He's bound—he's bound." David's voice reveals not only his blackness—his racial "family"—but also his immediate family, since Jennie's own vocal gifts presaged his. When she says that David is "bound," then, it has two meanings: he is bound through his family ties to Jennie and to the wider black community, and he is bound to the enraptured white audiences who figuratively enslave him when they "won't let him go." David's ambiguity extends beyond his voice. Like Biddy, he is phenotypically unintelligible, one of the "colored folks as white as white folks" or "the other way 'round too." Although "his skin is dark and his hair is curly . . . they don't betray him none," and this racial multiplicity is explained as an outgrowth of the western environment: "Yes, he is dark; but his boyhood home is on the western plains, where unfettered winds blew free, to tan his cheek." This racial indeterminacy is coded not only as western but also as American. David is described as one "of whom America is so arrogantly proud. Proud, that he is no foreigner, come to us from across the sea, but truly ours. A product of America."[48]

With this, Coleman gestures toward a mixed-race America epitomized by the racial complexities of the borderlands West—yet an America with black identity at its core. For her, the West provides a place to imagine the black family and the black home as a site of power and autonomy; at the same time, it participates in wider cross-racial networks. Looking at this region and the racial networks it elicits in Coleman's work becomes a way to see, as bell hooks puts it, "the margin" as "much more than a site of depravation." It can also be seen as "the site of radical possibility, a space of resistance" that "offers . . . radical perspective from which to see and create, to imagine alternatives, new worlds." Indeed, in much of her writing, Coleman presents the borderlands West as a land of hope. Yet she never forgets the depravation—the deferral—implicit in hope: in "Hands," she describes the black washerwoman whose exploitation is stopped only by "the quiescent pose of death." Even for Coleman, the land of *esperanza* is tempered by *esperando*—by waiting.[49]

PART II

*

Those Who Went Away

And over it all the joyous freedom of the West. The
unlimited resourcefulness of the boundless space—that
either bids them stay—or baffles with its vastness—until
it sends them scuttling to the North, the South, the East
whence-so-ever they have come.
—*Anita Scott Coleman, "Arizona and New Mexico—The
Land of Esperanza" (1926)*

.

CHAPTER 2

The Two LAs

Los Angeles, Louisiana, and Geographies of Race

> Mudtown (like the Avenue) was more than a place; it was
> a period and a condition.
> —*Arna Bontemps, "The Chariot in the Cloud" (1929)*

Archived with the Arna Bontemps Papers at Syracuse University is an undated scrap bearing a typewritten, autobiographical blurb. The first line, which has been crossed out, reads, "Arna Bontemps is a writer." The second, presumably revised, says, "ARNA BONTEMPS is a Californian, born in Louisiana, and living in Tennessee." Another set of notes contains the following:

> I consider myself a Californian, born in Louisiana and living
> in Nashville at present. My parents went West in the spring of
> 1906, when I was three. I grew up around Los Angeles, mostly,
> attending schools and colleges in the vicinity and graduating from
> Pacific Union College in Angwin, California, in 1923. Graduate
> work first in English and later in Graduate Library School was
> done at the University of Chicago. Meanwhile, however, I had
> taught school on and off over a period of twelve years on the
> high school level. And meanwhile, too, I had become a free-lance
> writer, I suppose.

A similar autobiographical description appeared on the dust jacket of Bontemps's edited collection of poetry, *Hold Fast to Dreams* (1969). He wrote his own copy, narrating in the third person: "When a magazine gave him a prize of $150 in 1926 for a poem he submitted and then asked him for an autobiographical note, Arna Bontemps described himself as 'a Californian, born in Louisiana and living in New York.'" Although he had planned to do so, Bontemps never wrote an autobiography. But these lines, taken together, contain some of the major geographic points on the map of his life experience: his birthplace in Alexandria, Louisiana; his seven years in New York during the New Negro movement; his time in Chicago doing graduate work and staffing the Illinois Writers' Project; his tenure as head librarian at Fisk University in Nashville; and the place where he spent his youth—Los Angeles.[1]

Heralded as a writer of both Harlem and the South, Arna Bontemps has rarely been considered a writer of the West. He is best known as a writer of Harlem, and he may have done more to establish this reputation for himself than any other critic. In the post–Harlem renaissance years, Bontemps stepped into myriad roles—scholar, activist, memoirist, critic, biographer, public intellectual, and historian—as well as maintaining his identity as a poet and a writer of fiction. His voluminous post-renaissance writing touches on many aspects of black history: the circum-Atlantic slave trade, figures such as Frederick Douglass and Booker T. Washington, the Fisk Jubilee Singers, slave narratives and uprisings. Yet as a witness to and a participant in the New Negro movement, his work as an editor and critic of the New Negro renaissance is of particular note. His edited anthology *The Harlem Renaissance Remembered* (1972), in tandem with his introduction to the 1969 reissue of Jean Toomer's *Cane*, serve as testimony to his dedication to preserving the legacy of the artists and literature of the New Negro movement, ensuring that neither the movement nor his participation in it would be forgotten. The unsurprising result is that Bontemps has been strongly associated with Harlem, placed alongside other young, prominent, rebellious African American literary innovators such as his good friends Langston Hughes and Wallace Thurman. Furthermore, in his memories of the New Negro movement, he consistently iterates how important this black community of artists was to him, even referring to his time in Harlem as "The Awakening" in one essay to emphasize how the milieu changed and cultivated his artistic and racial consciousness. In "The Awakening" he describes his arrival in Harlem in 1924, when he first set foot on New York's pulsing artery of black life, Lenox Avenue: "I came up out of the subway at 125th Street and Lenox Avenue and stood blinking in the sun," he writes—his emergence from the tunnel and into the light nothing less than a metaphorical rebirth. After seven years among the movers and shakers of the black literary renaissance, Bontemps's time in Harlem came to an abrupt end during the Depression when he, along with many others, was forced to move elsewhere to find work that would pay the bills. Without the financial support of a patron, and with the added pressure of providing for his growing family, he left Harlem for Huntsville, Alabama, in 1931, and took a teaching position at Oakwood College. Long after 1931, however, due to his writing about the renaissance and his continued collaboration with its key figures such as Langston Hughes, scholarly understandings of Bontemps are largely based on his reputation as a Harlem writer.[2]

Scholars have also pointed to Bontemps's engagement with the intricate dialectic of North and South. It was not uncommon for members of the cosmopolitan artistic coterie of Harlem to consider their relationship to the past (particularly enslavement), to rural folk life, and to working-class black experience characterized largely as southern. New Negro writers trod a line between the elite, as part of the so-called talented tenth, and the proletarian and vernacular cultures they often chose to represent in their work. As David G. Nicholls has suggested, this created "a dynamic relation between metropolitan artistic culture and its popular referents," which was often expressed geographically as the relation between New York and the South. When Bontemps left Harlem for Huntsville, his decision to do so was undoubtedly based on economic necessity, yet it was also the fulfillment of a preexisting fixation with the southern milieu as a representative black space. Critics such as Houston A. Baker Jr. have contended that the South provides the inescapable core of African American modernism, African American history, and African American experience in general: "Where the South and the black southern being are concerned," he writes, "I believe such [deeply ambivalent rehashing of the past] forms the crux of a psychodrama of framing, performance, signification, and ultimately *being* for the black American." More recently, Thadious Davis has coined the term

"southscapes" to describe geographies of race and region, clearly center-
ing the South in African American literature and history and "placing
African Americans at the center of current discourses on 'the South' and
'Southern Literature' as categories of critical inquiry, literary analysis,
and theoretical positioning." Bontemps himself went so far as to insist
(interestingly, in a written response to Baker's *Long Black Song*), "The
folk sources are the taproot of conscious literature by Negroes in the
United States. There is no other background against which the writing
can be clearly seen and understood. Nearly every story can be read as
an updated slave narrative, an account of bondage and freedom. Nearly
every essay, as plantation oratory." Although the drama of slavery and
freedom, for example, was not exclusive to the South, it most frequently
emerged from this regional context. As Baker points out, "The South
defined itself in *difference* through the 'peculiar institution' of black slavery." By the time he was a young man, Bontemps had long "conclud[ed]
that for him a break with the past and the shedding of his Negro-ness
was not only impossible but unthinkable." It thus makes sense that—
after he "went to New York in the twenties" and "met young Negro
writers and intellectuals who were similarly searching"—he would end
up in the Jim Crow South and become immersed in its living legacies
of slavery for the first time since he was a small child.[3]

Scholars, in kind, have situated Bontemps within a tradition of black
writers who turned toward the South almost as frequently as they have
situated him among writers of Harlem. Kirkland C. Jones's biography
does so even in its title: *Renaissance Man from Louisiana: A Biography
of Arna Wendell Bontemps*. Jones identifies Louisiana as the key site in
Bontemps's experience and only gestures toward his activity in Harlem.
He argues that the few years Bontemps spent in Louisiana, together
with the stories and memories of Louisiana shared by his family, left
an indelible mark on him as a writer. In an essay, Jones writes, "By
the time of his death, Arna Bontemps had established Louisiana as his
favorite and most productive topic. Using autobiographical and genealogical themes and devices, he achieved a level of variety that keeps his
reader enthralled. Old Louisiana and the Old South became the most
profound sources of meaning in his works." Jones is not alone in his
assessment, and it is not uncommon to see Bontemps considered among

southern writers. Jill Leroy-Frazier suggests that his work represents an "othered Southern" counterpoint to the fugitive agrarians of the 1930s, one that disrupts their fantasies of the preindustrial South by revealing its dependence on slavery. Take together, she insists, both the southern agrarians and black writers like Bontemps constitute the complex and often contradictory whole of southern modernism. In an early piece, Nicholas Canaday emphasizes the impact of Louisiana on Bontemps's writing and suggests that it manifests largely through representations of his great-uncle Buddy, such as the character of Augie in his first published novel, *God Sends Sunday* (1931). Literary critics and historians alike have seen these representations of Buddy as Bontemps's efforts to center an "authentic" black identity in his writing, one that is not stifled by the bourgeois aspirations central to the politics of racial uplift and conservative religious observance that characterized his home life with his father, Paul Bontemps. In short, Bontemps's birthplace of Alexandria, his three years in Huntsville in the 1930s, and his time in Nashville provide frequent touchstones throughout his work dealing with black history, literature, and experience.[4]

Critics have often painted Bontemps's relationship to the South as an affectionate one—evident, for example, in his love for family members such as his great-uncle and his grandmother. This affection is cast as symptomatic of a racial nostalgia, a deep yearning for an authentic black folk past during a period of rapid modernization. In a letter from 1941, Bontemps wrote of his relationship to the South and juxtaposed it with his time in California: "My parents were always anxious to put the South (and the past) as far behind as possible. They were quick to correct any hint of Southern dialect that might creep into my speech. . . . One by one, however, our relatives migrated to Southern California during my childhood, and [a] link with the past was established for me in spite of all efforts to the contrary." In this geography, Southern California stands in for a modern and perhaps deracinated future, while the South represents a black past. To know that past, Bontemps moved to Huntsville in the 1930s and spent "three years in the South, remedying a lack."[5]

Alongside this palpable sense of longing, Bontemps describes his years in Huntsville as "horrifying," "crude," and "frightening." "We had fled here to escape our fears in the city," he wrote in his introduction to the 1968 edition of *Black Thunder* (his second novel, originally published in 1936), "but the terrors we encountered here were even more upsetting than the ones we had left behind." When Bontemps and his family moved to Alabama, they lived in the shadow of the Scottsboro trial, which writ large the oppression of blacks by the southern legal system, by white-supremacist ideology, by cultural taboos and pathologies surrounding miscegenation, and by the constant threat of racial violence. Like Jean Toomer, whose southern sojourns were characterized by "lyric images, pastoral landscapes, and spontaneous folksongs," on the one hand, and "the threat of violence, lynching, and surveillance that would define Southern society," on the other, Bontemps found the South to be a place of both tremendous beauty and tremendous horror. This is evident in his short story "Saturday Night: Portrait of a Small Southern Town, 1933," based on his experiences in Huntsville; it was originally published in *Opportunity* in 1933 and republished in the collection *The Old South* (1973). It begins by describing a pastoral scene: "Day ends abruptly here. The Alabama twilight is brief and lovely as a rainbow." Yet before long, "terror is on the street" as Huntsville's black residents rapidly and surreptitiously vacate the public space in an act of preemptive self-preservation after hearing that a white man has been hit by a car and "it might o' been a cullud man what did that killin." The beauty and terror of the South are inextricably joined, Bontemps suggests: "The beauty of this town is solely the beauty of its sins."[6]

In addition to Harlem and the South, Bontemps has less frequently been associated with Chicago. The Bontempses left Huntsville in 1933, paused briefly in Los Angeles, where Bontemps completed *Black Thunder*, and then moved to Chicago in 1935. They stayed there until 1943, during which time Arna taught, attended graduate school, and worked at the Illinois Writers' Project. Bontemps, like so many other black migrants, was disappointed to discover that the conditions in Chicago were not greatly improved from those his family had endured in Huntsville: "We had fled from the jungle of Alabama's Scottsboro area to the jungle of Chicago's crime-ridden South Side, and one was as terrifying as the other," he recollected. Hemmed in by restrictive housing covenants and threatened by violence at the hands of neighboring white communities, African Americans in Chicago found that life could be

THE TWO LAs: LOS ANGELES AND LOUISIANA

difficult and desperate. As historian Davarian Baldwin records in *Chicago's New Negroes: Modernity, the Great Migration, and Black Urban Life*, the African American population of Chicago "exploded from 44,130 in 1910 to 233,903 in 1930," and "the force of racist restrictive covenants and racial violence . . . gave rise to overcrowded housing . . . [in] some of the city's most dilapidated neighborhoods." He also notes, "While Harlem has been heralded as the center of early-twentieth-century black culture, when most migrants connected freedom with the urban north, 'the mecca was Chicago.'" Bontemps became rapidly disillusioned with this redemptive narrative of Chicago, but he remained captivated by the city as a hub for twentieth-century black migration. While there, he collaborated with Jack Conroy on a collection of African American migration narratives, *Anyplace but Here* (1966; originally published in 1945 as *They Seek a City*). In it, Bontemps and Conroy acknowledge that the internal migration of African Americans from the South "followed no set route. Starting at any point in the South, they have moved in every possible direction." Yet they also claim, "Traditionally and geographically, the whole period of migration considered, the most important of these dispersal points has been Chicago." As a result, Chicago serves as a continual point of return for the stories narrated in their collection. Despite the city's magnetism, and although he found a supportive literary community there, Bontemps recalled, "I never felt I could settle permanently with my family in Chicago. I could not accept the ghetto, and ironclad residential restrictions against Negroes situated as we were made escape impossible."[7]

Given this attention to Harlem, the South, and Chicago, it is clear that Bontemps was a writer preoccupied with the meanings of place and, in particular, how place informs black experience. Yet with so much attention paid to these three locales, it is rather surprising that he retained his self-identification as a "Californian" throughout his career, from the note he sent to the *Crisis* upon winning a Spingarn prize in 1926 to the publication of *Hold Fast to Dreams* in 1969. Comparatively, Bontemps's published writing on California is sparse, largely represented by a section on "Mudtown" in *God Sends Sunday*. It also appears in unlikely places—in the prefaces, introductions, or first chapters of many of his books set elsewhere. This includes, oddly, the first essay in

The Old South, the prologue to the Chicago-driven *Anyplace but Here,* and the introduction to the 1968 edition of *Black Thunder,* a novel set in the South. These looks back at California, then, seem prefatory for Bontemps; they appear to be an explanatory framework for what comes afterward. Although it may be tempting to dismiss California as merely the setting of Bontemps's youth, its presence in these texts suggests that an understanding of California is necessary to an understanding of the other geographies of Bontemps's writing and biography. When he writes of the South, of Harlem, or of Chicago, these sites often draw meaning from a dialogue with California. And when California becomes part of this network of black experience, the relationship between particular places and racial formations—such as the South and what Bontemps describes as "Negro-ness"—can be understood in new ways. Turning to Bontemps's lesser-known and unpublished work reveals that Los Angeles and the South have far more in common than his published work alone suggests.

Bontemps's life in California began in 1906 when his father, Paul, brought his family west from Alexandria, Louisiana, in search of an environment where racism would have less impact on their lives. Like many African Americans who arrived in Los Angeles during the Jim Crow era, Paul Bontemps was a striver who settled in a community where blacks tended to have similar middle-class aspirations. Black migration to Los Angeles had a different character than that to places like Chicago and Detroit around the time of World War I, when masses of black newcomers from the rural South and sharecropping communities were wooed northward by the promise of factory jobs in large industrial cities. In *Bound for Freedom: Black Los Angeles in Jim Crow America,* historian Douglas Flamming demonstrates that early black migrants to Los Angeles were largely from the urban South, had bourgeois mores and aspirations, and were looking for improved race relations rather than job opportunities. In 1915, when Arna was thirteen years old and the family had been living in Los Angeles for nine years, Frederick Madison Roberts, editor of the newspaper the *New Age,* wrote an essay describing the possibilities the city offered to blacks: "The West has been built upon . . . the belief of the pioneer builders in themselves," he contended, "and in their ability to create a community the equal of any in the world." He mobilized frontier tropes of individualism, hard work, and success to promote what Flamming terms the "Western Ideal." And situated within a black publication (Anita Scott Coleman's husband, James, would serve as an editor of the *New Age* in the mid-1920s), Roberts's claim that Los Angeles houses "a community the equal of any in the world" took on additional valence; he proclaimed not only regional equality but also racial equality. Roberts emphasized race and region together, suggesting "there isn't anything South or North or East which we can't duplicate or excel here" and stating, "individually and collectively we are doing better than any other equal number of a class of people in the country."[8]

These gentle gestures toward the intersection of race, class, and region echo Paul Bontemps's desires to ensconce his children in a place presumably more "race neutral" than the South, a place where they would have more educational opportunities, upward class mobility, and a lifestyle less hindered by Jim Crow. As a skilled tradesperson, a bricklayer, he was deeply invested in the ideologies of racial uplift characterized by "self-help, racial solidarity, temperance, thrift, chastity, social purity, patriarchal authority, and the accumulation of wealth." As historian Kevin K. Gaines points out, "Black elites sought status, moral authority, and recognition of their humanity by distinguishing themselves, as bourgeois agents of civilization, from the presumably un-developed black majority." For blacks in Los Angeles, the West became a vehicle to make this class-based vision of uplift possible. The language of racial uplift tended to replicate the language of American frontier fiction, which characterized the West as a place to pull oneself up by one's bootstraps and make a fortune. As a result, Los Angeles's African American community could be triply invested in this project: as blacks, as Americans, and as westerners, this rhetoric had tremendous appeal. At the end of his essay, Roberts clearly aligns race and region when he harnesses the language of class solidarity and respectability, bestowing upon his readers the rather muscular injunction that "whenever we find a lukewarm Angeleno, inject a little stiffening—Don't leave him until he realizes that he is living in the best part of the world and that his Race in this section is behind no one else. . . . If he will not be convinced put him down as either a fool or a jackass and as either, irresponsible."

Despite this conviction, Los Angeles, of course, was not free of racism, and in 1965 Watts, where the Bontemps family lived, would become a flash point for black rebellion against institutional racism outside of the South. Yet in the early twentieth century, black migrants like Roberts, the Bontempses, and the Colemans tended to envision Los Angeles as a place where the opportunity for middle-class success was better than it was elsewhere, including in Arna's birthplace of Louisiana.[9]

When early-twentieth-century black migrants arrived in Los Angeles, they found a multiethnic place. Bontemps's 1968 introduction to *Black Thunder* presents an idealized image of this community when he describes his father's neighborhood in Watts, where he had lived while finishing the novel in 1934: "A Japanese truck farmer's asparagus field was just outside our back door," he writes. "In the vacant lot across from us . . . a friendly Mexican neighbor grazed his milk goat. We could smell eucalyptus trees when my writing window was open and when we walked outside, and nearly always the air was like transparent gold in those days." Written in the wake of the 1965 unrest in Watts, this passage recalls a time before black ghettoization became entrenched in South Central Los Angeles, a time when, according to Flamming, black Angelenos lived in "quite possibly the most ethnically and racially diverse urban area in America," a community of Japanese, Mexican, and African Americans, as well as a "complicated mix of white folks," including Jews. In the 1930s Los Angeles had a marked East Side and West Side. The East Side, which included the Central Avenue district where most black migrants moved, was "poorer and ethnically diverse." This diversity was largely maintained until after World War II, when the construction of Interstate 10 made it attractive for mobile whites to move out of the East Side, at which point African Americans, due to restrictive covenants and racism, were left behind.[10]

By 1960, Watts was "virtually all black. The Central Avenue district had been pushed south and the black community in Watts had expanded northward until the two were effectively joined—a seven-mile stretch of African Americans locked between Main Street and Alameda." Yet when Bontemps wrote *Black Thunder* in the early 1930s, racial multiplicity was still the defining characteristic of Watts, and his life alongside Japanese and Mexican American neighbors accounted for part of its idyllic beauty. However, he did not stay. When Bontemps returned to Watts, he was in a state of financial duress; he, his wife, and his children were crowded into his father's house. Bontemps had recently resigned from his job at Huntsville's conservative Oakwood College, largely because his association with the progressive politics of the New Negro movement had been frowned upon by the administration. Paul Bontemps, who had become a Seventh-Day Adventist preacher, shared the college's opinion of Arna's writing. Because Arna's political affiliations had both imperiled his financial status during these Depression years and placed him in conversation with bohemians and radicals such as Wallace Thurman and Langston Hughes, it flew in the face of his father's politics of respectability. As Gaines suggests, "Historically, the conditions for social mobility and class formation among all Americans, blacks, immigrant groups, and other racially marked groups, including whites, have been circumscribed by race and color." As a result, "elite African Americans" who promoted racial uplift "were replicating, even as they contested, the uniquely American racial fictions upon which liberal conceptions of social reality and 'equality' were founded." Flamming contends that when Paul Bontemps moved west, he took the internal logic of uplift politics a step further—he cast off African American culture, tradition, and history along with the yoke of oppression. The move to California provided a way for Paul to leave blackness, which he saw as southern, behind. He encouraged his son to do the same.[11]

These attempts, however, met with limited success. Not long after Paul and his family arrived in Los Angeles, Arna's great-uncle Buddy joined them. Characterized by Arna as a free-spirited alcoholic who took pleasure in folk traditions, black vernacular, and the blues, Buddy became the model for some of his fictional proletarian heroes. Flamming suggests that Bontemps "reduced the complex personalities of Paul and Buddy to their least common denominators"—Paul becoming the epitome of a deracinated, bourgeois West, and Buddy becoming the symbol of a black folk South. As a result, never the twain shall meet. When Bontemps writes of African America, no matter where it is located, it resembles the South. About Bontemps's *God Sends Sunday* Flamming argues, "Even the part of the novel situated in southern California is really about the South, not the West," since it is about black people.[12]

Flamming is one of the few scholars to seriously consider the interplay between the New Negro movement and the borderlands West, and his argument makes sense, particularly when derived from *God Sends Sunday*. A consideration of Bontemps's archived works, however, expands and complicates this neat regional schema. In part 2 of *God Sends Sunday*, Augie arrives in a black neighborhood in the Los Angeles area, which Bontemps names "Mudtown." Outside of Mudtown, Bontemps suggests, a far more typical black western experience exists, which he describes by painting black westerners as intrepid pioneers, emphasizing individualism and echoing paradigms of uplift. Taking the tone of a historian, he writes:

> In those days, fifteen or twenty years ago, Negroes were not plentiful in the far west. Least of all were they to be seen in the rural parts. A few of them, to be sure, had come as early as the historical gold rush with the forty-niners, working in personal service. Others had followed the conquest of the frontier. But the number had remained small until the great transcontinental railway lines established important terminals in Los Angeles and San Francisco. Then the real migration began.

He goes on to describe Pullman porters and their families, who ended up clustered in multiracial urban centers located near train stations throughout the West. This is the usual black western experience, Bontemps asserts, and it exists in contrast with Mudtown. There, he suggests, "the small group . . . was exceptional." They are unencumbered by the politics of respectability—"removed from the influences of white folks, they did not acquire the inhibitions of their city brothers" elsewhere in the Los Angeles region. Mudtown is characterized as a pastoral, preindustrial, and, indeed, southern place: "Throughout warm summer days toothless men sat in front of the little grocery store on boxes, chewing the stems of cob pipes, recalling the 'Mancipation, the actual beginning of their race. Women cooked over fireplaces in yards and boiled their clothes in heavy iron kettles. There were songs in little frail houses and over the steaming pots. Lilacs grew at every doorstep. In every house there was a guitar." In descriptions like this one, Bontemps seems to, indeed, create "a tiny section of the deep south literally transplanted" in the West."[13]

An examination of the unpublished predecessor to *God Sends Sunday*, however, complicates this representation of the black West. "The Chariot in the Cloud," dated December 31, 1929, was the first novel Bontemps wrote. By then, he had already gained notoriety as a poet, winning the *Crisis*'s inaugural Spingarn prize for "Nocturne at Bethesda" in 1926; the following year he won the Alexander Pushkin poetry prize from *Opportunity*. He had not, however, established much of a reputation for his prose, and "The Chariot in the Cloud" went unpublished, although it did provide some of the scaffolding for *God Sends Sunday*. Bontemps adapted the stories of Augie from "The Chariot in the Cloud," rearranged and expanded them, and made them the center of his first published novel. To readers of *God Sends Sunday*, then, parts of "The Chariot in the Cloud" would look familiar. However, the bulk of the unpublished novel is a bildungsroman that follows the autobiographical Alec Plum, who doesn't appear in *God Sends Sunday* at all.

The Mudtown of "The Chariot in the Cloud" resembles that in *God Sends Sunday;* it is a segregated community, "removed across the inter-urban tracks without so much as a street by which it could be directly approached." Here, Bontemps introduces the language he would later refine and reuse in *God Sends Sunday*: "Here the colored immigrants, un-abashed by the eyes of strangers, lost their inhibitions. It was as if a small section of the deep south had been literally transplanted." He continues:

Along three dusty, ungraded streets there were rows of pitiful little rough-board structures in which the folks lived. Usually these sat well away from the street, and in the front yards there were woodpiles and carts and rubbish and sometimes a horse or a cow. Part of Mudtown had formerly been a walnut grove and in many yards certain of the trees were still standing. In others there were castor bean trees and oleanders; no yard was without shade, and in a few the trees formed the main pillars for the huts erected beneath them. Flower beds and lawns had not yet been cultivated but every shack and out-house boasted a honeysuckle or a morning glory vine, and these sometimes covered an entire side or roof and, here and there, casually blotted out doors and windows.[14]

During Bontemps's time in Southern California, this area was known as the "Furlong Tract" (Bontemps, writing in the vernacular, calls it the "Furlough Track"). Situated between Watts to the south and the Central Avenue district to the north, the Furlong Tract was, according to Flamming, an "ethnically diverse area, a patchwork of black, white, and ethnic Mexican homes, varying widely in size and quality." It may have taken some imagination for Bontemps to describe it as a "small section of the deep south . . . transplanted," but it was one of the first areas of the city where African Americans were able to buy land. This occurred when a white farmer named James Furlong, the son of Irish immigrants, subdivided his property in 1905 and sold parcels to blacks for $750. The nearby industrial city of Vernon, which had yet to hit its prime, provided employment to residents of the working-class neighborhoods that surrounded it. The once underdeveloped tract grew, and Los Angeles's first public school to serve a black community opened there. In 1908, after the death of Bontemps's mother, his father moved the family to the Furlong Tract, where his grandmother helped take care of Arna and his siblings. These experiences provided the basis for Alec's narrative in "The Chariot in the Cloud."[15]

The Mudtown of "The Chariot in the Cloud" is an idealized black space. Bontemps describes "the menfolks" who "surrounded their yards with picket fences made of unrelated strips and stray boards, but the gates usually stood open," inviting neighbors in, which suggests that Mudtown is a cohesive community. He writes lovingly of "goats tethered in the vacant lots, chickens scratching on the streets and, in the backyards, big-hipped women bending over wash-tubs, their turbaned heads bobbing up and down in time with the disconsolate rhythms of their songs," emphasizing the agrarian and proletarian aspects of this place. His use of the words "folks" and "menfolks" and his somewhat predictably drawn black matrons intertwine tenderness and rural nostalgia to depict this working-class African American community.[16]

The Fifty-First Street School, 1915. This first African American school in Los Angeles was located in the Furlong Tract. (Los Angeles Public Library Photo Collection)

Mudtown appears throughout Bontemps's written corpus. When describing it, he moves between idyllic, pastoral scenes and documentation of its increasingly urban character. The attempted synthesis of the pastoral and the urban characterizes Bontemps's ongoing representations of the African American West and extends to other sites of black migration. In *Anyplace but Here*, Bontemps and Conroy inflate Mudtown to describe black settlement across the United States: "Mudtown is that embarrassing section of the Northern city in which the new people from the South erected those absurd little shacks to house themselves until they could move on—or perhaps do better. The Furlough Track in Los Angeles was one of the Mudtowns. Perhaps its history is typical." Here, it appears that Bontemps will remain faithful to his image of Mudtown as a "section of the deep south . . . transplanted." Certainly, Mudtown's lush fecundity is repeated:

> Cows and goats were tethered on that part of Holmes Avenue that reached into the neighborhood. A half-grown cinnamon bear was chained to a stake on a side lot. Flocks of pigeons circled over the rooftops and settled on the towering birdhouses that had been erected for them on twenty- and thirty-foot poles. Honeysuckle covered slat fences, tumble-down verandas, and outhouses, and filled the air with an unexpected sweetness.

Upon arriving, according to Bontemps and Conroy, the southern migrant finds Mudtown indistinguishable from other places he has lived. Again modeled on Bontemps's great-uncle Buddy, this "tired little man" is both saddened and unsurprised to see that Mudtown resembles the impoverished, marginalized communities he knew so well in the segregated South: "So this is where the colored folks live," he muses wistfully, "I mighta known."[17]

A committed settler, however, like the careful reader, will discover that the Mudtown of *Anyplace but Here* is not an entirely black space: "Those who remained longer made some surprising discoveries," Bontemps and Conroy insist. Those discoveries consist of the complicated networks of race and ethnicity in the borderlands West—networks elaborated through the authors' detailed look at the African Americans,

Mexican Americans, Filipinos, and whites that live in the community. They write of a place that fosters a racial egalitarianism—what they call "Mudtown's dream"—where, across the boundaries of race, the community is united by geography and class. The bridges across cultures are seen even within individuals. For instance, they describe Red Eagle as a "broad-shouldered Negro who lived alone, talked little, and dressed like an Indian. His parentage was obscure, but there was little doubt that he had grown up and lived most of his life among Indians in Oklahoma." On the one hand, he "knew all about ornaments made of silver, all about ropes and knots, but nothing much about the ways of his fellow Negroes and nothing at all about their songs and laughter." On the other hand, he is not completely detached from African American experience, for he knows that "even when one of [the Negro cowboys] was praised as 'the whitest man I've ever known,' he was not white." Red Eagle appears to have emerged from a tribal culture, yet he knows about African American oppression. His complicated identity is undoubtedly a marginal one—and decidedly nonwhite.[18]

Such complexity is not unusual in Mudtown, a community that is both African American and multiethnic. Although African American space is centered, the multiethnic West provides its context. For example, Bontemps and Conroy write of a black church in Mudtown: "Those who remember this community fondly mention unforgettable services in one or the other of the two little Mudtown churches, particularly the Sunday night when the quartet of boys from Tuskegee gave a program which started folks humming spirituals they thought had been left down home." Here, the South is clearly considered "home." But the easy transportability of African American folk culture from the South to California is undercut by Mudtown's irrepressible multiethnic westernness in the next line: "They still talk about the Mexican storekeeper and his pretty daughter Julia, and they remember the even prettier colored girl named Alameda who looked more Mexican than Julia." The first part of this sentence seems at odds with the prior description of the spirituals performed at Mudtown's churches, but the second part brings these two worlds together in a figure as complex as Red Eagle. Alameda's Spanish name and seemingly Mexican phenotype complicate her legibility as African American, yet this multiethnic ambiguity is also decidedly at home in a Mudtown that embraces both black churches and Mexican stores. Alameda is, after all, more than just the name of a pretty girl; it is also the name of the major north-south thoroughfare in the Furlong Tract. This black-Mexican woman is thus entirely allied with this locality.[19]

A closer look at the Mudtown of *Anyplace but Here* reveals its multiethnic landscape through figures such as Red Eagle and Alameda, distinguishing it somewhat from the monoethnic black communities of *God Sends Sunday* and "The Chariot in the Cloud." But rather than confining the Los Angeles–based narrative to a single and relatively autonomous black neighborhood, "The Chariot in the Cloud" describes a far more nuanced geography by also sketching the interplay between the "country" near Watts and the "city" or Central Avenue district. By attending to local geographies, Bontemps makes African

The Furlong Tract on the cusp of change—just before construction of the Pueblo del Rio housing projects, 1941. (Los Angeles Public Library Photo Collection)

American life multidimensional in an era plagued by overly simplified, primitivist representations of blacks. Although he describes, for example, how "the Clows, a peasant family from the southern plantations, had not caught on quickly in the west," he dwells less on the West-South dichotomy and more on the differences between the rural and urban dimensions of Los Angeles. While prevalent images of the West tend to focus on wilderness, or perhaps on quaint southwestern villages, and contemporary Los Angeles is envisioned as a sprawling concrete jungle, "The Chariot in the Cloud" shows both of these. Alec lives with his grandmother, Ma Pat, in the country near Watts. Ma Pat and her brother, Augie, grew up on a southern plantation, and their neighbors out on Bingham Road, the Clows, are depicted as irreducibly southern and "countrified," yet the country is far from an exclusively black rural space. Ma Pat, like the inhabitants of Mudtown in *God Sends Sunday*, is described as "an exception" to the general rule that African Americans "had the tendency to remain within the city and, particularly, in the neighborhood of the depot." Until the Clows move to the neighborhood, she is one of the only blacks in a predominantly Mexican American community. As a result, Ma Pat's son, Pig, "had always associated with the Mexicans" and "looked much like a Mexican himself and in their company was frequently taken for one." Pig is married to a Mexican American woman, and at a party thrown by the Clows, rife with the trappings of black vernacular culture, Pig "talked with [his Mexican friends] in Spanish and seemed as much out of his element as they."[20]

The country created by the novel grapples with images of inscrutable Mexicans, agricultural landscapes, and the trappings of ranch culture popular in depictions of the West. Bontemps describes a "gang of Mexicans" who arrive to work a sugar beet field adjacent to Ma Pat's: "Passing Alec at his gate, some of them greeted him in their own language. . . . They were men with grave, humorless faces, bountiful moustaches and eyes, the expressions of which Alec could not guess." While this encounter appears to highlight Alec's difference from the Mexican farmworkers, the next passages integrate the black experience into familiar representations of the greater Mexican borderlands. Bontemps writes, "In the level adjoining fields the beet harvest was finished. A herd of Texas steers had been brought in to fatten on the tops that were left on the ground.

A "country" backyard in Watts, 1919. (Los Angeles Public Library Photo Collection)

They were lean untamed animals with incredible horns and were tended by cowboys and dogs in the old romantic manner familiar to readers of western fiction." This passage, however, is sandwiched between two sets of lyrics sung by Augie. First he sings, "De boat's gone up de river / An' de tide's gone down," referring, most likely, to the Mississippi and its undeniable power in the African American imagination. In conjunction with these lines, the scene "familiar to readers of western fiction" is made unfamiliar through its juxtaposition with the Mississippi blues. But the second set of lyrics gestures toward a less acknowledged but no less powerful site in the black imagination: "I'm going to de nation an' marry me an Indian squaw," Augie sings, "An' let some Injun woman be ma mother-in-law." Resembling several classic blues songs, these lyrics allude to Indian country as another possible site for black freedom. By embedding the West in the blues, Bontemps suggests that black folk traditions are not, in fact, at odds with the West at all; they have been part of its multiethnic landscape all along. Thus, when Alec replies to the Spanish greetings of the Mexican farmworkers by "mumbling an answer without committing himself to any particular tongue," this is a moment of possible connection, a transcultural bridging, rather than a moment of oppositional difference.[21]

If the country is multiethnic, so too is the city in "The Chariot in the Cloud." When he describes the city, Bontemps most often means the Central Avenue district, describing it as the major location for black commerce, culture, and social life. He calls it "less . . . a place to live and more . . . a marketing place and bright-light district." Families shop there during the day, but at night "the lights blossomed, the brown wine-tinted chippies swept down like a flight of birds and the young blades appeared in their fine clothes, primed to spread joy." The nightclubs of the avenue are alluring to Alec, and Bontemps traffics in predictable descriptions of "far-away glamour" and "dancing so urgent and riotous that neither disaster nor sudden tragedy could impede it." However, Bontemps does not describe the avenue as exclusively black. As a commercial district, there is money to be made there, which brings whites and nonblack people of color into its orbit, with markets "run by foreigners for the colored trade" and the "Chinese laundry-man" who "carried on" a "lottery business . . . among the Negroes." Although they sometimes look similar, Central Avenue is not Lenox Avenue, and this neighborhood is not Harlem, just as the country near Watts is not the sharecropping plantations of the rural South.[22]

Triangulating the city, the country, and Mudtown enables Bontemps to depict a wide range of African American experience within the multiethnic context of the borderlands West. These neighborhoods represent the class and gender contours that are always intersecting in black Los Angeles, painting a far different picture than either the primitivist representations of African Americans in much modernist writing or the middle-class propriety in uplift literature. The seemingly countrified Clows, particularly the daughters Beulah and Azilee, complicate class- and gender-based notions of primitivist authenticity when Alec comes to understand their relationship to power. He is shocked to learn that the sisters, whom he had imagined as "natural and unspoiled," were "miserable" in their dependence on arduous domestic service, like so many of the black women in Coleman's writing. Although Bontemps seems to laud the Clows for their proletarian "Negro-ness," he also

African American women dressed in "Spanish" costumes at a Halloween party at La Veda Ballroom in South Central Los Angeles, 1929. Later, the ballroom also hosted dances sponsored by the Ex–New Orleaners Club. This photograph and its context, like Bontemps's writing, suggest that the two LAs—Los Angeles and Louisiana—are related to each other as part of the greater multiethnic borderlands. (Los Angeles Public Library Photo Collection)

acknowledges the layers of oppression that inform their experience. He mocks the patronizing naïveté of his own protagonist who, when contemplating Beulah's difficult, unfulfilling work as a laundress, first thinks, "This is her peasant blood." Then Alec "put[s] his arm around her shoulder" and tells her, "You are a great one around a house." Beulah's sister, Azilee, becomes a figure of resistance in the novel—a resistance allied with geographic space: "Living in [Mud]town had not yet proved what she expected; it got her nothing she valued, none of the things she associated with city life . . . ; she was beginning to feel that she might just as well have remained in the country." Yet when Azilee, desiring economic advancement and independence, establishes herself in the city, her move is complicated not only by class but also by gender. Her community sees her desire for liberation as evidence of sexual promiscuity, and her own mother accuses her of "aimin to go to the dogs with the rest of the chippies on the Avenue." As an urbane, modern woman seeking independence and self-determination, Azilee is accused, frankly, of "streetwalking" in the city—ultimately presenting a much different picture of black western womanhood than that constructed by Coleman's loyal wives and long-suffering domestics. In the work of both Bontemps and Coleman, however, class and gender, overlaid, become mapped onto place.[23]

These geographies of class, gender, and place in black Los Angeles become increasingly obvious as Alec begins "to drift away from his Mudtown associates and to spend most of his time on the West side," where "many of the young people whom he had met at school lived . . . , being the children of the more prosperous colored families." Alec is torn between the relative privilege of his West Side friends from school and the working-class existence of his childhood friends in the country, the city, and Mudtown; these are emblematic of competing visions of black America during the era of racial uplift. Alec's time on the avenue with Azilee troubles his father, whose pretenses to middle-class respectability are bared when he "grimly disapproved of his own people and their loose, care free proclivities." Yet when he confronts Alec, asserting that "the Avenue's done got you," Alec convinces him to soften his stance somewhat, particularly where Azilee is concerned: "Maybe I'm wrong," Alec's father muses as he gives Azilee the benefit of the doubt. "Maybe this man's town's jes too little fuh her." He seemingly recognizes that Azilee's behavior is a sign of her resistance to a matrix of domination. By the end of the novel, Azilee has artfully transformed her "fly" persona into successful entrepreneurship, becoming a beauty culturist in Harlem. There, her salon is a business, a community institution, and a site that engenders black political and intellectual thought by offering "current copies of *Opportunity, The Crisis, The Tattler* and several of the better known Negro newspapers" such as "*The Amsterdam News, The Courier, The Defender* [and] *The American*" to serve as points of exchange for her patrons. The character Azilee finds historical precedents in women such as famed hair tycoon Madam C. J. Walker, who, as Noliwe Rooks notes, "could not draw on ideologies that privileged education and middle-class notions of domesticity because her life did not include these things. As a result, she reconfigured the terms of the debate to include characteristics she did possess—money and a Protestant work ethic." This demonstrated Walker's desire for "African American women" to "gain a level of economic independence"—"not only freedom from economic dependence on dominant culture but also freedom from individual African American men within the institution of marriage." This is a very different view of autonomy and domesticity than that promoted by Coleman's western writing. Perhaps it is Azilee's move to Harlem—getting into "another man's town," as the novel puts it—that enables this difference.[24]

As characters like Azilee and, later, Alec leave California for other locations, Bontemps triangulates region in addition to neighborhood, placing California in dialogue with both the South (which is never seen but is frequently referred to) and Harlem. It is tempting to correlate these geographies, as Flamming does when he suggests that Bontemps's California is, essentially, the South. It is also tempting to pit these geographies against one another, seeing them as opposites by making the claim that, for example, the West and the South have nothing in common. But neither of these concepts sufficiently explains Bontemps's spatial imagination in "The Chariot in the Cloud." A more accurate way to understand his local and national geographies can be derived from the image of the railroad, which appears throughout the novel. The railroad (particularly the "interurban tracks") structures the network between Los Angeles neighborhoods in the novel, as well as the network between western and nonwestern black communities. Railroad tracks have often been seen as dividing lines—with a "right" and a "wrong" side, indicating the difference between working-class and bourgeois communities or between white and black communities. But "The Chariot in the Cloud" suggests that the railroad functions as a literal connector across geographic distance and as a figurative connector across divergent social locations and from the past to the present.[25]

For example, when Alec leaves Mudtown, he realizes he "did not really hate Mud Town at all. He hated its squalor and ugliness. But he loved the wretched handkerchief-headed black folks who lived there, for he understood every ripple of their existence. He was, peculiarly, their son—no matter how far life might remove him." At this point, musing on the working class of Mudtown, he determines he must "learn something about his race," a study he plans to undertake in Harlem. When he sets out on his journey, however, he cannot shake off his connections to Los Angeles, for he is beholden to the mechanisms of memory. Gazing through the train windows as he rushes eastward, he reflects on the "vast arid country" and his "ever increasing sense of distance, separation." Yet, as the empty western landscape echoes Alec's feelings of solitude, his mind is flooded "again and again" with images from "the period of time and the group of people from whom he was escaping." As he looks forward (and eastward) to his escape, he is already looking backward (and westward) by reminiscing about his hometown, his people, and his past, even dreaming of a contradictory, nostalgic future in which he and Azilee "might get together occasionally in that new place [New York] and thereby retain their memories of Mud Town and Bingham Road." The railroad separates Alec from his boyhood home and community, yet at the same time, he remains connected to this place and its people through both his memories and the miles and miles of railroad tracks stretching across the continent. No matter how far away he goes, or where, he will always be connected to Southern California. In a set of lyrical passages describing the scenery that darts past the train windows in fleeting glimpses, Bontemps creates a paean to the black diaspora in the American West. The train is a new geographic imagining of black experience as part of American multiethnic experience. "Railroad travel still being new to [Alec], he could not keep his eyes off the passing scene," writes Bontemps. Like a cinema flashback, "the things he saw he did not see as literal objects; they were of the quality of pictures, like scenes imagined." Here, Bontemps makes it clear that the tracks are important not only for their literal use in traversing space but also for their metaphorical gestures. When Alec envisions the tracks branching off in every conceivable direction, he imagines the nascent Great Migration radiating throughout the nation and even beyond it. No matter where he looks, black migrants are found, sometimes in the most surprising places, and the tracks connect them all, both immersing them in multiethnic communities and connecting regions such as the West and the South: "The trains . . . every day communicated between [dispersed blacks] and the south," Bontemps writes. Even when Alec arrives in Harlem, he is connected to the South—and to California.[26]

Engagement with a diasporic consciousness is evident in a scene in which Alec is at a Harlem café, "where a group of Negro scholars and artists" is discussing the meaning of African American identity. One, perhaps based on Alain Locke, argues, "The Negro artist's need . . . is a tradition. . . . Africa is our home." But "two young poets"—likely based on Langston Hughes and Bontemps himself—"could not agree. How should they think of themselves?—as Americans or Africans?" In response to this question, in language that seems to draw from Hughes's "The Negro Artist and the Racial Mountain" (1926), Bontemps writes, "For some time the Negro must say before each thought: 'I am black.' Later it was hoped he might add: 'but comely.' Eventually, perhaps, he might remember only: 'I am comely.'" This progression, however, is a complicated one, as Bontemps suggests when he writes, "In such case he would lose his blackness. Yes, he was already losing it. . . . Despite all efforts to the contrary the African strain was dissolving, becoming simply an element in a great racial composite. . . . Alec's race, as it now existed in America, began at Emancipation." Here, Bontemps traces US black identity from the African diaspora through the history of emancipation and beyond, ultimately gesturing at something new, a modern racial formation that he identifies as "composite"—a hybrid African American identity. Conceptualized through Alec's perspective in the novel, this is arguably an outgrowth of his western experience, which was shaped by the relationships between black people and other people of color in the multiethnic landscape of Los Angeles and within its local geographies: Mudtown, the country near Watts, and the avenue.[27]

At this moment, Alec is flooded with memories of his childhood friend and sweetheart Beulah Clow—the only one of his peers who remains in California throughout the narrative. He experiences an epiphany: the "mystery" of his affection for her is "clarified." Beulah, he realizes, "was to him his race. . . . Her problems were not personal, merely, but the well-known problems of hosts of blacks along the railroads and in the remote corners of the country." Beginning with Beulah in California and extending along the symbolic network of the railroad, the black western experience is not anomalous. Instead, it becomes generalized to African American experience overall, furthering the "double-consciousness" of being both an "American" and a "Negro" articulated by W. E. B. DuBois in *The Souls of Black Folk* (1903). In "The Chariot in the Cloud," it is not the veil but the railroad that symbolizes the complexities of African American experience and perspective. When he uses this as a symbol, emphasizing transregional migration and local geographies, Bontemps creates a new metaphor for the experiences of US blacks, one distinct from, for example, the slave ship used to describe trans-Atlantic black cultures, perspectives, and politics in Paul Gilroy's work. Ultimately, this is an image derived from the multiethnic American West, where the railroad is a central character in both stories of American progress and stories of the devastation of the Plains Indians or the abuse of the Chinese, African American, Mexican American, and white ethnic workers who laid its tracks—even though the economic utility of the railroad in the West, as Richard White has convincingly demonstrated, was always dubious.[28]

The images that flit across the "screen" of Alec's train window also document the history of black settlement in the West. One of the earliest scenes he sees is of Mexicans working in an agrarian landscape, as they did in the sugar beet fields surrounding Ma Pat's house: "By [the] roadside he saw a group of young Mexicans, apparently of the same family, waiting with cups while the tallest boy milked a small goat; a freckled youngster stood at curbside directing a flock of geese with a tree-switch; and on a hill, at sunset, a girl in heavy shoes guided a plow to which were teamed a milk-cow and a mule." When Alec looks more closely, he sees that African Americans also appear trackside, in conjunction with their Mexican American and Native American neighbors: "Most of the towns he saw had unfamiliar names, soft charming names from Indian and Spanish words. Alec noticed that in many of these as well as along the road there were black faces. He wondered if it were the same throughout the country, if everywhere the approach to an American city by rail were marked by the rude dwellings of Negroes." Bontemps situates black experience in the unlikeliest of places—the Native American and Mexican American towns of the borderlands West. In doing so, he creates a history of black settlement in these borderlands spaces, seeing them as natural landscapes, as Indian and Mexican places, and then as places that become increasingly black as the railroad attracts laborers. Together, these images foreshadow sweeping demographic changes. As Richard White points out, by the end of World War II, the West was, "above all, a metropolitan West." Bontemps imagines a West transitioning to an industrial economy and becoming increasingly urbanized. He even notes that in Mudtown, "a forest of smoke-stacks had arisen, surrounding it on two sides. Foundries and mills blazed day and night. Each week, it seemed, they crept nearer and nearer. It would only be a matter of months until they covered Mudtown completely." Bontemps's description of a future Mudtown overtaken by industry parallels his intimation that blackness was being lost in modern America in favor of a "composite" race. As a result, "The Chariot in the Cloud," like Jean Toomer's *Cane*, operates as both a tragic "swan-song" for African America and a triumphant proclamation of a new African American hybridity. This story of racial transformation is allied with that of technological and industrial innovation—a story perhaps best illustrated by turning toward California. Bontemps's work, then, may be a modern, more masculinist predecessor to the postmodern regionalism explored by Krista Comer's *Landscapes of the New West*. There, Comer argues that California is a "western continuum" on which the "various parts of the western problematic" can be mapped, particularly the tension between wilderness and economic, urban, and industrial expansion. "What more *western* story (either past or present)," she asks rhetorically, "can one think of than the battle between slow growth and urban development?"[29]

In *Anyplace but Here*, Bontemps and Conroy conclude their segment on Mudtown by comparing westward expansion with the Great Migration:

> The story of the internal migration of Negroes in the United States has perhaps as many threads as the story of the nation's westward expansion. The front is wide, and the period of the movements covers more than a hundred years. And just as every man who went West had his own personal experiences, so every Negro who left the South behind was motivated by a set of circumstances peculiar to himself.[30]

At first, this passage makes the story of the western frontier and the story of the Great Migration look incongruous—their only similarity being their complexity, their "many threads." But upon closer examination, they appear less divergent, both of them motivated by powerful fictions of American individualism—by "personal experiences." Although these stories are not necessarily the same, this passage insinuates that the story of the West and the story of the South have at least some connection. Once again, this returns to the question of the relationship between the West and the South in Bontemps's work. Whereas Flamming contends that Bontemps's Mudtown in *God Sends Sunday* is a simulacrum of the South, an examination of Bontemps's archived work makes it possible to modify this contention. As "The Chariot in the Cloud" suggests, Bontemps does more than simply re-create a monolithic black South in the West. Instead, he constructs intricate local and regional geographies that are aligned with complicated racial, class, and gender formations. Whereas Bontemps's representations of California, are, as Flamming argues, certainly somewhat "southern," his West and his South are far more multiethnic, complex, and—as his image of the train tracks implies—connected than *God Sends Sunday* alone allows readers to understand.

Nowhere is this more evident than in the final scenes of "The Chariot in the Cloud," when Alec returns to California. Once there, he takes the train to Blythe, a town located southeast of Los Angeles and along the Arizona border, "on the edge of the desert." There, he hopes to reconnect with Beulah, who has come to symbolize his relationship to African

America. When he arrives, Blythe is described as irreducibly western. Bontemps uses images and language reminiscent of the dime novels so popular during the 1920s. Blythe, he contends, is "the only remaining town in which the legendary west of fiction still existed. Cowboys, stores with hitching bars, blanketed Indians from the reservations, dusty unpaved streets, eating places where men lingered to chat, and painted meretricious women in the little bars." Yet at the same time, Blythe is remarkably southern, for it was "not gold, but cotton, that made this town boom." As already indicated by Coleman's "Arizona and New Mexico—The Land of Esperanza" and the memories of settlers from Blackdom and Vado, the early twentieth century saw the cotton industry take hold in the desert West. Cotton cultivation, however, had a long history in the arid lands of the Southwest (pima cotton, for example, is named for the Pima Indians of Arizona, who first cultivated it), so there was something western about the production of cotton long before it ruled the southern economy, contributed to white westward expansion, and fueled black oppression. In the twentieth century, however, southwestern cotton production expanded—largely due to the growing auto industry, which used cotton to make the threads that held tires together. During World War I, Goodyear established cotton farms in what is now Goodyear, Arizona, to make the tires used in the war effort. The southeastern boll weevil infestation during these years made southwestern cotton production even more attractive. For Bontemps, these vast western fields of cotton also represented a reckoning with the South: "As far as [Alec] could see there were cotton fields in blossom. This is what he imagined Ma Pat's former home [on a southern plantation] to have been like." Alec's arrival in Blythe and his meeting with Beulah are an immersion in African American history: it "was like going back into the past, into the beginnings of his people. A white man on horseback was riding across his acres. Nearby some black cotton pickers were kneeling around a fire over which they were preparing coffee and bacon. The smooth, well modulated quality of their voices seemed transmitted directly from the earth."[31]

If Southern California is both southern and western in "The Chariot in the Cloud," the connections between these locales are even clearer in another of Bontemps's unpublished works—an unfinished novel titled "The Prizefighter and the Woman," written in 1947. By then, the neighborhoods Bontemps first depicted in "The Chariot in the Cloud" had become increasingly urban, increasingly populated, and increasingly African American. Rather than functioning as sites where middle-class migrants promoted ideologies of uplift, bought houses, and pursued bourgeois lives, these communities now drew primarily working-class migrants seeking employment in the defense industries. Although "The Prizefighter and the Woman" was written after the neighborhoods of South Central Los Angeles had become more monolithically black, the Los Angeles depicted in this manuscript is even more racially diverse than that described in "The Chariot in the Cloud." "The Prizefighter and the Woman" takes place largely on John Street, near Watts, and it follows Eugene Holmes, a local African American boy nicknamed "Sweet Pea." At the outset of the novel, a gruff southern white woman named Dove takes in the orphaned Eugene. Following in the footsteps of some of his Filipino, Mexican, and African American friends and neighbors, Eugene becomes a boxer. Already acting as his guardian and supporter, Dove also becomes his manager, and the novel follows their relationship as they stave off both corrupt boxing impresarios and a range of opponents.

The setting of "The Prizefighter and the Woman" is easily recognizable as California, and Bontemps takes great care to document local geographies, including specific street and place names, that draw a detailed picture of the Los Angeles neighborhood where the novel takes place. Unlike in the Black Belt of the South, African Americans are not the most populous group in Eugene's neighborhood on John Street. There, near "the dusty intersection of Compton and Lindenwood roads" and "the flag station called Abila," is a "little tumbled down community of Mexicans, Negroes, and [like Dove] other unsettled migrants." Among Eugene's friends there is only one other "Negro in the bunch," the middle-class Eustace Ward. Eugene's best friends are Mexican American—Manuel De la Fuente, Joe Ramírez, and Joe's sister Raquel—and other friends are white. As the neighborhood children go to school, "little squads of Mexican, Negro, Oriental and white children came from across the interurban tracks, from over toward Alameda road, from John street and the section near Leak's lake, from along

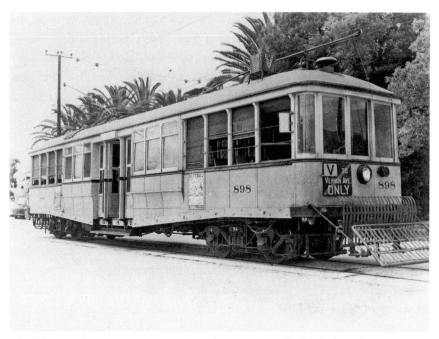

The Vernon Avenue streetcar, traversing Los Angeles's black and multiethnic geographies. (Los Angeles Public Library Photo Collection)

Compton avenue and from up toward Nadeau junction." As in "The Chariot in the Cloud," the railroad serves as both a dividing line and a connector—here connecting multiethnic communities in addition to the US black diaspora.[32]

"The Prizefighter and the Woman," like "The Chariot in the Cloud," creates a nuanced urban geography for Los Angeles, one that captures its racial multiplicity and relies on the image of railroad tracks to do so. Instead of the transcontinental railroads, however, Bontemps looks locally, at the interurban streetcars that crisscross the Southern Californian landscape. These represent not only the contours of black migration but also the small details of multiethnic, intraregional community. Even the station names and the streetcar lines become familiar to readers as passengers of all racial backgrounds ride to their jobs in the shipyards of San Pedro, up-and-coming fighters travel to their gym on Central Avenue, and a few members of the community commute to their classes at the University of California at Los Angeles. The intersections, businesses, and landmarks in the community become intimately familiar—the Mexican grocery store on John Street, the movie theater near Watts Station, the Pico Heights district on the West Side, the Southern Pacific tracks along Alameda Road, the burlesque on Los Angeles's Main Street, and the Humming Bird nightclub on Central Avenue. With Bontemps's characters, readers loiter at the corner of Ninth and Central, ride the streetcar to Long Beach, and wait for the train at Vernon Avenue and Long Beach Boulevard. Even the sport of boxing is intensely local—the industrial city of Vernon, which housed an outdoor and later an indoor coliseum, contributed to Los Angeles's reputation as a boxing capital during and between the world wars.

After Jack Johnson's famous "Fight of the Century" in 1910, when he defeated James Jeffries, the so-called Great White Hope, boxing continued to be intensely racialized. Los Angeles's working-class men—white, Mexican, Filipino, and African American, all of whom are represented in "The Prizefighter and the Woman"—provided a steady stream of local talent to electrify audiences on the basis of racial identity. This was not lost on Bontemps, who writes that, in the arena "on the fringe of the Negro community, [Eugene] was loved on sight," yet when he "met white boxers before white audiences, something else fell between him and the crowd." Although John Street seems to be a bubble of idealized working-class, cross-racial solidarity, California as a whole is certainly not depicted as free of racism. Dove advises Eugene to be aware that even Californians "ain't used to seeing a white woman take up with a boy of your color and doing for him like his own maw would, leastwise one from the South." She brings her knowledge of the South, including social and cultural pathologies surrounding miscegenation, to Eugene's multiethnic western experience, exposing these same pathologies in California. When Dove takes Eugene into her home, "just as if he belonged to her," she is easily mistaken for his mother, and the specter of miscegenation haunts their relationship. In one scene, an African American barber comments about Eugene, "He's got good hair. . . . Anybody can cut good hair. This boy could go to the Mexican barber if he wanted to—or the white one." This is less a discussion of Eugene's phenotype than a revelation of the discomfort produced by Eugene and Dove's interracial family. Even if it is not a biological family,

Joe Rivers, a notable Mexican American boxer, fights Freddie Walsh at the Vernon Arena, 1914. (Los Angeles Public Library Photo Collection)

the hint that it *could* be is enough to provoke discussion. The barber feels "uneasy in Dove's cold and sullen [and white] presence." Like Azilee in "The Chariot in the Cloud," Dove is seen as a ruined woman; even her name recalls tales of the "soiled doves"—nineteenth-century western prostitutes. And here, she is further sullied by the suggestion of interracial sexuality. By collaborating with those potentially tainted by interracial sex, Eugene's barber realizes he is putting himself at risk. And when Eugene and Dove leave the familiar and diverse landscape of John Street, they are faced with segregationist policies at restaurants that "didn't serve Indians, Orientals, Filipinos, Mexicans—nothing like that." Although Eugene is African American, he is "like that," and even in California, he becomes a target of white supremacy.[33]

In the opening pages of "The Prizefighter and the Woman," Dove is depicted as the potential bearer of such white-supremacist convictions. As a white southerner, she is characterized as an outsider to the John Street community—as solitary and unfriendly to her African American and Mexican American neighbors. One of these neighbors, loitering at the "little Mexican grocery store" that serves as a community meeting place throughout the novel, says, "That Dove is as mean as they come." Another neighbor, "a colored customer," sighs and says, "Two things I shun . . . rattlesnakes and evil women." The community's trepidation toward Dove is engendered by gender, sexuality, region, and race. She is a working-class, sexually suspect white woman; she is also southern. When these qualities are taken together, her neighbors—nearly all of whom are people of color—suspect that her hostility toward them is due to racism. When Dove first interacts with Eugene and his best friend, Joe Ramírez, she quickly codes them racially, asking, "You boys Mexicans?" Eugene admits, "I'm not." By disclaiming a Mexican identity, he reveals his blackness, to which Dove responds, "I used to know plenty of negras." Joe and Eugene both take "negras" as a slur, and Dove unsatisfactorily attempts to excuse her language by appealing to region: "I'm from the South." If Southern California in *God Sends Sunday* becomes, essentially, the South, it is done by constructing a wholly black space. Here, however, Dove is painted in contradistinction to Joe and Eugene as westerners. The southernness of Southern California, then, looks quite different; it is not an idyllic black folk past but an acknowledgment of pervasive white supremacy.[34]

Yet as the novel progresses, this depiction of Dove becomes more nuanced. Although she is white, she shares some of the same folk beliefs of Ma Pat in "The Chariot in the Cloud." And some blacks in the novel, such as Eugene and his stepfather, discount her superstitions: "Them signs," Eugene claims, "don't mean nothing, Dove." Later in the novel Eugene asks her, "Where did you come from, Dove? Where's your real home, and who are your people?" By coupling "home" and "people," Eugene allies region and race. But the South as a quintessentially black space is disrupted when he comments, "You sound like you come from down South. You sound more like down South than most colored folks." At this point in the novel, long after the establishment of their interracial family in California, Dove distances herself both temporally and spatially from her southern past, remarking, "Far back as you got knowledge, I been right here on John street. . . . My home is here with you." By doing so, both her regional and racial identities are called into question, and her southern whiteness is thrown somewhat off kilter. She is, as she puts it, "a southerner that's learned to see things different." Her identity becomes more inflected by her local, working-class, multiethnic community on John Street and more dislocated from the South—in a word, it becomes mobile. But like the interurban streetcars that she cleans for a living, it traverses some distance and crosses some boundaries, but it can never leave its tracks entirely.[35]

At first, it seems that the setting of "The Prizefighter and the Woman" can only be Southern California, with its carefully constructed local geography, its neighborhood landmarks, and its multifarious working-class community. Yet Bontemps's attention to the presence of "southern" racial anxieties calls this into question—for example, the gestures toward miscegenation, the depictions of segregation, and the hints of white mob violence among the fervent crowds at Eugene's boxing matches. In short, like "The Chariot in the Cloud," "The Prizefighter and the Woman" sees the South and the West as entwined. The mysterious figure of Dove, however, is unlike any other in Bontemps's work. As a white who is "more like down South than most colored folks," "a southerner that's learned to see things different," and an individual who ultimately becomes an accepted part of the multiethnic community on John Street, Dove calls into question not only visions of the multiethnic West but also understandings of "down south." In the character of Dove, it becomes clear that for Bontemps, both the West and the South are far more multiethnic than *God Sends Sunday* or even "The Chariot in the Cloud" would have us imagine.

Bontemps, after all, was interested primarily in a very particular South—his birthplace, Louisiana. His fixation on Louisiana is evident throughout both his published work and his archived manuscripts and letters. It is obvious in his interest in his own Creole family history and in his obsession with the lineage of his New Negro contemporary Jean Toomer, as exemplified by his introduction to the 1969 edition of *Cane* and his efforts to acquire Toomer's papers for the Fisk University Library. Bontemps was unusually interested in Toomer's relation to his grandfather, P. B. S. Pinchback, who was the first person of African descent to serve as Louisiana's governor, which he did for a little over a month during Reconstruction. Additionally, Bontemps wrote copiously on Creole performer Adah Isaacs Menken. As scholarship has shown, both Menken and Toomer had complicated racial identities and Louisiana connections. In short, the racial multiplicity—and perhaps even *mestizaje*—seen in Bontemps's western writing is not necessarily antithetical to his interests in the South, for Bontemps's South *is* Louisiana.[36]

Any rendering of a monoracial—or even a biracial—Louisiana would defy its history as a product of French, Spanish, and US imperial expansion and as a site of slavery. Bontemps's birthplace, Alexandria, was in the central part of the state, on the banks of the Red River and on the cusp of Cajun country; it was a hub for transportation and commerce and had long been a cultural crossroads. French, Spanish, and US rule; Caribbean immigration, including from Haiti; indigenous populations; and African chattel slavery all shaped Louisiana. As a result, it developed a complicated, multiracial social structure that stood in stark contrast to the racial bifurcation of "black" and "white" that was common elsewhere in the United States—except, perhaps, in the borderlands West. It was not until after the Civil War, the abandonment of Reconstruction, and the rise of Jim Crow that Louisiana's racial landscape became "Americanized"—that is, Louisiana's preexisting, multitiered racial ideology began to conform with the binary black-white understanding of race that was common elsewhere and writ large under Jim Crow. As Arnold R. Hirsch and Joseph Logsdon explain in reference to New Orleans, "Americanization . . . involved, for nearly a century, the curious coexistence of a three-tiered Caribbean racial structure alongside its two-tiered American counterpart in an ethnically-divided city. . . . The imposition of Jim Crow at the dawn of the twentieth century symbolized the ascendance of the new order . . . as a stark racial dualism." The most profound symbol of this new order was the *Plessy v. Ferguson* decision, and it is worth mentioning that Homer Plessy was a Creole of color from New Orleans. His lawsuit was a response to Louisiana's Separate Car Act (mandating separate railcars for blacks and whites), emphasizing the importance of the railroad to the black racial imagination and to lived experience. This occurred six years before Bontemps's birth and only ten years before the Bontemps family left Alexandria for Los Angeles.[37]

When Bontemps reaches back to the southern past and to his family history, he is reaching not for the Louisiana he left as a toddler in 1906 but for the older, complicated, multiracial Louisiana that flourished in the years before he was born—a Louisiana he himself hardly experienced at all. It is, frankly, a Louisiana that more closely resembles the other LA—Los Angeles—than it does the Huntsville of "Saturday Night: Portrait of a Small Southern Town, 1933." So when Bontemps writes of a Los Angeles that is simultaneously southern and western in "The Chariot in the Cloud" and "The Prizefighter and the Woman," this simultaneity is a result of the racial multiplicity that informs both places. This is clear in the latter novel when Eugene "went over to Alameda and wandered down the dusty wagon road that followed the railroad tracks." There, he comes upon a veritable wagon graveyard, the technological detritus of western expansion, a junk heap where outmoded forms of transportation—in use before the railroad, which Bontemps describes as a symbol of black western migration—have been deposited after outliving their usefulness. The dilapidated carriages inspire Eugene's imagination, and he wonders about the *Californio* and frontier past of the place he now inhabits: "Surely the best surrey had belonged to one of those elegant Spanish families of early California who planted avenues of palms on the approaches to their homes. Perhaps the Conestoga had come over the western passes with a white covered top," he muses. As an African American, however, Eugene is forced to ask, "But what was this to him?" The answer reveals itself when Eugene spies, for the first time, the great-uncle Buddy figure of this novel. Here, Bontemps rewrites a scene he had used before and would recycle again later. This scene features Augie in both *God Sends Sunday* and "The

Chariot in the Cloud" and features his own real-life great-uncle Buddy in a personal narrative titled "The Cure," which he wrote about living in the Furlong Tract and published in his collection *The Old South*. Eugene "recognized a small brown man, his ill-fitting suit and hat smeared, his feet heavy with mud, and saw him reach the road with arms full of white flowers. . . . The little fellow was quite drunk. He was crushing the flowers unmercifully." This figure is considered the representation of the black folk South throughout Bontemps's oeuvre. Here, he is Pierre Louis Laurent "from Barbin's Landing in Avoyelles Parish"—located just down the Red River from Alexandria. Yet throughout "The Prizefighter and the Woman," Pierre is a puzzling figure, both southern and of the borderlands, described as a "little Indian-like colored man" or a "tiny, Indian-like Negro." When Pierre appears, he answers Eugene's question about what Spanish colonialism and frontier conquest mean to an African American. His regional and racial complexity—he is both black and multiethnic, both southern and western—suggests that for Bontemps, the black West is not a simple replication of the black South. Instead, the South and, specifically, Louisiana are also like the borderlands West.[38]

If New Orleans is reconceptualized as part of the "Gulf of Mexico system"—an effort that reveals its "Latinness"—then Louisiana is also part of a greater Spanish borderlands where race is not historically binary but multiple, if no less fraught. New Orleans, as Kirsten Silva Gruesz unveils, has acted as "a liminal zone between the Anglo and Latin worlds—the North and the South, the future and the past, mingling in the Gulf like fresh water and saline." The city, she argues, "occupies a dual historical position: it is both a locus of power from which US hegemony over much of Latin America has been extended, and an abjected place within the national body of the US. . . . Both positions have been ideologically supported by the 'natural' fact of the city's access to the Gulf of Mexico" and to Mexico itself. Louisiana's enmeshment with the broader Spanish borderlands is a historical and cultural fact that was not lost on intellectuals of Bontemps's era—including Frederick Jackson Turner's student Herbert E. Bolton, who contested his mentor's frontier thesis. In Bolton's foundational 1921 work *The Spanish Borderlands* (often considered the initiator of border studies), Louisiana is the subject of a chapter—just preceding a chapter on California.[39]

Like Bolton's work, Bontemps's archived writing reveals the scale of the borderlands, stretching at least from the mouth of the Mississippi and the Gulf of Mexico to the harbor at San Pedro featured in "The Prizefighter and the Woman." Between these sites sprawl the railroads, and along with them the scattered black borderlands communities that are so integral to the multiethnic communities in Bontemps's fiction. From the interurban to the transcontinental, he constructs new representations of the greater Spanish borderlands. The two LAs do more than resemble each other; they are intrinsically connected through Bontemps's racial imagination.

CHAPTER 3

Revolt from the Provinces

Black Politics of Respectability
and Black Sexual Politics

> There is no typical Harlem Negro as there is no typical
> American Negro. There are too many different types
> and classes. White, yellow, brown, and black and all the
> intervening shades. North American, South American,
> African and Asian; Northern and Southern; high and
> low; seer and fool—Harlem holds them all, and strives
> to become a homogenous community despite its motley,
> hodge-podge of incompatible elements and its self
> nurtured or outwardly imposed limitations.
> —*Wallace Thurman, "Negro Life in New York's Harlem: A
> Lively Picture of a Popular and Interesting Section" (1927)*

In 1932 Theophilus Lewis, best known as the *Messenger's* drama critic, published a biographical sketch titled "Wallace Thurman Is Model Harlemite." The article was published on the heels of the production of Thurman's play *Harlem*, which he coauthored with white dramatist William Jourdan Rapp, and the near-simultaneous publication of Thurman's satirical novel *Infants of the Spring*, about bohemian life in New York's African American "culture capital" (as James Weldon Johnson called Harlem in 1925). Lewis's subtitle characterizes Thurman as "Leader of shock-proof young sophisticates. Born in Mormon state. Now professional New Yorker." Throughout, the article teasingly describes Thurman's cosmopolitanism. It insists that he fled to Harlem from the provinces and that, upon his arrival in New York, he finally found a suitable home for his brash cultural critiques and decadent artistic perspective. It paints him as a mover and shaker about town, one who flew in the face of propriety and convention, much to the chagrin of older black intellectuals such as W. E. B. DuBois, who embraced a black politics of respectability and the notion that, for African Americans, "all art is propaganda" to be utilized in the service of racial uplift. Lewis writes, "Thurman arrived in New York or as he would express it, he began to live on Labor Day 1925." Often serving as a hub for Harlem's artistic community, Thurman cultivated the perspective of a gadfly to African America, a cultural raconteur whose incisive and at times bombastic critiques filled the pages of the *Messenger*, the *World Tomorrow*, the *Independent*, the *Bookman*, and the *New Republic*. Cutting a consummately urbane figure, Thurman has been almost exclusively associated with Harlem in scholarship and memoir.[1]

Yet Lewis's article gestures toward a new location in which to read Thurman's biography and writing: Salt Lake City, Utah—his birthplace. Although Harlem is the stated focus of the piece, Salt Lake City provides its playful rhetorical force. No matter how avidly Lewis anoints Thurman a "model Harlemite," he cannot—and perhaps Thurman cannot—leave Salt Lake City behind. "Wallace Thurman Is Model Harlemite" both lauds and mocks Thurman's literary accomplishments and goals, and it both appreciates and critiques his cosmopolitan façade. These vacillations are tied to region throughout the piece, and the West is introduced as a foil to New York. The juxtaposition of these two sites accentuates Thurman's sophisticated persona while revealing it as an obvious construction. Lewis sometimes exhibits a wholesale disregard for the West, which is painted as utterly provincial, out of touch with the modern era, politically backward, and repressed. Yet at other times, he seems conscious of—and critical of—a metropolitan elitism that refuses to recognize the intellectual, political, artistic, and cultural contributions of the region as valid and worthwhile.

These complicated and at times contradictory regional constructions result in part from the article's shifting perspective. It appears to adopt Thurman's perspective almost as often as it adopts Lewis's. For example, Lewis writes, "[Thurman's] ambition, he says, is to be the editor of a financially secure magazine. I wonder if he knows his mind? I rather think his real aim is being a model Harlemite, dwelling in Sugar Hill and making flying trips through the West solely to disparage provincial ways and to enjoy the luxury of returning to New York." He continues, "The people who have influenced [Thurman's] life most are: Jean Toomer, Elisabeth Marbury, Richard Bruce, and—a break for the provinces—his grandmother. . . . He says his philosophy of life is Hedonism. That's the final mark of the ultra New Yorker. Who ever heard of Hedonism in the sticks?" Taken together, these lines shift between Lewis's narration and Thurman's outlook, creating what looks like, at times, a dialogue or a negotiation between these interlocutors throughout the piece. These lines also oscillate between the West and New York, and this dialogic imagination creates a sense of deep ambivalence about region. Although the article claims that Thurman is an adherent to a sort of New York chauvinism, the cultural preeminence of New York is called into question as well. The idea of Thurman traveling to the West solely to enjoy his return to New York is Lewis's fantasy, and Thurman's voice retains its fidelity to his western grandmother in what is otherwise a list of figures commonly thought of as urban sophisticates. (Toomer, of course, is addressed differently in chapter 5.) The sense of ambivalence toward region is, on the one hand, a result of Lewis's and Thurman's competing perspectives in the article and, on the other hand, evidence of the complicated spatial imagination developed within Thurman's perspective alone and articulated via Lewis as amanuensis. Some scholars have considered the spatial imagination of Thurman's work, particularly his work set in Harlem, as the mechanism through which he develops his mode of critique and aesthetic—particularly as it is inflected by sexuality. To complicate this spatial imagination by turning to the West, then, sheds new light on Thurman's queer black aesthetic. And ultimately, the West provides a milieu that is just as appropriate for its genesis as New York, if not more so.[2]

As Lewis's description intimates, Thurman trafficked in his urbane persona, patterning himself as an African American Oscar Wilde for the 1920s and 1930s. As an essayist, his publications tended to focus on the role of black art in modern America. He sought to promote a black modernist aesthetic of art for art's sake, and he found beauty, whimsy, humor, and pathos in the street life of New York. As a result, he reveled in descriptions of unabashed modern excess, and his writing across genres detailed numbers running, rent parties, dances, drinking, and

other colorful—and, to many of his older predecessors, seedy—aspects of
Harlem during the era of the renaissance. He was also a playwright, and
in that role he is best known for *Harlem* (1932), based on his short story
"Cordelia the Crude," which had appeared in *Fire!! Devoted to Younger
Negro Artists*, a short-lived but significant literary magazine. *Fire!!* was
edited by Thurman in association with Zora Neale Hurston, Langston
Hughes, Gwendolyn Bennett, Richard Bruce Nugent, Aaron Douglas,
and John Davis in 1926. Thurman's most notable legacy may indeed
be as an editor. In addition to *Fire!!* he founded the equally short-lived
and significant *Harlem: A Forum of Negro Life* (1928). He also worked in
editorial and managerial capacities at publications as diverse as the *Messenger* and the white-owned, Christian, pacifist the *World Tomorrow*, as
well as at the major publishing house Macaulay's, which was best known
for the modernist anthologies *The American Caravan* (1927), *The Second
American Caravan* (1928), and *The New American Caravan* (1929). In addition, Thurman published three novels in his short lifetime: *The Blacker
the Berry* (1929), *Infants of the Spring* (1932), and *The Interne* (1932), a
sensationalist exposé of conditions at New York's Welfare Island Hospital
coauthored with white writer A. L. Furman. All three novels take place
largely in New York City, and *The Blacker the Berry* and *Infants of the
Spring* are set primarily in Harlem. These settings certainly contribute
to Thurman's image as a "professional New Yorker," a reputation he
solidified through numerous journalistic pieces that served as tour guides
for readers seeking to experience Harlem's nightlife.

Given Thurman's expertise in Harlem living, the West—and particularly Salt Lake City—was a continual source of amusement for
Thurman's contemporaries and a rhetorical touchstone for their representations of him. An "ultra New Yorker" who was black, iconoclastic,
and—scholars have suggested—queer, he was seemingly everything that
Salt Lake City was not in New Yorkers' imaginations. Even the speech
delivered at his 1934 funeral at Harlem's St. James Presbyterian Church
emphasizes the surprising fact of Thurman's western upbringing, noting
in the first lines:

> In Salt Lake City, Utah, early in the year 1901, Beulah Thurman
> bore her husband, Oscar, a son whom they called Wallace. The

boy followed a routine of solid growth—play, the public schools, and then the steadying influence of College. He graduated from the University of Utah, leaping instantly after that mile-post of his life into the riotous sea of the thing which amazed him . . . —the reasonable and unreasonable conduct of men.

These lines are packed with factual errors: Thurman was born in 1902, not 1901, and he briefly attended but did not graduate from the University of Utah. The presence of such bald inaccuracy is a reminder that this speech—as well as other works memorializing and remembering Thurman—is rife with representational gymnastics. Even—and perhaps especially—at his funeral, the "facts" of Thurman's life are springboards for fantasies about bohemianism, African American culture, and the presumed dichotomy between the New Negro movement and the American West. The core concept of nearly all the pieces describing, remembering, and memorializing Thurman is the assumption of an irreducible difference between the character of Thurman's birthplace and the character of Harlem, where his life ended: "He came out of the West and into New York [C]ity," the eulogy proclaims, painting a picture of Thurman's emergence from western obscurity into eastern and urban notoriety. In New York it became possible for "the men and women who really mattered"—in other words, New Yorkers—to recognize his "worth and merit," and "he was received warmly and graciously." The assumption here, of course, is that Salt Lake City was far too provincial to appreciate Thurman's radicalism as a writer, an intellectual, and a public figure. Thurman's pervasive financial struggles in New York, his difficulty sustaining his editorial agenda, the failure of *Fire!!* and *Harlem: A Forum on Negro Life* (neither survived past its inaugural issue), the often cutting reviews of his novels in New York–based publications, and the wariness with which readers and critics, both black and white, approached him are reduced to the following narrative: "Mr. Thurman's adjustment [to New York life and to literary success] rose steadily," and "his life in his profession went up and up." This triumphant narrative depicts New York as meritorious, as the only place willing to give Thurman a chance, and, as a result, as a cultural vanguard. It becomes the central place in Thurman's life story, construed as a site of success, opportunity, and unhindered freethinking. In contrast, the West "wasn't ready yet" for Thurman's efforts to "establish the movement of the 'New Negro' there." The West is represented as unsophisticated, backward, and hostile to Thurman's progressive racial, sexual, and aesthetic outlook.[3]

Thurman has been represented and fictionalized in memoirs and novels by several key figures from the New Negro movement, including Dorothy West, Langston Hughes, Arna Bontemps, and Richard Bruce Nugent. None of them failed to remark on his Salt Lake City upbringing, and they often created similar stories about the relationship between Salt Lake City and Harlem. West's biographical essay "Elephant's Dance" describes Thurman's Utah birth, his literary aspirations in Los Angeles, and his move to New York. Ultimately, West determines that no one better symbolized the spirit of the New Negro movement than Thurman: "The name of Wallace Thurman," she writes, "is more typical of that epoch than the one or two more enduring names that survived the period." This is true, she asserts, because Thurman's racy life and early death served as a notice to New Negro writers that they "lack[ed] . . . immortality." West sees Thurman as representative of the New Negro movement, and she can only imagine him distancing himself from Salt Lake City. Like the eulogy delivered at Thurman's funeral, West's facts are skewed; for example, she insists that he "received his Bachelor of Arts degree from the University of California, where he had gone after four gainful years at the University of Utah" (Thurman took classes at both universities but never graduated from either). Her biography of Thurman is somewhat fictionalized, which allows her to heighten the sense of antipathy toward the West. Thurman's time spent not only in Salt Lake City but also in Los Angeles is depicted as stifling and intellectually dead: "He was writing a column called 'Inklings' in the *Pacific Defender*, a Negro paper, doing pieces of topical interest on mildly controversial subjects, when wind of the 'renaissance' blew West," she writes. "Thurman tried to organize a literary group in Los Angeles," she continues. "His friends, however, had not followed the Eastern activities with his interest. He tried to be a movement all by himself, and started a paper, which he personally financed. It failed, but he had a lot of fun doing it. After this abortive attempt to revolutionize the West, Thurman headed East."[4]

Although it is common for writers to squabble over the details of Thurman's biography, some aspects of his life seem fairly certain. He did write for the *Pacific Defender*, but none of the issues featuring his "Inklings" columns survive. Nor are there any extant samples of his short-lived Los Angeles–based literary magazine the *Outlet*—although it lasted longer than his New York–based magazines. He was the offspring of Oscar and Beulah Thurman but was raised largely by his grandmother, Emma Jackson, whom he called "Ma Jack." Her parents were not among the first Mormon pioneers in Utah, as claimed by some commentators; rather, she was born in Missouri in 1862 and traveled westward with her first husband, settling in Leadville, Colorado—a mining town—by the 1880s. There, her daughter Beulah was born. After Ma Jack remarried, the family moved to Salt Lake City in 1892, and Ma Jack became a founding member of the Calvary Missionary Baptist Church. After Thurman's birth, she was responsible for most of his care. In a 1929 letter Thurman called her "the only person in the family who seemed immune to neuroticism," and he dedicated *The Blacker the Berry* to her, even naming his protagonist Emma. In an autobiographical statement Thurman notes, "My parents and grandparents were pioneer Westerners who settled finally in Salt Lake City, Utah, thus enabling me to be born, twenty-six years ago, within the protective shadows of the Mormon Temple and the Wasatch Mountains." Thurman's parents divorced when he was quite young, and he lived with his mother, grandmother, and stepgrandfather Jesse Jackson. Beulah gained a reputation among Salt Lake City's black community—as her son would—for being smart, attractive, and a little racy. She was rumored to be a prostitute and married several times. As a result, Beulah moved often, accompanying her partners, and Thurman occasionally joined her. In his autobiographical statement he briefly describes spending time in Chicago, Omaha, and Pasadena with his mother, but he always returned to Salt Lake City until he moved to Los Angeles (where he stayed for three years) and then finally undertook his "hectic hegira to Harlem" in 1925. Other details of Thurman's life remain sketchy, and his archive is thin. What seems certain is that Wallace Thurman was born in Salt Lake City in 1902, where he lived for most of his youth—with relatively short, erratic stints elsewhere. After living in Harlem for nine years, in 1934 he briefly returned to

Los Angeles, where he wrote screenplays. Once he was back in New York City, he went on a whirlwind party tour, which exacerbated his long-term health problems. He lived fast and died young, passing away in 1934 in the same tubercular ward he had profiled in *The Interne*. He spent six months there before his death, lonely and pleading in letters to his friends for reading material until he became too weak to write.[5]

In the dominant narratives about Thurman's life, his intellectual and literary adventurousness make him incompatible with the West—only in New York can he realize his ambition. Indeed, in a letter to W. E. B. DuBois, Thurman claimed that the *Outlet* was "the first western Negro literary magazine," but it folded in 1924 after publishing only six issues. Thurman, however, made some lasting connections with writers, intellectuals, and publishers who would become important to the African American cultural wellspring in Los Angeles and across the nation during the 1920s and 1930s. These included Arna Bontemps, whom Thurman met while they both worked at a post office; Bontemps, of course, eventually moved to Harlem. Thurman's connections also included journalist Fay M. Jackson, who remained in Los Angeles throughout her career. The *Outlet* reportedly published both Bontemps's and Jackson's early work. Jackson, who had moved to Los Angeles from Dallas as a teenager, attended the University of Southern California in 1922, the same year Thurman did, and she too wrote for the *Pacific Defender*. They remained lifelong friends, reconnecting when Thurman returned to Los Angeles in the 1930s to write screenplays. In 1934 he joked to Langston Hughes in a telegram: "FAY AND I MARRIED TODAY." He followed up with another that read: "DONT YOU REALIZE DIFFERENCE BETWEEN GIN AND MARRIAGE." By this point, Jackson had founded a magazine titled *Flash*, which she edited from 1928 to 1930; it billed itself as "the only Negro newsmagazine" in Los Angeles. *Flash* reported with interest on the New Negro movement in Harlem, including contributions by Thurman, and it went beyond news to publish creative writing by local talent such as Anita Scott Coleman and book reviews, including one of Thurman's *The Blacker the Berry*. When these connections are taken into account, it is clear that Thurman had a lasting impact on the western literary scene—and it on him, if only indirectly. The neat opposition constructed between Harlem and the West in memoirs like West's "Elephant's Dance" doesn't account for these circuits of collaboration.[6]

Given the whiteness of Utah history and the sparseness of its African American population, it is not surprising that both Thurman's contemporaries and current scholars have given little thought to situating him—the enfant terrible of the New Negro movement in Harlem—in the context of his western birthplace. There had been a black presence in Utah since trapper and former slave James P. Beckworth traversed its mountain passes in the 1820s. In the early 1840s Jacob Dodson, an African American member of John C. Frémont's western expedition, explored its canyons. Black settlement did not begin, however, until the Mormon exodus later in that decade, when what is now Utah was still part of Mexico. African Americans accompanied the first Mormon pioneers to the territory they named "Deseret," and they were soon joined by others, including those enslaved by southern Mormons known as the "Mississippi Saints." Outsiders saw Mormon religious practice and racial politics as entwined. The 1856 Republican Party platform famously denounced the "twin relics of barbarism—polygamy, and slavery," painting both institutions as morally corrupt and sexually depraved. Leaders Joseph Smith and, later, Brigham Young saw slavery as biblically sanctioned but preached that slave owners should treat their slaves humanely. Under the Compromise of 1850, Utah's legalization of slavery was decided by popular sovereignty, but when the state instituted black codes, they tended to be milder than those enacted in the South. Slavery, however, never flourished in this Mormon "gathering place," and the number of black residents remained quite small both before and after emancipation. The Mormon Church began to ban blacks from the priesthood in the 1850s—a ban that was rescinded only in 1978. Although the Latter-Day Saints always baptized black adherents, African Americans long remained marginal in doctrine and in practice. Despite this marginalization, in the late nineteenth century the black population of Utah began to grow as the territory and then the state saw an influx of African American railroad workers, such as Pullman porters, and black soldiers. The Calvary Missionary Baptist Church and the Trinity African Methodist Episcopal Church were established in Salt Lake City to serve African American parishioners in the 1890s, and other black community organizations—literary societies, Masonic lodges, and social clubs—quickly followed. Salt Lake City, which had the largest black population in Utah, saw the publication of several black newspapers with various political perspectives in the same decade. Although the black population of Utah increased exponentially in the years leading up to Wallace Thurman's birth there in 1902, so too did the white population—which means that although blacks increased in number, they gained little in terms of percentage of the population. Even today, Utah's black population hovers at around only 1 percent.[7]

In addition to being relatively scarce, the black population of Utah, and particularly of Salt Lake City, was beset by spatial scatter, which made community building difficult. According to the 1920 census, conducted two years before Thurman left Salt Lake City, there were only 718 African Americans in the city. By 1930, four years before Thurman's death in New York City, the black population had actually shrunk to 681. In comparison, the total population of Salt Lake City grew from 118,110 in 1920 to 140,267 in 1930. Furthermore, African Americans in Salt Lake City were not housed in a single established neighborhood; they had no enclave to call their own. In 1920 Salt Lake City's African Americans were distributed across five city wards: Wards 1 and 5 had the largest black populations, with 213 and 251 black residents, respectively; Wards 2 and 3 had 142 and 85 black residents; and Ward 4 had only 27 black residents. There seemed to be no correlation between the wards that housed blacks and those that housed other communities of color. Of the 611 other nonwhites who were counted in the 1920 census, 330 lived in Ward 2, 142 lived in Ward 5, and the others were distributed across wards in numbers ranging from 7 to 35. In short, the African American population of Salt Lake City was not geographically cohesive during Thurman's lifetime, a fact that does not go unnoticed in his western writing. He actually overestimates Salt Lake City's black population, claiming in 1926 that although there are "about 1,800 colored people" in the city, "one can walk for hours . . . without meeting a colored person," since the city "has not become centralized and there is no Negro ghetto."[8]

Reviews of Thurman's work at the time of its initial publication—and much of the literary criticism since then—have focused on his challenges to an African American politics of respectability. These critiques have not, however, considered the role of the West in these challenges. Because the publishing industry, which both produced and reviewed Thurman's work, was located largely in the East, that is where most of these critiques originated. Reviews of Thurman's work were notoriously mixed and often quite negative. A few applauded his commitment to a modernist aesthetic, including his exploration of themes like alienation, and some praised his urbanity, seeing him as a black parallel to "high" modernist expatriates. The *Philadelphia Tribune*, for example, described *Infants of the Spring* as follows: "Harlem has gone so sophisticated that it has developed a 'lost generation' of its own. Wallace Thurman's new book . . . is also being referred to as 'The Sun Also Rises' of Negro America. Hard drinking and hard loving are the recourses of the artists, writers, and musicians in the story when they feel the futility of their life." An article in the *Baltimore Afro-American* went a step further and linked Thurman's depiction of modern artistic coteries to social justice issues: Thurman, like his characters, is "trying to solve the problem of admixture of race in this country. They are trying to take the problem of color out of American life by letting art break down the barriers." Art, this article suggests, speaks across the color line, and the production of art itself—even when it is doggedly disinterested in being "propaganda" for the race—is a form of antiracist activism. This politicized approach to Thurman's work, however, was quite unusual.[9]

Indeed, most critics were far less generous. In the mainstream press, reviewers of Thurman's work tended to be caustic. For example, the reviewer for the *New York Times* wrote, "By any standard, . . . 'Infants of the Spring' is a pretty inept book. . . . It is clumsily written. Its dialogue . . . is often incredibly bad. Its characters, men and women who rotate giddily and senselessly through the mazes of Harlem's Bohemia, are ciphers. For all its earnestness and its obvious sincerity, the book is merely a tedious dramatization of various phases of the Negro Problem." This reception undercuts both Thurman's abilities as a writer and the seriousness of persistent racism in the United States. Reviewers in African American publications were hardly more sympathetic. Some were lukewarm, like the reviewer for the *New York Amsterdam News*, who suggested, "In this recent book [Thurman] shows his talent for writing, but we do not think he has made the most of his ability." Dewey R. Jones of the *Chicago Defender* went so far as to label Thurman "the black sheep of the Race authors" and accused him of "frankly . . . writing for the favor of his white readers and catering to certain preconceived notions which white people have about Negroes—especially in Harlem." *Opportunity*'s 1929 review of *The Blacker the Berry* made a similar accusation:

> The vogue today . . . for literature by Negroes and about Negroes, is so great that there is no apparent incentive or compulsion to conform to any academic standards in the matter of construction, expression or finish. The more quickly the novelty of the Negro theme wears off and publishers and critics begin to extract from Negro writers that same high standard which they do from others, the more quickly we may expect something better from writers like Wallace Thurman who are capable of things infinitely better than they give.[10]

George Schuyler, a fellow African American writer and Thurman's predecessor at the *Messenger*, was one of only a few who took a more nuanced approach to Thurman's work. On the one hand, Schuyler employs a typically sarcastic, Menckenian tone when he acknowledges that *Infants of the Spring* "will not be nearly as popular among Negroes as was 'The Blacker the Berry,' and I cannot recall that there was any great shout of approval from Aframerica when that tome made its appearance." On the other hand, he admits that "there is much food for thought in this book." In particular, he suggests that the sense of modernist alienation and individuation calls into question the cheap generalizations about race made by Thurman's characters during their occasionally pompous, grandiose, and ill-founded exchanges. Schuyler proposes that by reproducing the figure of the alienated modern individual but placing this figure within the African American milieu, *Infants of the Spring* reveals that, for better or worse, "Thurman is sick and tired of Negroes as such and resents shouldering the burdens of an entire group because he happens to be of the same color. He sees the Negro as accomplishing things only as an individual, and perhaps he is right." Although Schuyler calls Thurman's work "devoid of conscious

humor," his careful reading of the text indicates that he verges on seeing it as satire. His analysis suggests that *Infants of the Spring* is less
of an endorsement of black primitivist stereotypes that pander to the
racist fantasies of a white audience and more of a demonstration of the
inauthenticity of such stereotypes through the mechanism of parody,
which Schuyler hints at when he comments that the novel is at times
"sadistically amusing" and "prankish." Schuyler was a satirist himself,
so it is perhaps no wonder that he was attuned to these inflections in
Thurman's work.[11]

The competing responses to Thurman's work all circle back to the
outsized role of respectability politics during the New Negro renaissance. Many writers remained fixated on the role of black art to earn
either the approbation or the contempt of white audiences. Some,
however, challenged these views, and Thurman often spearheaded
this dissent. W. E. B. DuBois, elder statesman of the "talented tenth,"
most famously sparked this debate with his 1926 essay in the *Crisis*
titled "Criteria of Negro Art." There, he argued that, given ongoing
racism in the United States, the material disadvantages faced by black
artists in realms such as education, and the widespread representation
of African American inferiority in art and other cultural products, "all
art is propaganda and ever must be, despite the wailing of the purists. I
stand in utter shamelessness and say that whatever art I have for writing
has been used always for propaganda for gaining the right of black folk
to love and enjoy. I do not care a damn for any art that is not used for
propaganda." DuBois, the frankest and best-known proponent of such
a position, was by no means its only promoter during the New Negro
movement. For years, discussions of art versus propaganda raged publicly
in the pages of the *Crisis* and in other forums of black print culture.[12]

As an aesthete, Thurman's approach to art was in stark contrast to
DuBois's. In a review of Walter White's novel *Flight* (1926), Thurman
argues that the problem with propagandists is not that they want to use
their writing to change the hearts and minds of America on the topic of
race but that they consider their writing to be art. "All art is no doubt
propaganda," he writes, "but all propaganda is most certainly not art.
And a novel must, to earn the name, be more than a mere social service
report, more than a thinly disguised dissertation on racial relationships

and racial maladjustment." In an essay titled "Negro Artists and the Negro," first published in the *New Republic* in 1927, Thurman extends this conversation about art and propaganda to a larger critique of a class-based politics of respectability. The black bourgeoisie, he suggests, are "angry because a few of [the New Negro writers who gained notoriety during the movement's heyday] had ceased to be what the group considered 'constructive' and had in the interim produced works that went against the grain, in that they did not wholly qualify for the adjective 'respectable.'" He continues by railing against individuals who hold such views:

> [They] feel certain that they must always appear in public butter side up. . . . They feel as if they must always exhibit specimens from the college rather than from the kindergarten, specimens from the parlor rather than from the pantry. They are in the process of being assimilated, and those elements within the race which are still too potent for assimilation must be hidden until they no longer exist. . . . It makes no difference if this element of their life is of incontestable value to the sincere artist. It is also available and of incontestable value to insincere artists and prejudiced white critics.[13]

Such debates on "high" and "low" culture in black America and on the duty of African American artists to either represent or obscure a range of black experiences, particularly in terms of class, sexuality, and concomitant ideas about respectability, drive the scholarly conversation about Thurman. These debates extend from a class-based tension whereby middle-class spokespeople for a politics of racial uplift condemn artists who reveal the presumably more sordid facets of African American life that are often associated with the working-class masses. Thurman is thus chastised by the black elite for capitalizing on white fantasies that insist on continued black degradation. He, however, may have seen himself as a champion of the black working class, giving voice and validity to experiences silenced in the name of respectability and finding beauty in black vernacular cultures rather than endorsing assimilation to white middle-class norms. On a superficial level, as the opening of

The Blacker the Berry demonstrates, Thurman's work arranges these debates geographically. He describes the provinces as being rife with black bourgeois pretensions—to the point where the black bourgeoisie would eliminate their blackness altogether. In contrast, the vibrant working class dominates the urban ethnic enclave of Harlem. Those who have resettled from the South constitute much of this working class. For example, Cordelia in Thurman's play *Harlem* is emblematic. Whereas she becomes a part of Harlem by latching onto men, attending parties, and getting involved in petty crime, her mother retains the provincialism of the South, refusing to assimilate to the street life of New York and maintaining a desire for class-based uplift through respectability. This pattern echoes the one detected by Douglas Flamming among the African American community in Los Angeles and in figures such as Paul Bontemps; there, too, the West becomes a rather deracinated site of middle-class uplift, while Harlem and the South become sites of a more vibrant black culture.[14]

As a result, much of Thurman's writing that addresses or is set in the West tends to treat it negatively. There is, it seems, very little ambivalence when Thurman writes: "Thus is Utah burdened with dull and unprogressive Mormons, with more dull and speciously progressive Gentiles, and with still more dull and not even speciously progressive Negroes. Everyone in the state seems to be more or less of a vegetable, self satisfied and complacent." In statements such as this one from "Quoth Brigham Young—This Is the Place," he appears to undercut the possibility of black intellectual, political, and artistic development in the West, and particularly in Utah. As Lewis notes, "As managing editor of the *Messenger*, . . . his most signal feat was outraging the black folks of his home state with a peppery contribution to a series of articles called 'These Colored United States.'" Published the month prior to Anita Scott Coleman's "Arizona and New Mexico—The Land of Esperanza," Thurman's essay for that series paints a far less congenial picture of the black American West. Whereas Coleman sees the West as a land of possible autonomy for the "Negro home seeker," Thurman begins his essay with characteristic sarcasm: "I am fully aware of what Brigham Young had in mind when he uttered the above enthusiastic statement ['This is the place'], yet try tho I might the most enthusiastic thing I can find to say about my home state and its capital city is that it invariably furnishes me with material for conversation."[15]

Superficially, this statement appears to be a wholly negative characterization of Utah—which for Thurman has produced nothing but "many dull hours" with "many dull people." Yet when he mentions that "it invariably furnishes me with material for conversation," his statement becomes just as much of a critique of New York and New Yorkers, whose cosmopolitan elitism makes it impossible for them to imagine the West and particularly Utah, which is especially foreign due to its Mormon history. So fantastical is Utah in the New Yorker's imagination, hints Thurman, that "I can even play this trick on the same group of persons more than once, for it seems as if they never tire of asking—Do Mormons still have more than one wife?—Do they look different from other people?—How many wives did Brigham Young have?—Are there any Negro Mormons?—Can one really stay afloat in the Great Salt Lake without sinking?" The questions he lists are predictable, focused on Mormonism (and polygamy), on the physical landscape, and on the presumed whiteness of the state, which renders Thurman an improbable spokesperson. This incongruity is what makes it safe to ask the same set of questions again and again. He is not what a New Yorker imagines a Utahan to be; he becomes an outsider within, a position that makes him appear to be a more objective and less invested interviewee ready to divulge the secrets of western difference. The reader of "Quoth Brigham Young—This Is the Place" identifies with these urban interrogators, and the rest of the essay duplicates the answers Thurman would likely give to such questions, beginning with a history of Utah from the time of Mormon settlement. Yet embedded in this attack on Utah is an implicit critique of the parochialism of New York and of the willfully naïve and uninformed questions of his New York associates and audience.[16]

Therefore, as with Bontemps, it is far too simple to set up a spatial, class, and racial dichotomy between Harlem and the West in Thurman's work. In Thurman's writing, it first appears as if a culturally uncorrupted, unassimilated black working class dominates Harlem, which therefore provides a more suitable home for Thurman's boundary-pushing writing and editorial labor. Yet this illusion is undermined by the many harsh critiques of Thurman's work that originated in Harlem-based venues, in the institutions of the black intellectual elite that also called the neighborhood home. Although Thurman's work depicts the racy world of Harlem's numbers runners, prostitutes, and bohemians, as well as the naïve newcomers who are eventually inducted into these neighborhood byways, it also recognizes (as does this chapter's epigraph) that there are multifarious racial, national, and class-based subcultures in Harlem. Among these, Thurman notes, are "a few aristocrats" and a "plethora of striving bourgeoisie," as well as "a few artistic spirits and a great proletarian mass." Although he perhaps rightfully insists that the last of these groups "constitutes the most interesting and important element in Harlem," he also acknowledges that the "aristocrats" and "bourgeoisie" may have louder voices. He accuses the Harlem elite of "wailing in the public places because white and black writers have seemingly overlooked them in their delineations of Negro life in Harlem," and he goes so far as to claim that "their most compelling if sometimes unconscious ambition is to be as near white as possible, and their greatest expenditure of energy is concentrated on eradicating any trait or characteristic commonly known as Negroid." If this echoes Thurman's critique of the West, it also undermines the presumed dichotomy between these sites, implicitly making a broader, class-based critique of African America at large.[17]

The targets of Thurman's critique were the educated African Americans who strove for social and economic advancement, those who supported the NAACP and the Urban League and contributed to, read, and staffed their publications, the *Crisis* and *Opportunity*. Unsurprisingly, this "talented tenth" objected to Thurman's obsession with what they saw as the baser elements of Harlem's African American community, and the largely negative reception of Thurman's work can be attributed in part to their control of Harlem's publishing world. Although Thurman's representation of Harlem in his creative writing tends to marginalize the black intellectual elite in order to focus on the proletarian mass, in reality, the Harlem where he lived, wrote, and published was a place where the "talented tenth" remained culturally dominant and, consequently, was able to direct public dialogue about the merit of Thurman's writing and subject matter. In short, although Thurman's work occludes the black bourgeoisie, their presence shaped his career, since they were perhaps the most powerful voice in Harlem due to their involvement in uplift organizations and publications and their access to resources—including, most obviously, the money it would have taken to sustain Thurman's publishing endeavors such as *Fire!!* or *Harlem: A Forum on Negro Life.*

As a result of these tensions, Thurman's depictions of New York are shaded by an ambivalence that is often neglected in the usual boosterish narratives about his life and work there. His descriptions of the West are no less ambivalent, and a closer look reveals that these presumably dichotomous sites are not as different as they first appear. To be sure, when Thurman narrates the history of Utah, he tells a much "whiter" history than that of New York, and this may be appropriate. In his most obvious piece of western writing, "Quoth Brigham Young—This Is the Place," it is not until well into the essay that Thurman acknowledges, "I have as yet made no mention of the Negro." And it is even later when he details, "There were two Negroes in the first overland Mormon train, a man and his wife (he had only one, for Mormons did not believe that a Negro could ever enter into Heaven as an angel, and that since because of Ham's sin he was to be deprived of full privileges in Heaven, he was not entitled to enjoy the full privileges of a good Mormon on earth)." After this, he describes the arrival of gold miners, domestics, gamblers, prostitutes, and ultimately Pullman porters ("plus more pimps and prostitutes"). Some members of this primarily transient population stayed, he contends, and from then on, there was little difference between Utah's African American "*haute monde*" and its "middle class white brethren. The only difference is one of color, and those Aframericans who have been in the state longest have done everything in their power to abolish even this difference." As he does later in *The Blacker the Berry*, Thurman critiques western blacks for their efforts to assimilate and cast off any cultural distinctiveness and even phenotypic differences. He goes so far as to claim, "Statistics will readily prove, I believe, that comparatively speaking the intermixing of races was as great or greater in Utah than in any other western state," suggesting that black Utahans were, en masse, attempting to eradicate their own blackness by intermarrying with whites. In short, he constructs a predominantly white history and forecasts a future in which the state gets even whiter demographically, phenotypically, and culturally.[18]

Thurman continues this type of narrative in what is perhaps the best known of his western writing, the opening chapters of *The Blacker the Berry*. He describes protagonist Emma Lou Morgan's upbringing in Boise, Idaho. In this depiction, the West is stifling, particularly to Emma, who has dark skin. The western blacks of the novel strive to be paragons of bourgeois respectability, breaking from their boisterous pioneer pasts that involved gambling, whoring, and drinking. In doing so, they manage to couple color with civilization. "Mulatto freedmen seeking a freer land" headed west, Thurman writes. Then, with characteristic sarcasm, he adds: they moved "to the Rocky Mountain States beyond the reach of [the] raucous and smelly rabble of recently freed cotton pickers." These western settlers conceived of themselves as a "superior class," "a very high type of Negro [who was] entitled to more respect and opportunity and social acceptance than the more pure blooded Negroes." Such intraracial color-based prejudice is the focus of Thurman's critique in *The Blacker the Berry*. The politics of color has long dominated readings of the novel and has overshadowed approaches to Thurman's life and work more generally. On the surface, this politics is attached to place, and Thurman appears to condemn the West for its elitism and internalized racism.[19]

This politics, however, is not confined to Boise. In *The Blacker the Berry*, Thurman depicts Boise, Los Angeles, and ultimately even Harlem as hostile to Emma Lou. Boise, for example, offers black freedom but exposes the limitations of that freedom. Thurman describes the "social intermixture between whites and blacks"; this occurs largely among the proletariat, where "white and black gamblers rolled the dice together," "white and black men amicably frequented the saloons," "white and black women leaned out of the doorways . . . of 'Whore Row,'" and "white and black housewives gossiped over back fences." Yet, he claims, "there was little social intercourse on a higher scale." Thurman describes African American society in Boise as impossibly stratified by color, which maps on to its politics of respectability. Emma Lou's uncle advises her, "People in large cities"—as opposed to those in the ramshackle, smaller, and western Boise—"are broad. . . . The people in Boise are fifty years behind the times, but you will find that Los Angeles is one of the world's greatest and most modern cities, and you will be happy there." Upon her arrival in Los Angeles, Emma Lou is hopeful that this is true, that "Boise was a provincial town, given to the molding of provincial people with provincial minds. Boise was a backward town out of the mainstream of modern thought and progress. Its people were cramped and narrow, their intellectual concepts stereotyped and static. Los Angeles was a happy contrast in all respects." Emma Lou, however, finds it difficult to associate with "the right kind of people," with the "children of fairly well-to-do families from Louisiana, Texas, and Georgia, who, having made nest eggs, had journeyed to the West for the same reasons that her grandparents at an earlier date had also journeyed West. They wanted to live where there would be greater freedom and greater opportunity for their children and themselves." These "right kind of people" are also lighter-skinned. When Emma fails to win acceptance among them, she determines that "Los Angeles, too, was a small-town mentally, peopled by mentally small southern Negroes. It was no better than Boise. She was now determined to go East where life was more cosmopolitan and people were more civilized."[20]

Needless to say, Harlem is no more accommodating. Emma Lou faces discrimination in employment, in housing, and in the social world. And Thurman makes it clear that because Emma Lou has been so cowed by racism and color prejudice—both real and perceived—she fails to make connections with the African Americans who try to befriend her in all three places she inhabits during the course of the novel; she either rebukes them for being too dark or refuses to believe that they could actually like her, given her complexion. This color prejudice, however, cannot be blamed on African Americans themselves. As the character Truman Walter (clearly Thurman's fictional double) notes, this color hierarchy is an outgrowth of the hegemony of white supremacy. Interestingly, Walter is not depicted as a Harlemite but rather as an outsider to Harlem; he recognizes Emma Lou from their years together at the University of Southern California. Walter is challenged by Cora Thurston (a character clearly modeled after Zora Neale Hurston) as an outsider to Harlem and the black community as it is imagined in the East. She remarks that, like a white man, he is a "foreigner" to Harlem and did not experience black folk culture as a child growing up in Salt Lake City.[21]

In short, Thurman's critique of US racism is transregional—it is located not only in the West, for Harlem is by no means a promised land. As Blake Allmendinger succinctly puts it, "For Thurman, the West was no better or worse than the rest of the nation." As a result, much of "Quoth Brigham Young" is an extensive meta-commentary on the *These "Colored" United States* series as a whole. Thurman contends, "To write of 'These Colored United States' is to be trying to visualize a phantom," for due to racism, "there are no Colored United States . . . , no state in the Union where the Negro has been an individual or vital factor." Black marginalization and disenfranchisement remain so entrenched throughout the United States, he implies, that blacks have been able to establish vibrant communities only on isolated and local levels. This is not necessarily a promotion of the East over the West; as examples of "colored cities" where "the Aframerican spirit manifests itself," Thurman lists Los Angeles's Central Avenue and Oakland's Seventh Street right alongside Harlem and Chicago's South Side. Instead, he suggests that the "Aframerican spirit"—at least at the time of his writing—exists in local units found across regional boundaries, but they exert little influence over the definition of those regions as a whole.[22]

These implied critiques of New York as well as the West—in short, a critique of the nation at large—explain why Thurman left Harlem frequently and suddenly, often returning to Salt Lake City and the home of Ma Jack, where he was refreshed by "the high altitude and my grandmother's care . . . milk, eggs, and cod liver oil." Although he frequently rhapsodizes about the splendor of New York, he cannot bring himself to leave Utah behind: "I miss New York," he writes, "yet I know should I be in New York no work would be done." In letters he jokes about his "ostracization among polite circles in Salt Lake," yet his comments are undercut by a sense of sadness. One example comes from a letter he wrote to William Jourdan Rapp in April 1929:

> I am fighting hard to refrain from regarding myself as a martyr and an outcast. I wish you could take my place in Negro society for about a week. Even on the train I was beset by a Pullman porter for my dastardly propaganda against the race. And here at home a delegation of church members (at my grandmother's

request) flocked in on me and prayed over me for almost an hour, beseeching the Almighty to turn my talents into the path of righteousness. All of which is amusing until the point of saturation is reached.

Here, it is clear that Thurman's sense of humor regarding his disrespectability has its limits, and his unpopularity among Salt Lake City's black community has taken its toll on him.[23]

New York and Salt Lake City, then, are closer together in Thurman's spatial imagination than they first appear. As literary critic Amritjit Singh remarks, Thurman "could not resolve the tension he felt between urban excitement and his urgent need for the peace and quiet of the beach or the country. While he was stimulated by the city and its abundant supply of freedom to experience a bohemian lifestyle, he realized that he could complete his writing projects much better in the relative calm of his grandmother's home in Salt Lake City." In letters written during Thurman's frequent "flying trips through the West," it appears that he found something reinvigorating in that environment, if not in the black community of Salt Lake City. In July 1929 Thurman lovingly described interacting with Utah's landscape:

> I had planned a hiking and camping trip with a group of former school chums this week but the doctor advised against it. I shall however go next week, and, coincidental with your advice, I have a friend who has a fruit farm on the outskirts of town, and I intend to spend a week with him sometime next month . . . picking fruit. I fear for the trees, the picked fruit and certain portions of my anatomy which might suffer when the earth calls its own and I tumble down from rickety stepladders.

In a later letter he describes his outdoor adventures in Utah. Despite his doctor's advice to stay indoors, he finds the environment healing: "I feel like a million dollars this morning. Spent Sunday, Monday and Tuesday in the canyon, hiking, chopping wood, fishing, roughing it in general." This, he suggests, increases his productivity: "And while in the woods and mountains I wrote scads of poetry," he reports (including a poem dedicated to Jean Toomer), even though, he admits, "none of it is worth a second look. . . . I am by no means a poet." As much as he lambasted Salt Lake City's African American community, Thurman recognized that the West offered him physical respite from the rigors of New York life, along with an opportunity to work uninterrupted and in a more settled environment. Though committed to an urbane cynicism, Thurman could also not help but be touched by the physical splendor of the West. About his prolific—if admittedly subpar—poetry writing in Salt Lake City, he jokes, "such is the result of spending three days in a canyon with a copy of *Cane* by Jean Toomer, *Thus Spake Zarathustra*, and *An Anthology of World's Poetry*." This sentence implies that the canyon setting was just as important as the books that inspire him.[24]

The physical setting, however, does little to help unravel the complicated intersections between racial and sexual politics in Thurman's work and, in particular, the relationship between these intertwined politics and region. Another letter from Salt Lake City, this one to Langston Hughes, gestures toward a new reading of Thurman, race, and place. In it, Thurman ties the West to his challenges to respectability politics and, in turn, the way these challenges inflect issues of race and sexuality. He writes:

> The only things of interest in Salt Lake are an epidemic of influenza, and the attitude of the older folk here toward me who have snubbed me with a vengeance because of an article I wrote three years ago in *The Messenger* about my home town and state. It seems as if I said that most of Utah's early Negro settlers were whores, gamblers and washerwomen, which is true of any of these western states. Somehow they got the idea that I said all of Utah's Negroes from the beginning until now were whores and gamblers. They didn't object to washerwomen. The younger folk have all been enjoying shot gun weddings since I left with the result that those whom I used to push around in a baby carriage are now pushing baby carriages of their own.

Here, he seems to be laughing at members of Salt Lake City's black community for their pretense of respectability, insinuating that this pretense is a denial of historical fact and also a denial of the present.

He observes that the community is still engaging in illicit and presumably disrespectable sexual behavior, but it is quickly covered up via the institution of marriage. Thurman points out the community's hypocrisy in matters of sexuality, as well as in its treatment of him as an outcast, even though he is one of the few "younger folk" who has not produced offspring by means of illicit sexual encounters. He paints an oppositional portrait of the West vis-à-vis Anita Scott Coleman, whose pictures of domesticity, family, and, indeed, washerwomen, often obscure black sexuality, particularly illicit aspects of sexuality such as prostitution, and trumpet the West as a land of *esperanza*—although one touched by ambivalence. According to Lawrence B. de Graff, black women in the West did not engage in prostitution to a greater extent than women of other groups. Yet stereotypes of rapacious black sexuality were widely held among whites, and these images, coupled with bawdy apocryphal depictions of western women overall, arguably made western blacks even more sensitive to accusations of sexual impropriety than their peers in other regions. Thurman suffers in kind.[25]

Much of Thurman's work has been read as a critique of black respectability politics as the basis for intraracial color prejudice. But his letter to Hughes suggests that it makes sense to consider Thurman's approach to respectability through the lens of sexuality in addition to color. The illicit sexualities Thurman detects in the West exceed the aforementioned premarital escapades and envelop a range of sexual postures. For example, Thurman accuses western blacks and the black bourgeoisie in general of desiring to become "whiter and whiter every generation," for "the nearer white you are the more white people will respect you." Here, he is alluding to the sexual taboo of miscegenation. This is not only an outgrowth of assimilative impulses in African America but also a nonnormative sexual configuration that Thurman characterizes as particularly western and particularly Utahan. For example, he discusses in "Quoth Brigham Young" his suspicion that statistics will show that the "intermixing of races" is greater in Utah than in any other western state. He goes on to describe houses of ill repute that cater only to the most taboo of interracial heterosexual encounters: "as late as 1915," he claims, "there was in Salt Lake a club catering only to Negro men and white women, and when I was last there, which was a year ago, there were three super-bawdy houses that I knew of, where white ladies of joy with itching palms cavorted for the pleasure of black men only." Although there is no denying that color prejudice is a major concern for Thurman, and miscegenation is part of the backdrop for these discussions, a critical focus solely on color ignores Thurman's larger critiques of respectability politics. If the analytical lens is widened to encompass the politics of sexuality in addition to the politics of color, Thurman's writing on the West looks quite different; the West may remain a place characterized by conservative or even reactionary racial politics, but it also becomes a place characterized by an expanded sexual politics.[26]

When sexuality is taken into account, it becomes possible to view the old debates about art and propaganda, about "high" and "low" culture, and about Harlem and the provinces in Thurman's work in new ways. For example, many recent critics have taken up these debates as a coded conversation about the representation of black sexuality, particularly black queer sexuality. Thurman was not "out," per se, as a queer black man. Nor were most other New Negro writers whose works have now been read in this context, such as Langston Hughes, Claude McKay, and Nella Larsen. Richard Bruce Nugent, Thurman's close friend and roommate in the famous "Niggeratti Manor" on West 136th Street—the setting for both Thurman's *Infants of the Spring* and Nugent's *Gentleman Jigger* (written in the late 1920s or early 1930s but not published until 2002)—was the only New Negro figure to write transparently about same-sex desire. Thurman, in a letter to Rapp, did disclose that he had at least one sexual experience with another man:

In 1925, a young colored lad anxious to enter a literary career came to New York. He had a little stake which was soon gone. He found no job. He owed room rent and was hungry. . . . At 135th St., he got off the Subway, and . . . went into the toilet. There was a man loitering in there. The man spoke. He did more than speak, making me know what his game was. I laughed. He offered me two dollars. I accepted.

At this point, he was arrested and subsequently fined. In the same letter, however, he vehemently denies a gay identity—perhaps due to closeting, and perhaps due to the fact that his then-wife, activist Louise Thompson, was suing for divorce and, he claimed, using this story to strengthen her case for alimony. Thurman's sexuality remains opaque; rather than identifying him as either heterosexual or homosexual, he is best read as queer or, in Lisa Duggan's definition, as "dissent[ing] from the dominant organization of sex and gender." As a result, literary scholars Granville Ganter, Eric King Watts, Eliza F. Glick, and others have insisted that the critical panning of Thurman's work in publications like *Opportunity* during the New Negro movement, as well as Alain Locke's cautious admonishment to Thurman's associates to avoid his "eccentricity," was a specific reaction to the queer currents running through his oeuvre. In scholarship like this, Thurman becomes one of the first writers, if not *the* first writer, to give voice to and theorize a queer black aesthetic.[27]

In scholarship, Thurman's queer black aesthetic has been depicted as emerging from urban experience—from the "sexual topography" of "gay New York," as George Chauncey puts it. Urban space—and Harlem in particular—has been imagined in this scholarship as queer space. David R. Jarraway, for example, endeavors to read gay identity through the representation of Harlem in Thurman's novels and therefore depicts Thurman as a black, gay urbanite. *The Blacker the Berry* at first seems to be congenial to a reading of Harlem as queer space, simply because all points in the novel that allude to same-sex desire take place in Harlem. For instance, when Emma Lou is looking for a room to rent, her potential landlady "tightened her arm around Emma Lou's waist" in a gesture of both sexual aggression and ownership; Thurman's use of italic in the landlady's name—"*Miss* Carrington"—calls attention to both her unmarried, spinster status and the intersection of her gender identity and her sexual advances. Later in the text, Emma Lou's sweetman, Alva, is "out with Marie, the creole Lesbian," again signaling Harlem's queer "sexual topography." Finally, Emma has an epiphany when she walks in and finds "Alva . . . sitting on the bed embracing an effeminate boy." All these encounters are depicted negatively—Miss Carrington's actions make Emma Lou tremendously uncomfortable, Marie signifies Alva's disrespectable ways, and Alva's embrace of the effeminate boy is the final affront that motivates Emma Lou to overcome her self-loathing. Thurman's representation of same-sex desire, then, is in line with modernist depictions of degeneration resulting from overcivilization and hypermodernity. In *The Blacker the Berry* this is also imbricated with color—it is embodied by the "creole Lesbian" and by the light-skinned Alva, who is half Filipino and half mulatto. Thurman uses same-sex sexuality to heighten his critique of the light-skinned for their "inbred" overcivilization. In contrast to someone like Jean Toomer (see chapter 5), Thurman does not see mixed-race subjects as imbued with a sort of "hybrid vigor"; rather, they are a dilution of vibrant blackness and a turn toward milquetoast white standards. It is no accident, then, that Alva and Geraldine's child—the offspring of two light-skinned characters—is born "sickly," "shrunken," and "deformed."[28]

As a result of this discourse of degeneration, *The Blacker the Berry*'s representation of same-sex sexuality complicates celebratory readings of Thurman as part of the vibrant queer underground that emerged in Harlem in the 1920s and 1930s. Watts's essay unveils this complication by exploring space and place in Thurman's *Infants of the Spring*. He examines Niggeratti Manor itself and argues that "although Harlem was revered as an African American 'homeland' that nurtured black artistic possibilities and was celebrated as an after-hours playground for Greenwich Village 'decadents' seeking safe haven for experiments with the exotic, New Negro racial politics were inhospitable to a black gay 'home.'" In other words, as an African American, Thurman was on the fringe of gay male, predominantly white Greenwich Village, even though he may have been exoticized via racial and sexual fetishism by downtown gay men who traveled to Harlem to engage in a kind of sexual "slumming." These Harlem nights may have provided a respite for white gay men from downtown, but unlike these sexual tourists, Thurman had to face Harlem days as well. And these days were saturated by a politics of respectability that rendered Harlem consistently uncomfortable for its queer black residents. Thurman, then, was marginal both to the Greenwich Village gay scene and to a Harlem dominated by the bourgeois imperatives of intellectuals and uplift organizations guided by a politics of respectability. This politics of respectability was often imbued by what historian Darlene Clark Hine identifies as a "culture of dissemblance" that obscured even the institutionalized rape of black women. As E. Frances White contends, it also silenced conversations about queer sexuality in African America.[29]

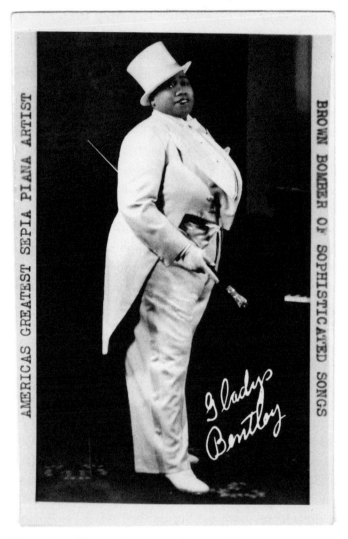

Blues singer Gladys Bentley, a fixture of Harlem's queer subculture. (Courtesy of J. D. Doyle, Queer Music Heritage)

In Thurman's work, then, the sexual politics of Harlem and of the West are far more similar than scholars imagined. Both sites are guided by a politics of respectability that serves to police sexual behavior. Like Harlem, the West—and Salt Lake City in particular—is home to nonnormative or disrespectable sexual postures, and miscegenation is just one of these. Thurman's erstwhile friend and collaborator Richard Bruce Nugent calls attention to the most disrespectable aspects of Salt Lake City through a fictionalized representation of Thurman in his novel *Gentleman Jigger.* Like Dorothy West and others, he sometimes relayed and sometimes contorted the facts of Thurman's life as the stuff of literature. This time, however, Salt Lake City is not depicted as backward and repressed. *Gentleman Jigger* tells largely the same story as Thurman's second novel, *Infants of the Spring.* But Nugent uses Thurman's western upbringing as the fodder for dramatic fiction, carving his character Henry Raymond Pelman (Ray) out of the material of western fantasy. In the novel, Ray's western genealogy is explained as follows: His maternal great-grandmother abandons her Mormon husband in protest of a black sister-wife. She marries a man who is half mulatto and half Jewish and has a dark-skinned daughter. This is Ray's grand-mother, who, like Thurman's real-life grandmother, is named Emma. Emma marries a mixed-race man and bears a daughter, Hagar, who becomes Ray's mother. Ray is the result of Hagar's torrid affair with a dark-skinned man. Perhaps predictably (Nugent was, after all, the author of a notorious contribution to *Fire!!* titled "Smoke, Lilies, and Jade," which Langston Hughes called a "green and purple story . . . in the Oscar Wilde tradition"), Nugent's scripting of Ray's genealogical and geographic origins is not only interracial but also polymorphously perverse. Nugent, always a provocateur, never passed up a chance to thumb his nose at the guardians of morality and respectability. In the short span of his six-page description of Salt Lake City, polygamy, miscegenation, incest, same-sex and intergenerational desire, rape, impotence, pimping, and prostitution all have a place.[30]

Nugent's representations of Salt Lake City and of Thurman are clearly fictionalized and fantastical, but it is noteworthy that he can imagine Salt Lake City as the opposite of stuffy and repressed. Thurman's other acquaintances, along with recent scholars, have insisted that Salt Lake City was so hostile to Thurman's self-described "erotic, bohemian life-style" that he "probably left the Mormon state after having a nervous breakdown, hoping to restore his failing health in California." Unfortunately, even California could not accommodate his racial and sexual identities and concomitant artistic vision. Yet Nugent's Salt Lake

City is a place built by taboo sexual configurations, including miscegenation, same-sex desire, and polygamy. That Nugent characterizes Salt
Lake City this way is perhaps little indication of Thurman's opinion
of the city. But it is worth noting that Nugent's *Gentleman Jigger* and
Thurman's *Infants of the Spring* are so similar that Nugent once accused
Thurman of plagiarizing his work. These allegations have never been
proved, but the parallels between the two texts provide clear evidence of
a deep collaboration and exchange. This might indicate that Thurman's
coy references to "more pimps and prostitutes" in "Quoth Brigham
Young" are part of a larger conception of the West undergirded by
sexual transgression.[31]

In kind, when Thurman turns to Utah's history, he must grapple
with the history of polygamy, one of the primary factors that delayed
Utah's statehood for forty-six years, from the territory's establishment
in 1850 until 1896. Plural marriage may have appalled nineteenth-
century Americans, who saw it as a form of female sexual slavery, but
for a twentieth-century iconoclast like Thurman, alternative configurations of marriage, family, and desire may have been alluring. Indeed, in
"Quoth Brigham Young" he writes rather longingly of a Utah he never
experienced, a Utah with radically different conceptions of intimacy,
marriage, and family life than those of the US mainstream. He writes
that after Brigham Young's death, "Utah was finally forced to come
into the Union, and for coming in she had to abolish polygamy, and
lose her individuality, for from that day on Utah was just another state,
peopled by a horde of typical American booboisie with their bourgeoisie
overlords, and today Utah is a good example of what Americanization
and its attendant spores can accomplish."[32]

Indeed, if Thurman's critique of black westerners and the black
bourgeoisie in general is that they accepted white middle-class norms
and pretensions, it is easy to see how this politics of respectability might
be driven in part by black westerners' efforts to distance themselves
from the history of polygamy in places like Salt Lake City. As historian
Sarah Barringer Gordon has argued, polygamy was long thought of as
a thoroughly un-American configuration of intimacy and family. In the
period after the Civil War, blacks were already seen as both morally
suspect and sexually unhinged, and they were thought to be particularly

susceptible to Mormon conversion. In the face of such stereotypes of African American sexuality, and amidst the continued black struggle for full, equal citizenship, western blacks, particularly those in largely Mormon regions, may have felt a singular pressure to use respectability to bolster their claims for racial equality. In 1890 (two years before Thurman's grandmother arrived in Salt Lake City) the Church of Latter-Day Saints proclaimed it would no longer expect its members to practice polygamy, officially backing away from its endorsement of "celestial marriage" in the hope of making Utah statehood more palatable to the mainstream United States.[33]

To Thurman, however, these claims for equality came at the cost of individuality. During this period he, like many modernists, perceived a dominant national trend toward conformity and standardization in an era characterized by Fordist mass production. As a result, his writings long for a Utah that existed before his family arrived there. Letters reveal that he was completing research for a play based on the life of Joseph Smith and, in particular, Smith's "vision authorizing polygamy." In a letter to Langston Hughes, he explained:

> I have began [sic] work on a perfectly intriguing play, again in collaboration with Wm. Jourdan Rapp. It is my idea. *Sultan Smith* is the title, it being woven around the experiences of Joseph F. Smith, founder of the Mormon religion. The scene of the action is Nauvoo, Ill., where for one brief moment the Mormons lingered before being driven out and forced to migrate to Salt Lake. It was at Nauvoo that Smith received his vision authorizing polygamy. That is the kernel of the play.

To date, this manuscript has not surfaced, and it may well be lost forever. However, Thurman's frequent mentions of its development indicate that he did not find Utah's history as "dull and unprogressive" as he claimed in "Quoth Brigham Young." Indeed, when he felt ostracized by Salt Lake City blacks, it may have been based not only on his candor about illicit sexuality in the community but also on his implied defense of Mormon polygamy. In "Quoth Brigham Young" he states, "The Mormons put up a brave battle while Brigham Young lived, but after his death there was a complete debacle." The implication is that Utah became respectable, bourgeois, and "Americanized"—to its detriment—through the abolishment of polygamy. Thurman buried himself in research during his 1929 trip to Salt Lake City, writing to Rapp, "Since I am now enthroned in the citadel of Mormonism, where all available records can be found there seems no better time than now [to work on *Sultan Smith*]. I shall hie myself to the library and the Mormon library and read all I can find on the subject." In another letter he reports, "My room is crowded with books on Joseph Smith and the early Mormons. I even have a Book of Mormon, confessions of one of Brigham's wives and much other juicy material, both scandalous and serious. Some emancipated Mormons I know here have aided me in gathering material, and I have gone directly to the Church library for the rest."[34]

Thurman's interest in plural marriage is apparent even in his fiction set in Harlem. In *The Blacker the Berry* Alva admits to Emma Lou that he "had already been married twice, and he hadn't even bothered to obtain a divorce from his first wife before acquiring number two." Alva's first wife is described as "an essential polygamous female." When Emma Lou questions him, he says, "I know plenty spades right here in Harlem get married any time they want to. Who in hell's gonna take the trouble getting a divorce when, if you marry and already have a wife, you can get another without going through all that red tape?" As for the law, Alva claims, "The only time they act about bigamy is when one of the wives squawk, and they hardly ever do that. They're only too glad to see the old man get married again—then they can do likewise."[35]

If Thurman's queer sexualities and fascination with Mormon plural marriage have perplexed both his contemporaries and various modern-day critics, a final complication is his apparent embrace of emergent notions of companionate marriage. *The Blacker the Berry* was published shortly after Thurman's marriage to Louise Thompson. Although Thompson was born in Chicago, she spent most of her youth—like Thurman's character Emma Lou—in Idaho and then in Oregon. She eventually moved to Sacramento and then attended the University of California at Berkeley, where she graduated in 1923. Thompson's archive, like Thurman's, indicates an interest in the African American West; she kept materials on blacks in California, Nevada, and Oregon.

During his study of Mormon polygamy, Thurman examined the religiously inflected intimacy and kinship structures of the past in order to envision new kinds of secular relations in the modern present. Indeed, when he first married Thompson he assured Claude McKay:

> I got married, which action I, who never and still do not believe in marriage for an artist of any type, will not try to explain. It's just one of those unexplainable things that happens to the best of us. My only point of extenuation is that I happen to have married a very intelligent woman who has her own career and who also does not believe in marriage and who is as anxious as I am to avoid the conventional pitfalls into which most marriages throw one. I assure you ours is a most modern experiment, a reflection of our own rather curious personalities.

Thurman's letter seems to support the idea of modern, companionate marriage.[36]

Two years before Thurman's marriage to Thompson, Colorado (and later California) judge Ben B. Lindsey coauthored with Wainwright Evans a book called *The Companionate Marriage* (1927). This book, extending the work of social scientists who had coined the term a few years earlier, described the tools necessary—such as birth control and easy access to divorce—for couples to enter into equal partnerships. The book, and Lindsey's nationwide promotion of its ideals, resulted in a firestorm of attention, both damning and supportive.

Although Thurman and Thompson began divorce proceedings only a few months after their marriage (Thompson traveled to Reno, Nevada, to initiate the process), their divorce was never finalized. Thus, when Thurman telegrammed Hughes from Los Angeles in 1934 to announce that "FAY [Jackson] AND I MARRIED TODAY," his joke is threefold: he undermines the respectable institution of marriage (the Thurman-Thompson divorce proceedings were, by all accounts, ugly—as was Fay Jackson's 1930 divorce from John Marshall Robinson Jr.), he questions heteronormativity (Thompson claimed their marriage was undermined by Thurman's homosexuality), and he hints at polygamy, given that Thurman was still legally married to Thompson, even though they had been separated for years. This telegram suggests, then, Thurman's complicated "sexual topography." It suggests a sexual politics that challenged conformist politics of respectability; that comprised the varied terrains of same-sex desire, miscegenation, polygamy, and companionate marriage; and that was derived from the West inasmuch as it was at home in "gay New York."[37]

CHAPTER 4

Technicolor Places

Race and Revolution in
Transnational America

I like the wild wild West
Because it's just
Like a movie to me.

I like Colorado,
It's always had a
Kick that's groovy to me.

I like all
Them wide open spaces.
I'm crazy about
Technicolor places.
—*Langston Hughes, "The Wild Wild West" (ca. 1940s)*

In the summer of 1920, one month after his high school graduation, a young aspiring writer traveled from Cleveland, Ohio, to Toluca, Mexico, to meet his father, who had been living in Mexico since 1903. Along the way, he crossed a railroad bridge over the Mississippi in St. Louis, Missouri. Gazing out the window over the muddy, churning waters, he thought of the stories his grandmother—a committed abolitionist whose first husband had been murdered while participating in John Brown's raid on Harpers Ferry and whose second husband was a groundbreaking black activist and politician—had told him about this place where North and South, East and West joined and shaped the experiences of so many African Americans, particularly under the regime of slavery.

153

The gravity of this history inspired him to compose a poem, which he hastily scribbled on the back of an envelope. He called it "The Negro Speaks of Rivers." He later sent it to the *Crisis*, which published the poem in 1921. The writer, of course, was Langston Hughes. "The Negro Speaks of Rivers" was one of his first published works and remains one of his best known and most celebrated poems.

Langston Hughes poses with pre-Columbian (or pre-Columbian inspired) statuary for African American photographer Gordon Parks, 1943. (Library of Congress, Prints and Photographs Division, FSA/OWI Collection)

"The Negro Speaks of Rivers," as many scholars have pointed out, uses the Mississippi, the Euphrates, the Congo, and the Nile as symbols that unify black diasporic history, memory, and experience:

> I bathed in the Euphrates when dawns were young.
> I built my hut near the Congo and it lulled me to sleep.
> I looked upon the Nile and raised the pyramids above it.
> I heard the singing of the Mississippi when Abe Lincoln
>   went down to New Orleans, and I've seen its muddy
>   bosom turn all golden in the sunset.

It was one of Hughes's first efforts to envision a transnational black culture. These efforts would continue throughout his life as he traveled around the world, visiting Africa and western Europe as a young adult, when he worked as a seaman, and later journeying to Haiti, Cuba, the Soviet Union, China, Spain, and elsewhere as he explored radical politics and antifascism in the 1930s. During these years he also traveled throughout the United States, where he gave readings and sought retreats where he could write in places as diverse as Florida, Chicago, Reno, and Carmel. He would return to many of these sites later in life as a lecturer, and travel continued to be an inspiration in his literature and other creative work. Hughes's titles for his later autobiographical writing, *The Big Sea* (1940) and *I Wonder as I Wander* (1956), could not be more fitting reflections of the circum-Atlantic and transnational experiences that characterized his often restless life. In a 1941 essay titled "Just Traveling," he proclaimed, "I like to travel. Just travel," and he admonished his reader not to "let anybody tell you it's too expensive to travel. It isn't—if you just like traveling. And traveling is my dish. Yeah, bo!" Hughes's journeys took many forms and resulted from a variety of circumstances (financial, political, and social). Regardless of whether he traveled due to necessity or for pleasure, he elevated it to a near vocation, and it became an important foundation for his thinking about how racial and class politics were shaped by location. All this began with his early journeys to Mexico, when Hughes crossed not only the Mississippi but also the Rio Grande.[1]

Hughes's writing is clearly informed by his multifaceted place-based experiences. He lived in Harlem longer than anywhere else, but he did not settle into his brownstone on East 127th Street, which he shared with nonbiological "aunt" Toy and "uncle" Emerson Harper, until the late 1940s. Up to that time, Hughes was rarely in one location for long, moving often as he sought to make ends meet through writing and lecturing. The impact of Hughes's migratory lifestyle on his vision of black culture and experience has not gone unconsidered by scholars, many of whom have written about Hughes, transnationalism, and diaspora. In *The Practice of Diaspora: Literature, Translation, and the Rise of Black Internationalism*, Brent Hayes Edwards, for example, reads Hughes's Paris-inspired poetry, such as "Jazz Band in a Parisian Cabaret" (1927), as a multilingual articulation of black international culture. In an essay titled "Langston Hughes and the Futures of Diaspora," Edwards argues that Hughes can be seen as a writer who critiques capitalist globalization as much as he expresses black diasporic longing and nostalgia, and by reading Hughes, it becomes possible to see the relations between these two forms of transnational engagement.

As Edwards noted in 2007, "It is by now commonplace to describe Langston Hughes as a writer of the 'African diaspora,'" but few scholars have discussed Hughes's transnationalism in the framework of the borderlands West or Greater Mexico. Edward Mullen provides information about Hughes's time south of the border in an essay "Langston Hughes in Mexico and Cuba," asserting that Hughes's Mexican experiences "were crucial in shaping his notions of race and class—elements so essential in his poetics." Astrid Haas addresses Mexico as part of Hughes's engagement with Latin America. Recently, Claudia Milian has examined Hughes's Latinness via Mexico in *Latining America: Black-Brown Passages and the Coloring of Latino/a Studies*. Hughes's Mexico, however, has not been considered in relation to the American West. Blake Allmendinger's *Imagining the African American West* is one of the only texts to center Hughes in the region; Allmendinger discusses Hughes's 1935 short story "Flora Belle" (later republished as "The Gun" in *Something in Common and Other Stories* [1963]), which takes place in Montana, the Pacific Northwest, and California. He then contemplates Hughes's *Not without Laughter* (1930), set in Kansas and Chicago—places that are western in relation to New York but were more commonly thought of as midwestern by the early twentieth century. Hughes's travels through and writings about the borderlands West—in particular, sites within the nation-state of Mexico (including Toluca and Mexico City) and the transnational space of Mexico's borderlands (including California, Texas, Nevada, and New Mexico)—bring these two approaches, the transnational and the regional, together, making it possible to explore discursive connections between the West, Mexico, and the world.[2]

"The Negro Speaks of Rivers" was not the only writing Hughes did during his 1920 journey to Mexico. With adolescent hopefulness and humor, he also kept a journal, which he titled "A Diary of Mexican Adventures (If There Be Any)." This diary reveals Hughes's desires for his time in Mexico and the connections he was making to geography and racial liberation even this early in his life. The journal begins as Hughes is traveling by rail across Texas: "All day long I have been riding thru Texas: heat and cotton fields, little forlorn villages, one with a large public well in the center of the main street, red and blue flowers singing their color song along the track, relieving the monotony of evergreen landscape, and always cotton growing, cotton growing—these thru my car window." Whereas waterways and currents describe transnational black experience in "The Negro Speaks of Rivers," here, Hughes writes of "cotton fields . . . always cotton growing, cotton growing," raising the specter of regional black history and experience in the South and Southwest under plantation and sharecropping systems. In both cases, geography serves as a metaphor for the black cultural memory. Indeed, Hughes suggests that region assists in the construction of race: "I am the only Negro in the car. Of course being in Texas I am not allowed to forget my color." Texas, he insists, shapes his experience of being black: "Last night at supper . . . a white Southerner left the table because he didn't care to sit opposite me."[3]

In later writings, Hughes would describe Texas as incontrovertibly part of the South because of its adherence to Jim Crow. His poem "West Texas," first published in *Shakespeare in Harlem* (1942), makes this clear: "Down in West Texas where the sun / Shines like the evil one / Ain't

Snapshot of Langston Hughes taken in Texas during his 1931–1932 lecture tour. (Beinecke Rare Book and Manuscript Library, Yale University; reprinted by permission from Harold Ober Associates, Incorporated, as agents for the Estate of Langston Hughes)

no place / For a colored / Man to stay!" Any affection Hughes felt for Texas was limited to border towns like El Paso, which he enjoyed because racial categories became confounded there. For example, in a draft of *I Wonder as I Wander*, Hughes recalls his 1931–1932 lecture tour and remarks, "Texans say that their state is not in the South, it's the Southwest. Be that as it may, Texas has southern ways, Jim Crow cars, and color lines all over the state." He continues, "I didn't like any part of it except El Paso. . . . Maybe I liked El Paso because it sits right on the Mexican border, is a partially Spanish-speaking town, and has no Jim Crow street cars. Whites, Negroes, and Mexicans ride anywhere in a public conveyance." Here, Hughes suggests that borderlands enhance mobility—although he also understands that borders serve as limitations. He takes up the border as both geopolitical and geographic—that is, it is determined politically and legally, on the one hand, but by the river and the land, on the other hand. Hughes relies on descriptions of the geography to emphasize attendant differences in the racial landscape: "And a short ten minute walk across the international bridge brings a man to soil where the color line melts away." He continues, "Merely by crossing a border—past the signs *U.S.A.-MEXICO* at the middle of the river—one can buy a beer in any bar, sit anywhere in the movies, or eat at any restaurant. It is regrettable, however, for a Negro in Texas to have to go outside his own country for these simple privileges." In this typescript, Hughes writes of borderlands as hybrid multiethnic and multilingual spaces, such as his comment that El Paso is "partially Spanish-speaking," and he describes borders as national dividers with real consequences for those who traverse them, such as his observations about blacks' relative freedom after crossing into Mexico. Hughes's writing about Mexico and its borderlands makes it possible to see him as more than a writer about the black diaspora; he is a writer who imagines multiethnic collaboration and exchange through transnational experience and its representation.[4]

Hughes contemplates the relationship between region and transnationalism later in his diary when he juxtaposes the racist, provincial southerner who refused to eat in the same dining car with another passenger on the train described as "a citizen of the world, a real cosmopolitan." In contradistinction to the bounded southerner, this "citizen of the world" "seems to have been everywhere from Tokio [*sic*] to Timbuctoo [*sic*]" and is "very friendly." Hughes takes particular care to note, "Today I had lunch with him and he did not get up from the table." The congenial relationship Hughes forms with this other passenger is a direct result, he suggests, of the man's embrace of transnational travel. As for the racist southerner, Hughes contends that the Texas environment shaped him. "I pity the man last night," he says—and asks rhetorically, "How could he be broadminded and live in Texas? (And I know he does.)" As this passage demonstrates, racism and provincialism are entwined in Hughes's mind. By extension, he suggests that the experience of transnational travel is one way to eradicate racial prejudice. With this in mind, Hughes's oeuvre—much of which can be loosely considered "travel writing," and much of which involves the translation of other poets into English—can be viewed as having a particular activist imperative. His writing does the work of travel for his readers, even those who remain static, thereby helping to eliminate racism in the United States and anywhere else he finds an audience.[5]

Hughes's efforts to align migration with antiracist perspectives are clear in his diary when he remarks, "Last night a fat old Jew informed me that he had known at once that I was a Mexican." Hughes seems quite troubled by this assumption. In a few short years he would write "The Negro Artist and the Racial Mountain," published in the *Nation* in 1926, and it would become one of his best-known essays. It is a manifesto of sorts for young African American artists, and in it, Hughes establishes himself as one of the most outspoken proponents of the New Negro ethos of black pride. He asserts that he wants to be known as nothing else but African American: "I am a Negro," he proclaims, "and beautiful!" Hughes defies the "mold of American standardization" that would strip him of "racial individuality" and demand that he be "as little Negro and as much American as possible." In his diary, however, he reveals the complexity of racial hierarchies beyond the binary of "Negro" and (white) "American." When the Jew on the train assumes that Hughes is Mexican, he clearly thinks he is paying Hughes a compliment—that is, he thinks Hughes is not black but something else. This is an affront to Hughes's sense of self, pride, and identity, but he is able to forgive this Jewish man because Jews, like African Americans, are racially subjugated. Hughes does not correct the man because, he contends, "Jews are a warmhearted people and seldom prejudiced." While Hughes makes a sweeping, essentialist statement about Jewish character and difference here, it is not biologically determined; instead, he attributes Jews' warmheartedness and lack of prejudice to their experiences as objects of discrimination and hate, their "persecution from Egypt to Russia." In other words, Jews can empathize with African Americans not only because of their shared experiences of oppression but also because of their shared experiences of diaspora ("from Egypt to Russia") due to that oppression. Migration—often framed as exodus, which is a powerful concept for both Jews and African Americans, as scholars such as Eddie Glaude and Eric Sundquist have shown—shapes Jewish attitudes toward race, according to Hughes, as much as anti-Semitism does. Having spent his youth in Lawrence, Kansas, Hughes surely understood how the tale of exodus also shaped black western history. In the years after his grandmother moved there, the biblical story of Moses leading the Jews from bondage in Egypt inspired African American western migration to the state where John Brown (also inspired by the book of Exodus) had worked for black liberation. There, they would form all-black towns, generally with the aid of the Homestead Act.[6]

In "A Diary of Mexican Adventures" Hughes seems to suggest that a willingness to cross borders leads to expanded perspectives and more generous minds. The racism of the Texan in the dining car is attributable to his home state and the provincial attitude that prevails there. The broadmindedness of the "citizen of the world" is a result of his vast travels. The hierarchical view of race (with blacks on the bottom) implied by the Jewish man's comment is forgiven because of the diasporic memory that makes this particular individual an unfortunate exception to the general character Hughes ascribes to Jewish people. It does not bode well for racial equality in the United States when Hughes comments on the "giant government hydroplane" in the town of Laredo, Texas, "guarding Uncle Sam's border I suppose." Efforts to guard the border were likely ramped up in 1920 because of the ongoing Mexican Revolution, but Hughes's cynical tone suggests that this will lead not to security but to greater provincialism. When the borders of the nation are impermeable, he implies, white supremacy will remain. This is evident in the slippage in his phrasing in "The Negro Artist and the Racial Mountain," where "American" and "white" become interchangeable. Hughes opens his essay by describing his dismay at a colleague who claimed, "I want to be a poet—not a Negro poet." This statement, according to Hughes, ultimately means, "I would like to be white." By the end of this paragraph, Hughes stops using "white" and, in its place, begins using "American" as he describes those who seek to "become as little Negro and as much American as possible." Hughes critiques the alignment of the United States with whiteness, an outgrowth of the borders of both entities being jealously guarded. An exchange he has with a white southern woman (again, emphasizing provincialism) in Mexico reveals as much: "Why, Ah-Ah thought you was an American," she stammers, upon seeing him teaching English. Hughes can only reply, "I am an American!" It takes transnational travel for the woman to receive this lesson.[7]

By crossing the border into Mexico, the youthful Hughes longed to emerge somewhere that looked very different from the United States—he sought an egalitarian, multiethnic place rather than one dominated by white supremacy. He traveled to Mexico in both 1919 and 1920, visiting his father the summer before and the year after his senior year in high school. James N. Hughes had moved to Mexico when Langston was only an infant, and by this point he was essentially a stranger to his son. Hughes had not seen his father since he was a small child, when, during a brief period of reconciliation, he and his mother had moved to Mexico City. Eleven years later, he had already developed an acute racial consciousness, largely cultivated through his childhood years in Lawrence, where he was raised by his maternal grandmother, Mary Langston. Mary had a long history of engagement with the black freedom struggle, and she passed her knowledge on to her grandson. When Hughes was a child, she would tuck him in at night and cover him with the shawl her first husband, Lewis Sheridan Leary, had been wearing when he was killed at Harpers Ferry. She would tell him "long, beautiful stories about people who wanted to make the Negroes free," and by the time Hughes graduated from high school, he knew he wanted to write "seriously and as well as I knew how about the Negro people."[8]

Hughes brought his racial consciousness to bear on his travels to Mexico. He had high hopes for his time there and envisioned his father "as a kind of strong, bronze cowboy, in a big Mexican hat, going back and forth from his business in the city to his ranch in the mountains, free—in a land where there were no white folks to draw the color line, and no tenements with rent always due—just mountains and sun and cacti: Mexico!" Here, his grandmother's tales about black freedom intersect with images of the borderlands West. His youthful fantasy of Mexico is also informed by histories of black freedom. His grandfather, Charles Langston, had participated in the famed Oberlin-Wellington rescue in 1858, during which fugitive slave John Price was wrested from kidnappers who sought to reenslave him in Kentucky and ultimately escaped to Canada. Thirty-seven men (twelve of them free blacks) were indicted for aiding Price's rescue, but only two were prosecuted for their roles. Langston was one of them. He was found guilty of undermining the 1850 Fugitive Slave Act and imprisoned for a relatively short time. As a result of this family history, the potential power of transnational border crossings may have loomed large in Hughes's imagination as he traveled to Mexico. Many antebellum African Americans, perhaps most famously Frederick Douglass, did not see border crossing as a long-term solution to slavery. Preferring to dismantle the system within the United States, they critiqued the racism blacks experienced in adjacent countries and bristled at the colonization movement, which would have deported blacks to unfamiliar lands and thus whitened the nation. But for fugitives from the South (particularly Texas), Mexico and the West were far closer (both physically and temporally) and therefore more viable options for freedom. By 1851, as historian James David Nichols notes, Mexico may have harbored as many as 2,000 fugitive slaves. In terms of transnational escape, then, Mexico was arguably as powerful a site in the black imagination as Canada was—a geographic focus popularized largely by the northern white abolitionist imagination in texts such as Harriet Beecher Stowe's *Uncle Tom's Cabin* and carried into scholarship.[9]

According to historian Sarah E. Cornell, Mexico became more than a site of "persistent historical memory . . . as an asylum for fugitive slaves." In a very real sense, it also became a refuge where slaves from Texas and "large swaths of the South, including Louisiana, Mississippi, Alabama, and Arkansas also found freedom"—albeit a freedom still limited by racism and the contours of immigration law. Despite these limitations, "a potent vision of Mexico as an antiracist, antislavery refuge emerged" in the antebellum period. During Hughes's visits in 1919 and 1920, this vision of Mexico as an egalitarian society was reinvigorated due to the Mexican Revolution, which had been under way for ten years and was often seen as an effort to eradicate social and political hierarchies, including race and class. As historian Gerald Horne suggests, during the Mexican Revolution, "Mexico would serve as a beacon of hope for [US-born] Negroes." "The social explosion across the border," he contends, "created opportunities for them to address frontally and forcefully the oppression of white supremacy in the United States." In Hughes's diary he comments on the impact the revolution has had on his journey: "I have just heard that the rebels have attacked Nuevo Laredo and that the railroad line to Mexico City has been cut. Well, I can't go back to Cleveland, so I shall have to go on. Maybe there will be adventures. Who knows? I hope so." In this passage, Hughes certainly does not appear to be terribly disappointed that he cannot return to Cleveland. Indeed, the revolution only makes him more excited about his journey across the border. Perhaps this excitement is merely an adolescent longing for fun, but his hope for adventure may also indicate a broader desire for freedom, which seems more accessible in revolutionary Mexico than in the Jim Crow–era United States. Furthermore, for Hughes, freedom was not an esoteric ideal legible only to adults; he committed much of his writing to children, including the republication of many of his most poignant poems, such as "I, Too" ("I, too, sing America. / I am the darker brother. / . . . I, too, am America") and "The Negro Speaks of Rivers," in *The Dream Keeper and Other Poems* (1932), a compilation geared toward younger readers. As a result, it makes sense to take his teenaged writing, and the dreams it contains, seriously—for Hughes took youth seriously. Later in his diary he acknowledges the goals of the revolution, along with its costs: "The revolutions have made many poor; broken on the wheel of the freedom they are seeking."[10]

Hughes alludes to the revolution once again when he describes the broad sky full of impossibly bright stars that extends limitlessly over the border towns of Nuevo Laredo, Mexico, and Laredo, Texas:

Paris has nothing on the two Laredos when it comes to stars, for
tonight the sky is filled with those lovely jewels which evening
wears upon her velvet gown. High above the Rio Grande, above
the two cities, above the two countries they sparkle and glow,
and one big star is winking and twinkling as if he were laughing
at my littleness—at the little of all men with their . . . hatred and
war.

The borderless sky subverts any efforts to shore up permeable national
boundaries, and the big star "laugh[s]" at the pathetic perpetuators of
"hatred and war" that impact marginalized racial groups and poor people
in both nations. Hughes's description of a single bright star is reminiscent of the north star's mobilization as a beacon of hope for enslaved
African Americans in publications such as Douglass's *North Star.* As in
so many imaginings of fugitive slaves, Hughes writes of a star that leads
to freedom across an international border—but here, that border is with
Mexico rather than Canada. The span of stars reaching across the border
serves as a metaphor for the bridging of difference that Hughes hopes
will eliminate Jim Crow in the United States and class- and race-based
inequality in Mexico. The revolutionary climate of Mexico, however,
seems to hold much more promise at this moment in Hughes's life. After he crosses the border he notes in his diary, "Here nothing is bared
[*sic*] from me. I am among my own people, for Nuevo Laredo is a dark
skinned city and Mexico is a brown man's country. Do you blame them
for fearing 'gringo' invasion with its attendant horrors of color hatred?"
Here, Hughes pays more attention to the encroachment of the United
States and its white-supremacist hegemony on Latin America than he
does to the complicated race and class politics still being sorted out in
revolutionary Mexico. The United States had indeed made military
excursions into Mexico during the revolution—in Veracruz in 1914; in
pursuit of Pancho Villa after his raid on Columbus, New Mexico, in
1916; and in subsequent border skirmishes for the remainder of the revolution. During his travels, Hughes sensed that Mexicans were suspicious
of growing US imperialism (particularly in former Spanish colonies),
enabled by the Monroe Doctrine and following the Spanish-American
War. He viewed this as a rational response to the white supremacy that

both undergirded manifest destiny and guided the racial order in the United States during the Jim Crow era.[11]

Hughes's critiques of US encroachment on its neighbor to the south help explain his comparative admiration of racial and class elites in Mexico during these early years. Mexico, of course, was by no means free of racism; both antiblack and anti-Indian racism were persistent, and despite the revolution and later efforts to proclaim and promote a unifying national *mestizaje*, Mexican society remained racially stratified. Yet on his initial journeys there, Hughes imagined that even its whitest and richest residents were at least friendly to its poorer people of color. Upon a chance encounter with the son of the German-descended Toluca industrialist to whom his father had sold an electric company, he comments, "You would not think him wealthy. His manners are too good. He has been talking to one of the poorest Indian women in the coach and with her we shared our supper. . . . But all the Mexicans I've talked to have been kind, friendly, jolly. It seems to be a national virtue—this friendliness to strangers and their courteousness to one another that is seen in all Mexican railway trains." Hughes is hopeful that these egalitarian attitudes are a "national virtue" of revolutionary Mexico. Given the racially charged nature of rail travel in the United States since *Plessy v. Ferguson*, it is no wonder that Hughes sees the networks of railroads connecting the Mexican nation as a prime place to make these somewhat ethnographic observations of Mexican character. But later in his life, on a 1934 trip to Mexico City to settle his father's estate, his assessment of Mexican elites seems to have changed, for he was inspired to jot down the following note in a journal: "Somehow I have a great dislike for the best society. Almost always, beauty and strength and tolerance and kindness lie elsewhere. I am not speaking of America alone. Take Haiti—take France, Russia, etc." By this time—spurred perhaps by the onset of the Great Depression, which widened the wealth gap between the prosperous and the impoverished in the United States; by his soured relationship with his business-minded father; by the loss of his wealthy white patron, Charlotte Osgood Mason; and by his travels to the Soviet Union—Hughes had developed a sharper proletarian consciousness that enabled him to critique class inequality transnationally. He could see the connections between poverty and racial oppression, and he was far less likely to lionize the wealthy, even in countries that feared subjugation by increasing US power. As Edwards points out, in a 1938 speech Hughes made to the International Writers Association for the Defense of Culture in Paris, he states, "because our world is . . . today so related and inter-related, a creative writer has no right to neglect to understand clearly the social and economic forces that control our world," making a link between transnationalism and class and articulating his understanding of capitalist globalization.[12]

Although Hughes began his 1920 trip to Mexico with optimism about the freeing experience of living in "a brown man's country," his early years there were unsatisfying and he chose to flee Mexico for Harlem, "the greatest Negro city in the world." When he recalls his teenaged experiences in Mexico in *The Big Sea*, Hughes expresses primarily regret and disappointment. His writings during that 1920 train ride to Mexico indicate that he was thinking about the complicated relationship between place and race, looking at how mobility and location might forge and undermine hierarchical arrangements of race and class. When he fantasized about his mysterious father as a "strong, bronze cowboy" who was "free," this was easy to do, for James Hughes's geographic trajectory appeared to link place and liberation. The son of former slaves, James had moved from Indiana in search of opportunity—first to Louisville, then westward to Kansas, and then to Guthrie, Oklahoma, in 1899, where he homesteaded 160 acres of land. As illustrated by the Exodusters and the founders of Blackdom, New Mexico, homesteading was one tool used by western blacks to gain increased autonomy, and it was the reason for a considerable amount of African American westward migration. By 1900, blacks owned 1.5 million acres of land in the Oklahoma Territory, much of it homesteaded. Oklahoma was the site of more black towns than any other territory or state in the West, as blacks worked toward a vision of collective uplift. These towns included Langston—located about twelve miles from Guthrie and named for Hughes's great-uncle, abolitionist activist and politician John Mercer Langston. In Guthrie, James met the woman who would become Hughes's mother, Carrie Langston, and married her in 1899. When James could not gain admittance to the Oklahoma bar due to his race, he moved again—first to Cuba and then, before his son was even one year old, to Mexico. In the

James N. Hughes's Oklahoma homestead claim, 1899. (Beinecke Rare Book and Manuscript Library, Yale University)

aftermath of Turner's proclamation that the frontier was closed, James Hughes—like the United States did through the Spanish-American War—created new frontiers abroad.[13]

Hughes encountered problems in Mexico because he disagreed with his father—not about the power of place to change people's lives but about the use of border crossing and mobility in both real and metaphorical senses, as well as about what constituted liberation. When the young Hughes arrived in revolutionary Mexico brooding about race- and class-based injustice, he hoped he would find an alternative to Jim Crow. Hughes was interested in large-scale, systemic changes in the racial and class order, and Mexico seemed to be undergoing such radical change. As Hughes wrote of a later trip to Mexico in the 1930s, "I was then all in favor of working to change the basic economics of the world" (if he sounds a little conservative here, it may be because *I Wonder as I Wander* was published shortly after his appearance before the House Un-American Activities Committee). In contrast, when James Hughes arrived in Mexico before the revolution, he hoped to achieve the financial success foreclosed to him in the United States by taking advantage of the rapidly growing economy fostered by Porfirio Díaz's dictatorship, which benefited its foreign investors while leaving the majority of the Mexican population destitute. James left the United States because of the racial order, but he was more interested in his own individual advancement than in eliminating the social hierarchy. The *Porfiriato* made James's move to Mexico possible; then, unwittingly, he also benefited from the revolution. As Hughes notes, "All the white Americans had to flee from the Toluca district of Mexico, because of the rising nationalism," so his father's complexion, somewhat unexpectedly, enabled him to become "the general manager of an electric light company belonging to an American firm in New York."[14]

Despite his bitterness toward the United States and the racism that impacted his life there, James Hughes was not terribly interested in community uplift. In a 1931 letter to his son he acknowledges, "The revolution has done more good for this country than the thirty years peaceful reign of Porfirio Díaz, and the Indian has taken advantage of his changed condition to improve himself"; however, more than anything else, James was concerned for his own personal economic success. As Hughes notes in *The Big Sea*, his father "wanted to go away to another country, where a colored man could get ahead and make money quicker." In this way, James Hughes's vision of his own freedom, tied largely to moneymaking, had more in common with the classic individualist ethos of the frontier and less in common with the communal visions of racial progress promoted by western blacks like Anita Scott Coleman. After James's death, Langston compiled a list of the books in his father's library, reflecting the frontierist lifestyle and persona he had cultivated: books on rifle firing, irrigation, swine husbandry, peach culture, and horse breeding, for example, paint a picture of James Hughes as a frontiersman trying to tame and civilize the wilderness. According to his son, once James found a place where he could pull himself up by his bootstraps, he remained there—isolating himself from his family, from his past, and from his race. Rather than remaining mobile, he became static, in a sense building borders around himself to create distance from African Americans and other people of color. In *The Big Sea*, Hughes reveals that his father accused him and his mother of being "just like niggers. . . . Always moving!" This comment emphasizes the

ties Hughes sees between place and race, between mobility and antiracist attitudes. Hughes is a traveler who dreams of racial liberation; his
father, on the contrary, is a critic of both mobility and African America.
Although encounters like this one may have caused Hughes to become
disenchanted with his father, his affection for revolutionary Mexico and
its democratic possibilities remained salient to him for the rest of his
life. In "Just Traveling" he points out the following irony: "My father
took me right down into a revolution," he writes, "and ever since I've
been a revolutionary."[15]

Given their different political, economic, racial, and personal stances,
it is unsurprising that Hughes's portrayal of his father in *The Big Sea* is
unrelenting in its criticism. There, he proclaims that his 1919 "summer
in Mexico was the most miserable I have ever known." Interestingly,
although James Hughes remained committed to Mexico after his move
there in 1903—never returning to the United States for more than a
business trip—Hughes describes him as *"muy americano,"* as not Mexican
at all. He writes, "My father was what the Mexicans called *muy americano,*
a typical American. He was different from anybody I had ever known.
He was only interested in making money." Hughes emphasizes his father's individualism and goes on to explain that this solitude is not just
interpersonal but also geographic. The black community in the United
States, he suggests, was also interested in making money, but "they were
always moving around from job to job and from town to town" to make
the necessary funds to spend—not surplus to keep.[16]

Although his son, adopting the Mexican perspective, saw James
Hughes as *muy americano,* particularly in relation to capitalism, he may
not have seen himself that way. Father and son had very different ideas
about what it meant to be American—and both were complicated and,
at times, paradoxical. Hughes contested a hegemonic Americanness
(here, I refer specifically to the United States, not to a hemispheric
American identity), which he saw as aligned with provincialism, white
supremacy, and classism. Despite his critiques of the United States and
his wide-ranging travels elsewhere, however, he retained his abiding love
for the nation and its promises. He turned to its working classes and
people of color as the subjects of his literature, and he used his writing
to work for justice, as evidenced by his famous poem "I, Too." James,

in contrast, entirely rejected the United States on account of its racism; he would never return to the land of his birth. His bitterness in the face of racism, however, never inspired him to work for systemic change or caused him to have much empathy for the oppressed working classes and people of color in the United States (or, for that matter, in Mexico). Instead, his attitude toward African Americans and Indians was largely disdainful, despite his personal experiences with institutional oppression. Hughes, of course, chalks this up to his father's patterning himself after hegemonic Americanness, particularly the white US capitalists whose moneymaking James so admired. But how could James both embrace "typical Americanness" and reject the United States with such virulence? It may make more sense to see James Hughes's contempt for African Americans and the working class as an outgrowth of the prerevolutionary Díaz regime and its positivist philosophy, which resulted in a widespread belief in social Darwinism among Mexico's elites. This marries his pro-capitalist sentiments (made possible by the *Porfiriato*'s efforts to attract foreign investment)—as well as his disparaging attitudes toward African Americans, Indians, and the poor—to his abandonment of the United States. This also makes it possible to refigure James Hughes's frontierism. Rather than seeing it as a wholly US-derived set of characteristics, it can be thought of in terms of the northern Mexican frontiersman. As anthropologist Ana María Alonso notes, *norteños*—generally thought of as white, whereas southern Mexicans are generally thought of as indigenous—"were and are considered to be brave, independent, rebellious, self sufficient, and hardworking." Thus, what looks to Hughes to be *"muy americano"* is actually quite Mexican—albeit often reflective of Mexico's aristocracy.[17]

James Hughes also felt some fidelity to the traditions of his adopted home. These, however, were the traditions of the Spanish-descended *criollo* elite, not the traditions of Mexico's indigenous and mestizo proletariat. For example, in a 1931 letter to his son, James complained that Americans are generally rude: "You know manners—such as they are—is the principle [*sic*] thing in Mexico and elsewhere, except in the U.S." (This proclamation is in response to a visit by Louise Thompson, who failed to offer James a cigarette.) Here, however, he does not claim a Mexican identity (he emphasizes "Mexico and elsewhere"); rather, he disclaims Americanness—at least the Americanness of blacks and the working class. Arguably, to claim Mexican identity in 1931 would be to align too closely with the *indios* and mestizos, who had gained a greater foothold in Mexican politics and the arts. James's only friends and support system in Mexico were three elderly *criollo* women, the Patiño sisters. Hughes describes them as "the color of parchment, a soft ivory-yellow—the blood of Spain overcast just a little by the blood of Mexico—for they were not Indians. And they were not revolutionists. They had adored the former dictator-president, Porfirio Díaz, and when they wanted to speak of some one as uncouth, they said: '*Muy indio.*' Very Indian!" These are the racial politics James Hughes adopted in Mexico; accordingly, he distanced himself from the poor and the indigenous, just as he distanced himself from African Americans. "My father hated Negroes," Hughes remarks in *The Big Sea*. And he hated Mexicans, too: "He said they were exactly like the Negroes in the United States, perhaps worse"; he characterized them as "ignorant and backward and lazy" and "very bad at making money." Even though James Hughes admired the elites of his adopted home, Langston did not consider his father Mexican—and neither did James himself, so shaped were his attitudes about white supremacy and individual financial gain. Distancing himself from both Mexico and the United States, James cultivated a radical individualism—isolated, selfish, and unmoored from ethnic and national communities, although informed by some of their ideologies, such as the frontier. James's transnational engagement was always an outgrowth of capitalist globalization, while his son's was both cross-cultural and modeled after proletarian internationalism; both their perspectives were complicated outgrowths of their mediations between Mexico and the United States. In later years, his politics would inspire Hughes to join the John Reed Club in Carmel, California, through which he supported a dockworkers strike in San Francisco. Reed, of course, was famous for *Ten Days that Shook the World* (1919), his document of the Russian Revolution. Before that, he had spent months alongside Pancho Villa, and he published *Insurgent Mexico* in 1914.[18]

When Hughes fled to Columbia University in 1921 to get closer to Harlem, it was less a flight away from Mexico and more a flight away from his father. As a result of their increasing estrangement, Hughes's time in Mexico did not meet his hopes and expectations. He made fewer connections with other people of color than he had envisioned, and he became more isolated. He describes Toluca as "a strange land in a mountain town, where there wasn't a person who spoke English." Indeed, Hughes paints a portrait of his lonesome, seventeen-year-old self in the mold of western solitude: "I took long rides on a black horse named Tito to little villages of adobe huts, nestled in green fields of corn and alfalfa, each with a big church with a beautiful tower built a hundred years ago, a white Spanish tower with great bells swinging in the turret." His rather cinematic description of himself as a borderlands loner is made even more so by his description of the "weekly movie show" in Toluca, the only social outlet for the town, so "you . . . stuck it out until the last cowboy had killed the last redskin and smothered the heroine in a kiss."[19]

Although his strained relationship with his father resulted in an overall negative experience, Hughes had some moments that were more like his dreams during his train ride—moments when he formed cross-racial alliances that subverted his father's ideologies, quite often by directly subverting his father. He describes how he and his father's housekeeper, a "tall Mexican woman with a kind, tan-brown face," "teamed up against" James to "order all kinds of good things to eat from the shops." This was in opposition to the frugal diet James usually adhered to in order to save money, but it was also a way to benefit a larger network of disadvantaged people. James had forbidden the housekeeper's children to eat at the house, so she was forced to take them leftovers. By ordering more food, she may have been able to provide more for her children. Hughes "would take the blame," using his modicum of privilege to benefit both himself and others—as well as to irk his father. He also reached out to his father's Indian *mozo* (servant boy) Maximiliano: "I gave Maximiliano my spare centavos and cigarettes, and we became very good friends," Hughes notes. "My father paid Maximiliano and the cook almost nothing," he continues, "but he gave me ten pesos a week allowance, which I used to share with the two servants." In exchange, Hughes earned not only Maximiliano's friendship but also the benefits of his indigenous knowledge: "He taught me how to ride a horse without saddle or stirrups, how to tell a badly woven serape from a good one, and various other

Hughes's Mexico, ca. 1919, including snapshots of James N.
Hughes (upper right) and Maximiliano (lower left). (Beinecke
Rare Book and Manuscript Library, Yale University; reprinted
by permission from Harold Ober Associates, Incorporated, as
agents for the Estate of Langston Hughes)

things that are useful to know in that high valley beneath the white volcanoes." These interactions with the Mexican proletariat exemplify Hughes's early gestures toward building cross-racial, transnational coalitions. He would continue to do this through his writing.[20]

By his second summer in Mexico, Hughes "began to wish for some Negro friends to pal along with," for "with my bad Spanish, I was still shy about making friends with the Mexicans." Despite his loneliness, he was able to form some cross-racial connections ideologically, if not interpersonally. With the revolution ongoing, Hughes had finally, by his father's estimation, learned to "ride rapidly enough and shoot straight enough to take care of myself in case of danger." He accompanied his father to his ranch outside of town, "a good day's ride over rocky roads and mountain trails, through majestic scenery." On the way, they passed the hanged bodies of three men who had been killed by "the Federal troops," who "left them hanging there as examples to others." Hughes describes this lynching scene in detail: "They were still there the day we passed, three poor Indian bandits with bare feet, strung from scrubby pine trees near the road, their thin dirty-white trousers flapping in the cold mountain wind. One had long black hair that lashed across his face. Their bodies swayed slowly in the high wind at the top of the pass, like puppets stiff across the sky." While the images Hughes employs—the rocky, mountainous terrain; the hanged bodies; the scrubby brush—are reminiscent of scenes from so many westerns, Hughes could not help but make parallels between these lynched, racialized bodies and the lynched bodies of African Americans in the United States, which also served as a public spectacle in the maintenance of a white-supremacist racial order. The NAACP had recently released its report titled *Thirty Years of Lynching in the United States, 1889–1918*, immediately preceding the "Red Summer," as James Weldon Johnson called it, of mob violence against African Americans. According to the Tuskegee Institute's data, seventy-six African Americans were lynched in 1919, the highest number in eleven years. The 1920 Republican Party platform encouraged the passage of antilynching legislation, but the Dyer antilynching bill would be defeated in 1922 and twice thereafter. During his lifetime, as W. Jason Miller points out, "Hughes addressed, referenced, responded, or alluded to lynching in nearly three dozen different poems." His chronicling of the lynching of the three Indians by Federal troops in Mexico echoes some of this poetry. Hughes describes the site of the lynching as "a high pass called *Las Cruces* (the Crosses)." The bodies of the three bandits at Las Cruces are thus not so subtly patterned after the crucifixion of Christ and the two thieves alongside him. In his poem "Christ in Alabama" (1931), Hughes uses similar references when he writes about the lynching of African Americans: "Most holy bastard / Of the bleeding mouth, / Nigger Christ / On the cross / Of the South."[21]

After seeing these bodies, Hughes's resistance to his father and his capitalist ideologies coalesces. As they ride through the ruins of a village, his father condemns the Zapatistas for being "bandits" who "loved to destroy property." Hughes pipes up: "I read somewhere that Zapata was a poor shoemaker, who wanted to get the land back for the peons." Their oppositional approaches to class politics are in stark relief here. Hughes's contention that Zapata—whose name means "shoe"—was a "poor shoemaker" can be juxtaposed with his description of the lynched bodies of "poor Indian bandits with bare feet." To do so reinforces Hughes's opinion of Zapata as one who worked to eradicate poverty and racism. Later, in *I Wonder as I Wander,* Hughes chooses a similar set of images to describe Haitian oppression during his travels there:

> Haiti was a land of people without shoes—black people, whose feet walked the dusty roads to the market in the early morning, or trod softly on the bare floors of hotels, serving foreign guests. Barefooted ones tending the rice and the cane fields under the hot sun, climbing mountain slopes, picking coffee beans, wading through surf to fishing boats on the blue sea. All of the work that kept Haiti alive, paid the interest on American loans, and enriched foreign traders, was done by people without shoes.

The wealthy of Haiti, he observes, emphasize their clothes and their shoes as markers of class privilege—about shoes, he muses, "perhaps they were symbols." In *The Big Sea,* when Hughes arrives in New York from Mexico, a Mexican he met on the ship "kept saying, . . . 'But where are all the poor people? *Caramba!* Everyone is dressed up here! Everybody wears shoes!'" Shoes serve as a symbol that has traction not only for Haiti but also for Mexico and the United States, transgressing national and racial lines. The image of shoeless people thereby expresses the transnational scope of Hughes's liberationist politics and poetics.[22]

Shortly after their conversation about the Zapatistas, Hughes declares to his father, "I think [I want to be] a writer." Whereas James envisions a life of moneymaking for his son during their trip to the ranch, Hughes envisions writing—and, specifically, writing in the service of social change—as his vocation. His father advises him to "learn something you can make a living from . . . , and don't stay in the States, where you have to live like a nigger with niggers." This statement encapsulates James Hughes's feelings about race and Americanness. He sees the racial order of the United States as limiting the moneymaking power of individual African Americans, but rather than staying to work for justice, he suggests resettlement and racial abandonment. Hughes replies, "But I like Negroes." Although he values travel as a way to expand perspectives and make transnational connections, he retains his fidelity to African America. At this point, he brings together his desire to write with his desire to work for liberation both in the United States and wherever global capitalism impacts the impoverished workers who are used to uphold it—from Haiti to Mexico and all the regions of the United States shaped by the Great Migration.[23]

Although Hughes was eager to leave Mexico, he found inspiration there for some of his early writings, which in turn became some of his first publications. As a young writer-activist, he aimed many of these early writings toward children—to whom he remained committed throughout his life and in much of his writing. In announcing in the *Crisis* the creation of the *Brownies' Book*, a magazine for children that published some of Hughes's early work, W. E. B. DuBois outlined the goals of the magazine, which included "to teach Universal Love and Brotherhood for all the little folk—black and brown and yellow and white." The *Brownies' Book* shared a transnational (even universal) and multiethnic perspective with Hughes, which made it a natural fit for some of his early writing. Its pedagogical imperatives, too, likely appealed to Hughes's commitment to social justice. Given Hughes's conviction that travel might serve a similar pedagogical function ("to teach Universal Love and Brotherhood"), it makes sense that his early contributions to the *Brownies' Book* would be travel writing from his time in Mexico. If, according to Hughes, travel can serve an important epistemic purpose to broaden perspectives and bridge differences, then by writing about Mexico in the *Brownies' Book*, he would be making these epistemic shifts accessible to African American children who—by virtue of race, class, and age—might otherwise be unable to experience new places.[24]

Hughes published four pieces in the *Brownies' Book* in 1921, before leaving Mexico for New York. The first was "Mexican Games," a description of children's games that Hughes addresses to his "Dear Little Friends." "These are three games which the children play in your beautiful neighbor country, Mexico," Hughes writes, simply. "I hope you will enjoy them." He also wrote a short morality play (the moral: give to the less fortunate) titled "The Gold Piece: A Play that Might Be True," which may or may not have a Mexican setting (its major characters are named Rosa and Pablo, suggesting a Latin American connection). In addition, he published two pieces of travel writing, "In a Mexican City" and "Up in the Crater of an Old Volcano." In these, Hughes makes clear efforts to connect his youthful readership with the culture, the landscape, and the people of Mexico, fulfilling the pedagogical goals of the *Brownies' Book* and his own desire to build cross-racial coalitions, particularly among the working class. Haas suggests that these publications from the *Brownies' Book* take a "tourist view" of Mexico, and "their focus on the picturesque sights of Mexico towns, landscapes, and local customs stress the country's otherness from the United States." While this may be true, Hughes's travel writing for the *Brownies' Book* also takes great pains to open up the nuances of race and class for its young readers. In this way, his writing is less about Mexican otherness and more about the impact of global capital on those living on the periphery of the United States.[25]

Even in this early writing for children, Hughes's attention to issues of race and class is obvious. In the opening paragraph of "In a Mexican City," he observes that "the poor folks never have shoes to wear" in Toluca, mobilizing early on what would become for him a symbol of the casualties of the wealth gap. He also mentions "a bare-footed old woman in a wide straw hat and long skirts" who "drives a little flock of white sheep down the street," gesturing toward the conditions of the working poor. He comments on the "Indians from the country" who sell goods in the marketplace, comparing the "Indian women with sacks of vegetables on their backs" to the "rich senorita with her black scarf draped gracefully about her shoulders"; he notes the "ragged brown boys seeking a chance to earn a few cents" and the "numberless beggars, blind, lame and sick beggars, all asking patiently for pennies or half-rotted fruits," thereby attending to the intersections of race and class. As Haas suggests, "In a Mexican City" is rather ethnographic in tone, but the core of Hughes's politics is implied when he comments about the role of economics in Toluca, making observations on the amount of furniture in the homes of the wealthy versus those of the middle or working class. He writes, "The poor here do not have much money"— presumably in comparison to the poor in the United States, thereby showing the differential impact of global capitalism in these locations.[26]

In "Up in the Crater of an Old Volcano," Hughes focuses more clearly on the development of cross-racial friendship than on the issue of class. In this essay, he tells the story of a two-day hike up the nearby volcano, Xinantecatl. Boys from the high school in Toluca invite Hughes to join them, and they share local knowledge with him, such as what he will need to take with him on the trip. Through this education in the local, Hughes is integrated into the community and gains a sense of belonging. This serves as a lesson to Hughes's readers in cross-racial understanding, as well as in the power of place to inspire and create a need for this understanding. At first, Hughes seems like an outsider to the group; he somewhat distances himself from the other boys when he remarks on their "Mexican politeness." Initially, their efforts to assimilate him seem to have the opposite effect, doing more to set him apart as a nonnative than to bring him into the fold. For instance, he expresses suspicion at their recommendation to bring onions as "the best things to smell if one began to feel ill" in the high altitudes. Yet before long, he determines, "These dark faced, friendly school boys were about like other dark-skinned boys of my own race whom I had known in the United States." As a result of this mutual recognition, it becomes possible for Hughes to claim a home in Toluca, no matter how disappointing his actual home life there was: "We in Toluca," he insists—including himself among its residents—"are not afraid of Xinantecatl. It is like a

well-known friend to us and one whom we see every day." Hughes not
only bridges the difference between himself and his Mexican companions
but also becomes part of the Mexican environment—the landscape itself
becomes a "well-known friend" to him.[27]

In addition to educating his "Dear Little Friends" in cross-racial
understanding and class-consciousness, Hughes submitted "The Negro
Speaks of Rivers" to *Crisis* editor Jessie Fauset, who was impressed with
his writing for the *Brownies' Book*. The *Crisis* also published another
poem by Hughes—"Mexican Market Woman" (1922)—and two essays featuring Mexico. "Mexican Market Woman," particularly when
read alongside "In a Mexican City," continues Hughes's focus on the
intersection of race and class in Mexico:

Langston Hughes (front row, third from left) with his Mexican companions,
ca. 1920. (Beinecke Rare Book and Manuscript Library, Yale University;
reprinted by permission from Harold Ober Associates, Incorporated, as
agents for the Estate of Langston Hughes)

This ancient hag
Who sits upon the ground
Selling her scanty wares
Day in, day round,
Has known high wind-swept mountains,
And the sun has made
Her skin so brown.

As revealed more directly in Hughes's "In a Mexican City," the market-place provides an opportunity to see "all sorts of people"—it becomes a microcosm of the society's class stratification. Here, in a simple, almost imagist poem, Hughes focuses on an indigenous peasant. Although he does not describe her in relation to other attendees at the market, her weathered brown skin reflects her class status. Later, Hughes would republish "Mexican Market Woman" in his book of poems for children, *The Dream Keeper and Other Poems.* "Mexican Market Woman" is thus a cross-written text aimed at both adults and children. Its lessons may be subtler than those taught in "In a Mexican City" or "Up in the Crater of an Old Volcano"—where they are absorbed not through pedantic statements but through affect—yet the poem retains the activist objectives of Hughes's work in the *Brownies' Book.*[28]

The same can be said of the Mexican essays Hughes published in the *Crisis:* "The Virgin of Guadalupe" (1921) and "The Fascination of Cities" (1926). "The Virgin of Guadalupe" tells the story of the revelation of Our Lady of Guadalupe to Indian peasant Juan Diego. Though Hughes makes no editorial comments about this narrative, there are several reasons why he might have thought the story was worth relaying to *Crisis* readers. First, Hughes's efforts to collect and replicate this story reflect his attraction to folk idioms, which he would utilize with respect to African America in his later writing. Second, the protagonist of this tale is a poor person of color, which appealed to his burgeoning racial politics. Third, the Virgin of Guadalupe as a syncretic religious figure—a hybrid figure that mediates between indigenous and non-indigenous sources for its mythos and symbolic language—may have been attractive to Hughes, who was interested in fostering cross-racial and cross-cultural exchange. Furthermore, he may have known that historical actors from Miguel Hidalgo to Emiliano Zapata had mobilized the image of the Virgin of Guadalupe in the service of indigenous liberation. Finally, the Virgin of Guadalupe—a product of colonialism and conquest, on the one hand, but a symbol of resistance, on the other hand—is also a transnational icon that, by the time of Hughes's visits to Mexico, had been declared "Queen of the Americas." As a result, when Hughes retells this story to the readership of the *Crisis*, it is suggestive of many of Hughes's more politicized preoccupations: to build a sense of pride in African American vernacular culture, to initiate cross-racial collaboration, to work against oppression, and to recognize both the pitfalls and the promises of transnational exchange—economically and culturally. "The Fascination of Cities" is also transnational, comprising short vignettes that describe fleeting moments in five different cities: Kansas City, Chicago, Mexico City, New York, and Paris. Each offers Hughes something different (an immersion in African American folk culture, an encounter with racism in an ethnically fragmented city, the excitement of an urban crowd, massiveness and anonymity, or an artistic avant-garde), yet taken together, they speak to the power of transnational urban experience to serve as inspiration for Hughes's aesthetic and political projects.

After these early pieces, Hughes did not write about Mexico again for almost a decade. During the 1920s he published the work that he has become most famous for—his groundbreaking poetry collections *The Weary Blues* (1926) and *Fine Clothes to the Jew* (1927). Then he wrote his first novel, *Not without Laughter* (1930). Beginning in 1931 James Hughes wrote his son a series of letters. James had suffered a stroke in 1922, and his health had gotten increasingly poor. After his son achieved some notoriety as a writer, he made an effort to reconnect with him. In the ten years since Hughes had left Mexico, however, it seems that his father's attitudes had changed very little. Common refrains in James's letters include queries about how much money Langston was making from his writing. He asks, "How many thousands of these books have been sold?" He advises Langston to scrimp and save: "If I had not saved my money when I was working and earned it I could not live today," he admits, "as I have been physically unable to do anything for over nine years, and have spent more money trying to get well than you will probably make out of these books." Later in the same letter he asks, "Are you saving your money, and have you got a bank account? If not, begin to do so at once, as brains are no account without money." Then—just in case his message is unclear—he adds a postscript: "Save your money. Don't let some nigger wench squander it all for you." He also suggests that his son cease writing in African American vernacular English. After reading *The Weary Blues* and *Not without Laughter,* James notes with some exasperation, "I think it's time for the old, Negro dialect to go out of date: in future writings, try to use good English, so that people can see that you are capable of doing so." Hughes, who was older now, had become more tolerant of his father's admonishments. He answers his father's letter by telling him about his book sales, although he admits he has published "three books and [has] practically no money." He closes with subtle sarcasm, which makes his continued adherence to a different set of perspectives clear: "If I make a lot of money from my next book I will come down and see you. . . . Thanks for all the good advice. I'm sure you're right." Hughes never saw his father again. James Hughes died later in 1934, and, pressured by family members who hoped for an inheritance, Hughes returned to Mexico to help settle his estate. Once there, he discovered that his father had indeed spent most of his savings on medical treatments and living expenses during the final years of his life. This discovery allowed Langston to shake off the cloying relatives who were pestering him to send them money. He was not mentioned in his father's will.[29]

On the one hand, this seems like a rather tragic ending to the turbulent relationship between father and son. They never truly reconciled. When James Hughes died, he was as difficult, as bitter, and as contrarian as ever; he never really acknowledged Langston's success. On the other hand, Hughes could finally experience Mexico unhindered by their strained relationship. He was able to immerse himself in the heady atmosphere of Mexico City after the revolution and partake of its thriving modernist scene, where the arts often harked back to indigenous themes and forms and flirted with the possibilities of leftist politics. In *I Wonder as I Wander* he writes, "the nearest I've ever come to *la vie de bohème* was my winter in Mexico." He shared an apartment with photographer Henri Cartier-Bresson and folklorist Andrés Henestrosa. "I met a number of painters," he relays, including "the sad Orozoco, the talkative Siqueiros, and the genteel Montenegro." He became good friends with Diego Rivera's second wife and muse, Lupe Marín, and was an acquaintance of Rivera himself. He reignited his friendship with artist Miguel Covarrubias, who had designed the cover of *The Weary Blues* back in Harlem and had recently returned to Mexico. From Rivera and Covarrubias, Hughes learned about Afro-Mexicans, "particularly in the Vera Cruz section of the coast where many of the people are dark indeed," thereby expanding his knowledge of the black diaspora. He admits, however, "In Mexico City I missed Negroes in larger numbers." Nonetheless, Hughes also wrote of his "affinity for Latin Americans, and the Spanish language." After Hughes and the Patiño sisters sorted out the details of his father's will, it was, he writes, "a delightful winter"— in stark contrast with his Mexican summers of misery as a youth. Again, in contrast with the time he lived under the thumb of his well-to-do but miserly father, he writes, "I can recall no period in my life when I've had more fun with less cash."[30]

A journal Hughes kept during his 1934–1935 winter in Mexico clearly articulates the ties he was making between nation, race, and class. It begins with an intensely local focus, replicating the immersion in the urban experience that his rather stream-of-consciousness "The Fascination of Cities" created in 1926, but centered on Mexico City. It is as though Hughes, wandering the avenues and plazas, used this notebook to jot down fragments of what he saw, creating memories and fodder for future writing. This record shows Hughes surrounded by the "scent of tortillas and damp masonry," "beggars and vendors walking in and out of restaurants," "lottery tickets everywhere," "street cars running close to the curb," "child vendors," "bull-fight posters," "lovers in the parks," and other fleeting images and sensory experiences. The most substantive part of this journal, however, is a section Hughes titled "Me and the White Race," in which the scope of his observations extends from the local to the transnational. "No hate—not bitter. Many friends," it begins. It then proceeds to list several topics—perhaps for future exploration: "race and bad manners," "race and economics," "race and ego," and "race and religion," among other themes familiar to readers of Hughes. The most revealing part of "Me and the White Race," however, may be

the following: "White liberals are not brave. [White] radicals are." He
continues, "Capital and spreading of international prejudice. Radicals
and international goodwill." This describes in more detail what was
only hinted at in Hughes's earlier Mexican writing: an awareness of the
impact of global capital on race and class politics. Hughes had begun to
develop this awareness during his early experiences of the revolution;
now, in the 1930s, he witnesses radical antiracist and proletarian politics gaining traction in the artistic and political circles within which he
moves in Mexico City. Interestingly, he also returns to a topic he first
considered during his 1920 train ride to Mexico: "Jews and Negroes"
as a way to articulate these politics. Again he points to the diasporic
experience that can serve as a point of departure for black-Jewish collaboration: "Jews are great internationalists," he writes. He continues,
perhaps thinking of his father, "Of course rich Jews and rich Negroes are
able to buy themselves out of the difficulties of race." Nonetheless, he
sees the possibility of cross-racial coalition building among the working
classes: "Therefore, to realize a new brotherhood, I count out the rich
of all races. They don't suffer enough. The poor, when they get wise
to themselves, will accomplish the real internationalism. Then me and
the white folks will be us. (In other words a united front from below.)"[31]

When Hughes returned to the United States in 1935, he remained
inspired by Mexico and once again used it as fodder for children's
literature. With Arna Bontemps (who also had experience with the
Mexican borderlands) he authored two books for young readers with
Mexican settings: *The Pasteboard Bandit* (written in 1935, published
1997) and *Boy of the Border* (written in 1939–1941, published 2009). As
Katharine Capshaw Smith argues in *Children's Literature of the Harlem
Renaissance*, the politics of *The Pasteboard Bandit* stems from postrevolutionary leftist ideologies in Mexico, for the figure of the "social
bandit" "bore immense symbolic power within Mexican popular culture" as a Robin Hood–like figure who swept in to save downtrodden
communities. "For Hughes and Bontemps," she suggests, "the bandit
represents the liberating possibilities of popular action, the capability
of overturning social oppression." This is also alluded to in *The Big
Sea*'s Christ-like portrayal of the three lynched bandits at the hands of
the Federal troops; likewise, James Hughes undermines the Zapatistas

by calling them "bandits," but they could be rethought as saviors of the people. In addition to being about class politics, *The Pasteboard Bandit* is a story of cross-racial and transnational coalition building, based on the friendship of mestizo Mexican and white American boys. As Smith writes, "the two African American writers depict the larger possibilities of cultural exchange" and "potential for the dissolution of national, cultural, and racial barriers."[32]

In *Boy of the Border*, Bontemps and Hughes use transnational travel as a mechanism to increase cross-racial understanding for their protagonist, Miguel, and for their readers. The story takes place in 1915, and the plot follows "a slender, brown boy" as he accompanies his uncle to drive a herd of horses from northern Mexico to Los Angeles. Along the way, Miguel befriends an Anglo-American boy in Arizona and is given a gift by a blanketed Navajo; he has a less positive experience with a "gypsy" boy. The authors' borderland and western experiences surely came into play as they collaborated on this book; the description of the protagonist's home and the presence of a worker named Maximiliano replicate Hughes's writing about his father's home in Toluca, and the descriptions of Los Angeles—including a chapter set in Watts—call to mind Bontemps's youthful experiences. And, like Hughes's other Mexican writing, the book includes as its backdrop the revolution: "There had been a revolution in Mexico and parts of the country were very unsettled," they write, which opened the door for bandits "raiding villages and stealing horses." In the beginning of the journey Miguel is the first to suspect that bandits are pursuing their party. On the way home from Los Angeles, when Miguel's new colt and its dam go missing, the party believes bandits stole them, but the horses are found later, having merely wandered off. As a result, the bandits' presence adds to Miguel's adventures, but they are never depicted as doing any damage in the narrative. Rather, when Miguel sees the bandits, "He could even make out that the bandit company wore no shoes," pointing to their poverty and making them more sympathetic and exciting than dangerous.[33]

Furthermore, *Boy of the Border* articulates a relationship involving Mexico, the United States, and Canada via a transnational American West. This becomes most evident when Miguel's uncle tells a folkloric story one night in camp. He sets the scene—the story takes place in "these [Mexican] plains and those that reach beyond them across the United States and to Canada."—and the legend has been told "from Mexico to the border of Canada," first among "different tribes of red men" and then among "white pioneers" as well, creating a narrative coherence across nation and race. These North American nations are unified by the depiction of the frontier as porous. Miguel does not even notice when he crosses the border: "he had been in the States several hours before he knew it," Bontemps and Hughes write. Miguel comments, "It doesn't look any different from Mexico." Although his uncle assures him that "Los Angeles will look different," even the city "seemed a good bit like his own village to Miguel."[34]

Boy of the Border thus acknowledges a transnational West, as well as the permeability and cultural hybridity of borderlands. But, at least according to Miguel's perspective, which side of the border one is on seems to make little difference. In Hughes's writing about African American experience in the borderlands, however, there is a difference. As he suggests when he writes of El Paso, borders have two sides, and for African Americans, life was sometimes better on one than the other. The same year Bontemps and Hughes wrote *The Pasteboard Bandit*, Hughes authored a short story titled "Flora Belle." The title character is an outcast, "the only Negro child" in Tall Rock, Montana. Later, she is one of only a few African Americans in Butte, and she remains distant from the others. She searches for a place to form community in the West, but Seattle, San Francisco, and Fresno all leave her lonely. Allmendinger draws a parallel to Thurman's *The Blacker the Berry* and suggests that, like Emma Lou, "Flora Belle discovers that the West offers no refuge for those who are racially ostracized." Yet whereas Emma Lou's family fled to the West to get away from southern blacks, Flora Belle's arrived in Tall Rock after fleeing a lynch mob in Texas that was pursuing her father, who had fought with a white man over his wages: "Her father had an idea of getting to Canada, fleeing like the slaves in slave days clean out of the United States, but gas and money ran out." The US West does not always offer black freedom—even in the economic sense that someone like James Hughes desired. Instead, freedom is imagined and at times accessed via transnational travel. The bounded US West in Hughes's writing seems to proffer little to African Americans—it is the borderlands that provide the critical difference for Hughes's place-based racial politics, enabling the imagination of cross-racial coalitions that lead to working-class liberation.[35]

PART III

One Who Arrived

Surely the best surrey had belonged to one of those
elegant Spanish families of early California who planted
avenues of palms on the approaches to their homes.
Perhaps the Conestoga had come over the western passes
with a white covered top. But what was this to him?
—*Arna Bontemps, "The Prizefighter and the Woman" (1947)*

What is Africa to me:
Copper sun or scarlet sea,
Jungle star or jungle track,
Strong bronzed men, or regal black
Women from whose loins I sprang
When the birds of Eden sang?
One three centuries removed
From the scenes his fathers loved
Spicy grove, cinnamon tree
What is Africa to me?
　　　　　—*Countee Cullen, "Heritage" (1925)*

CHAPTER 5

Mapping the New American Race

From New York to New Mexico—and Beyond

> Taos is an end-product. It is the end of the slope. It is
> an end-product of the Indians, an end-product of the
> Spaniards, an end-product of the Yankees and [P]uritans.
> It must be plowed under. Out of the fertility which death
> makes in the soil, a new people with a new form may
> grow. I dedicate myself to the swift death of the old,
> to the whole birth of the new. In whatever place I start
> work, I will call that place Taos.
> —*Jean Toomer, "A Drama of the Southwest: Notes" (ca. 1935)*

A photograph of Jean Toomer taken by Marjorie Content, his second wife, shows him posed at his typewriter, apparently at work. A piece of paper neatly winds its way through the typewriter rollers. On the table nearby are manuscript pages stacked haphazardly, a decanter, two casually tossed matchbooks, and an ashtray that barely peeks into the frame—the trappings of a modernist artist at work. Toomer seems to have paused in his writing, glancing up momentarily over the rims of his glasses, his hand poised lightly near his chin as he contemplates his next phrase, his brow slightly furrowed. The setting is perfectly staged. The items on the table are as carefully chosen and positioned as those in a still life. Books and trinkets are collected on the shelves as signifiers of cultural authority and erudition. Marjorie Content was far more than Toomer's wife; she was a noted photographer who ran in the same circles as Georgia O'Keeffe and Alfred Stieglitz, and this portrait has the posed look of a book jacket. Its artful arrangement makes one wonder whether Content simply took a snapshot of her husband, catching him during a lull in his work, or whether this tableau was planned and arranged, constructed to look spontaneous. Was Toomer even writing? Words are faintly visible on the paper emerging from his typewriter; the distance from which the photograph was taken obscures them. They are muted, apparitional, illegible.

The year is 1935, more than a decade after the publication of Toomer's *Cane* (1923). *Cane* has long been considered the harbinger of New Negro literature. The letters and memoirs of other New Negro writers such as Arna Bontemps and Wallace Thurman often cite *Cane's* publication as the moment in African American literary history when an experimental, modernist, New Negro aesthetic was born. Often these writers lament that *Cane* was Toomer's first and last published piece of avant-garde creative writing—and, many have argued, his first and last piece of New Negro writing. His cumulative output, as critics have noted time and time again, was small, comprising mainly poems and stories from *Cane* that appeared in modernist magazines such as the *Little Review, Broom,* and the *Dial* and were reprinted in foundational anthologies of New Negro writing such as Alain Locke's *The New Negro* (1925) and Countee Cullen's *Caroling Dusk* (1927). In addition to *Cane,* Toomer published only a handful of critical and political essays, some short stories and poetry, and a book of aphorisms titled *Essentials* (1931), based on his involvement with Russian mystic George Gurdjieff. Later in his life he published a series of short essays for the Religious Society of Friends. But by most accounts, this is a disappointing bibliography for an artist whose early career seemed so promising and whose first book inspired so many of his contemporaries. Toomer's literary history is, foremost, one of rejection. As a result, critical attention has focused largely on *Cane*; otherwise, it has fixated on the question of why Toomer failed to reproduce the kind and caliber of writing that characterized his early success. Such criticism, along with numerous biographies, have attempted to demystify Toomer's perceived failure as a writer after his stunning debut in 1923. As a result of this stubborn critical narrative, Content's portrait of Toomer posed at his desk, ready to write, can be viewed as pathetically contrived, as little more than a fantasy of authorship for a writer who, according to most critical accounts, had long been washed up by the time this photograph was taken.[1]

Jean Toomer in Taos, by Marjorie Content, 1935. (Copyright Estate of Marjorie Content; courtesy of Jill Quasha on behalf of Estate of Marjorie Content)

In essence, Content's photograph—and Toomer scholarship—represents the artist dichotomously. On the one hand, Toomer is the author of *Cane* and, as such, is conceived of as politically engaged, racially conscious, and aesthetically experimental. This Toomer—like so many New Negro writers who came after him—looks back to the southern past, the history of slavery, and black folk traditions as sources for emergent, modernist, New Negro sensibilities. On the other hand, there is the less celebratory post-*Cane* Toomer, who is thought of not as a poet but as a psychologist or a philosopher who has fallen hopelessly under the spell of his spiritual mentor Gurdjieff. This Toomer is less of a race man and more of a mouthpiece for "the harmonious development of man" described by Gurdjieff's psychological system. After *Cane*, Toomer left the New York literary scene behind. In doing so, he distanced himself from white avant-gardists such as Waldo Frank and the editors of the literary magazine *Broom*, who fostered his early work under the auspices of a primitivist fascination with black culture. He also left the burgeoning literary movement in Harlem behind—protesting his inclusion in Locke's *The New Negro* and refusing permission to reprint his work in James Weldon Johnson's revised *Book of American Negro Poetry* (1931). Toomer thereby deprives younger black writers of a model and a mentor and is depicted as increasingly reactionary, not only disclaiming New Negro writing but also rejecting an empowered, transnational black identity politics and perhaps even passing as white (particularly when he is married to white women). Toomer's adherence to Gurdjieffian teachings, his rejection of black heritage, and his departure from New York create the perfect storm for interpretations of him as failing to write anything approaching the literary merit of *Cane*. Thus, critics such as Charles Larson are left to wonder "why Jean Toomer failed as a writer after the publication of that one brilliant work. What diminished whatever potential there was in his later works?"[2]

These oppositional narratives of Toomer's life and career have remained relatively untroubled, but they are complicated by a closer look at Content's photograph. With the traces of writing barely visible on the manuscript pages that lay before him, this image does more than raise the question of whether and what Toomer was writing after *Cane*; it also expands an understanding of where Toomer was writing. The setting is not the familiar locations of *Cane* or of Toomer's life. It is not the lush Victorian interior of his childhood home in Washington, D.C., its propriety mimicked in the stifling, feminized, and bourgeois domestic realm of Mrs. Pribby's house in "Box Seat." It is not the dormitories where he lived and studied at Chicago's American College of Physical Training or at the University of Wisconsin–Madison, which may have been models for Paul's room in "Bona and Paul." It is not the smoky salons of the white Greenwich Village radical scene, where Toomer bantered with Waldo Frank and first encountered Georgia O'Keeffe, Lola Ridge, and Marjorie Content herself. Nor is it the eerie, gothic South woven throughout *Cane*'s first and third sections, beset by the terror of white-supremacist violence and inspired by Toomer's eight weeks as a substitute principal at an African American school in Sparta, Georgia. And finally, it is not the bustling streets of Harlem, its dimly lit clubs, or its raucous rent parties. Peering into the background of the photograph, beyond Toomer's table, one sees his books stacked neatly on the imperfectly curved shelves of a hand-built adobe house. He writes by the warmth of a semicircular kiva fireplace, a fixture of Pueblo architecture in New Mexico. The graceful, rounded pottery of southwestern tribal artisans is displayed on the mantel. Working against all the dominant narratives of Toomer's life, work, and geographies, Content's photograph finds him in the borderlands West, near Taos, New Mexico.

Like the words faintly visible on Toomer's manuscript in Content's photograph, the published footprint of Toomer's time in New Mexico is indistinct; the writing he produced there went largely unpublished during his lifetime and has rarely been republished in collections. The bulk of it—and other evidence of Toomer's life in New Mexico—remains archived. To read Toomer's archived work and explore his time in the borderlands West complicates previous understandings of him as a writer who, after *Cane*, never returned to "an open discussion of racial matters." The Toomer archive shifts the critical gaze away from *Cane*'s fragmented formal qualities, its postslavery folk South and bustling Great Migration North, and its modernist and New Negro sensibilities. While all these issues continue to define Toomer and his literary worth, his writing from New Mexico moves toward a more nuanced understanding of the matrix of race, location, and the modern as it proliferated in the contexts of both the New Negro movement and the interwar United States. This archive reveals that Toomer continued to discuss race, but this discussion took a different shape when it emerged from the United States–Mexico border region rather than from the locales that informed *Cane*—the rural South, the urban North, and the New York publishing milieu, with its burgeoning attention to black texts.[3]

For Toomer, place matters. When Content's photograph relocates Toomer in the Southwest, in an adobe house near Taos, it places him in a space connected with yet distinct from the sites that inform *Cane*, and it separates him from the Harlem scene within which he is usually read, however uncomfortably. Always informed by location, Toomer's writings about race differ depending on the locales they depict, within which they are produced, and where they are distributed and read. Despite his tenuous association with the Harlem scene (his activity there was largely limited to leading a short-lived Gurdjieffian group in the neighborhood), *Cane* is often read as presaging New Negro efforts to depict modern black urban life and mobilize folk traditions. *Cane*'s tripartite structure is organized by a North-South geography that has become familiar to readers of New Negro texts as the quintessential black geographic experience during these early years of the Great Migration. Indeed, it may be possible to claim that *Cane*'s three sections, curving from the South to the North and then returning to the South, set the precedent for this dialectic. When the text winds its way through the canebrakes, pine forests, obscure mill towns, and dusty back roads of rural Georgia, it tours the history of slavery and its living legacies under Jim Crow. When it dances through the vaudeville theaters, supper clubs, ballrooms, avenues, and college campuses of Washington and Chicago, it interrogates modern black urban life. And finally, when the last section of the book, "Kabnis," returns to the South, it constructs a disjointed gothic narrative in which the threat of racial violence and domination is ever present and the history of black enslavement is terrifyingly buried yet very much alive. When it moves from North to South, *Cane* defines the New Negro against the old; it examines the tensions between the younger generation and their older brethren who lived under and were conditioned by the regime of slavery and then the collapse of Reconstruction. Members of this older generation were, like Father John in

"Kabnis," becoming increasingly marginalized and forgotten, and by the early years of the 1920s, they were silent or dying.

Cane's power relies on the construction of these networks between the North and the South, as well as the racial configurations—sometimes radically different, but often troublingly similar—mapped onto them. And caught up in these geographic circuits are questions about racial ambiguity and passing (such as in "Fern" or "Bona and Paul")—topics rife in Harlem writing and outgrowths of the widespread anxiety about codifying black identity that had been present since colonial Virginia but was being revisited and growing more robust during the 1920s. This racial codification could work in two ways, with political imperatives that varied greatly: As a strategy among New Negroes, it could cohere the black community in the United States or even transnationally to make political gains. Yet among white-dominated institutions, such as the law, racial categorization was used to police the color line, maintain white supremacy, and uphold the dicta of Jim Crow. Nurtured and produced by the New York publishing scene and literati such as Waldo Frank, *Cane* falls in line with these classificatory impulses and uses geography to do so. Scholars have described Toomer as both validating and resisting these definitional projects. When they consider him solely as the author of *Cane*, critics tend to see Toomer as politically engaged. They detect in the text an investment in the politics of self-determination, in the recovery of black folk traditions, and in antilynching activism. When Toomer is seen as a writer of "a book by a negro about negroes" (as an early announcement in the *New York Times* described *Cane*), his work is typically thought to be a look back to an ancestral southern past and history of black enslavement, as well as to African American vernacular cultures as the source for emergent, empowered, and aesthetically experimental New Negro sensibilities. Unsurprisingly, during the watershed years of civil rights and black power in the 1960s, which led to the development of ethnic studies and increasing academic interest in African American writers, *Cane* was reintroduced to the public and, in particular, to the black community as a touchstone for black empowerment and pride. Upon its reissue in 1969, for example, one review triumphantly declared, "The Black Classic that Discovered 'Soul' Is Rediscovered after 45 Years."[4]

The characterization of Toomer as a rising star of the New Negro literati is complicated by his post-*Cane* biography. After 1923 he not only failed to publish widely but also distanced himself from African American identity. Although, as Content's photograph suggests, he continued to write throughout his life, a substantial amount of his work remains unpublished and unstudied. Although some of his post-*Cane* writing has been included in anthologies, much of it remains archived. And nearly all of it has been dismissed as inaccessible—and sometimes just plain terrible. Critics generally see the Toomer of this era as little more than a mouthpiece for his spiritual mentor Gurdjieff; they claim his writing became less experimental and adventurous and more autobiographical, a generic shift that tends to be misapprehended as a degraded form of writing because of its emphasis on realism and linear narration in lieu of fragmentation and aesthetic play. Toomer, then, has been characterized as a rather pathetic and solipsistic writer and rewriter of his autobiography, in the hope of using it as a parable for spiritual development and as a teaching tool for his reader-disciples—a hope dashed again and again when his work was rejected by publishers. As a result, the scholarly consensus is that Toomer never again achieved the "literary merit" of *Cane*. Rudolph P. Byrd writes, "After the discovery of Gurdjieff, the philosopher-poet of *Cane* vanished and in his place appeared a spiritual reformer and social critic whose obsession with Gurdjieff's theories weakened and then wasted his talent."[5]

Concomitant with his literary decline, Toomer scholars have to contend with his increasing detachment from the black community. He most famously distanced himself from his African American heritage on the occasion of his marriage to a white woman, modernist writer Margery Latimer, in 1931. He proclaimed:

> There is a new race in America. I am a member of this new race. It is neither white nor black nor in-between. It is the American race, differing as much from white and black as white and black differ from each other. It is possible that there are Negro and Indian bloods in my descent along with English, Spanish, Welsh, Scotch, French, Dutch, and German. This is common in America; and it

is from all these strains that the American race is being born. But the old divisions into white, black, brown, red are outworn in this country. They have had their day. Now is the time of the birth of a new order, a new vision, a new ideal of man. I proclaim this new order. My marriage to Margery Latimer is the marriage of two Americans.

Despite this pronouncement, the public saw the marriage as the racially transgressive union of a black man and a white woman. Toomer and Latimer were both well-known writers at the time—Latimer had recently published two positively reviewed novels, *We Are Incredible* (1928) and *This Is My Body* (1930)—so the news of their interracial marriage spread like wildfire. Newspapers hopelessly contorted Toomer's statement by focusing on the language of birth ("the American race is being born"), which suggests the scandal of interracial sex. According to biographers Cynthia Earl Kerman and Richard Eldridge, the "culmination of this unwanted publicity was in an article in *Time* under 'Races.' Entitled, 'Just Americans,' the article focused by innuendo on miscegenation and belittled what appeared to be Toomer's elaborate rationalization for marrying a white woman." Needless to say, articles of this type focused not only on Toomer's African heritage but also on Latimer's ancestry. Even reports of her death one year later emphasized, first, that Toomer was "part Negro" and then, not insignificantly, that Latimer was a descendant of poet Anne Bradstreet and Puritan clergyman John Cotton. This renders her not simply a white woman but one with a pure Anglo-Saxon lineage that could be traced to the early colonists and could not possibly remain unsullied by Toomer's "one drop" of black blood. Newspapers titillated their readers by printing lurid, sensationalist headlines announcing Latimer's death in childbirth: "Woman Novelist Called by Death: Death Ends Romance of Two Races—White Wife of J. Toomer, Novelist of Negro Blood, Expires in Childbirth." As a result, the birth of the new American race, literalized in Toomer and Latimer's child, becomes a tragic allegory for the perceived threat of miscegenation at a time when books like Lothrop Stoddard's *The Rising Tide of Color against White World-Supremacy* (1920) and fields like eugenics were at their peak of popularity.[6]

Around the same time as his proclamation about the new American race, Toomer began to speak out against his inclusion in *The New Negro* anthology. In an autobiographical piece written circa 1932 he complained, "I did not like the boosting and trumpeting and the over-play and over-valuation of the Negro, the products of Negro writers, which were springing up. I refused to have any part in this kind of displaying. I did not like the anthologizing which was springing up." Rather than seeing this anthologizing as a marginalized community's collaborative effort to gain a voice, he saw it as both a kind of racial chauvinism and a devaluing of African American experience as a generalizable human experience. Toomer even claimed that Alain Locke had used his short story "Fern" (from *Cane*) and a portrait of him in *The New Negro* without his permission. According to Locke, this foundational anthology's mission was to redefine and empower black America, to "document the New Negro culturally and socially, —to register the transformation of the inner and outer life of the Negro in America that have so significantly taken place in the last few years," and to enable the young black intellectual who arose from these changes to "speak for himself." As a result, when Toomer opposed his inclusion in Locke's anthology, he effectively rejected New Negro identity and, some have argued, African American identity altogether. He also famously turned down James Weldon Johnson's invitation to be included in his revised *Book of American Negro Poetry* (1931), although Toomer later regretted that decision, calling Johnson's anthology "one of the best." When Toomer refused these opportunities, he distanced himself not only from the African American community but also from the New York–based publishing houses that were seeking African American talent, which was particularly marketable during this period.[7]

Many of Toomer's contemporaries reacted to his departure from the New York publishing scene with lamentation and a sense of betrayal. Langston Hughes, in *The Big Sea*, recalls:

The next thing Harlem heard of Jean Toomer was that he married Margery Latimer, a talented white novelist, and maintained to the newspapers that he was no more colored than white—as certainly his complexion indicated. When the late James Weldon Johnson wrote him for permission to use some of his poems in the *Book of American Negro Poetry*, Mr. Johnson reported that the poet who, a few years before, was "caroling softly souls of slavery" now refused to permit his poems to appear in an anthology of *Negro* verse.

Although Kerman and Eldridge claim that black publications lauded Toomer and Latimer's marriage as a "form of race pride," comments such as Hughes's have a far different tenor. Although Hughes clearly respects Latimer's talent as a writer, he does not celebrate her pairing with Toomer as a meeting of minds or even as two people in love. Instead, he is somewhat disappointed, dismissing it as a symptom of Toomer's racial abandonment. For Hughes, Toomer's marriage signified, incontrovertibly, his departure from Harlem. And his departure from Harlem signaled his departure from the black community. In all, these events threatened Toomer's ability to produce the right kind of literature—or any literature at all. Hughes laments, "Harlem is sorry he stopped writing." Arna Bontemps's assessment of Toomer is even bleaker: Toomer "faded completely into white obscurity." He continues, "The rumor that Toomer had crossed the color line began circulating when his name stopped appearing in print," suggesting that Toomer "is on record as having denied later that he was a Negro. . . . At that point, it seems, Jean Toomer stepped out of American letters." Contemporary critics Rudolph P. Byrd and Henry Louis Gates Jr. have followed in the tradition of Hughes and Bontemps; they insist that when Toomer refuses essentialism, he begins passing.[8]

Oddly enough, although Harlem's New Negro movement was liberating and empowering for other young writers of color—some of whom, like Hughes, Thurman, and Bontemps, flocked to Harlem from the West to take part in it—Toomer came to see Harlem, and New York in general, as a place of classification and circumscription. And his resistance to such classification undoubtedly impacted his ability to publish. He turned down the black mentors and editors who wanted to provide him with a forum, and he sabotaged his relationships with white writers and editors who took an interest in his work, however puerile that interest was. The 1920s gave rise to a variety of projects that sought to define race, from Marcus Garvey's message of Pan-African unity and

his declaration that black is beautiful to the "one drop rule." As George
Hutchinson remarks:

> Indeed, the great irony of Toomer's career is that modern
> American racial discourse—with an absolute polarity between
> "white" and "black" at its center—took its most definite shape
> precisely during the course of his life. The United States would be
> more segregated at the time of Toomer's death than it had been at
> the time of his birth, despite the dismantling of some of the legal
> bulwarks of white supremacy.[9]

During Toomer's lifetime, legislation such as the 1924 Virginia Racial
Purity Act was one strong arm of a cultural imperative toward racial
determinacy. So too, however, was aesthetic production and literary publication, which were encouraged to represent authentic African American
experience, perhaps reducing its complexity in the process. This was
fostered not only by black nationalist politics, which surged through
Harlem in these days, but also by the white publishing marketplace,
which had what Toomer called a "thirst for the exotic." Narratives of
Toomer's career that focus on his failure after *Cane* are bound up in this
cultural imperative for racial codification. They suggest that if Toomer
had continued to write books "by a negro about negroes," he may have
achieved greater literary acclaim. Yet as Toomer's rebuffs of Locke and
Johnson and the regretful recollections by Hughes and Bontemps indicate, he was notoriously uncomfortable with these impulses toward racial
classification, definition, and self-definition and their relationship to the
literary marketplace. As he wrote in a letter to Johnson regarding *The
Book of American Negro Poetry*, "I do not see things in terms of Negro,
Anglo-Saxon, Jewish, and so on . . . I see myself as an American, simply
an American. . . . I see our art as primarily American art and literature.
I do not see it as Negro, Anglo-Saxon, and so on. Accordingly, I must
withdraw from all things that emphasize . . . racial or cultural divisions."
Such a withdrawal was necessary, he claimed, regardless of its impact
on his career as a writer. When he chose to distance himself from the
New Negro, he also chose to distance himself from New York and the
publishing industry that could have fostered and distributed his work.[10]

Whereas New York exerted a pull over writers such as Bontemps, Thurman, and Hughes, who sought a vibrant black community, for Toomer, it necessitated leave-taking. He first went to Chicago, but even there, "the anthologies had preceded me. . . . Some . . . did know of the collections, and they formed pictures and feelings about me based on their impressions of my work and my name appearing in these collections." He describes his response to this codification as "a general countermovement." On the one hand, this countermovement involved his refusal to be further anthologized and his disassociation from the New Negro. On the other hand, this countermovement was a literal movement across space and geography. Whereas legions of young African Americans migrated to Harlem to find themselves, their community, their artistic voice, their fortune, and their freedom in this vibrant urban geography, Toomer moved away from it. In *The Big Sea*, Hughes acknowledges this nexus of race and geography when he describes Toomer's travels and notes that Toomer is "never seen on Lenox Avenue any more." He goes on to ask rhetorically (and with a hint of snipe), "Why should Mr. Toomer live in Harlem if he doesn't care to? Democracy is democracy, isn't it?"[11]

The post-*Cane* Toomer who is so maligned by critics is the Toomer who left New York and the New Negro behind. But this portrayal is complicated when Toomer's experiences in New York and with the literary communities there are examined more closely. Toomer grew up in Washington, D.C., and spent time in the Midwest, where he attended schools in Chicago and in Madison, Wisconsin, in addition to his famous stint in Sparta, Georgia, that shaped *Cane*. In comparison and in total, the time Toomer spent in New York was brief; he was never really committed to the city. Furthermore, during his time in New York he was rarely in Harlem and never lived there. In these years, Harlem had not quite burst onto the literary scene the way it would after he left. Most of the time Toomer spent in Harlem consisted of brief visits after he published *Cane*, during which he tried (fairly unsuccessfully) to spread Gurdjieffian teachings to the black community. Although he was not in New York very often or for very long, he became somewhat involved with the bohemian—and largely white—literary circle in Greenwich Village, mainly through his association with Jewish writer and erstwhile friend and mentor Waldo Frank, who introduced him to Lola Ridge, an editor at the avant-garde magazine *Broom*. As a result of Toomer's links to this circle, critics Charles Scruggs and Lee VanDemarr have read Toomer in the tradition of Greenwich Village radicals like Randolph Bourne. They do not consider Toomer's disassociation with African American identity a racial betrayal; rather, they see it as engendering a "hyphenated," multiracial America that is parallel to the cosmopolitanism iterated by Bourne in his famous 1919 essay "Trans-National America." Because of his connections to this radical community, and because of the associations critics have made between *Cane* and the later imperatives of the New Negro movement that would follow in its wake, Toomer has often—and possibly incorrectly—been considered in the context of New York, despite the relatively little time he actually spent there.[12]

The problematic alliance between Toomer and New York is made easier by "Americans and Mary Austin," an essay he wrote for the radical *New York Call* in 1920. He composed this piece in response to an essay by Mary Austin titled "New York: Dictator of American Criticism" and published in the *Nation* three months earlier. In it, Austin rejects New York's centrality in American letters by suggesting that a turn toward regionalism would reveal a more authentic—and, ultimately, less ethnically inflected—America. She takes Waldo Frank's *Our America* (1919) to task in particular. This novel, she claims, is a misrepresentation of the nation because it refuses to go beyond its New York–based myopia. She suggests that the small-town Midwest or the American West would provide more realistic and authentic representations of the nation. Her text, however, smacks of anti-Semitism. This is implicit in her attack on Frank, and it is explicit when she states that New York's prominence is problematic because it is a "half-way house of immigration" and thus cannot produce truly American literature. "Can the Jew," she asks rhetorically, "become the commentator, the arbiter, of American art and American thinking?" If New York is an ethnic space, teeming with Jewish and other immigrants who threaten Anglo-American hegemony, Austin sees the provinces as a more authentic—and white—America. The West is not racially pure, but for Austin, people of color, including Native Americans, represent an eternal primitive. Unsurprisingly, she critiques Frank for his woefully inadequate treatment of indigenous people, claiming, "a chapter on the Southwest [is] stuffed with encyclopedic information about the Aztecs, who never occupied the territory of the United States, and some superficial observations of Pueblo Indians." But regardless of this critique, Austin's West is certainly not one that incorporates Jews or African Americans.[13]

Toomer's "Americans and Mary Austin" lambasts both her anti-Semitic version of American identity and her adherence to regionalism, and it is the first time he theorizes about a new, mixed American race. He writes, "We are some distance from a realization of the race to be known as the American, yet in general contour and aspirations it is visible to those who see. It is certain that it will be a composite one, including within itself, in complementary harmony, all races." If, as Toomer claims, American identity will consist of a "complementary harmony" of "all races," then New York—conceptualized as a space where ethnic mixture and multiplicity already occur (the very "half-way house of immigration" Austin attacks)—is certainly not incapable of representing American identity. On the contrary, it is the only place truly able to articulate it. As a result, Toomer writes, "I am led to conclude that New York and New Yorkers are dictators of American criticism [because] they are doing the job better than any others are capable of doing it." Scruggs and VanDemarr rearticulate Toomer's argument succinctly: he "defended New York's cultural ascension as having occurred through merit; the problem with the provinces was that they remained provincial." This essay, however, was written three years before *Cane*'s publication and long before the New Negro movement gained prominence on the American literary scene. New York was a place of possibility for Toomer in 1920, a place that foretold a mixed-race American future, and it remained that way throughout the years he was writing *Cane*. By the time the New Negro announced itself in Locke's anthology in 1925, Toomer had left the city and the black community.[14]

The year Locke's anthology was released saw Toomer's "general countermovement" away from the New Negro that brought him to New Mexico for the first time. Indeed, by the time Content took her photograph of Toomer in 1935, he was already a well-versed New Mexican traveler. He lived in the borderlands West sporadically and intermittently from 1925 to 1947. Like many artists and writers, Toomer was invited to Taos, New Mexico, for the first time by art patron, socialite, memoirist, and activist Mabel Dodge Luhan, who encouraged him to consider founding a Gurdjieffian center for spiritual development there. Although his work on behalf of Gurdjieff brought him to Taos, Toomer continued to visit New Mexico long after they severed ties, believing perhaps that New Mexico could provide the fulfillment that Gurdjieff ultimately could not. When Toomer arrived in Taos, it was already a landscape crowded with artists and writers. Realist painters, such as those involved with the Taos Society of Artists, had been active in the region since well before World War I, and the area opened up to modernists after Luhan's arrival in 1917, when she began promoting it to Willa Cather, D. H. Lawrence, Georgia O'Keeffe, and Andrew Dasburg, among others. Many of these figures represent New Mexico and the Greater Southwest as dehistoricized and timeless, and they often construct it in opposition to paradigmatically modern urban spaces, particularly New York. Creating nostalgic, primitive renderings of the landscape and of Native and Mexican Americans, they represent the Southwest, and especially the Pueblo Indians, as untouched by modernism's directive to "make it new." Needless to say, the primitivism of these writers and artists was similar to that of the whites who sought contact with black culture in New York. For instance, Charlotte Osgood Mason, one of the most well known white patrons of New Negro writers such as Zora Neale Hurston and Langston Hughes, had been fascinated with Native Americans.

After his initial visit to Taos in 1925, Toomer stayed in contact with Luhan and visited New Mexico often with his family in later years, taking up residence in Taos and other nearby towns. These visits included a trip in 1931, after Toomer's marriage to Latimer, and another in 1934, when he and Content were married by the Taos justice of the peace. They, along with Toomer and Latimer's daughter, Argie, returned in 1935 and again in 1939, after a trip to India. There were scattered trips in the 1940s, and they visited for the final time in 1947. During these stays, Toomer worked on a surprising array of texts: undated notes, drafts, manuscripts, and typescripts across literary genres that are, for the most part, autobiographical.

Toomer's time in New Mexico has largely escaped the gaze of criticism. The only published work consists of the fragments reproduced in

A Jean Toomer Reader: Selected Unpublished Writings, edited by Frederik L. Rusch, and contributions to the "New Mexican Writers" section of the *New Mexican Sentinel* that were reprinted and briefly addressed by Tom Quirk and Robert E. Fleming in *Jean Toomer: A Critical Evaluation*. Most of his writing from the West, and most of the evidence of his time there, remains archived. The most substantive texts in this archive include a series of essays, all undated but likely written around 1940, titled "Noises at Night," "New Mexico after India," and "To This Land Where the Clouds Fall." There is also a play titled "A Drama of the Southwest," undated but likely written around 1935. Toomer produced an undated draft titled "Sequences" after 1945, comprising a series of short sketches of New Mexico. Around the same time be began to draft what appears to be the foundation of a novel (untitled) in a notebook. While in New Mexico, Toomer likely continued to work on his long poem "The Blue Meridian," which contains southwestern imagery and was first published in *The New Caravan* in 1936, as well as his cryptically titled autobiography, "Book X." He wrote several other poems set in the borderlands West that remained unpublished until the 1988 compilation *The Collected Poems of Jean Toomer.*[15]

This work complicates previous understandings of Toomer as a writer who, after *Cane*, never again discussed racial matters. It reveals that, on the contrary, Toomer continued to discuss race, but he did so in a much different form. Looking westward shifts the critical optic away from *Cane*'s fragmented, formal qualities and its modernist, New Negro sensibilities and toward a more nuanced understanding of the geographic and discursive matrix of race and location. When Toomer is situated in the West, his writing about race does not disappear—far from it. Indeed, his message about racial mixing as the touchstone for American identity remains remarkably consistent throughout his written corpus, from "Americans and Mary Austin" onward. The West is ultimately a far more amenable environment for the construction and distribution of this message—an environment that makes this message legible, whereas before it was seen only as eccentric or reactionary. It is, in the end, not Toomer's discourse about race that changes throughout his career but the location within which he sees this race emerge: a shift from New York to New Mexico.

Like Toomer's previous work, his writing from New Mexico uses the spatial to describe the new and the old, as well as their relationship to ideas of race. In *Cane*, semicircles drawn on the first page of each section of the book demarcate the movement from South to North to South. These curves represent the geographic trajectory of the Great Migration, while the circular shape they form when imagined together is a way to visualize how the New Negro is distinct from the southern folk past yet, at the same time, looks back to, examines, and embraces this past as an inspiration for modernist aesthetics. In the notebook Toomer kept on New Mexico, he also employs drawn shapes, derived from geography, to describe racial identities. Here, he uses two slopes extrapolated from the mountain scenery surrounding the Taos Valley. In this notebook, the mountains, the rivers, the horizon, and other landmarks describe the emergence of the new American race realized in the West. Toomer writes:

> Two mountain ranges face each other across the river, across the valley. To the east is the Sangre de Cristo, to the west the Jémez. How far it is between them I do not know. Sometimes it seems that a mighty leap would swing you through the air from one to the other. Sometimes it seems that you would trudge on for days, through a sculptured land that defies description, before reaching the other side. If you arc between two worlds, which way?

This description of two mountain ranges, their faces descending toward each other to meet in the valley below, suggests the image of two slopes that reappears in Toomer's "Sequences." There, he muses, "Man, in the valley, has the choice of climbing one or the other" of "two slopes (symbolized by the Sangre and the Jémez ranges)." The epigraph of Toomer's play "A Drama of the Southwest" also mentions these slopes and ultimately ties them to his vision for a multiethnic new American race that emerges from the desert landscape of the borderlands West: "Taos is the end-product. It is the end of the slope. It is an end-product of the Indians, an end-product of the Spaniards, an end-product of the Yankees and [P]uritans. It must be plowed under. Out of the fertility which death makes in the soil, a new people with a new form may grow."

The language of fertility and fecundity in the arid desert soil mimics modernist tropes of regeneration. The "new people with a new form," regenerated from this environment, represent Toomer's multiethnic new American race.[16]

The New Mexican landscape is tied to this racial formation, and Toomer's western writings are rife with lyrical descriptions of it. He paints the mountains and the sky rising above the Taos Valley with the vivid poeticism he uses to describe the Georgia pines and canebrakes in *Cane*. Maintaining his interest in the earth (as a young man, Toomer studied agriculture at the University of Wisconsin, and he would later retire to a farm in Bucks County, Pennsylvania), Toomer frequently employs images of farming, particularly of tilling the soil, when he describes the preconditions for germinating the new American race. In "Sequences" he writes:

> Oh traveler, oh modern tourist rolling rubber, as you shuttle to and from auto court in Santa Fe to cabin camp in Taos, from auto motor court in Taos to motel in Santa Fe, stop your car just once where the highway passes the side of the Chama gap, get off the paved road and touch the earth and take into yourself the dust of your people. Those ancient people had red skins, and some dark skins, and a few white. What matter the skin color of them or yourself. They are your people. My people are the people of the earth. Today, yesterday, tomorrow.

At this point in the text, Toomer draws a triangle. Then he continues: "They touch at points, at angles only." When he scrawls this triangle, much like the curves drawn at the beginning of *Cane*'s three sections, Toomer provides a kind of geometry for his writing and his ideas about race. This triangle is a reminder of the northern New Mexico mountain ranges—the "slopes" of the Sangre de Cristo and Jémez. The triangular form replicates the mountain peaks visually on the page. Furthermore, its three sides join together like the Indian, black, and white influences that mingle in Toomer's conception of the new American race—the "red skins, . . . dark skins, and a few white." And especially, given its placement in the text, the three sides of the triangle join "today, yesterday, and tomorrow"—a temporal mapping that gestures toward the newness, the futurity of the new American race.[17]

This triangle is not the only map in Toomer's New Mexican writing. He also linguistically maps New Mexico in conjunction with other sites, both transregionally and transnationally. These are often familiar sites that appear in his biography, his experience, and his imagination. And, like so many writers associated with the New Negro movement and American modernism more generally, although he can leave it behind physically, Toomer cannot leave New York unconsidered. As a result, he places these sites in dialogue, constructing the geological terrain of New Mexico in relation to the "man-made canyons of New York." He writes:

> In times past, I had always come to New Mexico from the eastern states of America. I had greeted Raton Pass and the land extending southwestward and beyond, having in the background of my mind the low soft country of the eastern seaboard, the prairies of the middle west, commerce, industry, and of course the man-made canyons of New York. New Mexico had always looked grand, open, sunlit, a summit of ancient earth and historic peoples.

In this essay, titled "New Mexico after India," Toomer suggests that, when contrasted with New York, New Mexico becomes a space of the racialized, eternal primitive, as it is so often represented in the work of modernist artists. When he describes New York's high-rises and skyscrapers, its asphalt streets and concrete sidewalks as "man-made canyons," he emphasizes the human acts of technological modernization that enable the construction of this unnatural environment. In contrast, New Mexico's stunning geology is construed as entirely pristine, untouched, and premodern. While New York invokes modernity, New Mexico evokes the ancient in its sedimentary strata—in the canyon's earthen layers, history is seen baldly, written in the land itself.[18]

When he sets New Mexico in contradistinction to New York, thus viewing it as more primitive than the urban East, Toomer also describes it as a place where he is stripped of language. In the context of modernist primitivism, the West appears to be an atavistic, prelinguistic space:

I have never tried to put in words the unique gift of New Mexico to me. It is enough that I feel it, I know it, that I recognize it without need of words. Something of New Mexico came to me for the first time fifteen years ago. It was a penetration deep under the skin. Ever since then there has existed a special polarization between this human being and the people and earth of the Southwest.

Fifteen years prior to writing this essay, Toomer visited New Mexico for the first time. He had recently left his failed Gurdjieff workshop in Harlem. It was the same year *The New Negro* was published and "Harlem [became] sorry [Toomer had] stopped writing." His western wordless-ness, then, makes more sense in the context of his biography than in the context of a modernist primitivism that attempts to access an authentic, prelinguistic, premodern, and essentialized racial Other. When Toomer's struggles to publish after *Cane* are taken into account—struggles that are repeatedly documented in optimistic letters to acquaintances that insist his next publication is just around the corner—it enables an enhanced understanding of how this western writing could have been forgotten. His essay titled "To This Land Where the Clouds Fall" also addresses Toomer's struggles to write and publish:

Furthermore I am a writer. In any case, that is what I am supposed to be. I, descendant of magicians, am supposed to use words with magical effects. But what words can I use that affect these mountains? Besides, as I have said, this country takes words away from me. Not only do the important words of my vocabulary go, but also the little words of everyday use. Sometimes I can't call to mind the word for some simple thing. Silence is grand, but writers are voluble folk. Who ever heard of a silent writer?[19]

But there is more to New Mexico than linguistic absence. Although it may seem that Toomer's writing about New Mexico smacks of modernist primitivism, he takes a different tack. Rather than participating in the racial reification of primitivism, he provides an alternative to it. This is revealed by a further examination of "New Mexico after India." In this essay, New Mexico does not elicit writerly output; instead, it produces somatic experience. Toomer describes embodiment rather than word craft, suggesting that the West inspires physical sensation in place of intellectual analysis, thereby producing a mind-body split. This is not surprising, given that Toomer notoriously describes an out-of-body experience in his autobiographical "From Exile into Being," which went unpublished during his lifetime but was reprinted in part in *A Jean Toomer Reader*. In New Mexico, he writes, "I feel it" as "a penetration deep under the skin." He also feels this place in his heart, stating that New Mexico "retains its hold upon my heart as home." Of course, this tension between language and embodiment is somewhat paradoxical, given that both Toomer's wordlessness and his somatic feeling are being expressed in a written manuscript. Nonetheless, attention to these claims deepens the critical and biographical narrative constructed around his failure as a writer by revealing a new nexus of language, geography, and race. Recall that in "Sequences," Toomer relies on the skin as a signifier of racial identity when he writes, "Those ancient people had red skins, and some dark skins, and a few white." He then declares, "What matter the skin color of them or yourself." He carries this signification into "New Mexico after India" when he describes New Mexico as a "penetration deep under the skin." Here, as in "Sequences," he wants to get beyond race somehow—or at least the kind of racial difference that had become codified. New Mexico makes this possible for him; it is a place where he can reconcile, or get "deep under," the complexities of racial identity symbolized by "skin." Despite its early promise, he was never able to do this in New York. When New Mexico "retains a hold" on Toomer as "home," somewhat fixing him in this space, he is actually far less circumscribed and confined in terms of racial categorization than he had ever been previously. New Mexico becomes a location where racial identity is far more flexible and multiple than what he had experienced the year he left New York and supposedly stopped writing.[20]

The feeling of being at home that Toomer describes in "New Mexico after India" is never satisfied in *Cane*'s migratory narrative, where both the North and the South refuse to harbor racially ambiguous characters. Examples include Paul in "Bona and Paul" and Fern in "Fern." One can even see this in the title character in "Becky"—a white woman who has transgressed racial boundaries by having "two Negro sons" and is thereafter banished to a slim strip of land between the railroad tracks and the road, sequestered from both the white and the black communities. Contrary to scenes like this one in *Cane*, "New Mexico after India" creates a New Mexican "home" where racial binaries are abandoned and racial ambiguity is celebrated. It does this not only by contrasting New Mexico and New York—by now, a predicable pairing in these tales of the New Negro and the American West. It also does this by reaching transnationally, far beyond the scope of the black Atlantic and even the borderlands West, all the way to India.[21]

In 1939, when Toomer and his family traveled to India, he was, as usual, seeking spiritual fulfillment and renovation. But India failed him in this respect, and as a result, he became far more capable of recognizing the actualization he experienced in New Mexico. If Toomer had imagined New Mexico solely in conjunction with the pinnacle of the United States' urban modernity, New York, his vision of it likely would have had more in common with the essentialist, primitivist gestures that characterize the work of many Anglo modernist writers. Interestingly, D. H. Lawrence also traveled through Asia before visiting Taos, but he did so to avoid New York and envision New Mexico unspoiled by the rest of the modern United States. Toomer, instead, finds New Mexico to be an intermediary location—not only in terms of geography but also in terms of temporality—floating somewhere between New York and India. He writes, "Compared to New York the Southwest may seem slow and unchanging. Compared with the interior of India, the Southwest is in rapid change." He suggests that the act of arriving in New Mexico from the "far east" rather than the Eastern Seaboard reveals it to be a much more modern place than he otherwise would have realized. Indeed, this looks like a strange Orientalist ranking of primitivisms, whereby Toomer's voyage from India to New Mexico is used to claim that the latter is more modern than the former but less modern than New York. Toomer's journey, built on "a background of experience in India, Ceylon, Hong Kong, Shanghai, and Japan," exposes that, "by contrast, even the pueblos seem to have a touch of the modern world, the Mexican villages seemed to be growing and changing as young things grow, and Taos and Santa Fe seemed to be altering under the same impulse that had created Chicago in some fifty years." Although Toomer, to be sure, constructs this troubling hierarchy, in creating this problematic he also carves a space for himself in a world where he felt like he never really belonged, thereby making New Mexico ripe for the harvest of a mixed new American race.[22]

"New Mexico after India" proceeds in this vein by describing a multiethnic coterie in which Toomer sees the possibility of racial amalgamation and cooperation: "The Indian is upstanding," he writes. Likewise, "The Mexican is upstanding. The Negro is upstanding. The White is upstanding. Let us continue to upstand, and at the same time bend towards each other on the basis of a common humanity, and we would become one people in spirit and fundamental aim." New Mexico is the crossroads where this "common humanity" exhibits itself, according to Toomer, precisely because of its intermediary position that looks so uncomfortably like an Orientalist hierarchy. If there was a scale of modernity, Toomer would place New Mexico somewhere between India and New York. His experience in New York revealed it as impossibly racially reified. The answer to this reification is not, however, a turn to India. Although New York is depicted as modern and India is depicted as ancient, they find commonality in their restrictiveness, largely because of India's caste system. Toomer contends that this system ruled everywhere he traveled in India, and he describes it as so old, so deeply embedded that it is nearly primordial and impossible to dissolve. As a result, the caste system depletes India's potential to enable diverse peoples to "bend towards each other on the basis of a common humanity." But Toomer now realizes (it had not occurred to him previously) that, in comparison to India's fixedness, the "Southwest is young," a condition that can challenge "our own complexities, taboos, classes if not castes, racial prejudices, and knotty problems." It is a site where the possibility of racial intermingling is feasible in ways it was not in either New York or India.[23]

Contrary to static images of an eternal primitive, then, to enter New Mexico is to enter a place with real and palpable histories of colonial intervention and their attendant discursive legacies. It is these histories and discourses that inform Toomer's western writing and enable him to construct a counternarrative to the classificatory impulses that were so prevalent culturally and politically throughout the United States during this time. Toomer's representation of New Mexico resonates with many of the tropes rife within both avant-garde and popular writing about the West. When he sees it as a space where the new American race can fashion itself and come to fruition, he echoes regional literatures bound up in classic narratives of individualism and self-making that dominate both representations of the West and representations of American identity. Yet unlike many writers, Toomer does not evacuate this place of its history and its indigenous peoples to "make it new." Instead, he makes a keen, concerted effort to attend to and integrate regional history into his own writing. His notes document a wide range of sources that inform his work, and these would have given him vastly different perspectives on New Mexico based on race, gender, class, and discipline. For example, his notes indicate he consulted Erna Fergusson's *Our Southwest* (1940) and *Forgotten People: A Study of New Mexicans* (1940) by Mexican American writer, professor, and League of United Latin American Citizens (LULAC) president George I. Sánchez. He read *Indians of the Rio Grande Valley* (1937) by anthropologists Adolph F. Bandelier and Edgar L. Hewett, as well as Frank Waters's novel *The Man Who Killed the Deer* (1942). He was clearly making an effort to learn all he could about the histories and potentialities of New Mexico. One can imagine books like these on the shelf in Content's photograph, within easy reach of Toomer's desk, ready for consultation as he writes of a New Mexico to house his de-essentialized and flexible new American race.[24]

Indeed, "Sequences"—a series of short, impressionistic sketches that describe the New Mexican landscape, interspersed with the somewhat rambling philosophical musings characteristic of the late Toomer—is rife with allusions to regional history. For example, he mentions Bartolomé de Las Casas, who fought against the enslavement of Indian people in the Americas during Spanish conquest. Although Las Casas once proposed participating in the African slave trade as an alternative to Indian enslavement, he ultimately renounced both and became known as an early proponent of human rights. Toomer also mentions a "certain Spanish priest" in the eighteenth century who, he claims, followed in Las Casas's footsteps. This may be a reference to Miguel Hidalgo, leader of the mestizo and *indio* insurrection against Spain that ultimately prompted the war for Mexican independence in the nineteenth century. According to popular accounts, Hidalgo led his rebellion under a flag emblazoned with the image of the Virgin of Guadalupe, the mestizo Madonna. Toomer claims that both these figures "came upon a vision of what human life in the New World should be, but who never journeyed far enough to see this particular [New Mexican] sky and earth." Such passages seem pregnant with the kind of vague spirituality that Byrd, among others, claims "wasted [Toomer's] great talent"; however, their historical references move beyond the spiritual and into the concrete. These references are derived from New Mexico as a landscape that—as part of the Mexican borderlands—gave birth to both liberationist ideas and mixed racial identities, since both Las Casas and Hidalgo have been mythologized as antiracist and anti-imperialist icons, temporal bookends to the Spanish colonial period, and voices of resistance.[25]

This history and these allusions to Mexico enable Toomer to envision New Mexico as a site for the new American race. This race is not bound to the United States; it is transnational in scope. This transnationalism derives not only from Toomer's travels in India but also from his attention to regional history and emergent theories of race in Mexico and its borderlands. A reflection on colonial history and subsequent racial mixing is evident in Latin American discussions of race and nation that emerged at the same historical moment as Toomer's theories of the new American race. During the 1920s these discussions were most famously given voice by Mexican intellectual José Vasconcelos, whose book *La raza cósmica* (The Cosmic Race) was published in 1925, the same year as *The New Negro* and the same year that Toomer visited Taos for the first time. *La raza cósmica* was Vasconcelos's most influential work and is largely credited as a foundational articulation of *mestizaje*, a culture, philosophy, ethos, and politics of racial mixing that spread throughout Latin America. Vasconcelos's iteration of *mestizaje* was foreshadowed in earlier works by Símon Bolívar and José Martí, and according to Marilyn Grace Miller, it relied on an "often unwieldy interdependence on the mystical and the material," which "prompts many critics to label it inconsistent and contradictory." A similar statement can be made about responses to Toomer's later work, as well as his theorization of the new American race, imbued by his unique mystical leanings. In short, the similarities between these two writers are too great to ignore.[26]

There is no clear evidence that Toomer ever read Vasconcelos's work or that he had even heard of Vasconcelos's theories. It is obvious, however, that he was engaged in research on Mexico and its borderlands and was interested in linking this region to an articulation of mixed-race identity. Certainly he read Erna Fergusson, who played with and perhaps adapted the idea of *mestizaje* in *Our Southwest*. And it is quite possible that while doing his research Toomer read the many newspaper accounts of Vasconcelos's lectures in the United States, including at the University of Chicago in 1926, where Toomer had once taken classes. It is also possible that he read of Vasconcelos's activities as the Mexican secretary of education (1920–1924), during which time he supported the Mexican muralist movement, as well as Vasconcelos's unsuccessful bid for the Mexican presidency in 1929. Toomer may have read reviews of Vasconcelos's works, which were being translated into English. Finally, if Toomer had any interest in keeping abreast of his former mentor Waldo Frank's globe-trotting whereabouts, he would have learned of Frank's extensive Latin American tours and the writings that emerged from them, which may have led him to Vasconcelos. But whether or not Toomer was aware of Vasconcelos's theories, there are clear parallels between their writings and ideas. Tace Hedrick claims that both Toomer and Vasconcelos relied on modern images of a graft or hybrid when they articulated their racial theories:

> Two years after *Cane* was published, José Vasconcelos, former Mexican Secretary of Education (1920–1924), published his own wide-reaching book, *La raza cósmica* (*The Cosmic Race*) wherein he posited what he called an "esthetic eugenics" whereby the most beautiful and fit of all the Spanish, Anglo-Saxon, black, and Indian races would marry and produce a futuristic "cosmic race" south of the border with the United States. In this book Vasconcelos uses exactly the same analogy as Toomer . . . ; that of the graft, or hybrid.

When Toomer's writings from New Mexico are considered, the parallels between his work and Vasconcelos's become even easier to imagine.

Their similarities include not only their theories of racial mixture but also their engagement with a transnational cultural geography that bears the marks of both Spanish colonialism and US imperialism, their concerns with processes and products of modernization, and their vague, unwieldy, and visionary spiritual gestures.[27]

Biographically, too, Vasconcelos and Toomer have commonalities. After Vasconcelos lost his presidential bid, he became increasingly reactionary. He even contributed to a pro-Axis newspaper based in Mexico City during World War II. These later writings denounced the "esthetic eugenics" of *mestizaje* in favor of a eugenics of racial purity. Unsurprisingly, as Miller notes, they "received far less press and had much less impact than his earlier triumphant celebration." Like Toomer, Vasconcelos is a deeply contradictory figure, one with a clear disjuncture between his early and later works. He is frustrating to scholars: his early work seems to be a radical reconsideration of race, yet his later work is unpalatable to the same readers who were attracted to the social justice imperatives and the language of liberation that characterized his initial radical visions.[28]

Also like Toomer, Vasconcelos's theory of racial mixture is rooted in the history of Spanish colonialism. He interprets conquest—perhaps problematically—not solely as the annihilation of indigenous peoples but as the birth of a promising new racial order. In *La raza cósmica* he suggests, "Although [the Spanish] may have thought of themselves simply as colonizers, as carriers of culture, in reality, they were establishing the basis for a period of general and definitive transformation." He argues that colonization unwittingly set into motion an epoch of racial mixing, and the cosmic race is the result—an outgrowth of postcolonial modernity: "The days of the pure whites, the victors of the day," he writes, "are as numbered as the days of their predecessors. Having fulfilled their destiny of mechanizing the world, they themselves have set, without knowing it, the basis for a new period. The period of the fusion and mixing of all peoples." *Mestizaje*—the racial mixture of "the Black, the Indian, the Mongol, and the White"—is depicted as an outgrowth of modernization, made possible only after "mechanizing the world" via imperial conquest. Vasconcelos's work, like Toomer's pronouncement of the new American race, takes on prophetic tones: "At the beginning, the Whites will try to take advantage of their inventions for their own benefit, but since science is no longer esoteric, it is not likely that they will succeed. They will be absorbed in the avalanche of all other races, and finally, deposing their pride, they will combine with the rest to make a new racial synthesis, the fifth race of the future." Like many other modernist texts, and like Toomer's temporal and racial triangulation of New York, New Mexico, and India in "New Mexico after India," Vasconcelos's language of the "beginning" and the "future" suggests a theory of race that is also a theory of modernization. According to him, the modern era is one of mixed identities, which resonates with the "newness" of Toomer's new American race.[29]

Furthermore, the origin stories of mixed-race identity told by Vasconcelos and Toomer are incredibly similar. Both inspire dual interpretations. These stories can be told as narratives of racial abandonment and betrayal or as narratives of empowerment and subversion. Although Vasconcelos seizes on the figure of the mestizo as a point of empowerment—a figure that can be mobilized to unify a fragmented nation in the wake of the Mexican Revolution—the mestizo is also a figure of racial betrayal, a stain on Mexico and a reminder of the brutality of its colonial past. As Miller notes, discussions of *mestizaje* are polarized around a female figure: the mythology of *la Malinche*, slave and interpreter to Cortés and the storied mother of the first mestizo. *La Malinche* has been seen—particularly in more masculinist, nationalist discourses in Mexico (and the United States), such as Octavio Paz's *The Labyrinth of Solitude* (1950)—as a traitor to the Indian people, as assimilative, and as the midwife to Mexican conquest at the hands of the Spanish. Yet in more recent discourses—particularly those emerging from Chicana feminism, such as Gloria Anzaldúa's *Borderlands/La Frontera: The New Mestiza* (1987)—this mythologized figure has been seen as a radical hybrid, a model for subverting the limitations of prescriptive binary oppositions and hierarchical social locations. Toomer's proclamation of the new American race and the concomitant story of his disaffiliation with the New Negro have been similarly fragmented, rendering him somewhat of a male *la Malinche* for the New Negro. On the one hand, his marriages to white women, his rejection of the New Negro, his failure to publish, and his departure from Harlem are met with feelings of regret, betrayal, and bewilderment. On the other hand, when he is read within the discursive framework of *mestizaje* emerging from Mexico and percolating across the border, new possibilities emerge for the assessment of Toomer's story. Although many readings of his later work presume that his turn away from black identity is a turn toward whiteness (recall Bontemps's insistence that Toomer "crossed the color line"), if we see Toomer in the mold of Vasconcelos's mestizo, his new American race is not a strategy for deracination, whitening, or passing. Instead, it is a radical reenvisioning of race at a time when it was increasingly codified. In Toomer's construction of a multiple, mixed-race identity, amalgamation is not seen as degenerate; it is seen as enabling. It is not seen as destructive; it is seen as constructive. Positioning Toomer in the West and in the Mexican borderlands, and uncovering the archive he produced there, allows a view of Toomer's new American race not as a racial reversal, a turn away from African American identity, or an embrace of whiteness in a binary system. It is a form of *mestizaje*, a subversion of such a system altogether. This is accomplished through his imagination of the borderlands West as a place where the new American race can flourish.[30]

There is evidence that, in subtle ways, this imagination extends beyond Toomer. Even Hughes, who left Mexico for Harlem, envisioned the West as a site where interracial desire and, potentially, racial mixing could be enacted, such as in his early poem "A House in Taos" (1926). Bontemps, among others, insinuated that this poem was based on rumors of Toomer's early visits to the home of Mabel Dodge Luhan, when he allegedly seduced her, but Hughes denied that. Nonetheless, the poem characterizes New Mexico as a space for interracial sexuality, describing a multiethnic triangulation of desire—the "red, white, yellow skins"—situated in the high desert of Taos. Whether this racial mixing is lauded, as in Toomer's work, or viewed skeptically, as in Hughes's, the borderlands West as a site for such mixing remains consistent, and it is epitomized by the Toomer-Latimer marriage, which was both upheld and decried as the foundation of the new American race.[31]

The story of the new American race was sensationalized by the mass media, which played on stereotypes of black male predatory sexuality and white female purity. It was looked at disapprovingly in Harlem, where there was an expectation of racial fidelity, such as that which resonates with mestizo origin stories painting *la Malinche* as a race traitor. But placing the new American race in the spatial context of the borderlands West can lead to an interpretation of this new racial formation as subversive instead of reactionary. Both essentialist racial stereotypes and expectations of racial fidelity rely on an understanding of race as bifurcated, a view instituted and perpetuated in the United States thanks to persistent ideas of hypodescent and the "one drop rule." When the new American race is placed outside this context—in the spatial and discursive zone of the Mexican borderlands—it is rendered legible, and its revolutionary aspects are illuminated. In "To This Land Where the Clouds Fall," Toomer expands on his role as the progenitor of this new American race. Here, he envisions fecundity, much like Margery Latimer did when she wrote to a friend in October 1931 and described her marriage: "You don't know how marvelously happy I am and my stomach seems leaping with golden children, millions of them." Toomer asserts:

> I am one. Here I am I. In these grand spaces I feel grand, with largeness in me, and my body in the world. I tell myself that this geography must in the future as it has in the past produce a great race. I see this future, mountains beyond mountains, and the sun. I buy land, a large tract. I build a big house and smaller ones. I have fields and cattle. My children grow up. Their children grow up. With my friends and workers I inhabit it, building in New Mexico my world of man.

In this passage, as in "New Mexico after India," Toomer imagines New Mexico as an ideal homeland for a mixed-race subject. The space is intrinsically connected to Toomer's "great race." Toomer, himself a mixed-race subject (a condition Hughes describes as "the problem of those so-called 'Negroes' of immediate white-and-black blood"), is at home in the New Mexican environment. "Here I am I," Toomer writes, and his racially ambiguous body is peaceful "in the world" of the borderlands West. He describes members of the new American race springing from the earth, almost as if they had been farmed there, like his "fields and cattle." His offspring, and his offspring's offspring—the millions of golden children leaping from Latimer's womb—circumvent images of New Mexico's desert landscape as barren.[32]

The dreamy optimism and hopeful, anticipatory future described here, however, is undercut by ambivalence in some of Toomer's other western writing. Despite his claims in "New Mexico after India" that New Mexico "retains its hold upon [his] heart as home," his failure to permanently settle there is foreshadowed by the hedging detectable elsewhere in his western work. For example, in "A Drama of the Southwest," Lewis Bourne (Toomer's dramatic double) weighs the pros and cons of buying land in Taos, similar to Toomer's impulse to "buy land, a large tract." Bourne's ambivalence about buying land is based on his suspicion—shared by Toomer in his first-person writings about New Mexico—that the West might become too modern too soon. In short, he fears it is dangerously close to becoming like New York. In "To This Land Where the Clouds Fall," Toomer describes the endless deferral of his own New Mexican land purchase: "My wife [Content] and I are looking at land. We looked last year. We will look the next. We will look every time we come until we buy." Although this land is crucial to Toomer's regenerative project, he never finds the perfect property:

> Day after day I go through the drama of it, night after night, affirming and denying, glad I am here, wanting to be somewhere else. This hour I would build my home forever on this earth, just this earth of sagebrush, tumble weed, piñon and cottonwood trees, the Rio Grande and streams from the mountains. The next hour I am in rebellion and want to fly away, critical of adobe, disliking the attitude of fast heartbeats and restlessness, scornful and depressed that so many small people have come to live small rancorous lives in this great region of the Western continent.

Toomer, however, may have considered himself among the "small people" leading "small rancorous lives" in the desert West. In a series of handwritten notes he prepared while drafting "New Mexico after India," he calls himself a "small man in big spaces. Not just any man. Not just any great space. Just myself in the spaces of the region of the Southwest between Taos and Santa Fe." As a "small man in big spaces," Toomer is in danger of becoming one of the "small people" in this "great region," reduced to a "small rancorous" life, dwarfed by the size and openness of the New Mexican landscape. All this adds to his ambivalence about the place itself.[33]

In "To This Land Where the Clouds Fall," Toomer provides more detail about this ambivalence: "I am attracted and repelled, attracted by the actual magnificence of physical New Mexico, attracted by my visions of the potentialities of life here, yet repelled by a number of trivial matters, all of which I know to be trivial, nevertheless they pester and obsess me as expressions of some deep undiscovered protest." His language of attraction and repulsion—of positively and negatively charged particles—is also scientific language. And despite prevailing descriptions of New Mexico as premodern, it is actually befitting for this space during this historical moment. This language suggests there is a tipping point when technological modernization will no longer allow the "visions of the potentialities of life" in New Mexico, which Toomer is otherwise so attracted to. This technological modernization, threatening the regenerative possibilities of New Mexico, is epitomized by the development of the atomic bomb at the Los Alamos National Laboratory, founded in 1943. In "Sequences," Toomer returns to the image of the sloping New Mexican landscape as a metaphor for the development of the new American race. This time, however, he links it to a discussion of modern nuclear science: "Until men are strong in their ascent up the spiritual slope, the existence of atomic energy will block the spiritual climb and enforce still more 'progress' up the material slope. Given men as they now are, its use in society would be an unqualified disaster. It should not be used, except in medicine." At the time "Sequences" was written, the Manhattan Project—its very name signifying its relation to a spatialized concept of modernity—was under way a mere sixty-five miles from Taos. The atomic bomb erupts in doomsday visions within the otherwise pristine, idyllic landscape Toomer constructs in the West. In his notebook on New Mexico he writes:

"The mountain will smoke, great winds will come up, the world will be destroyed by fire." So say the old men of the pueblo, some of whom may have true vision and gift of prophecy. Do we not hear the same prediction in different terms from scientists who know the fearful potential of the atomic bomb?

Who I do not know is—Do the elders of Taos vision the coming destruction as the end of man, or as the matrix of a new birth? Will resurrection follow this death? And, if so, who will be resurrected? White men? Red men? Black men? An entirely new race?

Despite his apocalyptic vision, Toomer continues to insist that "new men and women are as possible as war. I will hold to the faith that we will be reborn until I see destruction sweep the earth and I am knocked to smithereens." But regardless of Toomer's faith in the possibility of New Mexico providing a home for his "entirely new race," the fact remains that he never settled there permanently. He continued to look for land to purchase until his final trip in 1947, but he never discovered the tract he required to harvest his subversive racial vision.[34]

Rather than retire to New Mexico and his own piece of fertile land, Toomer remained in the East. He spent the final years of his life at a farm in Doylestown, a small community in Bucks County, Pennsylvania, where he had first moved in the late 1930s. At the time, Bucks County, only ninety miles from New York City, was a rural community that attracted a group of artists and writers who set up their studios there. Now it is essentially a Philadelphia suburb and was the site of the second Levittown, built in the 1950s. In Doylestown, the county seat, Toomer was once asked to define his race at a public "inquiry" (as Larson describes it) focused on whether his daughter—whose birth had caused such a scandal in 1932—could attend an all-white school. During the course of this inquiry, Toomer was able to convince his audience that he was not African American. He could not, however, pass as white. In any case, in Bucks County, Toomer was unable to inhabit the mixed-race, multiple-subject position he had always envisioned as truly "American"—a position he had theorized about and sought out personally, spiritually, and geographically for most of his life. One resident of Bucks County (interviewed in Larson's *Invisible Darkness: Jean Toomer and Nella Larsen*) related that he had once been "told . . . with a straight face, that Mrs. Toomer was married to an East Indian," because "the farmers around here are very narrow. If they thought Mrs. Toomer, white, was married to a Negro, they would make life miserable for both of them. An East Indian they can live with so, remember, Jean Toomer is East Indian." In Doylestown, Toomer's mixed new American race was disabled, and he was forced to pass—although not as white. But for Toomer, who had once conceptualized India as a limiting space—just as limiting as New York—passing as Indian was little consolation. Like New York, New Mexico, and India, Bucks County can be mapped geographically and racially in this unwieldy and unstable network of race relations and transregional and transnational geographies. In New Mexico, Toomer described the new American race emerging from the desert soil, made fertile through its regional history, its cultural crosscurrents, and the discourses of Mexico and its borderlands. In Bucks County, in contrast, it is the farmers, the tillers of the land themselves, who are "narrow"— so different from the "great region," the "big spaces," of the vast New Mexican earth.[35]

Coda

Bring me all of your dreams,
You dreamers,
Bring me all of your
Heart melodies
That I may wrap them
In a blue cloud-cloth
Away from the too-rough fingers
Of the world.
    —Langston Hughes, "The Dream Keeper" (1925)

The Borderlands of Blackness

The Formation of a Multiethnic
American Imagination

Africa! Africa!
Black soul with a song
And a chain. . . .

But in spite of the chains
The song remains,
I can hear it echoing yet . . .

May you never forget.
—*Américo Paredes, "Africa" (1935)*

In the opening of *Playing in the Dark: Whiteness and the Literary Imagination*, Toni Morrison writes that she intends to "draw a map, so to speak, of a critical geography and use that map to open up as much space for discovery, intellectual adventure, and close exploration as did the original charting of the New World—without the mandate for conquest." In this sentence, Morrison uses spatial metaphors to describe her critical approach to literature. Her reference to "the New World" and processes of conquest also gesture toward the outcome of her "mapping" practices—a definition of American literature that coalesces around encounters with blackness: "Through significant and underscored omissions, startling contradictions, heavily nuanced conflicts, through the way writers peopled their work with signs and bodies of this presence," she argues, "one can see that a real or fabricated Africanist presence was crucial to their sense of Americanness." For Morrison, American literature is constituted, no matter how subtly, by blackness. Her major question is "whether the major and championed characteristics of our national literature—individualism, masculinity, social engagement versus historical isolation; acute and ambiguous moral problematics; the thematics of innocence coupled with an obsession with figurations of death and hell—are not in fact responses to a dark, abiding, signing Africanist presence."[1]

Morrison's list of quintessentially American characteristics does not depart significantly from those long ascribed to the experience of the frontier. Indeed, Morrison relies on a lengthy passage from historian Bernard Bailyn's *Voyagers to the West: A Passage in the Peopling of America on the Eve of Revolution*, which uses the traits of colonist and planter William Dunbar as an apt description of what came to be considered American: "Endlessly enterprising and resourceful, his finer sensibilities dulled by the abrasions of frontier life, and feeling within himself a sense of authority and autonomy he had not known before, a force that flowed from his absolute control over the lives of others, he emerged as a distinctive new man, a borderland gentleman, a man of property in a raw, half-savage world." While Bailyn attributes Dunbar's Americanizaton to the "frontier," rendering him a "borderland" subject, Morrison refocuses this passage on his "absolute control over the lives of others"—his slave ownership. Morrison does not substitute blackness for the frontier; rather, she sees encounters with blackness as a crucial component of meditations on the frontier. One cannot imagine borderlessness, freedom, mobility, and limitless opportunity without having as their counterpoints circumscription, enslavement, bondage, and oppression. Through deft readings of classic American literature—from Poe, Twain, Hawthorne, and Melville to Hemingway, Faulkner, and Cather—Morrison convincingly demonstrates that these American cultural characteristics arise from fantasies of blackness. As she asks rhetorically, "How could one speak of . . . the frontier . . . without having as a referent, at the heart of the discourse, at the heart of definition, the presence of Africans and their descendants?" Perhaps this is why her initial explanation of her method for charting the centrality of this Africanist presence to American literature is best expressed through the geographic metaphor of mapping.[2]

Morrison's *Playing in the Dark* is a succinct and adept statement about the importance of the Africanist presence to an American literary canon in which whiteness has been taken as the unspoken norm and white authorial fantasies, such as that of the frontier, are undergirded by the presence of blacks. Anglo-American writers like Melville or Hemingway, however, are not the only ones whose writings about American identity have been built around an Africanist presence. Although African Americans often constituted a minority in the West during the years of the New Negro renaissance, more than just a small cadre of black western writers acknowledged the community's presence; in fact, Mexican American, Native American, and Asian American writers emerging from this geography also acknowledged it. Through brief, subtle mentions and quick gestures, non–African American multiethnic western writers— such as self-described proto-Chicano Américo Paredes, mixed-blood Osage John Joseph Mathews, Filipino American Carlos Bulosan, and Mexican American Josefina Niggli—evidence an Africanist presence in their own texts. Taken in concert with African American western writers, Paredes, Mathews, Bulosan, and Niggli demonstrate that African American experience was essential to the establishment of American identity—not only for whites but also for nonblack ethnic American writers who were negotiating their own places in the national imagination, in the racial order, and in American literary history, sometimes in solidarity with blacks under the regime of Jim Crow and sometimes in distinction to them.

In the prologue to his collection of poetry *Between Two Worlds* (1991), renowned folklorist, creative writer, and forebear of Chicana and Chicano studies Américo Paredes explains the belated publication of his poetry. In this prologue, written in 1989, Paredes notes that much of the collection consists of his juvenilia, written as early as the 1930s, which he had always intended to destroy. In the years following the Chicana and Chicano movement of the 1960s, however, he decided to preserve his work and, he jokes, "compete for the title of Grandpa Moses of Chicano literature, depending on how you define Chicano and literature." Downplaying any aesthetic achievement, Paredes suggests that the collection is most useful as a "historical document" that charts a long Chicana and Chicano movement—with its foment of cultural nationalism and identity politics for Mexican Americans—dating back to the 1930s and preserved in "the scribblings of a 'proto-Chicano' of a half-century ago."[3]

While Paredes's description of his youthful self as "proto-Chicano" gestures toward a nationalist politics, the first poem in the volume, "The Rio Grande" (1934), immediately reminds the reader that a proto-Chicano politics is also a transnational politics. The twists and turns of the Rio Grande that mark the border of south Texas and northern Mexico are a metaphor for Chicana and Chicano history and identity. The river's "swirls and counter currents" that constantly "turn back" on themselves—here, toward the North and the United States; there, toward the South and Mexico—reflect the speaker's search for origin and belonging in the United States–Mexico border region. The speaker notes, "I was born beside your waters / And since very young I knew / That my soul had hidden currents / That my soul resembled you." Here, Paredes uses the physical geography of the border to symbolize the racial and national complexity of proto-Chicano identity in a way that is similar to many later writers, most famously "new *mestiza*" writer and theorist Gloria Anzaldúa in *Borderlands*.[4]

Literary critic Ramón Saldívar—who, incidentally, helped Paredes choose the poems to include in *Between Two Worlds*—has recently extended Paredes's transnationalism beyond the interplay of Mexico and the United States. In *The Borderlands of Culture: Américo Paredes and the Transnational Imaginary*, Saldívar argues that Paredes's multigeneric oeuvre—from his folklore scholarship to his poetry, from his novel *George Washington Gómez* to his work as a journalist—exhibits "a tension between national and transnational perspectives" that is "exceptionally significant for how we think about 'America' today. His overlapping identities as a scholar of regional nationalist culture and as a transnational journalist and writer taught him to see the struggle for Mexican American social justice as part of a much larger and more elaborate geopolitical puzzle." Saldívar locates the origins of this "transnational imaginary" in the time Paredes spent in Japan as a journalist after World War II. It was then, he suggests, that Paredes formed a transnational understanding of imperialism, occupation, and citizenship, among other things, which enabled him to crystallize the concept of "Greater Mexico" to describe a Mexican diasporic experience. Paredes's engagement with the notion of diaspora, however, is also visible in a poem he wrote shortly after "The Rio Grande" that was also published in *Between Two Worlds:* "Africa" (1935).[5]

Saldívar does not let "Africa" go unmentioned in *The Borderlands of Culture*. He focuses on the repetition of "the music of drums"—"Of the drums! / Of the drums!! / Of the drums!!!"—suggesting that the drums' insistence is a reminder of an African past; the beat of the drum is the eruption of ancestral diasporic memory and history, as well as an indication of "a modern American idiom in which the achieved promise of America will someday exist." In tone and subject matter, "Africa" clearly resonates with contemporaneous writing from the New Negro movement. Saldívar mentions, as corollaries, Toomer's "Song of the Son" from *Cane* and Lewis Alexander's "Enchantment," which was published in *The New Negro*. He does not, however, mention Countee Cullen's "Heritage" (1925), which also features the allure of "great drums throbbing through the air"; Cullen's speaker, who is "three centuries removed" from the continent's shores, asks, "What is Africa to me?" This question is also introduced by Langston Hughes in "Afro-American Fragment" (1930), where he suggests, "Subdued and time-lost / Are the drums—and yet / Through some vast mist of race / There comes this song / I do not understand."[6]

When Cullen's and Hughes's presumably African American speakers ask, essentially, "What is Africa to me?" it makes Paredes's "Africa" look even stranger. If this question illuminates the tensions of an African American double consciousness rather than asserting a uniform Pan-Africanism, what does it do for a proto-Chicano? If Paredes's concept of Greater Mexico is used to describe a Mexican diaspora throughout the Americas and the larger transnational world, perhaps it makes sense to see this formation as emerging not from his engagement with Asia but from his more subtle engagement with Africa and African America—including black writers from the borderlands West. One can see such a reckoning with Africa and its diaspora in the work of New Negro poet and visual artist Gwendolyn Bennett, whose poem titled "Heritage" was published in *Opportunity* two years before Cullen's. Bennett was born in Giddings, Texas, and spent her early childhood in Wadsworth,

Nevada, where her parents were teachers at the nearby Pyramid Lake Paiute Indian Reservation. The family later moved to Washington, D.C., and then to Brooklyn, New York. Yet, like Paredes's "Africa," Bennett's "Heritage" is located far from these sites and from the borderlands West. The speaker longs for an Africa never experienced, where "I want to feel the surging / Of my sad people's soul / Hidden by a minstrel-smile."[7]

Bennett's and Paredes's work suggests a connection between the diasporic consciousness of African Americans and Mexican Americans, as both writers consider a nostalgia for a homeland never experienced. Given Paredes's "Africa," one must consider "The Rio Grande" more closely. When Paredes is imagined in dialogue with New Negro writers, his writing about the borderlands river exists in a wider tradition of poetry that links such waterways with the diasporic imagination. Clearly, the images of the currents, eddies, and wending shorelines of the Rio Grande, which always double back on themselves toward the United States and then toward Mexico, suggest a kind of double consciousness for proto-Chicano subjects. Saldívar usefully suggests that "The Rio Grande," as well as Paredes's Spanish-language version of the poem, "El Rio Bravo," can be read in concert with transnational modernist poetry about rivers, such as Wallace Stevens's "The River of Rivers in Connecticut" (1954). He also places "The Rio Grande" alongside Langston Hughes's "The Negro Speaks of Rivers" (1920), noting Hughes's story about composing the poem on the way to visit his father in Mexico and suggesting that "Paredes . . . looks at rivers . . . for the same reasons. He focuses on the ways that rivers as metaphors of deep tradition and symbols of music can express an understanding of the course of history."[8]

One could also compare "The Rio Grande" with Jean Toomer's "The Blue Meridian" (1936), the first 125 lines of which were originally published in *Pagany* as "Brown River, Smile" (1932), two years before Paredes's "The Rio Grande." Toomer's poem refigures the Mississippi as a "sacred river" like India's Ganges. Images of currents and waves are used to bring together "great European races" that "send wave after wave / That washed the forests" and "great African races" that sent "a single wave / . . . singing riplets to sorrow in red fields," invoking colonization, the Middle Passage, and the black Atlantic. Even the borderlands West and its indigenous inhabitants are described through images of water: "The great red race was here / In a land of flaming earth and torrent-rains / Of red sea plains and majestic mesas." Toomer uses the image of the river to describe how "growth is by admixture" of humanity across racial lines. To express this mixing he uses the flow of the Mississippi: "The Mississippi, . . . / Is a sacred river / In the spirit of our people; / Whoever lifts the Mississippi / Lifts himself and all mankind." The river traverses the North and South, demarcates the East and West, and meanders through other geographic borderlands: "The west coast is masculine, / The east coast is feminine, / The middle region is the child— / Reconciling force / And generator of new symbols." Even more than "The Negro Speaks of Rivers," Toomer's "The Blue Meridian" is a text of both the African diaspora and the Mexican borderlands, composed during Toomer's time in New Mexico and containing lines describing the southwestern landscape as a conceptual twin to the river, since both serve as connectors across difference. In 1938 Toomer published a poem in the *New Mexican Sentinel* titled "Imprint for Rio Grande," in which he turns to that river—albeit the section that flows through New Mexico rather than at the Texas-Mexico border—as a site that engenders the connectedness he sought throughout his life, both spiritually and racially, through the birth of the new American race: "There is a Being in me," he writes. "Sometimes . . . I am him, / and when I am there is such marvel in the Rio Grande, such ecstasy of / inner sun to outer sun, or inner breath to the blazing winds, that I / and everyone seem re-born."[9]

When Paredes's poetry—particularly "Africa" and "The Rio Grande"— is placed alongside the work of Hughes, Toomer, Cullen, and Bennett, he can be seen as accomplishing two things: First, both of Paredes's poems, as Saldívar suggests, gesture to a feeling of kinship with African Americans based on shared histories and experiences of oppression and diaspora. Second, Paredes alludes not only to a shared transnational experience but also to a shared regional experience as the foundation for this kinship—the local experience of a borderlands West where African Americans, like Mexican Americans, had a long history. As an example, his brief mention of Bagdad, Mexico, in "The Rio Grande" is notable: "We shall wander through the country / Where your banks in green are clad, / Past the shanties of rancheros, / By the ruins of old Bagdad." This stanza is the only place in the poem where the singular "I" used by the speaker turns into the plural "We," suggesting a collective history exemplified by the mention of "the ruins of old Bagdad." Bagdad, Mexico, located across the river from Paredes's hometown of Brownsville, Texas, was the site of the Confederacy's largest shipping port during the Civil War, the place where the Rio Grande meets the Gulf of Mexico. Deemed international waters under the Treaty of Guadalupe-Hidalgo, this waterway remained accessible to the Confederacy even during the years of Lincoln's blockade. Bagdad thereby sustained the cotton trade, the Confederacy's economy, and slavery. "We," then, may refer to the shared Mexican and African American past at this site, constituted by interlocked histories of imperial expansion and the spread of chattel slavery. These connections between the local and the transnational, illuminated when Paredes is read in conjunction with African American writers, seem to verify José E. Limón's assertion that although Paredes "occasionally lend[s] himself to" Saldívar's interpretation of him as a "critically postcolonial transnational cultural critic," he is also "a more complex and ultimately national and regional figure." When Paredes is assessed alongside contemporaneous African American writers, and particularly those of the borderlands West, he can be seen as gesturing—as Toomer, Bontemps, and Hughes do —to the myriad connections between the region and the world.[10]

In 1934, the same year Paredes published "The Rio Grande," a mixed-blood Osage Indian named John Joseph Mathews released his first novel, *Sundown*. Mathews had written *Sundown* upon his return to the Osage Agency in Oklahoma after spending years living in Europe and then in California during the 1920s. He had attended Oxford University, traveled around Europe on a motorcycle, lived in Geneva, sold real estate in Los Angeles, and participated in hunting excursions to North Africa. Once he was back in Oklahoma, Mathews began to write both fiction and nonfiction. In the 1970s he told an apocryphal story about his decision to return to Oklahoma. Sometime around 1921, he told an interviewer, he took a hunting trip to Algeria. While there:

Some Kabyles . . . came racing across the sand. I think there were about six or eight of them firing their Winchesters. . . . I thought, here, we're in trouble. . . . Then I got to thinking about it, and I thought that's exactly what happened to me one day when I was a little boy riding on the Osage prairies. Osage warriors with only their breech clouts and their guns had come up and surrounding me—firing. . . . That's what we called joy-shooting, you see, just joy. So, I got homesick, and I thought, what am I doing over here? Why don't I go back to the Osage?

Here, Mathews describes his affiliation with a group of Arabs. As I have argued elsewhere, this affiliation is based on tribalism via gender, which helps him form connections between the local (his allotment on the Osage Agency) and the transnational (his experiences at Oxford and in Algeria, for example). In this story, Mathews's transnational experiences (like those of Paredes or of Bontemps, Hughes, and Toomer) help him understand the experiences of people of color in local environments—in his case, the Osage in Oklahoma.[11]

There is a critical difference between Mathews's and Paredes's geographies, however. While both turn to Africa, Paredes—like many New Negro writers—turns specifically to sub-Saharan Africa. Mathews does not, thereby avoiding engagement with black Africans and with their descendants in the diaspora. Furthermore, as Susan Kalter has discovered through an examination of Mathews's archived diaries, "his reactions towards blacks in general . . . were ambivalent at best." Although he showed some sympathy toward the African American civil rights movement in the early 1960s, "in the 1920s, he was telling 'nigger stories' to his pals at Oxford"; by the late 1960s, he thought the civil rights movement would not be successful if African Americans "continue through riots and screaming." Kalter suggests that although Mathews was likely in favor of the goals of the civil rights movement, he had deep-seated prejudices against blacks. These feelings were shared by some Native American Oklahomans who had a long history of entanglement with African Americans, including slave ownership. In Mathews's own complicated family history, his Anglo paternal grandfather—married to a half-Osage woman, through whom Mathews received his agency allotment—was a slave owner from Kentucky. According to Mathews, after his grandfather moved to Kansas:

> [He was] killed by Free Staters in 1861. His trading posts were burned, his property confiscated. His sons, aged ten and twelve years of age, set out for Texas, under the protection of a Confederate-sympathizing family. . . . They could take nothing from their home before it was burned except the clothes they wore. Two of the Mathews slaves fled with them: one "Ole Aunt Millie," the nurse, and the stable man, "Uncle Ned."

Here, Mathews's recollection of his father's childhood reveals some bitterness toward the "Union Bush-Whackers," and he participates in paternalistic fantasies of loyal slaves who did not flee to freedom but chose to accompany their masters. Mathews does not mention that his grandfather, John Allen Mathews, was the leader of an 1861 guerrilla raid on Humboldt, Kansas. The *Daily Cleveland Herald* reported that "125 rebels under the command of Mathews and Livingston . . . surrounded the town, searched houses, outraged women, stole everything of value, kidnapped twelve free negroes, and treated the people with great cruelty. . . . The marauders . . . had promised the lands to the Osage Indians—their allies." According to correspondence from the Office of Indian Affairs, however:

> The feeling of the Osages is favorable to the Union, the loyalty of most of the tribe still unshaken, although a few of their half-breeds have been found in company with roving bands of white vagabonds and thieves who have been employed in robbing and driving Union men and their families from their homes. The ringleader, John Mathews, has, through the prompt action of General James H. Lane, already met a traitor's doom.

The Osage's ambivalent allegiances in the early years of the Civil War are reflected in Mathews's representations of the interstices of Native American and African American experience even in the twentieth century.[12]

Later in his autobiography *Twenty Thousand Mornings* (written in 1966–1967 and published in 2012), Mathews mocks the descendants of slave-owning southerners who were his classmates at the University of Oklahoma. He suggests they were "eager and serious and staunchly believed in Christian brotherhood, but there was no test facing them at the University, since no Negro was allowed to stay in the town of Norman overnight." He comments on the class pretensions of these students and extends his critique by derisively referring to Confederates as "Slaveocrats" at one point in the text, pointing out the planter class's reliance on black slavery to uphold its power. When he describes his fellow students, he points out the hypocrisy of those who preach brotherhood but maintain segregated institutions and race-based hegemony; he goes on, however, to romanticize the Lost Cause, imagining himself, at the beginning of World War I, as participating in "something akin . . . to the romantic unreason and the dramatics of protective maleness, when the South took up arms for the beginning of the Civil War." And later, he uses dialect in his writing to mock an African American who asks him about flying airplanes in the Signal Corps. Mathews, the first-person narrator, could not make himself appear more patrician and modern, whereas the African American man could not be made to seem more undereducated and backward: "Yas'suh, hit's the fust [airplane] Ah evah seed, and you de fust aeroventilatah Ah evah seed," says the "veritable 'Uncle Tom,'" as Mathews calls him. To this, Mathews crisply answers, "If you want to ask questions, go ahead." The representation of this African American man is saturated with minstrel stereotypes, which serve to degrade African Americans while at the same time elevating Mathews, a mixed-blood Osage, by asserting his distinction from blacks through his Anglicized and arrogant dialogue.[13]

If Paredes suggests that black diasporic histories can be instructive for proto-Chicano experiences, then Mathews's writing shows some of the limitations of African American and Native American solidarity. This occurs as early as Mathews's *Sundown*, which follows a mixed-blood protagonist, Chal Windzer, through the heady days of modernist excess both outside and inside the Osage Agency—from World War I through the frenetic Oklahoma oil boom of the 1920s. Chal—constantly on the move on his pony, in his airplane, in his roadster—is depicted as a

Ponca Indians at the 101 Ranch Wild West Show, ca. 1907. (Research
Division of the Oklahoma Historical Society)

wanderer in search of belonging; he is, as Christopher Schedler points
out, a paradigmatic alienated modern individual due to both his mixed-
blood status and the rapid changes taking place within the agency.[14]

Chal's anxious, ambivalent alienation is not only constructed in relation to the Osage and white worlds, however. It is also revealed through
his interactions with African Americans and African American culture.
In one scene in the novel, Chal takes his white female friends to a tribal
dance. Although this is a social dance, not a ceremonial one, Chal feels
uneasy about violating the cultural fidelity of the event by bringing white
spectators. But whites routinely attended such tribal dances, and once he
is there, Chal notices an Indian performer who is clearly catering to their
primitivist fantasies. This dancer is, the narrator notes, a Ponca—not
an Osage: "He stamped and twisted, and jerked his head fantastically,"
Mathews writes. "He did the black bottom, the Charleston, and other
clownish tricks until Chal looked away in disgust, but he could hear
murmurs of approval from the visitors on the benches. The Ponca had
been on the vaudeville stage, and he knew how to please white people."
Chal's reaction to the Ponca dancer is the result of several factors. First,
the Ponca is an outsider who has "desecrate[d]" the Osage dance through

his presence. Second, the Ponca has introduced the influence of African American culture through his performance of "the black bottom" and "the Charleston." Third, these are not just popular dances with roots in African American culture (which, when described as "clownish," seems somewhat denigrating); they are also cultural forms that were already

Bill Pickett, African American rodeo cowboy at the 101 Ranch Wild West Show, ca. 1890–1916. (Research Division of the Oklahoma Historical Society)

being marketed to white audiences through vaudeville entertainment, from minstrel shows to jazz.[15]

The perversion of black cultural forms for modern white audiences seeking to consume the "primitive" is a reminder that Indian cultures could be similarly manipulated for the pleasure of Anglos. Indeed, by the 1920s, they were already being exoticized by some of the same figures, such as Charlotte Osgood Mason, who cultivated an interest in African Americans. That the Charleston and the black bottom could garner applause from white viewers at an Indian dance indicates a lack of white engagement with specific cultures in favor of broad primitivist fantasies that allowed one group to be substituted with another. Finally, the Ponca dancer's effort to appeal to white audiences is a sad reminder of the complicated outcomes of allotment. After the 1906 Dawes Act, "surplus" Indian land was sold to white settlers. For the Ponca, these buyers included the Miller brothers, sons of a Confederate veteran. They established not only the largest cattle ranch in the United States but also a Wild West show (possibly the "vaudeville" mentioned in *Sundown*), both of which employed Ponca from the region. The Millers thus made a (short-lived) fortune on Ponca land at their ranch and through distortions of Native American history and culture in their show. They profited, too, from African Americans. One of the biggest stars of the 101 Ranch Real Wild West Show was Bill Pickett, the son of former slaves; Pickett wrestled steers as the "Dusky Demon." The show relied on African American roustabouts until its demise in 1931.[16]

During the oil boom years, both Oklahoma Indians and whites employed African Americans in low-wage positions. Those who worked for the Osage are not unaccounted for in *Sundown*, and they provide another opportunity for Chal to find his place in Oklahoma's rapidly changing racial landscape by considering his relation—and sometimes his opposition—to blacks. In one scene, Chal seeks his friend Sun-on-His-Wings, who has gone "back to the blanket" and turned toward the peyote religion, a pan-tribal syncretic religion developed in the 1880s that mediated between tradition and modernity. Arriving at the home of his friend, Chal encounters a "slovenly negro" who tells him that Sun-on-His-Wings is at his "old man's." The reference to Chief Watching Eagle as simply "the old man" sends Chal into a rage, and

African American roustabouts at the 101 Ranch Wild West Show, July 1931. (Research Division of the Oklahoma Historical Society)

he chastises this African American worker for his "disrespect." Chal not only distinguishes himself from this black man in terms of race and class; he also distinguishes both of them from whites—placing himself in an intermediary position in a hierarchy of dominance and submission: "You know you're treated better when you work for an Indian than when you work for white men in town," Chal snarls. This results in "the negro [becoming] quite frightened"—an outcome that makes Chal, who has used white supremacy to assert his own limited privilege, feel better as he departs.[17]

Readers, however, do not necessarily affiliate with Chal's aggression—he is the protagonist, but he is not a hero in this novel. As he speeds dangerously in his motorcar, traversing the Oklahoma landscape in an alcohol-induced haze, he appears morally and culturally bankrupt. The sense of pathos conveyed by Chal's interaction with the black laborer is heightened by the unsettling juxtaposition of humor and fear described in its aftermath: "He thought of that black man's face and he realized how very funny it was," writes Mathews. "The emotion of humor was intensified by the fumes in his brain. . . . There was something in him which magnified the humor inspired by that fear on the negro's

African Americans in Indian country, 1899. (Research Division of the
Oklahoma Historical Society)

face." In this moment, Chal appears to have hit rock bottom; he is cold
and lacking in empathy, and he cultivates pleasure through his domination of others. Rather than finding commonalities in Indian and black
experiences of institutional and individual racism, Chal seems willing to
perpetuate black oppression in order to feel a sense of superiority and

control in his otherwise unanchored life. The figure of the black laborer does nothing to entertain the reader, which may have been the purpose of Mathews's use of dialect in *Twenty Thousand Mornings*. Instead, his presence elicits revulsion toward Chal.[18]

At the end of this scene, Chal seeks an explanation for his complicated response to the black laborer in the tales he learned from "the old men of his people." When Mathews uses the term "old men" to respectfully describe the tribal elders, it points out the wrongfulness of Chal's treatment of the African American worker at Sun-on-His-Wings's house, whom he chastised for calling Chief Watching Eagle "the old man." Mathews writes, "The old men of his people always said the Great Mysteries had sent the Black Rears to their people to make them laugh and forget their troubles. They came with the white man who brought trouble; they said the Black Rears had come for that reason; to make them laugh and forget those troubles which the white man had brought to them. They said the Black Rears came from the South; from the direction of Good." This passage is rife with contradictions. First, the suggestion that blacks are inherently comedic perpetuates minstrel stereotypes of African Americans used for popular entertainment (much like the exaggerated dialect Mathews creates in *Twenty Thousand Mornings*), and it recalls paternalist fantasies of happy-go-lucky, childish black slaves. Second, although this passage may reference Osage cosmology, by envisioning the South as the "direction of Good," the narrative effaces the history of African American oppression during slavery and the Jim Crow era, as well as Indian removal from the region. Third, this passage makes it clear that both African Americans and Indians suffer in a white-supremacist regime—they both experienced loss at the hands of "the white man who brought trouble." Although this passage continues to traffic in paternalistic myths about African Americans, it also describes them as suffering along with Indians under a common oppressor. For Chal—and perhaps for Mathews—race is always treated with ambivalence. The presence of African Americans in this text of Indian country expands this ambivalence beyond the critical conversations about *Sundown* as a "mixed-blood" novel and Mathews as a "mixed-blood" writer.[19]

A very different picture of the relationships between people of color in the borderlands West is presented in the 1943 autobiographical novel *America Is in the Heart: A Personal History*, by Filipino American writer Carlos Bulosan. Featuring a first-person narrator and protagonist, *America Is in the Heart* describes Carlos's upbringing in the Philippines and his arrival in Seattle during the first year of the Great Depression, a time when the Philippines was still a US territory but Filipinos were not eligible for US citizenship. Following Carlos throughout the West—from Alaska to California's Imperial Valley, from Idaho to New Mexico—the narrative ends shortly after the bombing of Pearl Harbor. At that point, the Philippines became a crucial site in the Pacific war, and Filipinos were able to curry favor with the US government, ultimately resulting in the Filipino Naturalization Act of 1946. This periodization places Carlos in a liminal position—without US citizenship and with no home government to protect him, he exists on the national margins. This liminality is often expressed through narratives of geographic mobility that follow not only Carlos's immigration from the Philippines but also his migration throughout the American West as he works as a laborer and a union organizer. This narrative takes place largely in California, and Carlos's experience is unified by the legacies of both Spanish colonialism and US imperialism. As a result, his youth in the Philippines is remarkably consistent with his adulthood in the United States, and the lessons he learns early in life about class, organizing, race, literacy, and literature are brought to bear later, underscoring the relationship between the borderlands West and the Pacific. Impacted by these multiple imperial histories, Carlos is a figure without a country, and Bulosan's text charts the process of creating one, as an aspiring writer, through literature.[20]

As Lisa Lowe has argued, *America Is in the Heart* is largely a book about Carlos's self-education; some sections read like rhapsodic bibliographies of American, European, and world literatures, and these traditions influence Bulosan's authorial style. Carlos's encounters with the written word enable him to construct his identity; when Bulosan's subtitle, *A Personal History*, is taken into account, *America Is in the Heart* can be seen as the product of these literary encounters, as an autobiographical excursion that locates Carlos and other Filipinos within the interwoven national, regional, and racial threads that make up the American fabric. Carlos's upbringing in the Philippines and his experiences in the United States are both punctuated by his encounters with literature. His brother reads him *Robinson Crusoe*, which serves as a cautionary tale about race, migration, and colonialism; however, his encounter with a biography of Abraham Lincoln is one of the first moments when dreams of both class and racial equality crystallize for him. During his first faltering steps toward literacy, Carlos is able to glean the mythology that "Lincoln was a poor boy who became president of the United States," but Lincoln represents more than just an exceptional individual who pulled himself out of poverty by his own bootstraps. Rather, Lincoln's story serves as a foundation for Carlos's project as a union organizer and his commitment to better the lives of working-class people through cross-racial solidarity. Carlos is less inspired by the individualist mythos of a poor boy becoming president and more inspired by what an Anglo-American librarian in the Philippines, Mary Strandon, tells him about Lincoln: "When he became president he said that all men are created equal. . . . But some men, vicious men who had Negro slaves, did not like what he said. So a terrible war was fought between the states of the United States, and the slaves were freed and the nation was preserved." After this revelation, Carlos asks with wonderment, "Abraham Lincoln died for a black person?" It is this—the potential of a cross-racial national imagination—that inspires him. From the moment of this epiphany, Bulosan writes, "this poor boy who became president filled [Carlos's] thoughts."[21]

While Bulosan's representation of Lincoln's biography allows Carlos to dream of cross-racial, democratic nation-building efforts, his other tales of literacy reveal the colder truth about racism in the United States. About Mary Strandon and her library, Carlos notes, "In later years I remembered this opportunity when I read that the American Negro writer, Richard Wright, had not been allowed to borrow books from his local library because of his color." The mythology of Lincoln's self-education through voracious reading (Carlos learns that Lincoln "walked miles and miles to borrow a book so that he would know more about his country") is juxtaposed with the reality of Wright's survival in the segregated South, which he discusses in "The Ethics of Living

Jim Crow." Wright contends, "I learned to play the dual role which every Negro must if he wants to eat and live." For instance, Wright describes the subterfuge he engages in to get books from the library. A coworker (whom Wright suspected "was a Roman Catholic and felt a vague sympathy for Negroes, being himself an object of hatred") gave Wright his library card along with a signed note reading, "Please let this nigger boy have the following books." This is just one example of how Wright learned "to live as a Negro" in the Jim Crow United States. As a new immigrant, Carlos must learn similar methods for survival, which hinge on the question of where he and other Filipinos fall in the American racial landscape. When the biographies of Lincoln and Wright are placed side by side in his narrative, Carlos finds himself believing in the lessons of both their stories. He finds in Lincoln an optimistic hope for cross-racial collaboration, and he finds in Wright a dissection of the mechanisms of systemic racism.[22]

This "paradox of America," as it is called in the text, often finds its greatest expression in the West, where the stunning brutality of racism, poverty, and union busting in the 1930s is counterpoised with idyllic descriptions of the Western landscape, such as the fertile fields of California's Central Valley, the "primitive beauty" of Santa Fe, and the citrus groves of San Fernando. As Carlos negotiates this paradox, African American characters serve as his guides. In one scene, a name-less "Negro boy" whom Carlos meets while train hopping serves as an informant to both the western geography and the US racial order. Carlos notes that this boy "kept playing [a harmonica] for hours, stopping only to say 'Salem!' 'Eugene!' 'Klamath Falls!' when we passed through those places." With his knowledge of western geography, this boy serves as Carlos's actual guide when he redirects Carlos to a train to California after he accidentally ends up in Reno: "'Boy, boy, boy!' he screamed, 'This is Reno, Nevada.'" In addition, this African American character serves as Carlos's guide figuratively. "It was the first time I had ever seen a black person," Carlos recalls, exposing his naïveté about race in the United States. He refers to the African American as "sir," a term of address that evokes both surprise and laughter from this character, who clearly, as Wright puts it, had a "Jim Crow education." In contrast, he calls Carlos "boy," such as when he declares, "Boy, you are far from

California." Through this pairing of "sir" and "boy," this character is able to instruct Carlos about the status of African Americans in the United States and also suggest the status of Filipinos, hinting at the "education" Carlos still needs to acquire.[23]

Near the end of the book, after Carlos has acquired such an education, he is surprised to be called "Mr. Bulosan": "It was the first time that anyone had addressed me that way," he remarks. Shortly thereafter, the United States declares war against Japan, giving Carlos and the Filipino community an opportunity, through military service, to prove their loyalty and commitment to the nation and, they hope, improve conditions for Filipinos by securing citizenship rights. This hope, of course, also informed the choices of other people of color to join the military, including African Americans. African Americans still served in segregated units during this war proclaimed in defense of democracy, an irony not lost on Langston Hughes. In a column titled "Nazi and Dixie Nordics," published in the *Chicago Defender* on March 10, 1945, Hughes remarked, "As the Hitlerites treat the Jews, so [white southerners] treat the Negroes." Filipino Americans also served in segregated regiments—but not always. After the battle of Corregidor in 1942, Carlos's older brother and mentor, Macario, enlists in the army. His last words to Carlos are instructions: "He remembered something of great importance," Carlos narrates, and "gave me ten cents. 'Don't forget to give this to the Negro bootblack across from my hotel,' he said. 'I forgot to pay him today.'"[24]

When Carlos fulfills his brother's request, Larkin, the bootblack, shows the other side of the "paradox of America"—its possibilities, including for cross-racial coalition building and understanding based on shared experiences of prejudice and discrimination. As Joseph Keith suggests, "the scene . . . speaks to a broader tradition of Filipino and African American solidarity . . . forged out of a common condition of exploitation as racialized labor [and] affiliation and exchange [and] within but in counterpoint to the prevailing economic and social logic." Indeed, once Macario leaves Los Angeles, Larkin becomes a surrogate brother to Carlos. Larkin reveals that he, like Macario, is joining the military. And when Carlos shakes Larkin's hand, he notes, "His hand, too, was like my brother's—tough, large, toil-scarred." Larkin and

Macario are bound together by the exploitative conditions of their labor and by the possibility of inclusion in the US body politic through their military service. When Larkin uses Macario's dime to share a beer with Carlos, this moment is emblematic of a cross-racial brotherhood. This brotherhood, however, is not confined to marginalized groups in the United States. Indeed, for Macario, for Carlos, and for Larkin, this is one of the potentialities of America. When Larkin leaves Carlos, he tells him, "I'll remember [Macario] every time I see the face of an American dime. Good-bye, friend!" Here, Larkin is not associating Macario with monetary greed in a capitalist regime where they have both been used as inexpensive labor. Instead, he is associating Macario with the "face of an American dime" because, until 1945, it featured an allegorical female representation of Liberty, the nation's promise to oppressed people. After this encounter with Larkin, Carlos has his final epiphany—the novel's surprisingly optimistic ending, which takes place as he travels from Los Angeles to Portland. His sense of comradeship across racial difference and his ideal of liberty lead to a new feeling of possibility as he gazes across the western landscape. For him, as for so many others, the West is a synecdoche of the imagined national community, multiethnic in scope and comprising those working together to achieve liberty: "I glanced out of the window again," he narrates, "to look at the broad land I had dreamed so much about, only to discover with astonishment that the American earth was like a huge heart unfolding warmly to receive me."[25]

In 1945, two years after *America Is in the Heart* was released, Mexican American writer Josefina Niggli published her first novel, *Mexican Village*, which takes place near Monterrey, in northern Mexico. Up until that time, Niggli had been best known as a playwright. She trained, beginning in 1935, at the University of North Carolina with the Carolina Playmakers, a theater company founded by Frederick H. Koch in 1918 to produce "folk plays"; its alumni includes the likes of Thomas Wolfe, Paul Green, and Betty Smith. As a result of Niggli's Playmakers' training, it makes sense to think of her in conversation with writers of the New Negro movement, particularly Zora Neale Hurston, whose work on African American folk life was informed by her mentorship by anthropologist Franz Boas and her patronage by Charlotte Osgood Mason. As William Orchard and Yolanda Padilla point out, "Niggli did not face the economic hardships that plagued Hurston throughout her life, nor did she achieve the same heights or depths of fame and infamy. The primitivism that was in vogue during the early decades of the twentieth century, however, profoundly shaped the careers of both authors."[26]

In addition to *Carolina Folk Plays*, published in the 1920s, the Play-makers and the University of North Carolina Press published Niggli's *Mexican Folk Plays* in 1938. In "The Playmaker's Aim," Koch enumerates his theater company's goals: "FIRST: To promote dramatic art, especially in the production and publishing of native plays"; "SECOND: To serve as an experimental theatre for plays representing the traditions and present-day life of the people"; and "THIRD: To extend its influence to create native theatre throughout America." He goes on to define "folk" as "the legends, superstitions, customs, environmental differences, and the vernacular of the common people. For the most part they are realistic and human; sometimes they are imaginative and poetic." The purpose of the Playmakers, then, was to create a national American theater, one that was not imitative of European forms, by turning to folk sources. Interestingly, in addition to her own collection of plays, Niggli's writing on Mexico was included in Koch's edited volume *American Folk Plays* (1939). Whereas Koch may have considered his definition of "folk" as simply being transportable to other nations, Niggli may have seen herself as contributing to a transnational understanding of America. She was born in Monterrey, the daughter of white Americans who had moved to Mexico, and she grew up mainly in northern Mexico, the border town of Eagle Pass, Texas, and San Antonio. And like so many others, Niggli developed an understanding of American identities, in part, through her engagement with ideas about blacks.[27]

As one might suspect, many of the Playmakers' folk plays were what Koch called "negro drama[s]." Of course, during the years Niggli studied at the University of North Carolina, it did not accept African American students. The "negro drama[s]" produced by the Playmakers, then, were generally written and performed by whites. Commenting on a 1935 Playmakers tour during which the troupe performed at the historically black Hampton Institute in Virginia, Niggli wrote, "This play had great interest here since it presented the struggle of a Negro

The Playmakers' performance of *Companion-Mate Maggie, A Negro Comedy*, showing the use of blackface, 1929. (North Carolina Collection, University of North Carolina Library at Chapel Hill)

share-cropper." During the play, she continued, "racial feeling was running high. . . . However, as the play progressed and the audience understood, the disturbance ceased and at the reception tendered us by the Hampton Players afterwards, there was much generous praise for the author and his play." This suggests there was some suspicion among black audiences about the Playmakers' representation of African American folk life, which was probably heightened by the use of blackface, the signal element of racial parody. Niggli, then, may have felt the burden of authenticity when writing about Mexican folk themes, considering her complicated relationship to Mexican identity as the white child of American parents who grew up in Mexico during the years *mestizaje* was deployed to unify the postrevolutionary nation.[28]

When Niggli turned to writing fiction in *Mexican Village*, folk elements remained a central focus. She transcribes songs, includes traditional beliefs, refers to superstitions, and, although she writes in English, makes an effort to replicate Spanish-language idioms and syntax for her Mexican characters. The theater, too, remains a central focus. The novel opens with a dramatis personae, much like a script does, and is composed of loosely connected chapters that read like scenes of a play. Niggli's background as a student of drama clearly influenced her prose. The novel, furthermore, transforms a classic dramatic device—a play within a play—into, in this case, a play within a novel that is written somewhat like a play. Such a *mise en abyme* is traditionally a smaller version of a larger whole, a scene that speaks to and makes revelations about the entirety of the dramatic piece. In *Mexican Village*, the *mise en abyme* is a dramatic rendition of *Uncle Tom's Cabin*, performed in blackface by a traveling theater troupe in the northern Mexican village of Hidalgo.

Scholars such as Alexander Saxton and Eric Lott have written about blackface minstrelsy as a way for working-class northerners and new immigrants (such as the Irish in the mid-nineteenth century or eastern European Jews in the early twentieth century) to make populist claims to an empowered white American identity. By performing in blackface, these marginalized subjects (and their audiences) distance themselves from the blacks they purport to represent. The humor of blackface performance, such as it is, rests in part on the knowledge that the actors are not *real* black people, although the representations they create can reflect negatively on African Americans. (This, of course, was complicated by African American actors who manipulated blackface performance to gain a foothold in the entertainment industry, change the stories told about African America, and entertain black audiences through satire.) In *Mexican Village*, however, rather than inserting the Mexican villagers into the American national imagination by, for example, presenting them in contradistinction to blacks and in allegiance with whites, the whole premise of the Tom Show suggests the utter foreignness of the United States, black or white, to the Mexican audience. The play opens with the prompter telling the audience: "This evening you are here to see a play" about "the Yanquis across the Río Bravo. . . . As you all know, there are many strange people among the Yanquis, and some of them are black—not just on face and hands, you understand, but black all over." The prompter's narration suggests that the critical difference here is not between blacks and whites (with Mexicans allying with one or the other) but between "strange . . . Yanquis" (some of whom are black) and Mexicans. Niggli's tale about the Mexican Tom Show does not rely on caricatures of black difference as a source of humor; indeed, the show itself is barely mentioned. The reader knows the actors are wearing black greasepaint, but little else is revealed about the content or form of the performance. The play is still a comedic event, but the humor rests on the hijinks of the Mexican villagers attending the play and their misunderstanding of the history and meaning of *Uncle Tom's Cabin*—and perhaps of the United States.[29]

As the play proceeds, the audience is riveted—partially because "the slave auction scene . . . was so interesting" and strange to Mexican viewers. The fact that "no one in the audience understood the story" is revealed when one of the audience members attempts to bid on Eliza during this scene. Later, when the theater troupe uses salt to simulate snow during Eliza's escape, "the audience, never having seen snow, could not understand why salt was raining on her." Although "the elemental passions involved" in *Uncle Tom's Cabin* "were clear" to the entire audience, only one audience member stands out: "a man who looked like a Yanqui . . . followed the Uncle Tom scenes with rapt attention, at times covering his face with his hands, his shoulders shaking with obvious emotion." Although he is unnamed here, this is presumably the Tejano Bob Webster, the protagonist of the novel and its only major Yanqui character. Despite the history of United States–Mexico relations during the Civil War (to which Paredes's mention of Bagdad, Mexico calls attention), and despite the existence of Afro-Mexicans (including those descended from black Seminole maroon colonies in northern Mexico), the drama of *Uncle Tom's Cabin* seems to affect only the mestizo Yanqui Webster. His emotion indicates his affiliation with this US-based story; the blackface performance incorporates him into the United States' national imagination not by distinguishing him from blacks but by distinguishing him from Mexicans, irrespective of race.[30]

Niggli's inclusion of *Uncle Tom's Cabin* as a *mise en abyme* helps make sense of the conclusion of *Mexican Village*, when Bob Webster, who has been depicted as an "outlander" to the village throughout the novel, discovers his true parentage. His great-grandfather was an *indio*, but his great-grandmother was a member of the Spanish elite, and through their son, his mestizo grandfather, he is the rightful heir to the lands of the Sabinas Valley in northern Mexico. Bob, however, does not expose his secret and claim the land. Instead, he remains silent and leaves the land to another character, his foil Joaquín, son of the Spanish-descended Don Saturnino. Joaquín had returned to the valley disguised as one of the actors in the Tom Show, and his "passionate tenderness for the Sabinas was too strong an emotion for Bob to parallel in his own lonely heart." At first, it looks as though Niggli reinscribes a prerevolutionary racial hierarchy onto Mexico, rendering the Spanish-descended elite as landowners while the mestizos and Indians of the valley remain landless. She takes great pains, however, to create in the figure of Joaquín a man who "agree[s] with the Revolutionary Party that all men are created equal, and an *indito* is as good as a Creole." And she exposes, through Bob's emotional reaction to *Uncle Tom's Cabin*, his knowledge of the problems with heredity. *Uncle Tom's Cabin*—particularly the tale of Eliza—is largely a story of hypodescent and family. The fact that enslavement was inherited through the condition of the mother, and black family ties were always at risk, serves as a counterpoint to the notions of inheritance and family in *Mexican Village*. Bob's understanding of the regime of slavery, then, informs his decision to shake off his hereditary ties to the valley, despite his growing affection for it and the feeling that it has become his home. As a result, Bob both retains his identification with the United States and develops his identification with Mexico; he becomes a border subject who muses, as he burns the letter revealing his lineage, "There are two sides to every coin, the side seen and the side unseen." Rather than simply eliding race and nation in the years after the Mexican Revolution, Niggli detaches them, creating far more complicated and often overlapping definitions of Americanness and Mexicanness based not on heredity but on affect. By doing so, Niggli, the Mexican-born daughter of white Americans, may have been claiming a dual Mexican and US identity—a transnational Americanness—at a time when folk authenticity was surging in popularity among the Playmakers, in Harlem, and in Mexico, even as it was troubled by the persistence of racial parody.[31]

This book has explored African American imaginings of the borderlands West as a multiethnic place, asking what happens when the New Negro is found outside of Harlem and in a place much more frequently associated with Mexican Americans, Native Americans, Anglo-Americans, and—to a lesser extent—Asian Americans. It has suggested that, by engaging with frontier fantasies and borderlands realities, this geography complicated New Negro identities and ideologies such as racial uplift and a coherent cultural nationalism. African Americans writing in the borderlands West both flirted with notions of radical hybridity and acknowledged the limitations of those notions. For Coleman, Bontemps, Thurman, Hughes, and Toomer, who wrote during the years of the New Negro renaissance, the borderlands West provided new ways to imagine blacks' relation to the nation, and this sometimes necessitated an extension of the definitions of the terms "nation," "Negro," and "the West." For Paredes, Mathews, Bulosan, and Niggli, who wrote during the same years, the borderlands West—from the banks of the Rio Grande to the roads of the Osage Agency, from the fields of central California to the ranges of northern Mexico—also demanded that the national imagination be investigated. Each of these writers used his or her literature to perform these investigations and to illustrate how Mexican Americans, Asian Americans, and Native Americans were included within or exiled from the nation. Although they did this through a variety of means, one tactic they all used—in subtle and often gestural ways—was to place non-black ethnic communities either in alliance with or in contradistinction to African Americans. While African Americans often constituted the smallest minority group throughout the borderlands West, their presence loomed large in the multiethnic American imagination. In *Freedom Dreams: The Black Radical Imagination*, historian Robin D. G. Kelley insists on the power of the imagination to inspire social and political movements for change. Even if black social movements have failed to eradicate racism, he contends, the dreams that anchor them are worth interrogating as they continue to inspire struggle. Taken together, the creative work of African American, Mexican American, Asian American, and Native American writers reveals that the borderlands West, long used as a synecdoche for the nation, was repurposed as one such dreamscape in the years of the New Negro renaissance. This dreamscape was never ignorant of reality and was always aware of the "wait" implied by "hope," yet these visions of the borderlands West still provide powerful alternative images of region, of nation, and of their ties to the world, where community empowerment, racial belonging, transnational harmony, sexual egalitarianism, and multiethnic collaboration become as possible as racism, conquest, capital, and individualism.[32]

Notes

Introduction: Going to the Territory

The epigraph is from Arna Bontemps to Langston Hughes, April 30, 1956, box 19, folder 416, Langston Hughes Papers, James Weldon Johnson Collection, Beinecke Rare Book and Manuscript Library, Yale University, New Haven, Conn. Reprinted by permission from Harold Ober Associates, Incorporated, as agents for the Estate of Arna Bontemps.

1. Frederick Jackson Turner, "The Significance of the Frontier in American History," in *The Norton Anthology of American Literature*, vol. C, *1865–1914*, 7th ed., eds. Nina Baym, Jeanne Campbell Reeseman, and Arnold Krupat (New York: W. W. Norton, 2007), 1152.

2. Frederick Douglass, "Frederick Douglass's Speech at Colored American Day (August 25, 1893)," in Christopher Robert Reed, *All the World Is Here! The Black Presence at White City* (Bloomington: Indiana University Press, 2010), 193–194. In an 1893 newspaper article, Willietta Johnson explained that when African Americans called for inclusion at the fair, they wanted to "make it a day which would stand in history commemorative of the mental, moral and physical progress of a people who are scoffed at and looked down upon. It was not intended that there should be minstrels, plantation scenes and such like, which do not show the improvement of the colored people in this country." See "Colored People's Day: They Will Have a Jubilee at the Columbian Exposition," *Boston Daily Globe*, March 22, 1893. Despite the demands of black activists, the fair introduced the stereotypical (and enduring) pancake spokesperson Aunt Jemima, who was played by fifty-nine-year-old domestic Nancy Green, a former slave. See M. M. Manring, *Slave in a Box: The Strange Career of Aunt Jemima* (Charlottesville: University Press of Virginia, 1998), 75. For more information on Colored American Day, see Robert W. Rydell, "Editor's Introduction: Contend! Contend!" in Ida B. Wells, Frederick Douglass, Irvine Garland Penn, and Ferdinand L. Barnett, *The Reason Why the Colored American Is Not in the World's Columbian Exposition* (Urbana: University of Illinois Press, 1999), xxx. For a scholarly appraisal of Colored American Day, see Reed, *All the World Is Here!*, 134–139.

3. Houston A. Baker Jr., *Long Black Song: Essays in Black American Literature and Culture* (Charlottesville: University Press of Virginia, 1972), 2. For a sustained examination of how African American culture engages with the frontier myth, contra Baker's assertion, see Michael K. Johnson, *Black Masculinity and the Frontier Myth in American Literature* (Norman: University of Oklahoma Press, 2002).

4. Richard White, "Frederick Jackson Turner and Buffalo Bill," in Richard White and Patricia Nelson Limerick, *The Frontier in American Culture*, ed. James R. Grossman (Berkeley: University of California Press, 1994), 45.

5. Douglass quoted in "Great Meeting in Faneuil Hall: Speeches of Samuel J. Mau, Frederick Douglass and Wendell Phillips," *Liberator*, June 8, 1849, 90 (Mexican War); Frederick Douglass and Richard T. Greener, "Frederick Douglass and Richard T. Greener on the Negro Exodus, 1879," in *A Documentary History of the Negro People in the United States*, ed. Herbert Aptheker (New York: Citadel Press, 1951), 724 (Exodusters).

6. Turner, "Significance of the Frontier in American History," 1150. For the most famous example of the furtherance of this western mythos, see Henry Nash Smith, *Virgin Land: The American West as Symbol and Myth* (1950; reprint, Cambridge, Mass.: Harvard University Press, 2007). In the years since the initial publication of *Virgin Land*, American studies scholars, particularly feminist scholars, have roundly contested Smith's gendered vision of "virgin land." See, among others, Annette Kolodny, *The Lay of the Land: Metaphor as Experience and History in American Life and Letters* (Chapel Hill: University of North Carolina Press, 1975), and *The Land before Her: Fantasy and Experience of the American Frontiers, 1630–1860* (Chapel Hill: University of North Carolina Press, 1984).

7. Ralph Ellison, "Going to the Territory," in *Going to the Territory* (New York: Vintage, 1995), 131.

8. Ibid., 126, 125, 131.

9. Owen quoted in Douglas Flamming, "'A Westerner in Search of Negroness': Region and Race in the Writing of Arna Bontemps," in *Over the Edge: Remapping the American West*, ed. Valerie J. Matsumoto and Blake Allmendinger (Berkeley: University of California Press, 1999), 91. For an extensive examination of the tension between an "authentic" unpopulated western landscape and the allegedly "nonwestern" urban space, see Krista Comer, *Landscapes of the New West: Gender and Geography in Contemporary Women's Writing* (Chapel Hill: University of North Carolina Press, 1999), particularly chap. 2, "Urbanscapes in the Golden Land: California as Western Continuum," 61–119.

10. Quintard Taylor, *In Search of the Racial Frontier: African-Americans in the American West, 1528–1990* (New York: W. W. Norton, 1999), 22.

11. Ellison, "Going to the Territory," 134.

12. Ibid., 131; Tiya Miles and Sharon P. Holland, "Introduction: Crossing Waters, Crossing Worlds," in *Crossing Waters, Crossing Worlds: The African Diaspora in Indian Country*, ed. Tiya Miles and Sharon P. Holland (Durham, N.C.: Duke University Press, 2006), 4; Johnson quoted in Taylor, *In Search of the Racial Frontier*, 17.

13. James Weldon Johnson, "Harlem: The Culture Capital," in *The New Negro: Voices of the Harlem Renaissance*, ed. Alain Locke (New York: Touchstone, 1997), 301–311. Recent work has tried to expand the scope of the New Negro movement beyond Harlem. See, for example, Davarian Baldwin and Minkah Makalani, eds., *Escape from New York: The New Negro Renaissance beyond Harlem* (Minneapolis: University of Minnesota Press, 2013).

14. Langston Hughes, *The Big Sea* (1940; reprint, New York: Hill & Wang, 1993), 223. The most obvious example of this assimilative impulse is Booker T. Washington. But New Negro artists even clashed with some of their more progressive mentors around issues such as the use of dialect in black literature. W. E. B. DuBois did not see this as representative of the "talented tenth" he wished to promote to signal black equality; "talented tenth" is one of DuBois's key terms in *The Souls of Black Folk* (1903; reprint, New York: Penguin, 1989). For representative scholarship that emphasizes Harlem, see James DeJongh, *Vicious Modernism: Black Harlem and the Literary Imagination* (New York: Cambridge University Press, 1990). Another example is Ann Douglas's *Terrible Honesty: Mongrel Manhattan in the 1920s* (New York: Noonday Press, 1995), which examines black-white collaboration in Manhattan and insists that Manhattan was the center of not only African American literature but all American literature during this period. Houston A. Baker's *Modernism and the Harlem Renaissance* (Chicago: University of Chicago Press, 1987) and its follow-up, *Turning South Again: Re-Thinking Modernism/Re-Reading Booker T.* (Durham, N.C.: Duke University Press, 2001), study the relationship between Harlem and the South in African American modernism.

15. Paul Gilroy, *The Black Atlantic: Modernity and Double-Consciousness* (Cambridge, Mass.: Harvard University Press, 1993), 15; Brent Hayes Edwards, *The Practice of Diaspora: Literature, Translation, and the Rise of Black Internationalism* (Cambridge, Mass.: Harvard University Press, 2003), 2–3, 13–15.

16. Gilroy, *Black Atlantic*, 17.

17. Thadious Davis, *Southscapes: Geographies of Race, Region, and Literature* (Chapel Hill: University of North Carolina Press, 2011), 19.

18. Arna Bontemps and Jack Conroy, *Anyplace But Here* (Columbia: University of Missouri Press, 1966), 315.

19. For examples of the new western history, see Patricia Nelson Limerick, *The Legacy of Conquest: The Unbroken Past of the American West* (New York:

W. W. Norton, 1987); Richard White, *It's Your Misfortune and None of My Own: A History of the American West* (Norman: University of Oklahoma Press, 1991); Susan Lee Johnson, *Roaring Camp: The Social World of the California Gold Rush* (New York: W. W. Norton, 2000). For the concomitant movement in literary studies, see, for example, Kolodny, *Land before Her*, and Comer, *Landscapes of the New West*. For a comprehensive historical work on the black West, see Taylor, *In Search of the Racial Frontier*. Other important works include Douglas Flamming, *Bound for Freedom: Black Los Angeles in Jim Crow America* (Berkeley: University of California Press, 2005); Daniel Widener, *Black Arts West: Culture and Struggle in Postwar Los Angeles* (Durham, N.C.: Duke University Press, 2010); Josh Sides, *L.A. City Limits: African American Los Angeles from the Great Depression to the Present* (Berkeley: University of California Press, 2003); Herbert G. Ruffin II, *Uninvited Neighbors: African Americans in Silicon Valley, 1769–1990* (Norman: University of Oklahoma Press, 2014). For an overarching book on African American literature in the West, see Blake Allmendinger, *Imagining the African American West* (Lincoln: University of Nebraska Press, 2005). Also see Eric Gardner, *Unexpected Places: Relocating Nineteenth-Century African American Literature* (Jackson: University Press of Mississippi, 2009); Johnson, *Black Masculinity and the Frontier Myth*; Michael K. Johnson, *Hoo-Doo Cowboys and Bronze Buckaroos: Conceptions of the African American West* (Jackson: University Press of Mississippi, 2014). In terms of the 1920s and 1930s, Allmendinger's book contains one chapter on the relationship between the New Negro renaissance and the West, titled "The Significance of the Frontier in the New Negro Renaissance" (46–65). Historian Douglas Flamming has written on New Negro writer Arna Bontemps and the West in his essay "'A Westerner in Search of Negro-ness,'" 85–104. An anthology of essays on the New Negro movement and the American West has also been published recently. Each essay is organized around a particular location and takes a largely historical approach to examining the black community in that locale during the New Negro movement. See Bruce A. Glasrud and Cary D. Wintz, eds., *The Harlem Renaissance and the American West: The New Negro's Western Experience* (New York: Routledge, 2011).

20. In popular culture, books like Zane Grey's *Riders of the Purple Sage* (1912) were best sellers, and these western fictions were carried over to the silver screen by directors such as John Ford, who began to make westerns during the silent era. For more on the rise of western tourism, see Hal K. Rothman, *Devil's Bargains: Tourism in the Twentieth Century American West* (Lawrence: University Press of Kansas, 2000). Critical texts that examine modernist primitivism include Marianna Torgovnick, *Gone Primitive: Savage Intellects, Modern Lives* (Chicago: University of Chicago Press, 1990). Native

Americans as the object of primitivism are examined in Helen Carr, *Inventing the American Primitive: Politics, Gender, and the Representation of Native American Literary Traditions, 1789–1936* (New York: New York University Press, 1996), and Mexican Americans as the object of primitivism are examined in Helen Dalpar, *The Enormous Vogue of Things Mexican: Cultural Relations between the United States and Mexico, 1920–1935* (Tuscaloosa: University of Alabama Press, 1995). Modernist primitivism was evident at a Dada exhibit at Paris's Centre Pompidou that ran from October 5, 2005, to January 6, 2006; it displayed southwestern Indian art alongside works by Man Ray and Marcel Duchamp. For more on white modernists in the West and their relationship to indigenous communities, see Flannery Burke, *From Greenwich Village to Taos: Primitivism and Place at Mabel Dodge Luhan's* (Lawrence: University Press of Kansas, 2008), and Audrey Goodman, *Translating Southwestern Landscapes: The Making of an Anglo Literary Region, 1880–1930* (Tucson: University of Arizona Press, 2002).

21. Carr, *Inventing the American Primitive*, 208–209.

22. Erna Fergusson, *Our Southwest* (New York: Alfred A. Knopf, 1940), 3–4. For additional information on Fergusson, see Robert Franklin Gish, *Beautiful Swift Fox: Erna Fergusson and the Modern Southwest* (College Station: Texas A&M University Press, 1996), 159.

23. José Vasconcelos, *The Cosmic Race/La raza cósmica*, trans. Didier T. Jaén (Baltimore: Johns Hopkins University Press, 1997), 19; DuBois, *Souls of Black Folk*, 1, 19. It is worth noting, of course, that antiblack racism persists in Latin America, and black history has been expunged at times in Mexico, often through ideologies of *mestizaje*. *Mestizaje* had traction as a national policy, so while it could be utilized to create a multiethnic community, it could also be used to create the illusion of racial sameness that occludes persistent racism. For more on Afro-Mexicans, see, for example, Ben Vinson III and Michael Restall, eds., *Black Mexico: Race and Society from Colonial to Modern Times* (Albuquerque: University of New Mexico Press, 2009).

24. Christine Stansell, *American Moderns: Bohemian New York and the Creation of a New Century* (New York: Henry Holt, 2000), 104–105. See also Mabel Dodge Luhan, *Movers and Shakers* (New York: Harcourt, Brace, 1936), and *Edge of Taos Desert: An Escape to Reality* (Albuquerque: University of New Mexico Press, 1987). In critiquing Luhan's antiblack racism, it is important to note that she did invite Jean Toomer to Taos; however, by that time, Toomer had self-identified as a member of a "new American race." For more on how Luhan's activism intersected with her primitivism, see Burke, *From Greenwich Village to Taos*, 114.

25. José David Saldívar, *Border Matters: Remapping American Cultural Studies* (Berkeley: University of California Press, 1997), 12, x–xi; Mary Pat Brady,

"Scaling the West Differently," *Western American Literature* 35, 1 (Spring 2000): 98; José E. Limón, *American Encounters: Greater Mexico, the United States, and the Erotics of Culture* (Boston: Beacon Press, 1998), 7–33. For work on the African American West in multiethnic contexts, see Scott Kurashige, *The Shifting Grounds of Race: Black and Japanese Americans in the Making of Modern Los Angeles* (Princeton, N.J.: Princeton University Press, 2008); David Chang, *The Color of the Land: Race, Nation, and the Politics of Landownership in Oklahoma, 1832–1929* (Chapel Hill: University of North Carolina Press, 2010); Stacy Smith, *Freedom's Frontier: California and the Struggle over Unfree Labor, Emancipation, and Reconstruction* (Chapel Hill: University of North Carolina Press, 2013); Shana Bernstein, *Bridges of Reform: Interracial Civil Rights Activism in Twentieth-Century Los Angeles* (New York: Oxford University Press, 2011); Mark Brilliant, *The Color of America Has Changed: How Racial Diversity Shaped Civil Rights Reform in California, 1941–1978* (New York: Oxford University Press, 2010); Kevin Leonard, *The Battle for Los Angeles: Racial Ideology and World War II* (Albuquerque: University of New Mexico Press, 2006); Mark Wild, *Street Meeting: Multiethnic Neighborhoods in Early Twentieth-Century Los Angeles* (Berkeley: University of California Press, 2005).

26. Saldívar, *Border Matters*, 13. For nineteenth-century black publications in the West, see Gardner, *Unexpected Places*. For more on Micheaux's western writing, see Allmendinger, *Imagining the African American West*, 13–32, and Johnson, *Black Masculinity and the Frontier Myth*, 69–97. See also Taylor Gordon, *Born to Be* (Lincoln, Neb.: Bison Books, 1995); Kornel Chang, *Pacific Connections: The Making of the U.S.–Canadian Borderlands* (Berkeley: University of California Press, 2012); Claudia Sadowski-Smith, *Border Fictions: Globalization, Empire, and Writing at the Boundaries of the United States* (Charlottesville: University of Virginia Press, 2008).

27. Krista Comer, "West," in *Keywords for American Cultural Studies*, ed. Bruce Burgett and Glenn Hendler (New York: New York University Press, 2007), 242.

28. See Richard Slotkin, *Gunfighter Nation: The Myth of the Frontier in Twentieth-Century America* (Norman: University of Oklahoma Press, 1998).

29. Mary Pat Brady, *Extinct Lands, Temporal Geographies: Chicana Literature and the Urgency of Space* (Durham, N.C.: Duke University Press, 2002), 8–9; Gloria Anzaldúa, *Borderlands/La Frontera: The New Mestiza* (1987; reprint, San Francisco: Aunt Lute, 1999), 99; Mary Pat Brady, "Border," in *Keywords for American Cultural Studies*, ed. Bruce Burgett and Glenn Hendler (New York: New York University Press, 2007), 32. "Locational feminism" is more thoroughly addressed in Susan Stanford Friedman, *Mappings: Feminism and*

the Cultural Geographies of Encounter (Princeton, N.J.: Princeton University Press, 1998), 18.

30. bell hooks, *Feminist Theory: From Margin to Center*, 2nd ed. (Boston: South End Press, 2000), 12, 16.

31. Philip J. Deloria, *Indians in Unexpected Places* (Lawrence: University Press of Kansas, 2004), 6. For examples of feminist standpoint epistemology, see Sandra Harding, *Whose Science? Whose Knowledge? Thinking from Women's Lives* (Ithaca, N.Y.: Cornell University Press, 1991); Patricia Hill Collins, *Black Feminist Thought: Knowledge, Consciousness, and the Politics of Empowerment* (New York: Routledge, 2000), particularly her famous articulation of a "matrix of domination" understood via black feminist intellectual traditions; and Donna Haraway, "Situated Knowledges: The Science Question in Feminism and the Privilege of Partial Perspective," *Feminist Studies* 14, 2 (1988): 575–599.

32. Anita Scott Coleman, "Arizona and New Mexico—The Land of Esperanza," in *Western Echoes of the Harlem Renaissance: The Life and Writings of Anita Scott Coleman*, ed. Cynthia Davis and Verner D. Mitchell (Norman: University of Oklahoma Press, 2008), 283–284; Claude McKay, *Home to Harlem* (Lebanon, N.H.: University Press of New England/Northeastern University Press, 1987). The rediscovery and dominant critical appraisal of Coleman's work can be credited to Davis and Mitchell, *Western Echoes of the Harlem Renaissance*, and Laurie Champion and Bruce A. Glasrud, eds., *Unfinished Masterpiece: The Harlem Renaissance Fiction of Anita Scott Coleman* (Lubbock: Texas Tech University Press, 2008).

33. Flamming, "'A Westerner in Search of Negro-ness,'" 85–91.

34. Wallace Thurman, "Quoth Brigham Young—This Is the Place," in *These "Colored" United States: African American Essays from the 1920s*, ed. Tom Lutz and Susanna Ashton (New Brunswick, N.J.: Rutgers University Press, 1996), 265–267.

35. Coleman, "Arizona and New Mexico—The Land of Esperanza," 385; Langston Hughes, "Harlem (2)," in *The Collected Poems of Langston Hughes*, ed. Arnold Rampersad and David Roessel (New York: Vintage Books, 1995), 426.

Part I: One Who Stayed

The epigraph is from "Harlem (2)," in *The Collected Poems of Langston Hughes* by Langston Hughes, edited by Arnold Rampersad with David Roessel, associate editor, copyright © 1994 by the Estate of Langston Hughes. Used by permission of Alfred A. Knopf, an imprint of the Knopf Doubleday Publishing Group, a division of Random House LLC. All rights reserved.

Chapter 1. Home on the Range

The epigraph is from "After the Bloodbath," *Newsweek*, August 30, 1965. © 1965 IBT Media. All rights reserved. Used by permission and protected by the copyright laws of the United States. The printing, copying, redistribution, or retransmission of this content without express written permission is prohibited.

1. D. H. Lawrence, *Studies in Classic American Literature* (1923; reprint, New York: Penguin, 1977), 7–14; Beulah Amidon Ratliff, "Mississippi: Heart of Dixie," in *These United States: Portraits of America from the 1920s*, ed. Daniel H. Borus (Ithaca, N.Y.: Cornell University Press, 1992), 202; Clement Wood, "Alabama: A Study in Ultra-Violet," ibid., 35; Ludwig Lewisohn, "South Carolina: A Lingering Fragrance," ibid., 326; Douglas Freeman, "Virginia: A Gentle Dominion," ibid., 379; Elizabeth Shepley Sergeant, "New Mexico: A Relic of Ancient America," ibid. 249; Mary Austin, "Arizona: The Land of Joyous Adventure," ibid., 39.

2. *Messenger* quoted in Tom Lutz, "Introduction: Diversity, Location, and Ideology in 'These "Colored" United States,'" in *These "Colored" United States: African American Essays from the 1920s*, ed. Tom Lutz and Susanna Ashton (New Brunswick, N.J.: Rutgers University Press, 1996), 6.

3. *Messenger* quoted in Cynthia Davis and Verner D. Mitchell, "Preface," in *Western Echoes of the Harlem Renaissance: The Life and Writings of Anita Scott Coleman*, ed. Cynthia Davis and Verner D. Mitchell (Norman: University of Oklahoma Press, 2008), xiii; the review of *Negro Voices* is in Frank M. Davis, "Book Review: Poetry by Colored Writers," *New Journal and Guide*, December 25, 1938, 9; Hughes's mention of Coleman is in Langston Hughes, "Here to Yonder: Mugging," *Chicago Defender*, May 1, 1943, 14.

4. When Coleman received third prize for her short story "Three Dogs and a Rabbit" (written under the pseudonym Elizabeth Stokes) in 1925, second prize went to Colorado Springs resident Marie French (writing as Jean France) for a short story titled "There Never Fell a Night so Dark." The same year, Myrtle Athleen Smith from Greeley, Colorado, won third prize for plays. See "Krigwa," *Crisis*, October 1925, 275–276. In 1926, when Coleman (writing under the pseudonym Annie Hawkins) received an honorable mention for her short story "Flaming Flame," other prizewinners included an honorable mention for the essay "Vagabonding in a City of Opera Seats" by San Francisco's Julian Elihu Bagley (writing as I. D. Evans). See "Krigwa," *Crisis*, December

1926, 70. *Tuneful Tales* has been republished; see Bernice Love Wiggins, *Tuneful Tales*, ed. Maceo C. Dailey Jr. and Ruthe Winegarten (Lubbock: Texas Tech University Press, 2002). The Ink Slingers are mentioned briefly, alongside other African American literary societies, in Elizabeth McHenry, *Forgotten Readers: Recovering the Lost History of African American Literary Societies* (Durham, N.C.: Duke University Press, 2002), 293.

5. See Laurie Champion and Bruce A. Glasrud, eds., *Unfinished Masterpiece: The Harlem Renaissance Fiction of Anita Scott Coleman* (Lubbock: Texas Tech University Press, 2008); Davis and Mitchell, *Western Echoes of the Harlem Renaissance*; Alice Walker, "In Search of Zora Neale Hurston," *Ms. Magazine*, March 3, 1975, 74–79, 84–89.

6. Population statistics for Los Angeles are from Quintard Taylor, *In Search of the Racial Frontier: African-Americans in the American West, 1528–1990* (New York: W. W. Norton, 1999), 193, 223, 286; population statistics for New Mexico are from United States Bureau of the Census, *1890 Census of Population and Housing*, vol. 1, *Report on Population of the United States at the Eleventh Census*, pt. 1 (Washington, D.C.: Government Printing Office, 1895), 390–422.

7. Rodman Wilson Paul, *Mining Frontiers of the Far West, 1848–1880*, rev. and exp. Elliot West (Albuquerque: University of New Mexico Press, 2001), 159; "Silver Ores from New Mexico," *Washington Post*, April 15, 1881, 2; H. B. Ailman, *Pioneering in Territorial Silver City: H. B. Ailman's Recollections of Silver City and the Southwest, 1871–1892* (Albuquerque: University of New Mexico Press, 1983), 29, 39, 48; "A Great Silver Country," *Chicago Daily Tribune*, September 1, 1873, 5; James A. Hall, "Once Mining Center of Fabulous Wealth, Now Grewsome Ghost," *Atlanta Constitution*, February 2, 1902, A3; Ailman, *Pioneering in Territorial Silver City*, 56. In 1915 an African American resident wrote to the NAACP in an effort to establish a chapter in the mining community of Bisbee, Arizona, on the grounds that "colored citizens . . . are debarred from all labor except Janitoring." See Katherine Benton-Cohen, *Borderline Americans: Racial Division and Labor War in the Arizona Borderlands* (Cambridge, Mass.: Harvard University Press, 2009), 103. For the assignment of domestic duties to men of color in mining camps, see Susan Lee Johnson, *Roaring Camp: The Social World of the California Gold Rush* (New York: W. W. Norton, 2000), 99–139.

8. Verner D. Mitchell, "A Family Answers the Call: Anita Scott Coleman, Literature, and War," *War, Literature, and the Arts* 20, 1/2 (2008): 303–304.

9. United States Census Bureau, *1900 Census of Population and Housing*, vol. 1, *Population: Population of States and Territories*, sec. 9 (Washington, D.C.: U.S. Census Office, 1901), 486; Hall, "Once Mining Center of Fabulous Wealth," A3; William A. Doback and Thomas D. Phillips, *The Black Regulars*,

1866–1898 (Norman: University of Oklahoma Press, 2001), 271; Davis and Mitchell, "Introduction: Anita Scott Coleman in the Southwest," in *Western Echoes of the Harlem Renaissance*, 9; Anita Scott Coleman, "Arizona and New Mexico—The Land of Esperanza," in Lutz and Ashton, *These "Colored" United States*, 283; Davis and Mitchell, "Introduction," 12. For an example of social events reported from Silver City nationwide, see "New Mexico: Silver City, New Mexico," *Chicago Defender*, September 11, 1937, 22; "Silver City, New Mexico," *Pittsburgh Courier*, October 8, 1938, 6.

10. For more on the railroad and black activism, see Eric Arnesen, *Brotherhoods of Color: Black Railroad Workers and the Struggle for Equality* (Cambridge, Mass.: Harvard University Press, 2002).

11. William D. Carrigan and Clive Webb, "The Lynching of Persons of Mexican Origin or Descent in the United States, 1848 to 1928," *Journal of Social History* 37, 2 (2003): 413.

12. Advertisement quoted in Taylor, *In Search of the Racial Frontier*, 144–145; Gerald Horne, *Black and Brown: African Americans and the Mexican Revolution, 1910–1920* (New York: New York University Press, 2005), 61; lore surrounding Boyer and Keyes's journey in Barbara J. Richardson, comp., *Black Directory of New Mexico, Bicentennial Edition, 1776–1976: Black Pioneers of New Mexico—A Documentary and Pictorial History* (Rio Rancho, N.M.: Panorama Press, 1976), 151; Lucy M. Henderson, "Free Land for the Race in New Mexico," *Chicago Defender*, December 21, 1912, 3. For more on the Exodusters, see Nell Irvin Painter, *Exodusters: Black Migration to Kansas after Reconstruction* (New York: W. W. Norton, 1992).

13. Delegates from Arizona, *Protest against Union of Arizona with New Mexico*. 59th Cong., 1st sess., February 12, 1906, S. Doc. 216, serial 4913, 1; F. Chris Garcia, Paul L. Hain, Gilbert K. St. Clair, and Kim Seckler, eds., *Governing New Mexico* (Albuquerque: University of New Mexico Press, 2006), 217. For more on New Mexico statehood, see David Van Holtby, *Forty-Seventh Star: New Mexico's Struggle for Statehood* (Norman: University of Oklahoma Press, 2012).

14. W. R. Cummins, "White Man's Country," *Artisian Sun* (Artisia, N.M.), October 3, 1903, quoted in Maisha Baton and Henry Walt, *A History of Blackdom, N.M. in the Context of the African American Post Civil War Colonization Movement* (Albuquerque: Historic Preservation Division, New Mexico Office of Cultural Affairs, 1996).

15. "Interview with Roosevelt Boyer, Sr. conducted by Maisha Baton," quoted in Baton and Walt, *History of Blackdom*, 7; Cummins, "White Man's Country." The Ku Klux Klan's terrorism of Vado is narrated as follows in Richardson, *Black Directory of New Mexico*, 91:

Not only the elements of nature conspired to defeat Boyer and his fellow-pioneers. The Ku Klux Klan resented the presence of Negroes, and one night burned a fiery cross in the center of the settlement. The settlers held their ground. The Klan threatened and burned more crosses but Vado refused to budge. Finally it was the Cotton King that settled the dispute. The discovery that cotton would thrive near Vado and the realization that the Negro farmers were the only ones in the area who knew how to cultivate it, caused the Klansmen and their backers to cease the assault. The Klan never rose again.

See chapter 2 for more on cotton agriculture in the borderlands West.

16. *Roswell (N.M.) Record*, September 10, 1915, quoted in Baton and Walt, *History of Blackdom*, 7.

17. W. E. "Old Man" Utterback, *Looking Back 73 Years* (Roswell, N.M.: Hall Poorbaugh Press, 1978), v, 12. Scholars who address the impact of the "Fight of the Century" include Gail Bederman, *Manliness and Civilization: A Cultural History of Gender and Race in the United States, 1880–1917* (Chicago: University of Chicago Press, 1995), and Theresa Runstedtler, *Jack Johnson, Rebel Sojourner* (Berkeley: University of California Press, 2012). For more on the intersection of African American and Native American literature and folklore, see Jonathan Brennan, ed., *Where Brer Rabbit Meets Coyote: African–Native American Literature* (Urbana: University of Illinois Press, 2003).

18. Coleman, "Arizona and New Mexico," 284; Davis and Mitchell, "Introduction," 21; "Wanted," *Crisis*, August 1913, 197.

19. Anita Scott Coleman, "Rich Man, Poor Man," in Davis and Mitchell, *Western Echoes of the Harlem Renaissance*, 139–140; Houston A. Baker Jr., *Long Black Song: Essays in Black American Literature and Culture* (Charlottesville: University Press of Virginia, 1972), 2.

20. Coleman, "Arizona and New Mexico," 283.

21. Ibid.

22. A facsimile of Blackdom's Articles of Incorporation is contained in the appendix to Baton and Walt, *History of Blackdom*; "Interview with Lillian Westfield Collins conducted by Maisha Baton," ibid., 9.

23. Ibid., 11; "Joann Coleman Weds U.S. Air Force Man," *Los Angeles Sentinel*, July 26, 1962, B3; Coleman quoted in Melvin J. Chisum, "Ivory and Gold," *Baltimore Afro-American*, December 26, 1931, 13.

24. The demise of Blackdom is recorded in Rodger D. Hardaway, "African American Communities on the Western Frontier," in *Communities in the American West*, ed. Stephen Tschudi (Reno: Nevada State Humanities Committee,

1999), 138. For the suggestion that the Colemans were relatively unaffected by Jim Crow, see Davis and Mitchell, "Introduction," 12–17.

25. For the 1859 New Mexican slave code, see Taylor, *In Search of the Racial Frontier*, 75. For the school segregation statute, see Soledad C. Chacon (Secretary of State), comp., *Laws of the State of New Mexico* (Albuquerque: Valliant Printing, 1925), 109.

26. Coleman, "Arizona and New Mexico," 284–285; Davis and Mitchell, "Introduction," 18.

27. Coleman quoted in Laurie Champion and Bruce A. Glasrud, "Introduction: Anita Scott Coleman's Short Stories and the Harlem Renaissance," in *Unfinished Masterpiece*, 6.

28. William Deverell, *Whitewashed Adobe: The Rise of Los Angeles and the Remaking of Its Mexican Past* (Berkeley: University of California Press, 2004), 2; Paul Robinson, "Race, Space, and the Evolution of Black Los Angeles," in *Black Los Angeles: American Dreams and Racial Realities*, ed. Darnell Hunt and Ana-Christina Ramón (New York: New York University Press, 2010), 21–34; Douglas Flamming, *Bound for Freedom: Black Los Angeles in Jim Crow America* (Berkeley: University of California Press, 2005), 1. For more on African American Los Angeles, see Josh Sides, *L.A. City Limits: African American Los Angeles from the Great Depression to the Present* (Berkeley: University of California Press, 2003), among others.

29. Hughes quoted in Arnold Rampersad, *The Life of Langston Hughes*, vol. 1, *1902–1941: I, Too, Sing America* (New York: Oxford University Press, 2002), 236; W. E. B. DuBois, "Colored California," *Crisis*, August 1913, 193; Flamming, *Bound for Freedom*, 51; Taylor, *In Search of the Racial Frontier*, 233.

30. Davis and Mitchell, "Introduction," 5; Anita Scott Coleman, "The Little Grey House," in Davis and Mitchell, *Western Echoes of the Harlem Renaissance*, 98, 100, 102. For more on *Half-Century Magazine* and its readership, see Noliwe M. Rooks, *Ladies' Pages: African American Women's Magazines and the Culture that Made Them* (New Brunswick, N.J.: Rutgers University Press, 2004).

31. Coleman, "Little Grey House," 101, 104, 98–99, 105.

32. Ibid., 100, 105.

33. Statistics on black women's domestic labor in Los Angeles are from Edna Bonacich, Lola Smallwood Cuevas, Lanita Morris, Steven Pitts, and Joshua Bloom, "A Common Project for a Just Society: Black Labor in Los Angeles," in *Black Los Angeles: American Dreams and Racial Realities*, ed. Darnell Hunt and Ana-Christina Ramón (New York: New York University Press, 2010), 392. Flamming, *Bound for Freedom*, 71, also comments on black women's labor in the West:

A smaller number of [black women] *had* to work for wages. From 1900 to 1920 in Atlanta, New Orleans, and San Antonio, women constituted about half the black workforce. In major western cities, women made up only 20 to 40 percent of the black labor force. In Los Angeles, women represented less than one-third of the black workforce in 1900, and slightly more than one-third in 1920. These figures reflect the middle-class nature of black migration to Los Angeles, as well as the higher wages that black husbands could earn out West.

34. Announcement for Coleman's forthcoming short story, "Love for Hire," accompanying Gwendolyn Williams, "Bow to the Sun," *Pittsburgh Courier*, August 14, 1943, 13 ("Love for Hire" appeared in the *Pittsburgh Courier*, August 21, 1943, 13); Anita Scott Coleman, "Hands," in Davis and Mitchell, *Western Echoes of the Harlem Renaissance*, 195–196 (Copyright 2008 University of Oklahoma Press. Reproduced with permission. All rights reserved); Anita Scott Coleman, "Idle Wonder," ibid., 202.

35. Claudia Tate, *Domestic Allegories of Political Desire: The Black Heroine's Text at the Turn of the Century* (New York: Oxford University Press, 1992), 8; W. E. B. DuBois, "Criteria of Negro Art," in *Double-Take: A Revisionist Harlem Renaissance Anthology*, ed. Venetria K. Patton and Maureen Honey (New Brunswick, N.J.: Rutgers University Press, 2001), 49.

36. Anita Scott Coleman, "Jack Arrives," in Davis and Mitchell, *Western Echoes of the Harlem Renaissance*, 113, 115, 114, 115, 117, 116, 117.

37. Anita Scott Coleman, "Rich Man, Poor Man," ibid., 140–141, 145, 146, 143, 146, 140, 141.

38. Anita Scott Coleman, "Phoebe and Peter up North," ibid., 187, 181–182, 184, 185; Anita Scott Coleman, "Phoebe Goes to a Lecture," ibid., 189, 188, 191, 192.

39. Austin, "Arizona," 42; Vera Norwood and Janice Monk, "Introduction: Perspectives on Gender and Landscape," in *The Desert Is No Lady: Southwestern Landscapes in Women's Writing and Art*, ed. Vera Norwood and Janice Monk (Tucson: University of Arizona Press, 1997), 9; Flannery Burke, "An Artists' Home: Gender and the Santa Fe Culture Center Controversy," *Journal of the Southwest* 46, 2 (2004): 352.

40. Nancy F. Cott, *The Bonds of Womanhood: "Woman's Sphere" in New England, 1780–1835*, 2nd ed. (New Haven, Conn.: Yale University Press, 1997); Aileen S. Kraditor, "Introduction," in *Up from the Pedestal: Selected Writings in the History of American Feminism*, ed. Aileen S. Kraditor (Chicago: Quadrangle Books, 1968), 3–24; Barbara Welter, "The Cult of True Womanhood:

1820–1860," *American Quarterly* 18, 2 (1966): 151–174; Elsa Barkley Brown, "To Catch the Vision of Freedom: Reconstructing Southern Black Women's Political History, 1865–1880," in *African American Women and the Vote, 1837–1965*, ed. Ann D. Gordon with Bettye Collier-Thomas, John H. Bracey, Arlene Voski Avakain, and Joyce Avrech Berkman (Amherst: University of Massachusetts Press, 1997), 66–67.

41. Daylanne K. English, *Unnatural Selections: Eugenics in American Modernism and the Harlem Renaissance* (Chapel Hill: University of North Carolina Press, 2004). See also Harry Bruinius, *Better for All the World: The Secret History of Forced Sterilization and America's Quest for Racial Purity* (New York: Vintage Books, 2007); Deborah Kuhn McGregor, *From Midwives to Medicine: The Birth of American Gynecology* (New Brunswick, N.J.: Rutgers University Press, 1998); Harriet Washington, *Medical Apartheid: The Dark History of Medical Experimentation on Black Americans from Colonial Times to the Present* (New York: Doubleday, 2006).

42. E. Frances White, "Africa on My Mind: Gender, Counter Discourse, and African American Nationalism," in *Is It Nation Time? Contemporary Essays on Black Power and Black Nationalism*, ed. Eddie S. Glaude Jr. (Chicago: University of Chicago Press, 2002), 133; Audre Lorde, "The Master's Tools Will Never Dismantle the Master's House," in *Sister Outsider: Essays and Speeches* (Berkeley, Calif.: Crossing Press, 1984), 110–113; Houston A. Baker, *Workings of the Spirit: The Poetics of Afro-American Women's Writing* (Chicago: University of Chicago Press, 1991), 32–33; Lora Romero, *Home Fronts: Domesticity and Its Critics in the Antebellum United States* (Durham, N.C.: Duke University Press, 1997), 67. For more on how black power movements considered the black family, see Robin D. G. Kelley, *Freedom Dreams: The Black Radical Imagination* (Boston: Beacon, 2002), 142–143.

43. Coleman, "Arizona and New Mexico," 283.

44. Mehlop quoted in Richardson, *Black Directory of New Mexico*, 77–78. For more on California's Alien Land Law and mixed marriages, see Karen Leonard, "Punjabi Farmers and California's Alien Land Law," *Agricultural History* 54, 1 (1985): 552–553; Karen Isaksen Leonard, *Making Ethnic Choices: California's Punjabi Mexican Americans* (Philadelphia: Temple University Press, 1992).

45. Anita Scott Coleman, "Three Dogs and a Rabbit," in Davis and Mitchell, *Western Echoes of the Harlem Renaissance*, 87, 92, 87, 93.

46. Anita Scott Coleman, "The Brat," ibid., 76, 77, 78, 80.

47. Ibid., 80, 81, 82, 82.

48. Ibid., 83, 82–83, 83.

49. bell hooks, "Choosing the Margin as a Space of Radical Openness," in

Yearning: Race, Gender, and Cultural Politics (Boston: South End Press, 1990), 149–150.

Part II: Those Who Went Away

The epigraph is from "Arizona and New Mexico—The Land of Esperanza," from *Western Echoes of the Harlem Renaissance*, by Anita Scott Coleman. Copyright 2008 University of Oklahoma Press. Reproduced with permission. All rights reserved.

Chapter 2: The Two LAs

The epigraph is from Arna Bontemps, "The Chariot in the Cloud," box 64, Arna Bontemps Papers, Special Collections Research Center, Syracuse University Libraries, Syracuse, N.Y. Reprinted by permission from Harold Ober Associates, Incorporated, as agents for the Estate of Arna Bontemps.

1. Arna Bontemps, "Autobiographical Material," box 1, Arna Bontemps Papers, Special Collections Research Center, Syracuse University Libraries, Syracuse, N.Y.; Arna Bontemps, "Dust Jacket Copy: *Hold Fast to Dreams*," box 31, ibid. Both reprinted by permission from Harold Ober Associates, Incorporated, as agents for the Estate of Arna Bontemps.

2. Arna Bontemps, "The Awakening: A Memoir," in *The Harlem Renaissance Remembered*, ed. Arna Bontemps (New York: Dodd, Mead, 1972), 16.

3. David G. Nicholls, *Conjuring the Folk: Forms of Modernity in African America* (Ann Arbor: University of Michigan Press, 2000), 2; Houston A. Baker Jr., *Turning South Again: Re-Thinking Modernism/Re-Reading Booker T.* (Durham, N.C.: Duke University Press, 2001), 18; Thadious Davis, *Southscapes: Geographies of Race, Region, and Literature* (Chapel Hill: University of North Carolina Press, 2011), 2; Arna Bontemps, "A Response to *Long Black Song: Essays in the Black Literary Tradition*, by Houston Baker, Jr.," box 34, Bontemps Papers (reprinted by permission from Harold Ober Associates, Incorporated, as agents for the Estate of Arna Bontemps); Baker, *Turning South Again*, 19; Arna Bontemps, "Why I Returned," in *The Old South* (New York: Dodd, Mead, 1973), 12.

4. Kirkland C. Jones, *Renaissance Man from Louisiana: A Biography of Arna Wendell Bontemps* (Westport, Conn.: Greenwood Press, 1992); Kirkland C. Jones, "Bontemps and the Old South," *African American Review* 27, 2 (1993):

185; Jill Leroy-Frazier, "Othered Southern Modernism: Arna Bontemps's *Black Thunder*," *Mississippi Quarterly: The Journal of Southern Culture* 63, 1/2 (Winter 2010): 3–29; Nicholas Canaday, "Arna Bontemps: The Louisiana Heritage," *Callaloo: A Journal of African American Arts and Letters* 1–3, 11–13 (1981): 163–169.

5. Arna Bontemps, "Letter to Verna Avery [December 29, 1941]," box 2, Bontemps Papers (reprinted by permission from Harold Ober Associates, Incorporated, as agents for the Estate of Arna Bontemps).

6. Arna Bontemps, "Introduction to the 1968 Edition," in *Black Thunder* (Boston: Beacon, 1992), xxi–xxv; Charles Scruggs and Lee VanDemarr, *Jean Toomer and the Terrors of American History* (Philadelphia: University of Pennsylvania Press, 1998), 9–13; Arna Bontemps, "Saturday Night: Portrait of a Small Southern Town, 1933," in *The Old South*, 157–168.

7. Bontemps, "Why I Returned," 18; Davarian Baldwin, *Chicago's New Negroes: Modernity, the Great Migration, and Black Urban Life* (Chapel Hill: University of North Carolina Press, 2007), 24, 14; Arna Bontemps and Jack Conroy, *Anyplace but Here* (Columbia: University of Missouri Press, 1966), 11; Bontemps, "Why I Returned," 18. For more on black migration patterns from the South to Chicago, the West, and New York City, see Isabel Wilkerson, *The Warmth of Other Suns: The Epic Story of America's Great Migration* (New York: Vintage, 2011).

8. Douglas Flamming, *Bound for Freedom: Black Los Angeles in Jim Crow America* (Berkeley: University of California Press, 2005), 55–58; Frederick Madison Roberts, "For the West," *New Age*, March 12, 1915.

9. Kevin K. Gaines, *Uplifting the Race: Black Leadership, Politics, and Culture in the Twentieth Century* (Chapel Hill: University of North Carolina Press, 1996), 2; Roberts, "For the West."

10. Bontemps, "Introduction to the 1968 Edition," xxii; Flamming, *Bound for Freedom*, 99, 93.

11. Flamming, *Bound for Freedom*, 378; Gaines, *Uplifting the Race*, 3.

12. Douglas Flamming, "'A Westerner in Search of Negro-ness': Region and Race in the Writing of Arna Bontemps," in *Over the Edge: Remapping the American West*, ed. Valerie J. Matsumoto and Blake Allmendinger (Berkeley: University of California Press, 1999), 86, 95.

13. Arna Bontemps, *God Sends Sunday* (New York: Washington Square Press, 1959), 118–119.

14. Arna Bontemps, "The Chariot in the Cloud," 75, box 64, Bontemps Papers (reprinted by permission from Harold Ober Associates, Incorporated, as agents for the Estate of Arna Bontemps). In "The Chariot in the Cloud," Bontemps spells "Mud Town" as two words—the only place he does so, even

though he mentions "Mudtown" in a number of his writings. For the sake of consistency, I have chosen to spell "Mudtown" as one word throughout.

15. Flamming, *Bound for Freedom*, 64.

16. Bontemps, "The Chariot in the Cloud," 76.

17. Bontemps and Conroy, *Anyplace but Here*, 5–6.

18. Ibid., 6–7.

19. Ibid., 8.

20. Bontemps, "The Chariot in the Cloud," 11, 3, 14–15.

21. Ibid., 60, 65, 60. For more on the image of Indian Territory in the blues, see Chris Smith, "Going to the Nation: The Idea of Oklahoma in Early Blues Recordings," *Popular Music* 26, 2 (2007): 83–96.

22. Bontemps, "The Chariot in the Cloud," 75–77.

23. Ibid., 83, 90, 86, 91. For more on modern female identity and conceptions of the street, see Deborah L. Parsons, *Streetwalking the Metropolis: Women, the City, and Modernity* (New York: Oxford University Press, 2000).

24. Bontemps, "The Chariot in the Cloud," 111, 109, 114, 115, 164; Noliwe M. Rooks, *Hair Raising: Beauty, Culture, and African American Women* (New Brunswick, N.J.: Rutgers University Press, 1996), 95, 135. "Another Man's Town" is the title of book 3 of "The Chariot in the Cloud."

25. The "interurban tracks" demarcate Los Angeles neighborhoods in Bontemps, "The Chariot in the Cloud," 129.

26. Ibid., 132, 141, 156, 159.

27. Ibid., 204–205.

28. Ibid., 206; Richard White, *Railroaded: The Transcontinentals and the Making of Modern America* (New York: W. W. Norton, 2011).

29. Bontemps, "The Chariot in the Cloud," 159; Richard White, *It's Your Misfortune and None of My Own: A History of the American West* (Norman: University of Oklahoma Press, 1991), 542; Bontemps, "The Chariot in the Cloud," 128; Jean Toomer, "The *Cane* Years," in *The Wayward and the Seeking: A Collection of Writings by Jean Toomer*, ed. Darwin T. Turner (Washington, D.C.: Howard University Press, 1982), 123; Krista Comer, *Landscapes of the New West: Gender and Geography in Contemporary Women's Writing* (Chapel Hill: University of North Carolina Press, 1999), 118–119.

30. Bontemps and Conroy, *Anyplace but Here*, 10.

31. Bontemps, "The Chariot in the Cloud," 213–214.

32. Arna Bontemps, "The Prizefighter and the Woman," 96, 22, 49, box 74, Bontemps Papers (reprinted by permission from Harold Ober Associates, Incorporated, as agents for the Estate of Arna Bontemps).

33. Ibid., 147, 49, 29, 26, 134. For "soiled doves" as a euphemism for nineteenth-century western prostitutes, see Anne M. Butler, *Daughters of Joy,*

Sisters of Misery: Prostitutes in the American West, 1865–90 (Urbana: University of Illinois Press, 1985), 82.

34. Bontemps, "The Prizefighter and the Woman," 1–2, 8.

35. Ibid., 24, 191, 49.

36. See Arna Bontemps, "Introduction," in Jean Toomer, *Cane* (New York: Perennial, 1969), vii–xvi; Arna Bontemps, "Material Related to the Jean Toomer Papers at Fisk University" and "Arna Bontemps to Marjorie Content Toomer," box 26, Bontemps Papers; Arna Bontemps, "Adah," box 64, ibid. For more on Toomer's racial identity, see chapter 5 of this volume; for more on Menken, see Daphne A. Brooks, "The Deeds Done in My Body: Performance, Black(ened) Women, and Adah Isaacs Menken in the Racial Imaginary," in *Bodies in Dissent: Spectacular Performances of Race and Freedom, 1850–1910* (Durham, N.C.: Duke University Press, 2006), 131–206.

37. Arnold R. Hirsch and Joseph Logsdon, "Introduction: Part III, Franco-Africans and African-Americans," in *Creole New Orleans: Race and Americanization*, ed. Arnold R. Hirsch and Joseph Logsdon (Baton Rouge: Louisiana State University Press, 1992), 189–190.

38. Bontemps, "The Prizefighter and the Woman," 53–54, 54, 141, 101–104, 143.

39. Kirsten Silva Gruesz, "The Gulf of Mexico System and the 'Latinness' of New Orleans," *ALH: American Literary History* 18, 3 (2006): 469–470; Herbert Eugene Bolton, *The Spanish Borderlands: A Chronicle of Old Florida and the Southwest* (New Haven, Conn.: Yale University Press, 1921).

Chapter 3. Revolt from the Provinces

The epigraph is from Wallace Thurman, "Negro Life in New York's Harlem: A Lively Picture of a Popular and Interesting Section," in *The Collected Writings of Wallace Thurman: A Harlem Renaissance Reader*, ed. Amritjit Singh and Daniel M. Scott III (New Brunswick, N.J.: Rutgers University Press, 2003).

1. "Wallace Thurman Is Model Harlemite, Lewis Announces," *Atlanta Daily World*, March 13, 1932, A6. An earlier clipping of this article, with Lewis's byline, is contained in "Clippings re: Wallace Thurman," box 3, folder 60, Wallace Thurman Collection, James Weldon Johnson Collection, Beinecke Rare Book and Manuscript Library, Yale University, New Haven, Conn. See James Weldon Johnson, "Harlem: The Culture Capital," in *The New Negro: Voices of the Harlem Renaissance*, ed. Alain Locke (New York: Touchstone, 1997).

2. "Wallace Thurman Is Model Harlemite," A6.

3. "Personal Papers—Biographical Sketches of Wallace Thurman by Harold

Jackman and Hughes Allison," box 3, folder 59, Thurman Collection. Notes indicate this speech was written by playwright Hughes Allison and delivered at Thurman's funeral by the Reverend William Lloyd Imes.

4. Dorothy West, "Elephant's Dance," in *The Richer, the Poorer* (New York: Anchor Books, 1995), 215–216.

5. Wallace Thurman, "Letter to William Jourdan Rapp [August 1929]," in Singh and Scott, *Collected Writings of Wallace Thurman*, 158; Wallace Thurman, "Autobiographical Statement," ibid., 91–92; Wallace Thurman, "Letter to Langston Hughes [Thursday, September 1934]," ibid., 130–131. For the only attempt at a full-length biography of Wallace Thurman, see Eleonore van Notten, *Wallace Thurman's Harlem Renaissance* (Amsterdam: Rodopi, 1994).

6. Wallace Thurman, "Letter to W. E. B. DuBois, [March 8, 1926]," in Singh and Scott, *Collected Writings of Wallace Thurman*, 163; Wallace Thurman, "Telegram to Langston Hughes [April 24, 1934]" and "Telegram to Langston Hughes [April 29, 1934]," ibid., 129. For information on the *Outlet*, see van Notten, *Wallace Thurman's Harlem Renaissance*, 91. For more on Fay M. Jackson, see Lael L. Hughes-Watkins, "Fay M. Jackson: The Sociopolitical Narrative of a Pioneering African American Female Journalist" (MA thesis, Youngstown State University, 2008), 12, 18–20.

7. To date, the only essay that has given considerable thought to situating Thurman in the western context is Gerald Haslam, "Wallace Thurman: Western Renaissance Man," *Western American Literature* 6 (1971): 53–59. Blake Allmendinger includes some information on Thurman and the West in *Imagining the African American West* (Lincoln: University of Nebraska Press, 2005), 53–55. For a more comprehensive history of blacks in Utah, see Ronald G. Coleman, "A History of Blacks in Utah, 1825–1910" (Ph.D. diss., University of Utah, 1980). Population statistics are from United States Bureau of the Census, *State and County QuickFacts: Utah*, http://quickfacts .census.gov/qfd/states/49000.html (accessed July 17, 2013), and United States Bureau of the Census, *Profile of General Population and Housing Characteristics: 2010*, http://factfinder2.census.gov/faces/tableservices/jsf/pages/productview .xhtml?src=bkmk (accessed July 17, 2013).

8. Wallace Thurman, "Quoth Brigham Young—This Is the Place," in *These "Colored" United States: African American Essays from the 1920s*, ed. Tom Lutz and Susanna Ashton (New Brunswick, N.J.: Rutgers University Press, 1996), 266. Population statistics are from United States Bureau of the Census, *Fourteenth Census of the United States: State Compendium—Utah* (Washington, D.C.: Government Printing Office, 1924), 29, 8; United States Bureau of the Census, *Fifteenth Census of the United States—1930 Population*, vol. 3, pt. 2, *Montana–Wyoming* (Washington, D.C.: Government Printing Office, 1932), 1113.

9. Joseph Baker, "By Midnight Oil: Of Making Books," *Philadelphia Tribune*, February 11, 1932, 16; "Is the Late A'Leila Walker the 'Amy Douglas' of Thurman Novel?" *Baltimore Afro-American*, April 9, 1932, 17.

10. "'Call Home the Heart' and Other Works of Fiction," *New York Times*, February 28, 1932, BR22; N. G., "New Books," *New York Amsterdam News*, March 16, 1932, 8; Dewey R. Jones, "Books by Race Authors Prove Disappointing as 1932 List Is Scanned," *Chicago Defender*, January 7, 1933, 10; Eunice Hunton Carter, "Review of *The Blacker the Berry*, by Wallace Thurman," *Opportunity: Journal of Negro Life*, May 1929, 162–163.

11. George S. Schuyler, "Views and Reviews," *Pittsburgh Courier*, February 6, 1932, 10. For more on Schuyler and Thurman as satirists, see J. Martin Favor, "George Schuyler and Wallace Thurman: Two Satirists of the Harlem Renaissance," in *The Cambridge Companion to the Harlem Renaissance*, ed. George Hutchinson (New York: Cambridge University Press, 2007), 198–212.

12. W. E. B. DuBois, "Criteria of Negro Art," in *Double-Take: A Revisionist Harlem Renaissance Anthology*, ed. Venetria K. Patton and Maureen Honey (New Brunswick, N.J.: Rutgers University Press, 2001), 49.

13. Wallace Thurman, "A Thrush at Eve with an Atavistic Wound: Review of *Flight*, by Walter White," in Singh and Scott, *Collected Writings of Wallace Thurman*, 183; Wallace Thurman, "Negro Artists and the Negro," ibid., 196–198.

14. For an example of the power of the debates about respectability as applied to Thurman, see Amritjit Singh, "Introduction: Wallace Thurman and the Harlem Renaissance," in Singh and Scott, *Collected Writings of Wallace Thurman*, 1–28.

15. Thurman, "Quoth Brigham Young," 267; "Wallace Thurman Is Model Harlemite," A6; Anita Scott Coleman, "Arizona and New Mexico—The Land of Esperanza," in *Western Echoes of the Harlem Renaissance: The Life and Writings of Anita Scott Coleman*, ed. Cynthia Davis and Verner D. Mitchell (Norman: University of Oklahoma Press, 2008), 285; Thurman, "Quoth Brigham Young," 263.

16. Thurman, "Quoth Brigham Young," 263.

17. Thurman, "Negro Life in New York's Harlem," 45–46.

18. Thurman, "Quoth Brigham Young," 264, 265–266, 266, 265.

19. Wallace Thurman, *The Blacker the Berry* (Mineola, N.Y.: Dover Publications, 2008), 6, 5, 6.

20. Ibid., 5–6, 11, 13, 30, 37.

21. Ibid., 95.

22. Allmendinger, *Imagining the African American West*, 55; Thurman, "Quoth Brigham Young," 264–265.

23. Wallace Thurman, "Letter to Langston Hughes [Friday, c. July 1929]," in Singh and Scott, *Collected Writings of Wallace Thurman*, 120; Wallace Thurman, "Letter to William Jourdan Rapp [n.d.]," ibid., 149; Wallace Thurman, "Letter to William Jourdan Rapp [Sunday midnight, August 1929]," ibid., 159; Wallace Thurman, "Letter to William Jourdan Rapp [c. April 1929]," ibid., 135.

24. Singh, "Introduction," 16; Wallace Thurman, "Letter to William Jourdan Rapp [Thursday, c. July 1929]" and "Letter to William Jourdan Rapp [c. July 1929]," in Singh and Scott, *Collected Writings of Wallace Thurman*, 151, 153–154.

25. Wallace Thurman, "Letter to Langston Hughes [Tuesday, December 5, 1928]," in Singh and Scott, *Collected Writings of Wallace Thurman*, 117; Lawrence B. de Graff, "Race, Sex, and Region: Black Women in the American West, 1850–1920," *Pacific Historical Review* 49, 2 (1980): 305.

26. Thurman, *The Blacker the Berry*, 13; Thurman, "Quoth Brigham Young," 265.

27. Wallace Thurman, "Letter to William Jourdan Rapp [Tuesday, May 7, 1929]," in Singh and Scott, *Collected Writings of Wallace Thurman*, 138–139; Lisa Duggan, "Making It Perfectly Queer," in *Theorizing Feminism: Parallel Trends in the Humanities and Social Sciences*, ed. Anne C. Herrmann and Abigail J. Stewart (Boulder, Colo.: Westview Press, 2000), 223; Granville Ganter, "Decadence, Sexuality, and the Bohemian Vision of Wallace Thurman," *MELUS: Multi-Ethnic Literature of the United States* 28, 2 (2003): 83–84; Eric King Watts, "Queer Harlem: Exploring the Rhetorical Limits of a Black Gay 'Utopia,'" in *Queering Public Address: Sexualities in American Historical Discourse*, ed. Charles E. Morris III (Columbia: University of South Carolina Press, 2007), 174–175; Elisa F. Glick, "Harlem's Queer Dandy: African-American Modernism and the Artifice of Blackness," *MFS: Modern Fiction Studies* 49, 3 (2003): 414–415. Watts's essay suggests that Locke's attitude toward Thurman's "eccentricity" is an example of the imposition of a politics of respectability onto Thurman's queer sexual politics. Eminently cultured and mannered, Locke was, indeed, a paragon of respectability. But as a philosopher, Locke patterned his aesthetic sensibilities and his mentorship of his New Negro protégés after homoerotic classical traditions. See A. B. Christa Schwarz, *Gay Voices of the Harlem Renaissance* (Bloomington: Indiana University Press, 2003), 12–13.

28. George Chauncey, *Gay New York: Gender, Urban Culture, and the Making of the Gay Male World, 1890–1940* (New York: Basic Books, 1994), 23; David R. Jarraway, "Tales of the City: Marginality, Community, and the Problem of Identity in Wallace Thurman's 'Harlem' Fiction," *College English* 61, 1 (2002): 36–52; Thurman, *The Blacker the Berry*, 73–74, 117, 144, 124.

29. Watts, "Queer Harlem," 175; Darlene Clark Hine, "Rape and the Inner

Lives of Black Women: Thoughts on the Culture of Dissemblance," in *Hine Sight: Black Women and the Re-construction of American History* (Bloomington: Indiana University Press, 1997), 37–58; E. Frances White, *The Dark Continent of Our Bodies: Black Feminism and the Politics of Respectability* (Philadelphia: Temple University Press, 2001). For more on queer Harlem, see Schwarz, *Gay Voices of the Harlem Renaissance*; Eric Garber, "A Spectacle in Color: The Gay and Lesbian Subculture of Jazz Age Harlem," in *Hidden from History: Reclaiming the Gay and Lesbian Past*, ed. Martin Duberman, Martha Vicinus, and George Chauncey (New York: Meridian, 1990), 318–331; Eric Garber, "'T'ain't Nobody's Bizness': Homosexuality in 1920s Harlem," in *Black Men/White Men: A Gay Anthology*, ed. Michael J. Smith (San Francisco: Sunshine Press, 1983), 7–16; James F. Wilson, *Bulldaggers, Pansies, and Chocolate Babies: Performance, Race, and Sexuality in the Harlem Renaissance* (Ann Arbor: University of Michigan Press, 2011); Michael L. Cobb, "Insolent Racing, Rough Narrative: The Harlem Renaissance's Impolite Queers," *Callaloo* 23, 1 (2000): 328–351; Stephen Knadler, "Sweetback Style: Wallace Thurman's Harlem Renaissance," *MFS: Modern Fiction Studies* 48, 4 (2002): 898–936.

30. Richard Bruce Nugent, *Gentleman Jigger: A Novel of the Harlem Renaissance* (Philadelphia: Da Capo Press, 2008), 13–18; Langston Hughes, *The Big Sea* (New York: Hill & Wang, 1993), 237.

31. Mae Gwendolyn Henderson, "Portrait of Wallace Thurman," in *The Harlem Renaissance Remembered*, ed. Arna Bontemps (New York: Dodd, Mead, 1972), 147, 149. Nugent's close friend and confidant writes of Nugent's allegations of plagiarism in his introduction to Nugent's novel; see Thomas H. Wirth, "Introduction," in Nugent, *Gentleman Jigger*, xiii–xiv.

32. Thurman, "Quoth Brigham Young," 264.

33. For more on polygamy and Mormonism in American culture and law, see Sarah Barringer Gordon, *The Mormon Question: Polygamy and Constitutional Conflict in Nineteenth-Century America* (Chapel Hill: University of North Carolina Press, 2001).

34. Wallace Thurman, "Letter to Langston Hughes [Wednesday, n.d.]," in Singh and Scott, *Collected Writings of Wallace Thurman*, 126; Thurman, "Quoth Brigham Young," 264; Thurman, "Letter to William Jourdan Rapp [c. July 1929]," in Singh and Scott, *Collected Writings of Wallace Thurman*, 153; Wallace Thurman, "Letter to William Jourdan Rapp [Saturday, n.d.]," ibid., 156.

35. Thurman, *The Blacker the Berry*, 100–102.

36. Wallace Thurman, "Letter to Claude McKay [October 4, 1928]," in Singh and Scott, *Collected Writings of Wallace Thurman*, 164–165. For Thompson's material on the West, see Louise Thompson Patterson, "Blacks in the West, sources," box 2, folder 20; "Blacks in the West: California, East Bay

sources," box 2, folder 21; "Blacks in the West: California, Oakland pioneers," box 2, folder 22; "Blacks in the West: Nevada, correspondence, 1987," box 2, folder 23; "Blacks in the West: Nevada, early sources," box 2, folder 24; "Blacks in the West: Nevada, Goldfield and Tonopah," box 2, folder 25; "Blacks in the West: *Nevada Historical Quarterly*, photocopied articles," box 2, folder 26; "Blacks in the West: Nevada, history," box 3, folder 1; "Blacks in the West: Nevada, University of Nevada (Reno), oral history program," box 3, folder 2; "Blacks in the West: Nevada, vital statistics, early 1900s," box 3, folder 3; "Blacks in the West: Oregon, Kathryn Bogle," box 3, folder 4; "Blacks in the West: Oregon, Coos Bay," box 3, folder 5; "Blacks in the West: Oregon, correspondence, 1987," box 3, folder 6; "Blacks in the West: Oregon, *History of Portland's African American Community (1805 to the Present)*, February 1993," box 3, folder 7; "Blacks in the West: Oregon, Marshfield and Coos Bay, historical sketches," box 3, folder 8; "Oregon, Oregon Black History Project, 1980," box 3, folder 9; "Blacks in the West: Oregon, research materials," box 3, folder 10; "Blacks in the West: Oregon, school records," box 3, folder 11; "Blacks in the West: University of California (Berkeley), memorabilia," box 3, folder 12, all in Louise Thompson Patterson Papers, Emory University, Atlanta, Ga. For more on companionate marriage, see Rebecca L. Davis, "'Not Marriage at All, but Simple Harlotry': The Companionate Marriage Controversy," *Journal of American History* 94, 4 (2008): 1137–1163.

37. For more on Reno divorces, see Jani Scandura, *Down in the Dumps: Place, Modernity, American Depression* (Durham, N.C.: Duke University Press, 2008).

Chapter 4. Technicolor Places

The epigraph is from Langston Hughes, "The Wild Wild West," box 387, folder 7133, Langston Hughes Papers, James Weldon Johnson Collection, Beinecke Rare Book and Manuscript Library, Yale University, New Haven, Conn. Reprinted by permission from Harold Ober Associates, Incorporated, as agents for the Estate of Langston Hughes.

1. Langston Hughes, "The Negro Speaks of Rivers," in *The Collected Poems of Langston Hughes*, ed. Arnold Rampersad and David Roessel (New York: Vintage Books, 1995), 23 ("The Negro Speaks of Rivers," from *The Collected Poems of Langston Hughes*, by Langston Hughes, edited by Arnold Rampersad with David Roessel, associate editor, copyright © 1994 by the Estate of Langston Hughes. Used by Permission of Alfred A. Knopf, an imprint of the Knopf Doubleday Publishing Group, a division of Random House LLC. All rights reserved.); Langston Hughes, "Just Traveling," in *The Collected Works of Langston Hughes*,

vol. 9, *Essays on Art, Race, Politics, and World Affairs*, ed. Christopher C. De Santis (Columbia: University of Missouri Press, 2002), 142, 146.

2. Brent Hayes Edwards, *The Practice of Diaspora: Literature, Translation, and the Rise of Black Internationalism* (Cambridge, Mass.: Harvard University Press, 2003), 63–68; Brent Hayes Edwards, "Langston Hughes and the Futures of Diaspora," *ALH: American Literary History* 19, 3 (2007): 691; Edward Mullen, "Langston Hughes in Mexico and Cuba," in *Review: Latin American Literature and Arts* 47 (1993): 23–27; Astrid Haas, "A Continent of Color: Langston Hughes in Latin America," in *Expanding Latinidad: An Inter-American Perspective*, ed. Luz Angélica Kirschner (Tempe, Ariz.: Bilingual Review Press, 2012), 177–194; Claudia Milian, *Latining America: Black-Brown Passages and the Coloring of Latino/a Studies* (Athens: University of Georgia Press, 2013), 80–87; Blake Allmendinger, *Imagining the African American West* (Lincoln: University of Nebraska Press, 2005), 56–61.

3. Langston Hughes, "A Diary of Mexican Adventures (If There Be Any)," box 492, folder 12432, Langston Hughes Papers, James Weldon Johnson Collection, Beinecke Rare Book and Manuscript Library, Yale University, New Haven, Conn. (reprinted by permission from Harold Ober Associates, Incorporated, as agents for the Estate of Langston Hughes).

4. Langston Hughes, "West Texas," in Rampersad and Roessel, *Collected Poems of Langston Hughes*, 252 ("West Texas," from *The Collected Poems of Langston Hughes*, by Langston Hughes, edited by Arnold Rampersad with David Roessel, associate editor, copyright © 1994 by the Estate of Langston Hughes. Used by Permission of Alfred A. Knopf, an imprint of the Knopf Doubleday Publishing Group, a division of Random House LLC. All rights reserved.); Langston Hughes, "I Wonder as I Wander: Drafts, Typescript, Carbon and Holograph, Corrected," 136, box 305, folder 5001, Hughes Papers (reprinted by permission from Harold Ober Associates, Incorporated, as agents for the Estate of Langston Hughes).

5. Hughes, "Diary of Mexican Adventures."

6. Ibid.; Langston Hughes, "The Negro Artist and the Racial Mountain," in *Double-Take: A Revisionist Harlem Renaissance Anthology*, ed. Venetria K. Patton and Maureen Honey (New Brunswick, N.J.: Rutgers University Press, 2001), 43, 40; Hughes, "Diary of Mexican Adventures"; Eddie S. Glaude Jr., *Exodus! Religion, Race, and Nation in Early Nineteenth Century Black America* (Chicago: University of Chicago Press, 2000); Eric J. Sundquist, *Strangers in the Land: Blacks, Jews, Post-Holocaust America* (Cambridge, Mass.: Harvard University Press, 2005). For more on the Exodusters, see Nell Irvin Painter, *Exodusters: Black Migration to Kansas after Reconstruction* (New York: W. W. Norton, 1992). For John Brown and the book of Exodus, see John Coffey, *Liberation and Exodus: Deliverance Politics from John Calvin to Martin Luther King, Jr.* (New York: Oxford University Press, 2014), 133–134.

7. Hughes, "Diary of Mexican Adventures"; Hughes, "The Negro Artist and the Racial Mountain," 40; Langston Hughes, *The Big Sea* (New York: Hill & Wang, 1993), 78.

8. Arnold Rampersad discusses Leary's shawl in *The Life of Langston Hughes*, vol. 1, *1902–1931: I, Too, Sing America* (New York: Oxford University Press, 2002), 6; Hughes describes his grandmother's stories of the black freedom struggle in *The Big Sea*, 17; Hughes on being a writer from Langston Hughes, *I Wonder as I Wander: An Autobiographical Journey* (New York: Hill & Wang, 1993), 5.

9. Hughes, *The Big Sea*, 36; James David Nichols, "The Line of Liberty: Slave and Fugitive Peons in the Texas-Mexico Borderlands," *Western Historical Quarterly* 44, 4 (2013): 414.

10. Sarah E. Cornell, "Citizens of Nowhere: Fugitive Slaves and Free African Americans in Mexico, 1833–1857," *Journal of American History* 100, 2 (2013): 352, 353–354, 357; Gerald Horne, *Black and Brown: African Americans and the Mexican Revolution, 1910–1920* (New York: New York University Press, 2005), 6; Hughes, "Diary of Mexican Adventures"; Langston Hughes, "I, Too," in Rampersad and Roessel, *Collected Poems of Langston Hughes*, 46; Hughes, "Diary of Mexican Adventures."

11. Hughes, "Diary of Mexican Adventures."

12. Ibid.; Langston Hughes, "Journal re: Mexico and Spanish Lessons," box 492, folder 12441, Hughes Papers (reprinted by permission from Harold Ober Associates, Incorporated, as agents for the Estate of Langston Hughes); Langston Hughes, "Writers, Words and the World," in De Santis, *Collected Works of Langston Hughes*, 9:199; Edwards, "Langston Hughes and the Future of Diaspora," 692.

13. Hughes, *The Big Sea*, 62. For information on James N. Hughes's and Carrie Langston's migration, see Rampersad, *Life of Langston Hughes*, 1:9–11. For more on black homesteading and black towns in Oklahoma, see Quintard Taylor, *In Search of the Racial Frontier: African-Americans in the American West, 1528–1990* (New York: W. W. Norton, 1999), 143–151.

14. Hughes, *I Wonder as I Wander*, 298; Hughes, *The Big Sea*, 39–40. For more on the economic policies of Porfirio Díaz and their impacts, see Juan Carlos Moreno-Brid and Jaime Ros, *Development and Growth in the Mexican Economy: A Historical Perspective* (New York: Oxford University Press, 2009), 45–67.

15. James N. Hughes, "Letter to Langston Hughes [January 13, 1931]," box 262, folder 4208, Hughes Papers (reprinted by permission from Harold Ober Associates, Incorporated, as agents for the Estate of Langston Hughes); Hughes, *The Big Sea*, 15; Langston Hughes, "Books in Father's Library," box

518, folder 12897, Hughes Papers; Hughes, *The Big Sea*, 37; Hughes, "Just Traveling," 142.

16. Hughes, *The Big Sea*, 39.

17. Ana María Alonso, *Thread of Blood: Colonialism, Revolution, and Gender on Mexico's Northern Frontier* (Tucson: University of Arizona Press, 1995), 15–16.

18. James N. Hughes, "Letter to Langston Hughes [August 4, 1931]," box 262, folder 4208, Hughes Papers (reprinted by permission from Harold Ober Associates, Incorporated, as agents for the Estate of Langston Hughes); Hughes, *The Big Sea*, 41, 40.

19. Hughes, *The Big Sea*, 46, 46–47, 44–45.

20. Ibid., 43, 44.

21. Ibid., 58, 59; National Association for the Advancement of Colored People, *Thirty Years of Lynching in the United States, 1889–1918* (New York: National Association for the Advancement of Colored People, 1919); James Weldon Johnson, *Along This Way: The Autobiography of James Weldon Johnson* (New York: Da Capo Press, 2000), 341; Monroe Work, "Lynching, Whites and Negroes, 1882–1968," Tuskegee University Archives Repository, Tuskegee Ala.; W. Jason Miller, *Langston Hughes and American Lynching Culture* (Gainesville: University Press of Florida, 2011), 1; Langston Hughes, "Christ in Alabama," in Rampersad and Roessel, *Collected Poems of Langston Hughes*, 143 ("Christ in Alabama," from *The Collected Poems of Langston Hughes*, by Langston Hughes, edited by Arnold Rampersad with David Roessel, associate editor, copyright © 1994 by the Estate of Langston Hughes. Used by Permission of Alfred A. Knopf, an imprint of the Knopf Doubleday Publishing Group, a division of Random House LLC. All rights reserved.).

22. Hughes, *The Big Sea*, 60; Hughes, *I Wonder as I Wander*, 27, 28; Hughes, *The Big Sea*, 80.

23. Hughes, *The Big Sea*, 61, 62.

24. W. E. B. DuBois, "The True Brownies," *Crisis*, October 1919, 286.

25. Langston Hughes, "Mexican Games," in *The Collected Works of Langston Hughes*, vol. 11, *Works for Children and Young Adults: Poetry, Fiction, and Other Writing*, ed. Dianne Johnson (Columbia: University of Missouri Press, 2003), 21; Haas, "Continent of Color," 180.

26. Langston Hughes, "In a Mexican City," in Johnson, *Collected Works of Langston Hughes*, 11:22, 24, 23.

27. Langston Hughes, "Up in the Crater of an Old Volcano," in Johnson, *Collected Works of Langston Hughes*, 11:31, 32, 31.

28. Langston Hughes, "Mexican Market Woman," in Rampersad and Roessel, *Collected Poems of Langston Hughes*, 25 ("Mexican Market Woman," from *The Collected Poems of Langston Hughes*, by Langston Hughes, edited by

Arnold Rampersad with David Roessel, associate editor, copyright © 1994 by the Estate of Langston Hughes. Used by Permission of Alfred A. Knopf, an imprint of the Knopf Doubleday Publishing Group, a division of Random House LLC. All rights reserved.).

29. James N. Hughes, "Letter to Langston Hughes [January 13, 1931]," and Langston Hughes, "Letter to James N. Hughes [June 30, 1931]," box 262, folder 4208, Hughes Papers (reprinted by permission from Harold Ober Associates, Incorporated, as agents for the Estate of Langston Hughes).

30. Hughes, *I Wonder as I Wander*, 295, 291, 294, 291, 293.

31. Hughes, "Journal re: Mexico and Spanish Lessons."

32. Katharine Capshaw Smith, *Children's Literature of the Harlem Renaissance* (Bloomington: Indiana University Press, 2004), 245–246, 251–252.

33. Arna Bontemps and Langston Hughes, *Boy of the Border* (El Paso, Tex.: Sweet Earth Press, 2009), 5, 56–63, 9, 21.

34. Ibid., 26, 28, 39, 38, 84.

35. "Flora Belle" was first published in the *Brooklyn Daily Eagle* in 1935; it was republished as "The Gun" in *Something in Common and Other Stories* (1963). Langston Hughes, "The Gun," in *The Collected Works of Langston Hughes*, vol. 15, *The Short Stories*, ed. R. Baxter Miller (Columbia: University of Missouri Press, 2002), 345; Allmendinger, *Imagining the African American West*, 57; Hughes, "The Gun," 345.

Part III. One Who Arrived

The first epigraph is from Arna Bontemps, "The Prizefighter and the Woman," box 74, Arna Bontemps Papers, Special Collections Research Center, Syracuse University Libraries, Syracuse, N.Y. Reprinted by permission from Harold Ober Associates, Incorporated, as agents for the Estate of Arna Bontemps. The second epigraph is from "Heritage" by Countee Cullen. Copyright Amistad Research Center, Tulane University. Administered by Thompson and Thompson, Brooklyn, N.Y.

Chapter 5. Mapping the New American Race

The epigraph is from Jean Toomer, "A Drama of the Southwest: Notes," box 44, folder 913, Jean Toomer Papers, James Weldon Johnson Collection, Beinecke Rare Book and Manuscript Library, Yale University, New Haven,

Conn. Reprinted by permission from Yale University, owner of literary property rights.

A version of this chapter originally appeared as "'A Small Man in Big Spaces': The New Negro, the *Mestizo*, and Jean Toomer's Southwestern Writing," *MELUS: Multi-Ethnic Literature of the United States* 33, 1 (2008): 11–32.

1. See Arna Bontemps, "Introduction," in Jean Toomer, *Cane* (New York: Perennial, 1969), vii–xvi; Wallace Thurman, "Letter to Langston Hughes [Thursday, c. July 1929]," in *The Collected Writings of Wallace Thurman: A Harlem Renaissance Reader*, ed. Amritjit Singh and Daniel M. Scott III (New Brunswick, N.J.: Rutgers University Press, 2003), 121–124; Wallace Thurman, "Letter to William Jourdan Rapp [c. July 1929]," ibid., 152–155.

2. Charles Larson, *Invisible Darkness: Jean Toomer and Nella Larsen* (Iowa City: University of Iowa Press, 1993), xiii.

3. Charles Scruggs and Lee VanDemarr claim that in 1935 (the same year Content took her photograph of Toomer in Taos) Toomer's writing returned to "a radical analysis of the politics of his time," although "not . . . an open discussion of racial matters" (Charles Scruggs and Lee VanDemarr, *Jean Toomer and the Terrors of American History* [Philadelphia: University of Pennsylvania Press, 1998], 219). Toomer's published New Mexican writing includes Jean Toomer, *A Jean Toomer Reader: Selected Unpublished Writings*, ed. Frederik L. Rusch (New York: Oxford University Press, 1993); Jean Toomer, *The Collected Poems of Jean Toomer*, ed. Robert B. Jones and Margery Latimer Toomer (Chapel Hill: University of North Carolina Press, 1988); Jean Toomer, *The Uncollected Work of American Author Jean Toomer, 1894–1967*, ed. John Chandler Griffin (Lewiston, N.Y.: Edwin Mellen Press, 2003); Jean Toomer, *The Wayward and the Seeking: A Collection of Writings by Jean Toomer*, ed. Darwin T. Turner (Washington, D.C.: Howard University Press, 1980). Toomer's major archival repository is the Jean Toomer Papers, James Weldon Johnson Collection, Beinecke Rare Book and Manuscript Library, Yale University, New Haven, Conn.

4. "Books and Authors," *New York Times*, August 12, 1923, BR26; Robert Bone, "The Black Classic that Discovered 'Soul' Is Rediscovered after 45 Years," *New York Times*, January 19, 1969, BR3.

5. Rudolph P. Byrd, *Jean Toomer's Years with Gurdjieff: Portrait of an Artist, 1923–1936* (Athens: University of Georgia Press, 1990), xv. See also Jon Woodson, *To Make a New Race: Gurdjieff, Toomer, and the Harlem Renaissance* (Jackson: University of Mississippi Press, 1999).

6. Jean Toomer, "A New Race in America," in Rusch, *A Jean Toomer Reader*, 105; Cynthia Earl Kerman and Richard Eldridge, *The Lives of Jean Toomer: A Hunger for Wholeness* (Baton Rouge: Louisiana State University Press, 1987), 202. The article mentioned by Kerman and Eldridge was "Races:

Just Americans," *Time*, March 28, 1932, 19. Latimer's ancestry is mentioned in "Margery Toomer, Novelist, Dies in West: Wife of Psychologist Was Descendant of Prominent New England Pioneers," *New York Times*, August 18, 1932, 19; "Woman Novelist Called by Death: Death Ends Romance of Two Races—White Wife of J. Toomer, Novelist of Negro Blood, Expires in Childbirth," *Los Angeles Times*, August 18, 1932, 3. See Lothrop Stoddard, *The Rising Tide of Color against White World-Supremacy* (New York: Charles Scribner's Sons, 1920).

7. Jean Toomer, "Fighting the Vice," in Rusch, *A Jean Toomer Reader*, 102–103; Alain Locke, "Foreword," in *The New Negro: Voices of the Harlem Renaissance*, ed. Alain Locke (New York: Touchstone Books, 1997), xxv; Toomer, "Fighting the Vice," 103.

8. Langston Hughes, *The Big Sea* (New York: Hill & Wang, 1993), 223; Kerman and Eldridge, *Lives of Jean Toomer*, 202; Hughes, *The Big Sea*, 243; Arna Bontemps, "Commentary on Jean Toomer and *Cane*," in Jean Toomer, *Cane*, ed. Darwin T. Turner (New York: W. W. Norton, 1988), 186–192; Rudolph P. Byrd and Henry Louis Gates Jr., "Introduction: 'Song of the Son': The Emergence and Passing of Jean Toomer," in Jean Toomer, *Cane*, 2nd ed., ed. Rudolph P. Byrd and Henry Louis Gates Jr. (New York: W. W. Norton, 2011), xix–lxx.

9. George Hutchinson, "Identity in Motion: Placing *Cane*," in *Jean Toomer and the Harlem Renaissance*, ed. Geneviève Fabre and Michel Feith (New Brunswick, N.J.: Rutgers University Press, 2001), 53–54.

10. Jean Toomer, "Not Typically American," in Rusch, *A Jean Toomer Reader*, 99; Jean Toomer, "Letter to James Weldon Johnson [July 11, 1930]," ibid., 106.

11. Toomer, "Fighting the Vice," 103; Hughes, *The Big Sea*, 243.

12. Scruggs and VanDemarr, *Jean Toomer and the Terrors of American History*, 82; Randolph Bourne, "Trans-National America," in *The Heath Anthology of American Literature*, ed. Paul Lauter, vol. D, *Modern Period, 1910–1945* (New York: Houghton Mifflin, 2006), 1637–1648.

13. Mary Austin, "New York: Dictator of American Criticism," *Nation*, July 31, 1920, 129–130.

14. Jean Toomer, "Americans and Mary Austin," in Scruggs and VanDemarr, *Jean Toomer and the Terrors of American History*, 228–229; Scruggs and VanDemarr, *Jean Toomer and the Terrors of American History*, 68.

15. See Jean Toomer, "To the Land of the People," "Rainbow," "The Dust of Abiquiu," "Taos Night," "New Mexico after India," "Part of the Universe," and "Santa Fe Sequence," in Rusch, *A Jean Toomer Reader*, 238–258; Tom Quirk and Robert E. Fleming, "Jean Toomer's Contributions to the *New Mexican Sentinel*," in *Jean Toomer: A Critical Evaluation*, ed. Therman B. O'Daniel (Washington, D.C.: Howard University Press, 1988), 64–73. See Jean Toomer, "Noises at

Night," box 48, folder 1012; "New Mexico after India: Notes and Drafts," box 48, folder 1011; "Unidentified: Typescript [To This Land Where the Clouds Fall]," box 48, folder 1014; "A Drama of the Southwest," box 44, folder 917; "A Drama of the Southwest: Notes," box 44, folder 913; "Sequences: Notes and Drafts," box 48, folder 1013, all in Toomer Papers and reprinted by permission of Yale University, owner of literary property rights. Some of "Sequences" was republished as "Rainbow," in Rusch, *A Jean Toomer Reader,* 240; "Part of the Universe" and "Santa Fe Sequence" also appear in ibid., 253–258. For the notebook containing the foundation of a novel, see Jean Toomer, "Notebook: Contains Notes about New Mexico," box 65, folder 1482, Toomer Papers (reprinted by permission of Yale University, owner of literary property rights); this notebook was partially reprinted as "The Dust of Abiquiu," in Rusch, *A Jean Toomer Reader,* 240–248. "The Blue Meridian" was republished in Jones and Latimer, *Collected Poems of Jean Toomer,* 50–75; other poems set in the West include "Lost Dancer," "Imprint for Rio Grande," "I Sit in My Room," "Rolling, Rolling," and "It Is Everywhere," ibid., 39, 81–87.

16. Toomer, "Notebook: Contains Notes about New Mexico"; Toomer, "Sequences: Notes and Drafts"; Toomer, "A Drama of the Southwest: Notes." The play's epigraph, which appears to have been extracted from "A Drama of the Southwest," was rewritten multiple times on pages labeled "From 'A Drama of the Southwest'" and is found only in Toomer's notes. The rewriting, however, seems to emphasize its importance.

17. Toomer, "Sequences."

18. Toomer, "New Mexico after India," in Rusch, *A Jean Toomer Reader,* 249–250. Although *A Jean Toomer Reader* states that "New Mexico after India" was previously unpublished, a published clipping of the essay exists, indicating that it originally appeared in a Santa Fe paper, the *New Mexican,* on June 26, 1940. See Mabel Dodge Luhan, "Subject Files: Toomer, Jean," box 102, folder 2397, Mabel Dodge Luhan Papers, Yale Collection of American Literature, Beinecke Rare Book and Manuscript Library, Yale University, New Haven, Conn.

19. Toomer, "New Mexico after India," 252; Toomer "Unidentified: Typescript [To This Land Where the Clouds Fall]." For an example of Toomer's letters regarding his publishing failures, see Mabel Dodge Luhan, "Correspondence: Toomer, Jean," box 34, folders 993–994, Luhan Papers; Jean Toomer, "Correspondence: Luhan, Mabel Dodge," box 5, folders 158–159, Toomer Papers.

20. Toomer, "New Mexico after India," 253; Toomer, "Sequences." For the published portions of "From Exile into Being," see Jean Toomer, "The Experience," in Rusch, *A Jean Toomer Reader,* 33–76.

21. Jean Toomer, *Cane*, 2nd ed., ed. Rudolph P. Byrd and Henry Louis Gates Jr. (New York: W. W. Norton, 2011), 11.

22. Toomer, "New Mexico after India," 253. For Lawrence's travels to Taos, see Mabel Dodge Luhan, *Lorenzo in Taos* (New York: Alfred A. Knopf, 1932).

23. Toomer, "New Mexico after India," 251.

24. Toomer, "Notebook: Contains Notes about New Mexico."

25. Toomer, "Sequences"; Byrd, *Jean Toomer's Years with Gurdjieff*, xv. The passage from "Sequences" discussing the "Spanish priest" was republished as Toomer, "A Part of the Universe," in Rusch, *A Jean Toomer Reader*, 253. There, it reads: "This was discovered in the sixteenth century by an uncommon Spanish priest who underwent transformation, who rose above himself and came upon a vision of what human life in the New World should be." But in Toomer's handwritten manuscript, "sixteenth," as Rusch has it, never appeared; he crossed out "seventeenth" and inserted "eighteenth." Toomer apparently fact-checked his writing and revised it at this point. As a result, I cite the archival materials.

26. Marilyn Grace Miller, *The Rise and Fall of the Cosmic Race: The Cult of Mestizaje in Latin America* (Austin: University of Texas Press, 2004), 29.

27. Tace Hedrick, "Blood-Lines that Waver South: Hybridity, the 'South,' and 'American Bodies,'" *Southern Quarterly* 42, 1 (2003): 47.

28. Miller, *Rise and Fall of the Cosmic Race*, 44.

29. José Vasconcelos, *The Cosmic Race/La raza cósmica*, trans. Didier T. Jaén (Baltimore: Johns Hopkins University Press, 1997), 9–10, 19, 9, 24.

30. Miller, *Rise and Fall of the Cosmic Race*, 23. For nonfeminist treatments of *la Malinche*, see Octavio Paz, *The Labyrinth of Solitude* (1950; reprint, New York: Grove Press, 1999); for more on feminist treatments of *la Malinche*, see Norma Alarcón, "*Tradutora, Traditora:* A Paradigmatic Figure of Chicana Feminism," in *Scattered Hegemonies: Postmodernity and Transnational Feminist Practices*, ed. Inderpal Grewal and Caren Kaplan (Minneapolis: University of Minnesota Press, 1991), 110–136.

31. Langston Hughes, "A House in Taos," in *The Collected Poems of Langston Hughes*, ed. Arnold Rampersad and David Roessel (New York: Vintage Books, 1995), 81. "A House in Taos" was first published in *Palms* in 1926 and won an undergraduate poetry prize judged by Witter Bynner, an intimate friend of Luhan's who had been living in New Mexico since 1922. In 1927 it appeared in Countee Cullen's edited anthology *Caroling Dusk: An Anthology of Negro Verse*, where excerpts from *Cane* also appeared. In his introduction to *Cane* (vii–xvii), Bontemps claims "A House in Taos" was based on the affair between Toomer and Luhan, but Hughes denies that in *The Big Sea*, 262.

32. Latimer's letter quoted in Kerman and Eldridge, *Lives of Jean Toomer*, 199; Toomer, "Unidentified: Typescript [To This Land Where the Clouds

Fall]"; Hughes, *The Big Sea*, 262–263 (this discussion, tellingly, immediately follows his narrative about "A House in Taos").

33. Toomer, "New Mexico after India," 253; Toomer, "Unidentified: Typescript [To This Land Where the Clouds Fall]"; Toomer, "New Mexico after India: Notes and Drafts."

34. Toomer, "Unidentified: Typescript [To This Land Where the Clouds Fall]"; Toomer, "Sequences," 63; Toomer, "Notebook: Contains Notes about New Mexico," 6, 9.

35. Larson, *Invisible Darkness*, 156.

Coda

The epigraph is from "The Dream Keeper," from *The Collected Poems of Langston Hughes* by Langston Hughes, edited by Arnold Rampersad with David Roessel, associate editor, copyright © 1994 by the Estate of Langston Hughes. Used by Permission of Alfred A. Knopf, an imprint of the Knopf Doubleday Publishing Group, a division of Random House LLC. All rights reserved.

The Borderlands of Blackness

The epigraph is from "Africa," reprinted with permission from the publisher of *Between Two Worlds* by Américo Paredes (© 1991 Arte Público Press–University of Houston).

1. Toni Morrison, *Playing in the Dark: Whiteness and the Literary Imagination* (New York: Vintage Books, 1992), 3, 6, 5.

2. Ibid., 42, 50.

3. Américo Paredes, *Between Two Worlds* (Houston: Arte Público Press, 1991), 9, 11.

4. Américo Paredes, "The Rio Grande," in *Between Two Worlds*, 15. "The Rio Grande" is reprinted with permission from the publisher of *Between Two Worlds* by Américo Paredes (© 1991 Arte Público Press–University of Houston).

5. Ramón Saldívar, *The Borderlands of Culture: Américo Paredes and the Transnational Imaginary* (Durham, N.C.: Duke University Press, 2006), 9. It is worth noting that another noted scholar of Chicano literature, José E. Limón, has contested Saldívar's insistence on the importance of Japan to Paredes, suggesting that it imagines an affiliation between Chicanos in the United States and the Japanese under US occupation that is impossible due to the history of

Japanese imperialism. See José E. Limón, "Imagining the Imaginary: A Reply to Ramón Saldívar," in *ALH: American Literary History* 21, 3 (2009): 595–603. See also José E. Límon, *Américo Paredes: Culture and Critique* (Austin: University of Texas Press, 2012).

6. Américo Paredes, "Africa," in *Between Two Worlds*, 18–19 ("Africa" is reprinted with permission from the publisher of *Between Two Worlds* by Americo Paredes [© 1991 Arte Público Press–University of Houston]); Saldívar, *Borderlands of Culture*, 259–261; Countee Cullen, "Heritage," in *The New Negro: Voices of the Harlem Renaissance*, ed. Alain Locke (New York: Touchstone Books, 1997), 250–253; Langston Hughes, "Afro-American Fragment," in *The Collected Poems of Langston Hughes*, ed. Arnold Rampersad and David Roessel (New York: Vintage Books, 1995), 129. "Afro-American Fragment" from *The Collected Poems of Langston Hughes*, by Langston Hughes, edited by Arnold Rampersad with David Roessel, associate editor, copyright © 1994 by the Estate of Langston Hughes. Used by permission of Alfred A. Knopf, an imprint of the Knopf Doubleday Publishing Group, a division of Random House LLC. All rights reserved.

7. Gwendolyn Bennett, "Heritage," in *Double-Take: A Revisionist Harlem Renaissance Anthology*, ed. Venetria K. Patton and Maureen Honey (New Brunswick, N.J.: Rutgers University Press, 2001), 508 (courtesy of the Schomburg Center for Research on Black Culture, The New York Public Library).

8. Saldívar, *Borderlands of Culture*, 255.

9. Jean Toomer, "The Blue Meridian," in *The Collected Poems of Jean Toomer*, ed. Robert B. Jones and Margery Toomer Latimer (Chapel Hill: University of North Carolina Press, 1988), 50, 52, 53, 51, 73, 73; Jean Toomer, "Imprint for Rio Grande," ibid., 81.

10. Paredes, "The Rio Grande," 16; Limón, *Américo Paredes*, 37. For more on Bagdad, Mexico, see David Montejano, "Mexican Merchants and Teamsters on the Texas Cotton Road, 1862–1865," in *Mexico and Mexicans in the Making of the United States*, ed. John Tutino (Austin: University of Texas Press, 2012), 141–170.

11. Mathews's story about Algeria quoted in Guy Logsdon, "John Joseph Mathews: A Conversation," *Nimrod* 16 (1972): 71. I suggest that Mathews creates "tribes of men" in Emily Lutenski, "Tribes of Men: John Joseph Mathews and Indian Internationalism," *SAIL: Studies in American Indian Literatures* 24, 2 (2012): 39–64.

12. Susan Kalter, "Introduction," in John Joseph Mathews, *Twenty Thousand Mornings: An Autobiography*, ed. Susan Kalter (Norman: University of Oklahoma Press, 2012), xxxviii; Mathews, *Twenty Thousand Mornings*, 24, 137; "The Recent Outrages at Humboldt, Kansas," *Daily Cleveland Herald*, September 28, 1861;

W. G. Coffin, "W. G. Coffin, Superintendent for Indian Affairs for the Southern Superintendency to Hon. Wm. P. Dole, Commissioner of Indian Affairs, October 2, 1961," in *Report of the Commissioner of Indian Affairs, Accompanying the Annual Report of the Secretary of the Interior for the Year 1861* (Washington, D.C.: Government Printing Office, 1861), 38. For more on the complexity of African American–Native American history, see Tiya Miles, *Ties that Bind: The Story of an Afro-Cherokee Family in Slavery and Freedom* (Berkeley: University of California Press, 2006); Tiya Miles and Sharon P. Holland, eds., *Crossing Waters, Crossing Worlds: The African Diaspora in Indian Country* (Durham, N.C.: Duke University Press, 2006); David Chang, *The Color of the Land: Race, Nation, and the Politics of Landownership in Oklahoma, 1832–1929* (Chapel Hill: University of North Carolina Press, 2010). For more on the Osage in the Civil War, see Louis F. Burns, *A History of the Osage People* (Tuscaloosa: University of Alabama Press, 2004), 246–268.

13. Mathews, *Twenty Thousand Mornings*, 138, 53, 160, 189.

14. Christopher Schedler, *Border Modernism: Intercultural Readings in American Literary Modernism* (New York: Routledge, 2002), 41–54.

15. John Joseph Mathews, *Sundown* (Norman: University of Oklahoma Press, 1988), 258.

16. See Michael Wallis, *The Real Wild West: The 101 Ranch and the Creation of the American West* (New York: St. Martin's, 1999).

17. Mathews, *Sundown*, 265. On the Native American Church and peyote religion, see Omer C. Stewart, *Peyote Religion: A History* (Norman: University of Oklahoma Press, 1987).

18. Mathews, *Sundown*, 265.

19. Ibid., 265–266. For criticism that considers Mathews's work as an illustration of "mixed-blood" hybridity, see, most famously, Louis Owens, *Other Destinies: Understanding the American Indian Novel* (Norman: University of Oklahoma Press, 1996). Owens's approach to Native American literature has been challenged as "doctrinaire postmodernism" by Jace Weaver, Craig Womack, and Robert Warrior, *Native American Literary Nationalism* (Albuquerque: University of New Mexico Press, 2006).

20. For more on the intersections between Filipino American identity construction via spaces of racial and national contestation, see Rick Bonus, *Locating Filipino Americans: Ethnicity and the Cultural Politics of Space* (Philadelphia: Temple University Press, 2000). For the contention that *America Is in the Heart* is an immigrant bildungsroman that relies on the generic conventions of self-education and self-making to both gain access to and expose the limitations of citizenship and national belonging, see Joseph Keith, *Unbecoming Americans: Writing Race and Nation from the Shadows of*

Citizenship, 1945–1960 (New Brunswick, N.J.: Rutgers University Press, 2013), 27–65.

21. Lisa Lowe, *Immigrant Acts: On Asian American Cultural Politics* (Durham, N.C.: Duke University Press, 1996), 45–48; Carlos Bulosan, *America Is in the Heart: A Personal History* (Seattle: University of Washington Press, 2002), 69–70.

22. Bulosan, *America Is in the Heart*, 71, 68; Richard Wright, "The Ethics of Living Jim Crow," in *Uncle Tom's Children* (New York: Harper Perennial, 2004), 13–14, 1. Wright's influence on Bulosan is discussed in Helen Jaskoski, "Carlos Bulosan's Literary Debt to Richard Wright," in *Literary Influence and African-American Writers: Collected Essays*, ed. Tracy Mishkin (New York: Garland, 1996), 231–243.

23. Bulosan, *America Is in the Heart*, 147, 168, 114–115; Wright, "The Ethics of Living Jim Crow," 7.

24. Bulosan, *America Is in the Heart*, 273; Langston Hughes, "Nazi and Dixie Nordics," in *Langston Hughes and the* Chicago Defender: *Essays on Race, Politics, and Culture, 1942–62*, ed. Christopher C. De Santis (Urbana: University of Illinois Press, 1995), 79; Bulosan, *America Is in the Heart*, 324. For a brief history of Filipinos in the United States, including the impact of World War II military service, see Yen Le Espiritu, "Introduction: Filipino Settlements in the United States," in *Filipino American Lives* (Philadelphia: Temple University Press, 1995), 17–19.

25. Keith, *Unbecoming Americans*, 62; Bulosan, *America Is in the Heart*, 324–325, 326.

26. William Orchard and Yolanda Padilla, "Introducing Josefina Niggli," in *The Plays of Josefina Niggli*, ed. William Orchard and Yolanda Padilla (Madison: University of Wisconsin Press, 2007), 9.

27. Frederick H. Koch, "The Playmaker's Aim," in *Carolina Folk Plays*, ed. Frederick H. Koch (New York: Henry Holt, 1941), vi; Frederick H. Koch, "The Carolina Playmakers," ibid., xiv. For more on Niggli, see Elizabeth Coonrod Martínez, *Josefina Niggli, Mexican American Writer: A Critical Biography* (Albuquerque: University of New Mexico Press, 2007).

28. Koch, "The Carolina Playmakers," xv; Martínez, *Josefina Niggli*, 30.

29. Josefina Niggli, *Mexican Village and Other Works* (Evanston, Ill.: Northwestern University Press, 2008), 470. For more on blackface performance, see Alexander Saxton, "Blackface Minstrelsy and Jacksonian Ideology," *American Quarterly* 27, 1 (1975): 3–28; Eric Lott, *Love and Theft: Blackface Minstrelsy and the American Working Class* (New York: Oxford University Press, 1993); W. T. Lhamon Jr., *Raising Cain: Blackface Performance from Jim Crow to Hip Hop* (Cambridge, Mass.: Harvard University Press, 1997).

30. Niggli, *Mexican Village and Other Works*, 471, 474, 472.

31. Bob is labeled an "outlander" even in the dramatis personae at the beginning of the novel. Niggli, *Mexican Village and Other Works*, 137, 558, 551, 558.

32. Robin D. G. Kelley, *Freedom Dreams: The Black Radical Imagination* (Boston: Beacon, 2002), ix.

Bibliography

Ailman, H. B. *Pioneering in Territorial Silver City: H. B. Ailman's Recollections of Silver City and the Southwest, 1871–1892.* Albuquerque: University of New Mexico Press, 1983.

Alarcón, Norma. "*Tradutora, Traditora:* A Paradigmatic Figure of Chicana Feminism." In *Scattered Hegemonies: Postmodernity and Transnational Feminist Practices,* ed. Inderpal Grewal and Caren Kaplan, 110–136. Minneapolis: University of Minnesota Press, 1991.

Allmendinger, Blake. *Imagining the African American West.* Lincoln: University of Nebraska Press, 2005.

Alonso, Ana María. *Thread of Blood: Colonialism, Revolution, and Gender on Mexico's Northern Frontier.* Tucson: University of Arizona Press, 1995.

Anzaldúa, Gloria. *Borderlands/La Frontera: The New Mestiza.* San Francisco: Aunt Lute, 1999.

Arnesen, Eric. *Brotherhoods of Color: Black Railroad Workers and the Struggle for Equality.* Cambridge, Mass.: Harvard University Press, 2002.

Austin, Mary. "Arizona: The Land of Joyous Adventure." In *These United States: Portraits of America from the 1920s,* ed. Daniel H. Borus, 37–44. Ithaca, N.Y.: Cornell University Press, 1992.

———. "New York: Dictator of American Criticism." *Nation,* July 31, 1920, 129–130.

Baker, Houston A., Jr. *Long Black Song: Essays in Black American Literature and Culture.* Charlottesville: University Press of Virginia, 1972.

———. *Modernism and the Harlem Renaissance.* Chicago: University of Chicago Press, 1987.

———. *Turning South Again: Re-Thinking Modernism/Re-Reading Booker T.* Durham, N.C.: Duke University Press, 2001.

———. *Workings of the Spirit: The Poetics of Afro-American Women's Writing.* Chicago: University of Chicago Press, 1991.

Baker, Joseph. "By Midnight Oil: Of Making Books." *Philadelphia Tribune,* February 11, 1932.

Baldwin, Davarian. *Chicago's New Negroes: Modernity, the Great Migration, and Black Urban Life.* Chapel Hill: University of North Carolina Press, 2007.

Baldwin, Davarian, and Minkah Makalani, eds. *Escape from New York: The New Negro Renaissance beyond Harlem.* Minneapolis: University of Minnesota Press, 2013.

Baton, Maisha, and Henry Walt. *A History of Blackdom, N.M. in the Context of the African American Post Civil War Colonization Movement.* Albuquerque: Historic Preservation Division, New Mexico Office of Cultural Affairs, 1996.

Bederman, Gail. *Manliness and Civilization: A Cultural History of Gender and Race in the United States, 1880–1917.* Chicago: University of Chicago Press, 1995.

Bennett, Gwendolyn. "Heritage." In *Double-Take: A Revisionist Harlem Renaissance Anthology,* ed. Venetria K. Patton and Maureen Honey, 508. New Brunswick, N.J.: Rutgers University Press, 2001.

Benton-Cohen, Katherine. *Borderline Americans: Racial Division and Labor War in the Arizona Borderlands.* Cambridge, Mass.: Harvard University Press, 2009.

Bernstein, Shana. *Bridges of Reform: Interracial Civil Rights Activism in Twentieth-Century Los Angeles.* New York: Oxford University Press, 2011.

Bolton, Herbert Eugene. *The Spanish Borderlands: A Chronicle of Old Florida and the Southwest.* New Haven, Conn.: Yale University Press, 1921.

Bonacich, Edna, Lola Smallwood Cuevas, Lanita Morris, Steven Pitts, and Joshua Bloom. "A Common Project for a Just Society: Black Labor in Los Angeles." In *Black Los Angeles: American Dreams and Racial Realities,* ed. Darnell Hunt and Ana-Christina Ramón, 360–381. New York: New York University Press, 2010.

Bone, Robert. "The Black Classic that Discovered 'Soul' Is Rediscovered after 45 Years." *New York Times,* January 19, 1969.

Bontemps, Arna. "The Awakening: A Memoir." In *The Harlem Renaissance Remembered,* ed. Arna Bontemps, 1–26. New York: Dodd, Mead, 1972.

———. "Commentary on Jean Toomer and *Cane.*" In *Cane,* by Jean Toomer, ed. Darwin T. Turner, 186–192. New York: W. W. Norton, 1988.

———. *God Sends Sunday.* New York: Washington Square Press, 1959.

———. "Introduction." In *Cane,* by Jean Toomer, vii–xvi. New York: Perennial, 1969.

———. "Introduction to the 1968 Edition." In *Black Thunder,* xxi–xxix. Boston: Beacon, 1992.

———. "Saturday Night: Portrait of a Small Southern Town, 1933." In *The Old South,* 157–169. New York: Dodd, Mead, 1973.

———. "Why I Returned." In *The Old South,* 1–25. New York: Dodd, Mead, 1973.

Bontemps, Arna, Papers. Special Collections Research Center, Syracuse University Libraries, Syracuse, N.Y.

Bontemps, Arna, and Jack Conroy. *Anyplace but Here.* Columbia: University of Missouri Press, 1966.

Bontemps, Arna, and Langston Hughes. *Boy of the Border.* El Paso, Tex.: Sweet Earth Press, 2009.

Bonus, Rick. *Locating Filipino Americans: Ethnicity and the Cultural Politics of Space.* Philadelphia: Temple University Press, 2000.

"Books and Authors." *New York Times,* August 12, 1923.

Bourne, Randolph. "Trans-National America." In *The Heath Anthology of American Literature,* vol. D, *Modern Period, 1910–1945,* ed. Paul Lauter, 1637–1648. New York: Houghton Mifflin, 2006.

Brady, Mary Pat. "Border." In *Keywords for American Cultural Studies,* ed. Bruce Burgett and Glenn Hendler, 29–32. New York: New York University Press, 2007.

———. *Extinct Lands, Temporal Geographies: Chicana Literature and the Urgency of Space.* Durham, N.C.: Duke University Press, 2002.

———. "Scaling the West Differently." *Western American Literature* 35, 1 (Spring 2000): 97–104.

Brennan, Jonathan, ed. *Where Brer Rabbit Meets Coyote: African–Native American Literature.* Urbana: University of Illinois Press, 2003.

Brilliant, Mark. *The Color of America Has Changed: How Racial Diversity Shaped Civil Rights Reform in California, 1941–1978.* New York: Oxford University Press, 2010.

Brooks, Daphne A. "The Deeds Done in My Body: Performance Black(ened) Women, and Adah Isaacs Menken in the Racial Imaginary." In *Bodies in Dissent: Spectacular Performances of Race and Freedom, 1850–1910,* 131–206. Durham, N.C.: Duke University Press, 2006.

Brown, Elsa Barkley. "To Catch the Vision of Freedom: Reconstructing Southern Black Women's Political History, 1865–1880." In *African American Women and the Vote, 1837–1965,* ed. Ann D. Gordon with Bettye Collier-Thomas, John H. Bracey, Arlene Voski Avakain, and Joyce Avrech Berkman, 66–99. Amherst: University of Massachusetts Press, 1997.

Bruinius, Harry. *Better for All the World: The Secret History of Forced Sterilization and America's Quest for Racial Purity.* New York: Vintage Books, 2007.

Bulosan, Carlos. *America Is in the Heart.* Seattle: University of Washington Press, 2002.

Burke, Flannery. "An Artists' Home: Gender and the Santa Fe Culture Center Controversy." *Journal of the Southwest* 46, 2 (2004): 351–357.

———. *From Greenwich Village to Taos: Primitivism and Place at Mabel Dodge Luhan's*. Lawrence: University Press of Kansas, 2008.

Burns, Louis F. *A History of the Osage People*. Tuscaloosa: University of Alabama Press, 2004.

Butler, Anne M. *Daughters of Joy, Sisters of Misery: Prostitutes in the American West, 1865–90*. Urbana: University of Illinois Press, 1985.

Byrd, Rudolph P. *Jean Toomer's Years with Gurdjieff: Portrait of an Artist, 1923–1936*. Athens: University of Georgia Press, 1990.

Byrd, Rudolph P., and Henry Louis Gates Jr. "Introduction: 'Song of the Son': The Emergence and Passing of Jean Toomer." In *Cane*, 2nd ed., by Jean Toomer, ed. Rudolph P. Byrd and Henry Louis Gates Jr., xix–lxvi. New York: W. W. Norton, 2011.

"'Call Home the Heart' and Other Works of Fiction." *New York Times*, February 28, 1932, BR7, BR19–BR22.

Canaday, Nicholas. "Arna Bontemps: The Louisiana Heritage." *Callaloo: A Journal of African American Arts and Letters* 1–3, 11–13 (1981): 163–169.

Carr, Helen. *Inventing the American Primitive: Politics, Gender, and the Representation of Native American Literary Traditions, 1789–1936*. New York: New York University Press, 1996.

Carrigan, William D., and Clive Webb. "The Lynching of Persons of Mexican Origin or Descent in the United States, 1848 to 1928." *Journal of Social History* 37, 2 (2003): 411–438.

Carter, Eunice Hunton. "Review of *The Blacker the Berry*, by Wallace Thurman." *Opportunity: Journal of Negro Life*, May 1929, 162–163.

Chacon, Soledad C. (Secretary of State), comp. *Laws of the State of New Mexico*. Albuquerque: Valliant Printing, 1925.

Champion, Laurie, and Bruce A. Glasrud. "Introduction: Anita Scott Coleman's Short Stories and the Harlem Renaissance." In *Unfinished Masterpiece: The Harlem Renaissance Fiction of Anita Scott Coleman*, ed. Laurie Champion and Bruce A. Glasrud, 3–13. Lubbock: Texas Tech University Press, 2008.

———, eds. *Unfinished Masterpiece: The Harlem Renaissance Fiction of Anita Scott Coleman*. Lubbock: Texas Tech University Press, 2008.

Chang, David. *The Color of the Land: Race, Nation, and the Politics of Landownership in Oklahoma, 1832–1929*. Chapel Hill: University of North Carolina Press, 2010.

Chang, Kornel. *Pacific Connections: The Making of the U.S.-Canadian Borderlands*. Berkeley: University of California Press, 2012.

Chauncey, George. *Gay New York: Gender, Urban Culture, and the Making of the Gay Male World, 1890–1940*. New York: Basic Books, 1994.

Chisum, Melvin J. "Ivory and Gold." *Baltimore Afro-American*, December 26, 1931, 13.

Cobb, Michael L. "Insolent Racing, Rough Narrative: The Harlem Renaissance's Impolite Queers." *Callaloo* 23, 1 (2000): 328–351.

Coffey, John. *Liberation and Exodus: Deliverance Politics from John Calvin to Martin Luther King, Jr.* New York: Oxford University Press, 2014.

Coffin, W. G. "W. G. Coffin, Superintendent for Indian Affairs for the Southern Superintendency to Hon. Wm. P. Dole, Commissioner of Indian Affairs, October 2, 1861." In *Report of the Commissioner of Indian Affairs, Accompanying the Annual Report of the Secretary of the Interior for the Year 1861*, 38–39. Washington, D.C.: Government Printing Office, 1861.

Coleman, Anita Scott. "Arizona and New Mexico—The Land of Esperanza." In Davis and Mitchell, *Western Echoes of the Harlem Renaissance*, 280–285.

———. "The Brat." In Davis and Mitchell, *Western Echoes of the Harlem Renaissance*, 75–84.

———. "Hands." In Davis and Mitchell, *Western Echoes of the Harlem Renaissance*, 195.

———. "Idle Wonder." In Davis and Mitchell, *Western Echoes of the Harlem Renaissance*, 202.

———. "Jack Arrives." In Davis and Mitchell, *Western Echoes of the Harlem Renaissance*, 112–117.

———. "The Little Grey House." In Davis and Mitchell, *Western Echoes of the Harlem Renaissance*, 98–108.

———. "Love for Hire." *Pittsburgh Courier*, August 21, 1943, 13.

———. "Phoebe and Peter up North." In Davis and Mitchell, *Western Echoes of the Harlem Renaissance*, 181–187.

———. "Phoebe Goes to a Lecture." In Davis and Mitchell, *Western Echoes of the Harlem Renaissance*, 188–192.

———. "Rich Man, Poor Man." In Davis and Mitchell, *Western Echoes of the Harlem Renaissance*, 139–146.

———. "Three Dogs and a Rabbit." In Davis and Mitchell, *Western Echoes of the Harlem Renaissance*, 85–93.

Coleman, Ronald G. "A History of Blacks in Utah, 1825–1910." Ph.D. diss., University of Utah, 1980.

Collins, Patricia Hill. *Black Feminist Thought: Knowledge, Consciousness, and the Politics of Empowerment*. New York: Routledge, 2000.

"Colored People's Day: They Will Have a Jubilee at the Columbian Exposition." *Boston Daily Globe*, March 22, 1893.

Comer, Krista. *Landscapes of the New West: Gender and Geography in Contemporary Women's Writing*. Chapel Hill: University of North Carolina Press, 1999.

———. "West." In *Keywords for American Cultural Studies*, ed. Bruce Burgett and Glenn Hendler, 238–242. New York: New York University Press, 2007.

Cornell, Sarah E. "Citizens of Nowhere: Fugitive Slaves and Free African Americans in Mexico, 1833–1857." *Journal of American History* 100, 2 (2013): 351–374.

Cott, Nancy F. *The Bonds of Womanhood: "Woman's Sphere" in New England, 1780–1835.* 2nd ed. New Haven, Conn.: Yale University Press, 1997.

Cullen, Countee. "Heritage." In *The New Negro: Voices of the Harlem Renaissance*, ed. Alain Locke, 250–253. New York: Touchstone Books, 1997.

Dalpar, Helen. *The Enormous Vogue of Things Mexican: Cultural Relations between the United States and Mexico, 1920–1935.* Tuscaloosa: University of Alabama Press, 1995.

Davis, Cynthia, and Verner D. Mitchell. "Introduction: Anita Scott Coleman in the Southwest." In Davis and Mitchell, *Western Echoes of the Harlem Renaissance*, 3–43.

———. "Preface." In Davis and Mitchell, *Western Echoes of the Harlem Renaissance*, xiii–xviii.

———, eds. *Western Echoes of the Harlem Renaissance: The Life and Writings of Anita Scott Coleman.* Norman: University of Oklahoma Press, 2008.

Davis, Frank M. "Book Review: Poetry by Colored Writers." *New Journal and Guide* (Norfolk, Va.), December 25, 1938, 9.

Davis, Rebecca L. "'Not Marriage at All, but Simple Harlotry': The Companionate Marriage Controversy." *Journal of American History* 94, 4 (2008): 1137–1163.

Davis, Thadious. *Southscapes: Geographies of Race, Region, and Literature.* Chapel Hill: University of North Carolina Press, 2011.

de Graff, Lawrence B. "Race, Sex, and Region: Black Women in the American West, 1850–1920." *Pacific Historical Review* 49, 2 (1980): 285–313.

DeJongh, James. *Vicious Modernism: Black Harlem and the Literary Imagination.* New York: Cambridge University Press, 1990.

Delegates from Arizona. *Protest against Union of Arizona with New Mexico.* 59th Cong., 1st sess., February 12, 1906. S. Doc. 216, serial 4913.

Deloria, Philip J. *Indians in Unexpected Places.* Lawrence: University Press of Kansas, 2004.

Deverell, William. *Whitewashed Adobe: The Rise of Los Angeles and the Remaking of Its Mexican Past.* Berkeley: University of California Press, 2004.

Doback, William A., and Thomas D. Phillips. *The Black Regulars, 1866–1898.* Norman: University of Oklahoma Press, 2001.

Douglas, Ann. *Terrible Honesty: Mongrel Manhattan in the 1920s.* New York: Noonday Press, 1995.

Douglass, Frederick. "Frederick Douglass's Speech at Colored American Day (August 25, 1893)." In *All the World Is Here! The Black Presence at White City*, by Christopher Robert Reed, 193–194. Bloomington: Indiana University Press, 2010.

Douglass, Frederick, and Richard T. Greener. "Frederick Douglass and Richard T. Greener on the Negro Exodus, 1897." In *A Documentary History of the Negro People in the United States*, ed. Herbert Aptheker, 724. New York: Citadel Press, 1951.

DuBois, W. E. B. "Colored California." *Crisis*, August 1913, 192–196.

———. "Criteria of Negro Art." In *Double-Take: A Revisionist Harlem Renaissance Anthology*, ed. Venetria K. Patton and Maureen Honey, 47–51. New Brunswick, N.J.: Rutgers University Press, 2001.

———. *The Souls of Black Folk*. New York: Penguin, 1989.

———. "The True Brownies." *Crisis*, October 1919, 285–286.

Duggan, Lisa. "Making It Perfectly Queer." In *Theorizing Feminism: Parallel Trends in the Humanities and Social Sciences*, ed. Anne C. Herrmann and Abigail J. Stewart, 215–231. Boulder, Colo.: Westview Press, 2000.

Edwards, Brent Hayes. "Langston Hughes and the Futures of Diaspora." *ALH: American Literary History* 19, 3 (2007): 669–711.

———. *The Practice of Diaspora: Literature, Translation, and the Rise of Black Internationalism*. Cambridge, Mass.: Harvard University Press, 2003.

Ellison, Ralph. "Going to the Territory." In *Going to the Territory*, 120–144. New York: Vintage, 1995.

English, Daylanne K. *Unnatural Selections: Eugenics in American Modernism and the Harlem Renaissance*. Chapel Hill: University of North Carolina Press, 2004.

Espiritu, Yen Le. "Introduction: Filipino Settlements in the United States." In *Filipino American Lives*, 1–36. Philadelphia: Temple University Press, 1995.

Favor, J. Martin. "George Schuyler and Wallace Thurman: Two Satirists of the Harlem Renaissance." In *The Cambridge Companion to the Harlem Renaissance*, ed. George Hutchinson, 198–212. New York: Cambridge University Press, 2007.

Fergusson, Erna. *New Mexico: A Pageant of Three Peoples*. New York: Alfred A. Knopf, 1951.

———. *Our Southwest*. New York: Alfred A. Knopf, 1940.

Flamming, Douglas. *Bound for Freedom: Black Los Angeles in Jim Crow America*. Berkeley: University of California Press, 2005.

———. "'A Westerner in Search of Negro-ness': Region and Race in the Writing of Arna Bontemps." In *Over the Edge: Remapping the American West*, ed. Valerie J. Matsumoto and Blake Allmendinger, 85–104. Berkeley: University of California Press, 1999.

Freeman, Douglas. "Virginia: A Gentle Dominion." In *These United States: Portraits of America from the 1920s*, ed. Daniel H. Borus, 374–381. Ithaca, N.Y.: Cornell University Press, 1992.

Friedman, Susan Stanford. *Mappings: Feminism and the Cultural Geographies of Encounter*. Princeton, N.J.: Princeton University Press, 1998.

Gaines, Kevin K. *Uplifting the Race: Black Leadership, Politics, and Culture in the Twentieth Century*. Chapel Hill: University of North Carolina Press, 1996.

Ganter, Granville. "Decadence, Sexuality, and the Bohemian Vision of Wallace Thurman." *MELUS: Multi-Ethnic Literature of the United States* 28, 2 (2003): 83–104.

Garber, Eric. "A Spectacle in Color: The Gay and Lesbian Subculture of Jazz Age Harlem." In *Hidden from History: Reclaiming the Gay and Lesbian Past*, ed. Martin Duberman, Martha Vicinus, and George Chauncey, 318–331. New York: Meridian, 1990.

———. "'T'ain't Nobody's Bizness': Homosexuality in 1920s Harlem." In *Black Men/White Men: A Gay Anthology*, ed. Michael J. Smith, 7–16. San Francisco: Sunshine Press, 1983.

Garcia, F. Chris, Paul L. Hain, Gilbert K. St. Clair, and Kim Seckler, eds. *Governing New Mexico*. Albuquerque: University of New Mexico Press, 2006.

Gardner, Eric. *Unexpected Places: Relocating Nineteenth-Century African American Literature*. Jackson: University Press of Mississippi, 2009.

Gilroy, Paul. *The Black Atlantic: Modernity and Double-Consciousness*. Cambridge, Mass.: Harvard University Press, 1993.

Gish, Robert Franklin. *Beautiful Swift Fox: Erna Fergusson and the Modern Southwest*. College Station: Texas A&M University Press, 1996.

Glasrud, Bruce A., ed. *African American History in New Mexico: Portraits from Five Hundred Years*. Albuquerque: University of New Mexico Press, 2013.

Glasrud, Bruce A., and Cary D. Wintz, eds. *The Harlem Renaissance and the American West: The New Negro's Western Experience*. New York: Routledge, 2011.

Glaude, Eddie S., Jr. *Exodus! Religion, Race, and Nation in Early Nineteenth Century Black America*. Chicago: University of Chicago Press, 2000.

Glick, Elisa F. "Harlem's Queer Dandy: African-American Modernism and the Artifice of Blackness." *MFS: Modern Fiction Studies* 49, 3 (2003): 414–442.

Goodman, Audrey. *Translating Southwestern Landscapes: The Making of an Anglo Literary Region, 1880–1930*. Tucson: University of Arizona Press, 2002.

Gordon, Sarah Barringer. *The Mormon Question: Polygamy and Constitutional Conflict in Nineteenth-Century America*. Chapel Hill: University of North Carolina Press, 2001.

Gordon, Taylor. *Born to Be*. Lincoln, Neb.: Bison Books, 1995.

"Great Meeting in Faneuil Hall: Speeches of Samuel J. Mau, Frederick Douglass and Wendell Phillips." *Liberator,* June 8, 1849, 89–91.

"A Great Silver Country." *Chicago Daily Tribune,* September 1, 1873, 5.

Grey, Zane. *Riders of the Purple Sage.* Mineola, N.Y.: Dover Publications, 2002.

Gruesz, Kirsten Silva. "The Gulf of Mexico System and the 'Latinness' of New Orleans." *ALH: American Literary History* 18, 3 (2006): 468–495.

Haas, Astrid. "A Continent of Color: Langston Hughes in Latin America." In *Expanding Latinidad: An Inter-American Perspective,* ed. Luz Angélica Kirschner, 177–194. Tempe, Ariz.: Bilingual Review Press, 2012.

Hall, James A. "Once Mining Center of Fabulous Wealth, Now Grewsome Ghost." *Atlanta Constitution,* February 2, 1902, A3.

Haraway, Donna. "Situated Knowledges: The Science Question in Feminism and the Privilege of Partial Perspective." *Feminist Studies* 14, 2 (1988): 575–599.

Hardaway, Rodger A. "African American Communities on the Western Frontier." In *Communities in the American West,* ed. Stephen Tschudi, 131–145. Reno: Nevada State Humanities Committee, 1999.

Harding, Sandra. *Whose Science? Whose Knowledge? Thinking from Women's Lives.* Ithaca, N.Y.: Cornell University Press, 1991.

Haslam, Gerald. "Wallace Thurman: Western Renaissance Man." *Western American Literature* 6 (1971): 53–59.

Hedrick, Tace. "Blood-Lines that Waver South: Hybridity, the 'South,' and 'American Bodies.'" *Southern Quarterly* 42, 1 (2003): 39–52.

Henderson, Lucy. "Free Land for the Race in New Mexico." *Chicago Defender,* December 21, 1912, 3.

Henderson, Mae Gwendolyn. "Portrait of Wallace Thurman." In *The Harlem Renaissance Remembered,* ed. Arna Bontemps, 147–170. New York: Dodd, Mead, 1972.

Hine, Darlene Clark. "Rape and the Inner Lives of Black Women: Thoughts on the Culture of Dissemblance." In *Hine Sight: Black Women and the Reconstruction of American History,* 37–58. Bloomington: Indiana University Press, 1997.

Hirsch, Arnold R., and Joseph Logsdon. "Introduction: Part III, Franco-Africans and African-Americans." In *Creole New Orleans: Race and Americanization,* ed. Arnold R. Hirsch and Joseph Logsdon, 189–200. Baton Rouge: Louisiana State University Press, 1992.

hooks, bell. "Choosing the Margin as a Space of Radical Openness." In *Yearning: Race, Gender, and Cultural Politics,* 145–153. Boston: South End Press, 1990.

———. *Feminist Theory: From Margin to Center.* 2nd ed. Boston: South End Press, 2000.

Horne, Gerald. *Black and Brown: African Americans and the Mexican Revolution, 1910–1920*. New York: New York University Press, 2005.

Hughes, Langston. "Afro-American Fragment." In Rampersad and Roessel, *Collected Poems of Langston Hughes*, 129.

———. *The Big Sea*. New York: Hill & Wang, 1993.

———. "Christ in Alabama." In Rampersad and Roessel, *Collected Poems of Langston Hughes*, 143.

———. "The Gun." In *The Collected Works of Langston Hughes*, vol. 15, *The Short Stories*, ed. R. Baxter Miller, 345–350. Columbia: University of Missouri Press, 2002.

———. "Harlem (2)." In Rampersad and Roessel, *Collected Poems of Langston Hughes*, 426.

———. "Here to Yonder: Mugging." *Chicago Defender*, May 1, 1943, 14.

———. "A House in Taos." In Rampersad and Roessel, *Collected Poems of Langston Hughes*, 81.

———. "I, Too." In Rampersad and Roessel, *Collected Poems of Langston Hughes*, 46.

———. "In a Mexican City." In *The Collected Works of Langston Hughes*, vol. 11, *Works for Children and Young Adults: Poetry, Fiction, and Other Writing*, ed. Dianne Johnson, 22–25. Columbia: University of Missouri Press, 2003.

———. *I Wonder as I Wander: An Autobiographical Journey*. New York: Hill & Wang, 1993.

———. "Just Traveling." In *The Collected Works of Langston Hughes*, vol. 9, *Essays on Art, Race, Politics, and World Affairs*, ed. Christopher C. De Santis, 142–146. Columbia: University of Missouri Press, 2002.

———. "Mexican Games." In *The Collected Works of Langston Hughes*, vol. 11, *Works for Children and Young Adults: Poetry, Fiction, and Other Writing*, ed. Dianne Johnson, 19–21. Columbia: University of Missouri Press, 2003.

———. "Mexican Market Woman." In Rampersad and Roessel, *Collected Poems of Langston Hughes*, 25.

———. "Nazi and Dixie Nordics." In *Langston Hughes and the* Chicago Defender: *Essays on Race, Politics, and Culture, 1942–62*, ed. Christopher C. De Santis, 78–80. Urbana: University of Illinois Press, 1995.

———. "The Negro Artist and the Racial Mountain." In *Double-Take: A Revisionist Harlem Renaissance Anthology*, ed. Venetria K. Patton and Maureen Honey, 40–44. New Brunswick, N.J.: Rutgers University Press, 2001.

———. "The Negro Speaks of Rivers." In Rampersad and Roessel, *Collected Poems of Langston Hughes*, 23.

———. "Up in the Crater of an Old Volcano." In *The Collected Works of Langs-*

ton Hughes, vol. 11, *Works for Children and Young Adults: Poetry, Fiction, and Other Writing*, ed. Dianne Johnson, 31–37. Columbia: University of Missouri Press, 2003.

———. "West Texas." In Rampersad and Roessel, *Collected Poems of Langston Hughes*, 252.

———. "Writers, Words and the World." In *The Collected Works of Langston Hughes*, vol. 9, *Essays on Art, Race, Politics, and World Affairs*, ed. Christopher C. De Santis, 198–199. Columbia: University of Missouri Press, 2002.

Hughes, Langston, Papers. James Weldon Johnson Collection, Beinecke Rare Book and Manuscript Library, Yale University, New Haven, Conn.

Hughes-Watkins, Lael L. "Fay M. Jackson: The Sociopolitical Narrative of a Pioneering African American Female Journalist." MA thesis, Youngstown State University, 2008.

Hutchinson, George. *The Harlem Renaissance in Black and White*. Cambridge, Mass.: Harvard University Press, 1995.

———. "Identity in Motion: Placing *Cane*." In *Jean Toomer and the Harlem Renaissance*, ed. Geneviève Fabre and Michel Feith, 38–56. New Brunswick, N.J.: Rutgers University Press, 2001.

"Is the Late A'Leila Walker the 'Amy Douglas' of Thurman Novel?" *Baltimore Afro-American*, April 9, 1932, 17.

Jarraway, David R. "Tales of the City: Marginality, Community, and the Problem of Identity in Wallace Thurman's 'Harlem' Fiction." *College English* 61, 1 (2002): 36–52.

Jaskoski, Helen. "Carlos Bulosan's Literary Debt to Richard Wright." In *Literary Influence and African-American Writers: Collected Essays*, ed. Tracy Mishkin, 231–243. New York: Garland, 1996.

"Joann Coleman Weds U.S. Air Force Man." *Los Angeles Sentinel*, July 26, 1962, B3.

Johnson, James Weldon. *Along This Way: The Autobiography of James Weldon Johnson*. New York: Da Capo Press, 2000.

———. "Harlem: The Culture Capital." In *The New Negro: Voices of the Harlem Renaissance*, ed. Alain Locke, 301–311. New York: Touchstone, 1997.

Johnson, Michael K. *Black Masculinity and the Frontier Myth in American Literature*. Norman: University of Oklahoma Press, 2002.

———. *Hoo-Doo Cowboys and Bronze Buckaroos: Conceptions of the African American West*. Jackson: University Press of Mississippi, 2014.

Johnson, Susan Lee. *Roaring Camp: The Social World of the California Gold Rush*. New York: W. W. Norton, 2000.

Jones, Dewey R. "Books by Race Authors Prove Disappointing as 1932 List Is Scanned." *Chicago Defender*, January 7, 1933, 10.

Jones, Kirkland C. "Bontemps and the Old South."*African American Review* 27, 2 (1993): 179–185.

————. *Renaissance Man from Louisiana: A Biography of Arna Wendell Bontemps.* Westport, Conn.: Greenwood Press, 1992.

Jones, Robert B., and Margery Toomer Latimer, eds. *The Collected Poems of Jean Toomer.* Chapel Hill: University of North Carolina Press, 1988.

Kalter, Susan. "Introduction." In *Twenty Thousand Mornings: An Autobiography*, by John Joseph Mathews, ed. Susan Kalter, xvii–lii. Norman: University of Oklahoma Press, 2012.

Keith, Joseph. *Unbecoming Americans: Writing Race and Nation from the Shadows of Citizenship, 1945–1960.* New Brunswick, N.J.: Rutgers University Press, 2013.

Kelley, Robin D. G. *Freedom Dreams: The Black Radical Imagination.* Boston: Beacon, 2002.

Kerman, Cynthia Earl, and Richard Eldridge. *The Lives of Jean Toomer: A Hunger for Wholeness.* Baton Rouge: Louisiana State University Press, 1987.

Knadler, Stephen. "Sweetback Style: Wallace Thurman's Harlem Renaissance." *MFS: Modern Fiction Studies* 48, 4 (2002): 898–936.

Koch, Frederick H. "The Carolina Playmakers." In *Carolina Folk Plays*, ed. Frederick H. Koch, ix–xxvi. New York: Henry Holt, 1941.

————. "The Playmaker's Aim." In *Carolina Folk Plays*, ed. Frederick H. Koch, vi. New York: Henry Holt, 1941.

Kolodny, Annette. *The Land before Her: Fantasy and Experience of the American Frontiers, 1630–1860.* Chapel Hill: University of North Carolina Press, 1984.

————. *The Lay of the Land: Metaphor as Experience and History in American Life and Letters.* Chapel Hill: University of North Carolina Press, 1975.

Kraditor, Aileen S. "Introduction." In *Up from the Pedestal: Selected Writings in the History of American Feminism*, ed. Aileen S. Kraditor, 3–24. Chicago: Quadrangle Books, 1968.

"Krigwa." *Crisis*, October 1925, 275–278; December 1926, 70–71.

Kurishage, Scott. *The Shifting Grounds of Race: Black and Japanese Americans in the Making of Modern Los Angeles.* Princeton, N.J.: Princeton University Press, 2008.

Larson, Charles. *Invisible Darkness: Jean Toomer and Nella Larsen.* Iowa City: University of Iowa Press, 1993.

Lawrence, D. H. *Studies in Classic American Literature.* New York: Penguin, 1977.

Leonard, Karen Isaksen. *Making Ethnic Choices: California's Punjabi Mexican Americans.* Philadelphia: Temple University Press, 1992.

———. "Punjabi Farmers and California's Alien Land Law." *Agricultural History* 54, 1 (1985): 549–562.

Leonard, Kevin. *The Battle for Los Angeles: Racial Ideology and World War II.* Albuquerque: University of New Mexico Press, 2006.

Leroy-Frazier, Jill. "Othered Southern Modernism: Arna Bontemps's *Black Thunder.*" *Mississippi Quarterly: The Journal of Southern Culture* 63, 1/2 (Winter 2010): 3–29.

Lewis, David Levering. *When Harlem Was in Vogue.* New York: Penguin, 1997.

Lewisohn, Ludwig. "South Carolina: A Lingering Fragrance." In *These United States: Portraits of America from the 1920s*, ed. Daniel H. Borus, 236–331. Ithaca, N.Y.: Cornell University Press, 1992.

Lhamon, W. T., Jr. *Raising Cain: Blackface Performance from Jim Crow to Hip Hop.* Cambridge, Mass.: Harvard University Press, 1997.

Limerick, Patricia Nelson. *The Legacy of Conquest: The Unbroken Past of the American West.* New York: W. W. Norton, 1987.

Limón, José E. *American Encounters: Greater Mexico, the United States, and the Erotics of Culture.* Boston: Beacon Press, 1998.

———. *Américo Paredes: Culture and Critique.* Austin: University of Texas Press, 2012.

———. "Imagining the Imaginary: A Reply to Ramón Saldívar." *ALH: American Literary History* 21, 3 (2009): 595–603.

Locke, Alain. "Foreword." In *The New Negro: Voices of the Harlem Renaissance*, ed. Alain Locke, xxv–xxvii. New York: Touchstone Books, 1997.

Logsdon, Guy. "John Joseph Mathews: A Conversation." *Nimrod* 16 (1972): 70–75.

Lorde, Audre. "The Master's Tools Will Never Dismantle the Master's House." In *Sister Outsider: Essays and Speeches*, 110–113. Berkeley, Calif.: Crossing Press, 1984.

Lott, Eric. *Love and Theft: Blackface Minstrelsy and the American Working Class.* New York: Oxford University Press, 1993.

Lowe, Lisa. *Immigrant Acts: On Asian American Cultural Politics.* Durham, N.C.: Duke University Press, 1996.

Luhan, Mabel Dodge. *Edge of Taos Desert: An Escape to Reality.* Albuquerque: University of New Mexico Press, 1987.

———. *Lorenzo in Taos.* New York: Alfred A. Knopf, 1932.

———. *Movers and Shakers.* New York: Harcourt, Brace, 1936.

Luhan, Mabel Dodge, Papers. Yale Collection of American Literature, Beinecke Rare Book and Manuscript Library, Yale University, New Haven, Conn.

Lutenski, Emily. "Tribes of Men: John Joseph Mathews and Indian Internationalism." *SAIL: Studies in American Indian Literatures* 24, 2 (2012): 39–64.

Lutz, Tom. "Introduction: Diversity, Location, and Ideology in 'These "Colored" United States.'" In *These "Colored" United States: African American Essays from the 1920s*, ed. Tom Lutz and Susanna Ashton, 1–12. New Brunswick, N.J.: Rutgers University Press, 1996.

Manring, M. M. *Slave in a Box: The Strange Career of Aunt Jemima*. Charlottesville: University Press of Virginia, 1998.

"Margery Toomer, Novelist, Dies in West: Wife of Psychologist Was Descendant of Prominent New England Pioneers." *New York Times*, August 18, 1832, 19.

Martínez, Elizabeth Coonrod. *Josefina Niggli, Mexican American Writer: A Critical Biography*. Albuquerque: University of New Mexico Press, 2007.

Mathews, John Joseph. *Sundown*. Norman: University of Oklahoma Press, 1988.

———. *Twenty Thousand Mornings: An Autobiography*, ed. Susan Kalter. Norman: University of Oklahoma Press, 2012.

McGregor, Deborah Kuhn. *From Midwives to Medicine: The Birth of American Gynecology*. New Brunswick, N.J.: Rutgers University Press, 1998.

McHenry, Elizabeth. *Forgotten Readers: Recovering the Lost History of African American Literary Societies*. Durham, N.C.: Duke University Press, 2002.

McKay, Claude. *Home to Harlem*. Lebanon, N.H.: University Press of New England/Northeastern University Press, 1987.

Miles, Tiya. *Ties that Bind: The Story of an Afro-Cherokee Family in Slavery and Freedom*. Berkeley: University of California Press, 2006.

Miles, Tiya, and Sharon P. Holland, eds. *Crossing Waters, Crossing Worlds: The African Diaspora in Indian Country*. Durham, N.C.: Duke University Press, 2006.

———. "Introduction: Crossing Waters, Crossing Worlds." In *Crossing Waters, Crossing Worlds: The African Diaspora in Indian Country*, ed. Tiya Miles and Sharon P. Holland, 1–24. Durham, N.C.: Duke University Press, 2006.

Milian, Claudia. *Latining America: Black-Brown Passengers and the Coloring of Latino/a Studies*. Athens: University of Georgia Press, 2013.

Miller, Marilyn Grace. *The Rise and Fall of the Cosmic Race: The Cult of Mestizaje in Latin America*. Austin: University of Texas Press, 2004.

Miller, W. Jason. *Langston Hughes and American Lynching Culture*. Gainesville: University Press of Florida, 2011.

Mitchell, Verner D. "A Family Answers the Call: Anita Scott Coleman, Literature, and War." *War, Literature, and the Arts* 20, 1/2 (2008): 301–313.

Montejano, David. "Mexican Merchants and Teamsters on the Texas Cotton Road, 1862–1865." In *Mexico and Mexicans in the Making of the United States*, ed. John Tutino, 141–170. Austin: University of Texas Press, 2012.

Moreno-Brid, Juan Carlos, and Jaime Ros. *Development and Growth in the*

Mexican Economy: A Historical Perspective. New York: Oxford University Press, 2009.

Morrison, Toni. *Playing in the Dark: Whiteness and the Literary Imagination.* New York: Vintage Books, 1992.

Mullen, Edward. "Langston Hughes in Mexico and Cuba." *Review: Latin American Literature and Arts* 47 (1993): 23–27.

N. G. "New Books." *New York Amsterdam News,* March 16, 1932, 8.

National Association for the Advancement of Colored People. *Thirty Years of Lynching in the United States, 1889–1918.* New York: National Association for the Advancement of Colored People, 1919.

"New Mexico: Silver City, New Mexico." *Chicago Defender,* September 11, 1937, 22.

New Mexico Constitution. http://www.sis.state.n.us/pdf/2007nmconst.pdf.

Nicholls, David G. *Conjuring the Folk: Forms of Modernity in African America.* Ann Arbor: University of Michigan Press, 2000.

Nichols, James David. "The Line of Liberty: Slave and Fugitive Peons in the Texas-Mexico Borderlands." *Western Historical Quarterly* 44, 4 (2013): 413–433.

Niggli, Josefina. *Mexican Village and Other Works.* Evanston, Ill.: Northwestern University Press, 2008.

Norwood, Vera, and Janice Monk. "Introduction: Perspectives on Gender and Landscape." In *The Desert Is No Lady: Southwestern Landscapes in Women's Writing and Art,* ed. Vera Norwood and Janice Monk, 1–9. Tucson: University of Arizona Press, 1997.

Nugent, Richard Bruce. *Gentleman Jigger: A Novel of the Harlem Renaissance.* Philadelphia: Da Capo Press, 2008.

Orchard, William, and Yolanda Padilla. "Introducing Josefina Niggli." In *The Plays of Josefina Niggli,* ed. William Orchard and Yolanda Padilla, 3–33. Madison: University of Wisconsin Press, 2007.

Owens, Louis. *Other Destinies: Understanding the American Indian Novel.* Norman: University of Oklahoma Press, 1996.

Painter, Nell Irvin. *Exodusters: Black Migration to Kansas after Reconstruction.* New York: W. W. Norton, 1992.

Paredes, Américo. "Africa." In *Between Two Worlds,* 18–19.

———. *Between Two Worlds.* Houston: Arte Público Press, 1991.

———. "Prologue." In *Between Two Worlds,* 9–11.

———. "The Rio Grande." In *Between Two Worlds,* 15–16.

Parsons, Deborah L. *Streetwalking the Metropolis: Women, the City, and Modernity.* New York: Oxford University Press, 2000.

Patterson, Louise Thompson, Papers. Emory University, Atlanta, Ga.

Paul, Rodman Wilson. *Mining Frontiers of the Far West, 1848–1880*, rev. and exp. Elliot West. Albuquerque: University of New Mexico Press, 2001.

Paz, Octavio. *The Labyrinth of Solitude*. New York: Grove Press, 1999.

Quirk, Tom, and Robert E. Fleming. "Jean Toomer's Contributions to the *New Mexican Sentinel*." In *Jean Toomer: A Critical Evaluation*, ed. Therman B. O'Daniel, 64–73. Washington, D.C.: Howard University Press, 1988.

"Races: Just Americans." *Time*, March 12, 1932, 19.

Rampersad, Arnold. *The Life of Langston Hughes*, vol. 1, *1902–1931: I, Too, Sing America*. New York: Oxford University Press, 2002.

———. *The Life of Langston Hughes*, vol. 2, *1941–1967: I Dream a World*. New York: Oxford University Press, 2002.

Rampersad, Arnold, and David Roessel, eds. *The Collected Poems of Langston Hughes*. New York: Vintage Books, 1995.

Ratliff, Beulah Amidon. "Mississippi: Heart of Dixie." In *These United States: Portraits of America from the 1920s*, ed. Daniel H. Borus, 196–204. Ithaca, N.Y.: Cornell University Press, 1992.

"The Recent Outrages at Humboldt, Kansas." *Daily Cleveland Herald*, September 28, 1861.

Richardson, Barbara J., comp. *Black Directory of New Mexico, Bicentennial Edition, 1776–1976: Black Pioneers of New Mexico—A Documentary and Pictorial History*. Rio Rancho, N.M.: Panorama Press, 1976.

Roberts, Frederick Madison. "For the West." *New Age* (Los Angeles), March 12, 1915.

Robinson, Paul. "Race, Space, and the Evolution of Black Los Angeles." In *Black Los Angeles: American Dreams and Racial Realities*, ed. Darnell Hunt and Ana-Christina Ramón, 21–59. New York: New York University Press, 2010.

Romero, Lora. *Home Fronts: Domesticity and Its Critics in the Antebellum United States*. Durham, N.C.: Duke University Press, 1997.

Rooks, Noliwe M. *Hair Raising: Beauty, Culture, and African American Women*. New Brunswick, N.J.: Rutgers University Press, 1996.

———. *Ladies' Pages: African American Women's Magazines and the Culture that Made Them*. New Brunswick, N.J.: Rutgers University Press, 2004.

Rothman, Hal K. *Devil's Bargains: Tourism in the Twentieth Century American West*. Lawrence: University Press of Kansas, 2000.

Ruffin, Herbert G., II. *Uninvited Neighbors: African Americans in Silicon Valley, 1769–1990*. Norman: University of Oklahoma Press, 2014.

Runstedtler, Theresa. *Jack Johnson, Rebel Sojourner*. Berkeley: University of California Press, 2012.

Rusch, Frederik L., ed. *A Jean Toomer Reader: Selected Unpublished Writings.* New York: Oxford University Press, 1993.

Rydell, Robert W. "Editor's Introduction: Contend! Contend!" In *The Reason Why the Colored American Is Not in the World's Columbian Exposition,* by Ida B. Wells, Frederick Douglass, Irvine Garland Penn, and Ferdinand L. Barnett, ed. Robert W. Rydell, xi–xlvii. Urbana: University of Illinois Press, 1999.

Sadowski-Smith, Claudia. *Border Fictions: Globalization, Empire, and Writing at the Boundaries of the United States.* Charlottesville: University of Virginia Press, 2008.

Saldívar, José David. *Border Matters: Remapping American Cultural Studies.* Berkeley: University of California Press, 1997.

Saldívar, Ramón. *The Borderlands of Culture: Américo Paredes and the Transnational Imaginary.* Durham, N.C.: Duke University Press, 2006.

Saxton, Alexander. "Blackface Minstrelsy and Jacksonian Ideology." *American Quarterly* 27, 1 (1975): 3–28.

Scandura, Janie. *Down in the Dumps: Place, Modernity, American Depression.* Durham, N.C.: Duke University Press, 2008.

Schedler, Christopher. *Border Modernism: Intercultural Readings in American Literary Modernism.* New York: Routledge, 2002.

Schuyler, George. "Views and Reviews." *Pittsburgh Courier,* February 6, 1932, 10.

Schwarz, A. B. Christa. *Gay Voices of the Harlem Renaissance.* Bloomington: Indiana University Press, 2003.

Scruggs, Charles, and Lee VanDemarr. *Jean Toomer and the Terrors of American History.* Philadelphia: University of Pennsylvania Press, 1998.

Sergeant, Elizabeth Shepley. "New Mexico: A Relic of Ancient America." In *These United States: Portraits of America from the 1920s,* ed. Daniel H. Borus, 249–255. Ithaca, N.Y.: Cornell University Press, 1992.

Sides, Josh. *L.A. City Limits: African American Los Angeles from the Great Depression to the Present.* Berkeley: University of California Press, 2003.

"Silver City, New Mexico." *Pittsburgh Courier,* October 8, 1938, 6.

"Silver Ores from New Mexico." *Washington Post,* April 15, 1881, 2.

Singh, Amritjit. "Introduction: Wallace Thurman and the Harlem Renaissance." In *The Collected Writings of Wallace Thurman: A Harlem Renaissance Reader,* ed. Amritjit Singh and Daniel M. Scott III, 1–28. New Brunswick, N.J.: Rutgers University Press, 2003.

Singh, Amritjit, and Daniel M. Scott III, eds. *The Collected Writings of Wallace Thurman: A Harlem Renaissance Reader.* New Brunswick, N.J.: Rutgers University Press, 2003.

Slotkin, Richard. *Gunfighter Nation: The Myth of the Frontier in Twentieth-Century America*. Norman: University of Oklahoma Press, 1998.

Smith, Chris. "Going to the Nation: The Idea of Oklahoma in Early Blues Recordings." *Popular Music* 26, 2 (2007): 83–96.

Smith, Henry Nash. *Virgin Land: The American West as Symbol and Myth*. Cambridge, Mass.: Harvard University Press, 2007.

Smith, Katharine Capshaw. *Children's Literature of the Harlem Renaissance*. Bloomington: Indiana University Press, 2004.

Smith, Stacy. *Freedom's Frontier: California and the Struggle over Unfree Labor, Emancipation, and Reconstruction*. Chapel Hill: University of North Carolina Press, 2013.

Stansell, Christine. *American Moderns: Bohemian New York and the Creation of a New Century*. New York: Henry Holt, 2000.

Stewart, Omer C. *Peyote Religion: A History*. Norman: University of Oklahoma Press, 1987.

Stoddard, Lothrop. *The Rising Tide of Color against White World-Supremacy*. New York: Charles Scribner's Sons, 1920.

Sundquist, Eric J. *Strangers in the Land: Blacks, Jews, Post-Holocaust America*. Cambridge, Mass.: Harvard University Press, 2005.

Tate, Claudia. *Domestic Allegories of Political Desire: The Black Heroine's Text at the Turn of the Century*. New York: Oxford University Press, 1992.

Taylor, Quintard. *In Search of the Racial Frontier: African-Americans in the American West, 1528–1990*. New York: W. W. Norton, 1999.

Thurman, Wallace. "Autobiographical Statement." In Singh and Scott, *Collected Writings of Wallace Thurman*, 91–92.

———. *The Blacker the Berry*. Mineola, N.Y.: Dover Publications, 2008.

———. "Negro Artists and the Negro." In Singh and Scott, *Collected Writings of Wallace Thurman*, 195–200.

———. "Negro Life in New York's Harlem: A Lively Picture of a Popular and Interesting Section." In Singh and Scott, *Collected Writings of Wallace Thurman*, 39–62.

———. "Quoth Brigham Young—This Is the Place." In *These "Colored" United States: African American Essays from the 1920s*, ed. Tom Lutz and Susanna Ashton, 261–267. New Brunswick, N.J.: Rutgers University Press, 1996.

———. "A Thrush at Eve with an Atavistic Wound: Review of *Flight*, by Walter White." In Singh and Scott, *Collected Writings of Wallace Thurman*, 183–184.

Thurman, Wallace, Collection. James Weldon Johnson Collection, Beinecke Rare Book and Manuscript Library, Yale University, New Haven, Conn.

Toomer, Jean. "Americans and Mary Austin." In *Jean Toomer and the Terrors of American History*, by Charles Scruggs and Lee VanDemarr, 228–231. Philadelphia: University of Pennsylvania Press, 1998.

———. "The Blue Meridian." In Jones and Latimer, *Collected Poems of Jean Toomer*, 50–75.

———. *Cane*, ed. Darwin T. Turner. New York: W. W. Norton, 1988.

———. *Cane*, 2nd ed., ed. Rudolph P. Byrd and Henry Louis Gates Jr. New York: W. W. Norton, 2011.

———. "The *Cane* Years." In *The Wayward and the Seeking: A Collection of Writings by Jean Toomer*, ed. Darwin T. Turner, 116–127. Washington, D.C.: Howard University Press, 1982.

———. *The Collected Poems of Jean Toomer*, ed. Robert B. Jones and Margery Toomer Latimer. Chapel Hill: University of North Carolina Press, 1988.

———. "The Dust of Abiquiu." In Rusch, *Jean Toomer Reader*, 240–248.

———. "The Experience." In Rusch, *Jean Toomer Reader*, 33–76.

———. "Fighting the Vice." In Rusch, *Jean Toomer Reader*, 101–104.

———. "Imprint for Rio Grande." In Jones and Latimer, *Collected Poems of Jean Toomer*, 81–82.

———. "I Sit in My Room." In Jones and Latimer, *Collected Poems of Jean Toomer*, 83.

———. "It Is Everywhere." In Jones and Latimer, *Collected Poems of Jean Toomer*, 85–87.

———. *A Jean Toomer Reader: Selected Unpublished Writings*, ed. Frederik L. Rusch. New York: Oxford University Press, 1993.

———. "Lost Dancer." In Jones and Latimer, *Collected Poems of Jean Toomer*, 39.

———. "New Mexico after India." In Rusch, *Jean Toomer Reader*, 248–253.

———. "A New Race in America." In Rusch, *Jean Toomer Reader*, 105.

———. "Not Typically American." In Rusch, *Jean Toomer Reader*, 95–101.

———. "Part of the Universe." In Rusch, *Jean Toomer Reader*, 253–257.

———. "Rainbow." In Rusch, *Jean Toomer Reader*, 240.

———. "Rolling, Rolling." In Jones and Latimer, *Collected Poems of Jean Toomer*, 84.

———. "Santa Fe Sequence." In Rusch, *Jean Toomer Reader*, 257–258.

———. "Taos Night." In Rusch, *Jean Toomer Reader*, 249.

———. "To the Land of the People." In Rusch, *Jean Toomer Reader*, 238–239.

———. *The Uncollected Work of American Author Jean Toomer, 1894–1967*, ed. John Chandler Griffin. Lewiston, N.Y.: Edwin Mellen Press, 2003.

———. *The Wayward and the Seeking: A Collection of Writings by Jean Toomer*, ed. Darwin T. Turner. Washington, D.C.: Howard University Press, 1980.

Toomer, Jean, Papers. James Weldon Johnson Collection, Beinecke Rare Book and Manuscript Library, Yale University, New Haven, Conn.

Torgovnick, Marianna. *Gone Primitive: Savage Intellects, Modern Lives*. Chicago: University of Chicago Press, 1990.

Turner, Frederick Jackson. "The Significance of the Frontier in American History." In *The Norton Anthology of American Literature*, vol. C, *1865–1914*, 7th ed., ed. Nina Baym, Jeanne Campbell Reeseman, and Arnold Krupat, 1149–1153. New York: W. W. Norton, 2007.

United States Bureau of the Census. *1890 Census of Population and Housing*, vol. 1, *Report on Population of the United States at the Eleventh Census*, pt. 1. Washington, D.C.: Government Printing Office, 1895.

———. *Fifteenth Census of the United States—1930 Population*, vol. 3, pt. 2, *Montana–Wyoming*. Washington, D.C.: Government Printing Office, 1932.

———. *Fourteenth Census of the United States: State Compendium—Utah*. Washington, D.C.: Government Printing Office, 1924.

———. *1900 Census of Population and Housing*, vol. 1, *Population: Population of States and Territories*, sec. 9. Washington, D.C.: United States Census Office, 1901.

———. *Profile of General Population and Housing Characteristics: 2010*. http://factfinder2.census.gov/faces/tableservices/jsf/pages/productview.xhtml?src=bkmk.

———. *State and County QuickFacts: Utah*. http://quickfacts.census.gov/qfd/states/49000.html.

Utterback, W. E. "Old Man." *Looking Back 73 Years*. Roswell, N.M.: Hall Poorbaugh Press, 1978.

Van Holtby, David. *Forty-Seventh Star: New Mexico's Struggle for Statehood*. Norman: University of Oklahoma Press, 2012.

van Notten, Eleonore. *Wallace Thurman's Harlem Renaissance*. Amsterdam: Rodopi, 1994.

Vasconcelos, José. *The Cosmic Race/La raza cósmica*, trans. Didier T. Jaén. Baltimore: Johns Hopkins University Press, 1997.

Vinson, Ben, III, and Michael Restall, eds. *Black Mexico: Race and Society from Colonial to Modern Times*. Albuquerque: University of New Mexico Press, 2009.

Walker, Alice. "In Search of Zora Neale Hurston." *Ms. Magazine*, March 3, 1975, 74–79, 85–89.

"Wallace Thurman Is Model Harlemite, Lewis Announces." *Atlanta Daily World*, March 13, 1932, A6.

Wallis, Michael. *The Real Wild West: The 101 Ranch and the Creation of the American West*. New York: St. Martin's, 1999.

"Wanted." *Crisis*, August 1913, 197.

Washington, Harriet. *Medical Apartheid: The Dark History of Medical Experimentation on Black Americans from Colonial Times to the Present.* New York: Doubleday, 2006.

Watts, Eric King. "Queer Harlem: Exploring the Rhetorical Limits of a Black Gay 'Utopia.'" In *Queering Public Address: Sexualities in American Historical Discourse*, ed. Charles E. Morris III, 174–194. Columbia: University of South Carolina Press, 2007.

Weaver, Jace, Craig Womack, and Robert Warrior. *Native American Literary Nationalism.* Albuquerque: University of New Mexico Press, 2006.

Welter, Barbara. "The Cult of True Womanhood: 1820–1860." *American Quarterly* 18, 2 (1966): 151–174.

West, Dorothy. "Elephant's Dance." In *The Richer, the Poorer*, 215–227. New York: Anchor Books, 1995.

White, E. Frances. "Africa on My Mind: Gender, Counter Discourse, and African American Nationalism." In *Is It Nation Time? Contemporary Essays on Black Power and Black Nationalism*, ed. Eddie S. Glaude Jr., 130–155. Chicago: University of Chicago Press, 2002.

———. *The Dark Continent of Our Bodies: Black Feminism and the Politics of Respectability.* Philadelphia: Temple University Press, 2001.

White, Richard. "Frederick Jackson Turner and Buffalo Bill." In *The Frontier in American Culture*, by Richard White and Patricia Nelson Limerick, ed. James R. Grossman, 7–65. Berkeley: University of California Press, 1994.

———. *It's Your Misfortune and None of My Own: A History of the American West.* Norman: University of Oklahoma Press, 1991.

———. *Railroaded: The Transcontinentals and the Making of Modern America.* New York: W. W. Norton, 2011.

Widener, Daniel. *Black Arts West: Culture and Struggle in Postwar Los Angeles.* Durham, N.C.: Duke University Press, 2010.

Wiggins, Bernice Love. *Tuneful Tales*, ed. Maceo C. Dailey Jr. and Ruthe Winegarten. Lubbock: Texas Tech University Press, 2002.

Wild, Mark. *Street Meeting: Multiethnic Neighborhoods in Early Twentieth-Century Los Angeles.* Berkeley: University of California Press, 2005.

Wilkerson, Isabel. *The Warmth of Other Suns: The Epic Story of America's Great Migration.* New York: Vintage, 2011.

Williams, Gwendolyn. "Bow to the Sun." *Pittsburgh Courier*, August 14, 1943.

Wilson, James F. *Bulldaggers, Pansies, and Chocolate Babies: Performance, Race, and Sexuality in the Harlem Renaissance.* Ann Arbor: University of Michigan Press, 2011.

Wintz, Cary D. *Black Culture and the Harlem Renaissance.* Houston: Rice University Press, 1988.

Wirth, Thomas H. "Introduction." In *Gentleman Jigger: A Novel of the Harlem Renaissance*, by Richard Bruce Nugent, x–xviii. Philadelphia: Da Capo Press, 2008.

"Woman Novelist Called by Death: Death Ends Romance of Two Races—White Wife of J. Toomer, Novelist of Negro Blood, Expires in Childbirth." *Los Angeles Times*, August 18, 1932, 3.

Wood, Clement. "Alabama: A Study in Ultra-Violet." In *These United States: Portraits of America from the 1920s*, ed. Daniel H. Borus, 29–36. Ithaca, N.Y.: Cornell University Press, 1992.

Woodson, Jon. *To Make a New Race: Gurdjieff, Toomer, and the Harlem Renaissance.* Jackson: University of Mississippi Press, 1999.

Work, Monroe. "Lynching, Whites and Negroes, 1882–1968." Tuskegee University Archives Repository, Tuskegee, Ala.

Wright, Richard. "The Ethics of Living Jim Crow." In *Uncle Tom's Children*, 1–15. New York: Harper Perennial, 2004.

Index

317